PRINCIPLES OF FEDERAL INDIAN LAW

Matthew L.M. Fletcher

Professor of Law & Director of the Indigenous Law & Policy Center
Michigan State University College of Law

CONCISE HORNBOOK SERIES™

WEST
ACADEMIC
PUBLISHING

© 2017 LEG, Inc. d/b/a West Academic
 444 Cedar Street, Suite 700
 St. Paul, MN 55101
 1-877-888-1330

Printed in the United States of America

ISBN: 978-1-63460-623-3

Summary of Contents

Table of Contents

PRINCIPLES OF FEDERAL INDIAN LAW

Chapter 1

AMERICAN INDIANS AND FEDERAL INDIAN LAW

Analysis

§ 1.1   Foundational Principles of Federal Indian Law

There are three kinds of sovereigns within the United States—federal, state, and tribal. The Constitution delineates the authorities, duties, and limitations of the United States in relation to the state governments, but the structure and text of the Constitution recognizes two other kinds of sovereign entity—foreign nations and Indian tribes.[1] As Justice O'Connor once stated, Indian tribes are the "third sovereign."[2]

The constitutional text, as consistent with the practice of Congress before the ratification of the Constitution, provides for two means by which Indian tribes and the United States will interact. First, the so-called Indian Commerce Clause provides that Congress has authority to regulate commerce with the Indian tribes. One of the first acts of the First Congress was to implement the Indian Commerce Clause in the Trade and Intercourse Act of 1790.[3] Second, the federal government's treaty power provides an additional form by which the United States deals with Indian tribes. There are hundreds of valid and extant treaties between the United States and various Indian tribes. The structure of the Constitution and the treaties established a relationship between sovereigns akin to a trust relationship, with the federal government in the position of trustee and Indian nations and Indian people in

---

[1]   Const. Art. I, § 8, cl. 3 (the Interstate, Foreign Nations, and Indian Commerce Clauses).

[2]   Sandra Day O'Connor, Lessons from the Third Sovereign: Indian Tribal Courts, 33 Tulsa L. J. 1 (1997).

[3]   An Act to regulate trade and intercourse with the Indian tribes, July 22, 1790, 1 Stat. 137, now codified as amended at 25 U.S.C. §§ 177, 261–65; 18 U.S.C. § 1152.

1

the position of trust beneficiary. The trust relationship is not merely metaphorical, as the federal government holds and administers billions of dollars of Indian and tribal assets in the form of land, natural resources, and cash.

The Supreme Court interpreted the meaning of the Indian Commerce Clause and how it interacts with Indian treaties in the so-called Marshall Trilogy of early Indian law cases. In *Johnson v. McIntosh*,[4] an early Indian lands case, Chief Justice Marshall held that the federal government had exclusive dominion over affairs with Indian tribes—exclusive as to individual American citizens and, implicitly, as to state government. In *Cherokee Nation v. Georgia*,[5] Chief Justice Marshall's lead opinion asserted that while Indian tribes were not state governments as defined in the Constitution, nor were they foreign nations—they were something akin to "domestic dependent nations." And, finally, in *Worcester v. Georgia*,[6] Chief Justice Marshall confirmed that the laws of states have "no force" in Indian Country, and that the Constitution's Supremacy Clause gave powerful effect to Indian treaties as "the supreme law of the land." However, largely because Congress has authority to abrogate ratified treaties, Congress may also abrogate Indian treaty rights, as the Supreme Court recognized in *Lone Wolf v. Hitchcock*,[7] but only so long as Congress pays just compensation for any takings.[8]

The Constitutional text, Indian treaties, Acts of Congress, and the Supreme Court's jurisprudence can be reduced to a few general, fundamental principles of federal Indian law. *First*, Congress's authority over Indian affairs is plenary and exclusive. As a concomitant principle, the federal government holds obligations to Indian tribes and individual Indians known as the trust responsibility. *Second*, state governments have no authority to regulate Indian affairs absent express Congressional delegation or granted in accordance with the federal government's trust obligations *Third*, the sovereign authority of Indian tribes is inherent, and not delegated or granted by the United States, but can be limited or restricted by Congress in accordance with its trust responsibilities. Congress must clearly express its intent to abrogate an aspect of tribal sovereignty.[9]

---

4   21 U.S. 543 (1923).

5   30 U.S. 1 (1831).

6   31 U.S. 515 (1832).

7   187 U.S. 553 (1903).

8   E.g., United States v. Sioux Nation, 448 U.S. 371 (1980).

9   Felix S. Cohen, Handbook of Federal Indian Law xxiii, 122 (1941 ed.); Cohen's Handbook of Federal Indian Law 2 (2012 ed.).

A key element in these three principles is the legal term of art, "Indian Country," which is defined by Act of Congress to include all reservation lands and other kinds of Indian lands.[10] These foundational principles are in strongest force within the boundaries of Indian Country.

Congressional Plenary Power and the Trust Responsibility

Congress's plenary and exclusive power allows Congress to enact statutes defining the "metes and bounds" of tribal and state sovereignty in Indian affairs.[11] Congress has delegated enormous authority to implement federal Indian policy to the Executive branch, particularly the Secretary of Interior.[12] Congressional plenary power, along with the treaty relationship between the United States and hundreds of tribes, forms the foundation of the federal government's trust responsibility to Indian tribes.[13]

The federal government's plenary power over Indian affairs provides the authority for the United States to recognize Indian tribes. There are now 567 federally-recognized Indian tribes.[14] Many of these tribes are signatories to treaties with the United States. Federal recognition has import in numerous ways. For example, Congress appropriates money to the Bureau of Indian Affairs, the Indian Health Service, and the Department of Housing and Urban Development, each of which then spend that money (or deliver that money) to federally-recognized tribes, who use the money to operate tribal government services ranging from health care to public safety to housing to employment training and education, and many other services. Indian tribes also use their own, independently-generated revenues to fund these programs. Key government services paid for by federal and tribal money includes courts of record developed and operated by the tribes, law enforcement departments, and jail facilities.

Exclusive Federal Authority

Second, there is a long tradition of excluding state governments from Indian Country, dating back to the Constitution. According to James Madison, one of the serious flaws of the Articles of Confederation was the failure of the Articles to exclude state

---

[10] 18 U.S.C. § 1151.

[11] United States v. Lara, 541 U.S. 193, 201 (2004).

[12] 25 U.S.C. §§ 2, 9.

[13] Sunderland v. United States, 266 U.S. 226, 233 (1924); Tiger v. Western Investment Co., 221 U.S. 286, 310 (1911); United States v. Kagama, 118 U.S. 375, 383–84 (1886).

[14] Indian Entities Recognized and Eligible to Receive Services from the United States Bureau of Indian Affairs, 82 Fed. Reg. 4915 (Jan. 17, 2017).

governments from Indian affairs.[15] The Framers intended the Indian Commerce Clause to exclude state governments from the field of Indian commerce, while the federal government's Treaty Power would be used to deal with Indian tribes as independent sovereign nations.[16] The First Congress enacted the Trade and Intercourse Act as a means to fulfill its obligation under the Indian Commerce Clause. But States continued to assert authority to deal in Indian affairs, including executing treaties with Indian tribes, negotiating major Indian land purchases, and asserting their police powers on Indian lands, but they did so in violation of federal law. The situation came to a head in the Cherokee cases, in which the Supreme Court finally declared the State of Georgia's efforts to assert control over the Cherokee Nation null and void. The Court held that state laws had "no force" in Indian Country.[17]

In the modern era, the notion that state laws have no force in Indian Country is riddled with exceptions, both statutory and in the common law, but the general rule remains. The Supreme Court in 1973 stated, "The modern cases thus tend to avoid reliance on platonic notions of Indian sovereignty and to look instead to the applicable treaties and statutes which define the limits of state power."[18] States may not tax on-reservation income,[19] the land,[20] or the reservation-based property of individual Indians,[21] and have no authority to enforce state law against Indian nations whatsoever due in large part to tribal sovereign immunity.[22] States have no authority to regulate Indian lands, except in extremely narrow circumstances.[23] State courts have no jurisdiction over civil cases

---

[15]   The Federalist No. 42, at 284–85 (Madison) (J.E. Cooke ed. 1961).

[16]   Robert N. Clinton, The Dormant Indian Commerce Clause, 27 Conn. L. Rev. 1055, 1149 (1995); Robert N. Clinton, There Is No Federal Supremacy Clause for Indian Tribes, 34 Ariz. St. L.J. 113, 118 (2003); Richard Pomp, The Unfilled Promise of the Indian Commerce Clause and State Taxation, 63 Tax Law. 897 (2010). Contra Robert G. Natelson, The Original Understanding of the Indian Commerce Clause, 85 Denv. U. L. Rev. 201 (2007); Saikrishna Prakash, Against Tribal Fungibility, 89 Cornell L. Rev. 1069, 1103 (2004).

[17]   Worcester v. Georgia, 31 U.S. 515, 561 (1832).

[18]   McClanahan v. State Tax Commission of Arizona, 411 U.S. 164, 172 (1973). But the Court still held in that case, after parsing through the relevant treaties and Acts of Congress, that Arizona's taxation of the income of reservation Indians was invalid. See id. at 165.

[19]   Oklahoma Tax Commission v. Sac and Fox Nation, 508 U.S. 114, 124 (1993).

[20]   McClanahan v. State Tax Commission of Arizona, 411 U.S. 164, 172 (1973); Mescalero Apache Tribe v. Jones, 411 U.S. 145, 148 (1973).

[21]   Bryan v. Itasca County, 426 U.S. 373, 377 (1978).

[22]   Michigan v. Bay Mills Indian Community, 134 S.Ct. 2024, 2031–32 (2014); Oklahoma Tax Commission v. Citizen Band of Potawatomi Indian Tribe, 498 U.S. 505, 509–10 (1991).

[23]   New Mexico v. Mescalero Apache Tribe, 462 U.S. 324, 332 (1983).

brought against individual Indians for disputes arising in Indian country, with limited exceptions.[24] And states have no authority to prosecute on-reservation crimes committed by Indians, also with limited exceptions.[25]

Inherent Tribal Authority and the Clear Statement Rule

The third major federal Indian law principle is the inherent sovereignty of Indian tribes. Because Indian tribes have independent and inherent sovereignty, tribes retain the authority to make laws and be ruled by them.[26] Since before the beginning of the American Republic, some Indian tribes have exercised their sovereignty to enact criminal codes, establish courts, and exercise governmental authority over individuals, Indian and non-Indian. Indian nations long have exercised law enforcement authority, and some still do exercise this kind of governmental authority. It was the Cherokee Nation of Georgia in the 1820s that likely was the first Indian nation to establish a written constitution and criminal code, a court system, and a formalized law enforcement mechanism.[27] By the 1970s, several dozen Indian nations exercised criminal jurisdiction over individuals, including non-Indians.[28] And now, perhaps hundreds of Indian nations exercise criminal jurisdiction, or soon will.[29]

It is a common misconception that Indian treaties constituted a federal grant of land and authority to Indian tribes, when the reverse is true. Indian treaties are *reservations* of land and authority by Indian tribes. If a tribe did not relinquish a sovereign right in the treaty, it remains.[30] The exception to this rule is that Congress has authority, according to the Supreme Court, to divest aspects of tribal sovereignty if it so wishes.[31] And finally, the

---

[24]   Williams v. Lee, 358 U.S. 217, 220–21 (1959).

[25]   Langley v. Ryder, 778 F.2d 1092, 1095 (5th Cir. 1985) (citing Oliphant v. Suquamish Indian Tribe, 435 U.S. 191, 208 n. 17 (1978)).

[26]   Williams v. Lee, 358 U.S. 217, 220–21 (1959).

[27]   Rennard Strickland, Fire and the Spirits: Cherokee Law from Clan to Court (1975); J. Matthew Martin, The Nature and Extent of the Exercise of Criminal Jurisdiction by the Cherokee Supreme Court: 1823–1835, 32 N.C. Cent. L.J. 27, 57–60 (2009).

[28]   Oliphant v. Suquamish Indian Tribe, 435 U.S. 191, 196 n. 7 (1978); Roxanne Dunbar Ortiz, The Great Sioux Nation: Sitting in Judgment of America 175 (1977).

[29]   Bureau of Justice Assistance, Pathways to Justice: Building and Sustaining Tribal Justice Systems in Contemporary America 6 (October 2005).

[30]   United States v. Winans, 198 U.S. 371, 381 (1905) (holding that Indian treaties are "not a grant of rights to the Indians, but a grant of rights from them—a reservation of those not granted.").

[31]   E.g., Johnson v. McIntosh, 21 U.S. 543 (1823) (holding in dicta that Congress can divest Indian tribes and individual Indians of the authority to alienate certain forms of Indian property).

Supreme Court engages in interpreting what authority tribes have retained over the course of history.[32]

Tribal authority may be divested by agreement with an Indian nation, such as a treaty, or by Act of Congress, which is governed by the clear statement rule. In short, courts will not find a limitation of tribal governance authority absent a clear statement by Congress to that effect.[33]

The clear statement rule is a defining rule in federal Indian law. The clear statement rule is, simply put, that courts will not find a limitation of tribal governance authority absent a clear statement by Congress to that effect. The Supreme Court in *Michigan v. Bay Mills Indian Community*,[34] articulated the clear statement rule as "an enduring principle of Indian law: Although Congress has plenary authority over tribes, courts will not lightly assume that Congress in fact intends to undermine Indian self-government."[35]

§ 1.2   Eras of Federal Indian Law

Federal government policymaking has outlined American Indian affairs throughout American history, driven by changes in relationships between Indian nations and state and federal interests. The fluctuating history of federal-tribal legal affairs is extremely well documented.[36] Federal policy toward Indian tribes has moved in various decades from physical extirpation to measured separatism to removal to assimilation to self-determination—sometimes at the same time.[37] This section will canvas those eras.

---

[32] E.g., Oliphant v. Suquamish Indian Tribe, 435 U.S. 191 (1978) (holding that Indian tribes have no authority to prosecute non-Indians, even absent an Act of Congress stating so); Montana v. United States, 450 U.S. 544 (1981) (holding that Indian tribes have no civil regulatory authority over nonmembers unless nonmember activity meets one of two limited exceptions).

[33] Michigan v. Bay Mills Indian Community, 134 S.Ct. 2024, 2031–32 (2014); Santa Clara Pueblo v. Martinez, 436 U.S. 49, 60 (1978).

[34] 134 S.Ct. 2024 (2014).

[35] Id. at 2031–32 (citations omitted).

[36] E.g., William C. Canby, American Indian Law in a Nutshell 13–34 (6th ed. 2015); Mr. Justice Joseph Story, A Familiar Exposition of the Constitution of the United States 13–14 (1840); Charles F. Wilkinson, American Indians, Time, and the Law 14–19 (1987); Vine Deloria, Jr., "Congress in its Wisdom": The Course of Indian Legislation, in The Aggressions of Civilization: Federal Indian Policy Since the 1880s 105 (Sandra L. Cawalader & Vine Deloria, Jr., eds. 1984); Michael Gross, Indian Self-Determination and Tribal Sovereignty: An Analysis of Recent Federal Policy, 56 Tex. L. Rev. 1195 (1978); Judith V. Royster, The Legacy of Allotment, 27 Ariz. St. L.J. 1, 7–9 (1995).

[37] See generally Duro v. Reina, 495 U.S. 676, 709 (1990) (Brennan, J., dissenting) ("This country has pursued contradictory policies with respect to the Indians.").

Treaty Era

The American treaty era began at the Founding of the Republic and continued formally until 1871.

Treaties between the European powers and Native nations largely governed pre-Republic relations.[38] The American treaty era began in the 1770s, during the American Revolution. Eventually, the First Congress enacted the Trade and Intercourse Act to fulfill its treaty obligations in Indian country and to establish policy under its Indian Commerce Clause authority.[39] In the Indian Commerce Clause, the Framers had moved away from vesting any reserved authority in the states. In the first important Indian law cases that reached the Supreme Court—*Johnson v. McIntosh,*[40] *Cherokee Nation v. Georgia,*[41] and *Worcester v. Georgia*[42]—the Marshall Court held that federal authority in Indian affairs was exclusive as to the states. *Worcester v. Georgia* also confirmed that state laws had no force in Indian country.[43] The Trade and Intercourse Acts established federal Indian policy, much of which survived as effective policy for more than a century.

In 1871, Congress passed a statute that purported to eliminate the authority of the President and the Senate to negotiate and ratify treaties with Indian tribes, although Congress continued to recognize as valid any treaty rights effective on that date.[44] From that point, the United States continued to negotiate with Indian tribes, but the resulting agreements would have to be adopted by Congress as legislation.[45]

Removal Era

The removal era began formally in 1830 with the enactment of the Removal Act and eventually gave way to the reservation era in the mid-1850s. During the removal era, the United States forcibly removed most American Indians and Indian nations east of the Mississippi River to foreign lands in the west.

---

[38]   Stuart Banner, How the Indians Lost Their Land: Law and Power on the Frontier 85–111 (2005).

[39]   An Act to regulate trade and intercourse with the Indian tribes, July 22, 1790, 1 Stat. 137. Congress reenacted the Trade and Intercourse Act multiple times, until finally enacting a permanent statute in 1834.

[40]   21 U.S. 543 (1823).

[41]   30 U.S. 1 (1831).

[42]   31 U.S. 515 (1832).

[43]   Id. at 559–61.

[44]   16 Stat. 566, codified at 25 U.S.C. § 71.

[45]   Antoine v. Washington, 420 U.S. 194, 203–04 (1975) ("[The Act of 1871] meant no more, however, than that after 1871 relations with Indians would be governed by Acts of Congress and not by treaty.").

"Despite the treaties and federal trade and intercourse laws, non-Indians continually encroached on the lands reserved to tribes on the Indian side of the frontier boundary line."[46] Many American people, particularly in the southern states, desired to control the large treaty-reserved areas of unceded Indian lands within and on their borders. The southern states came to view the treaties themselves as the primary impediments to desired control of all the lands east of the Mississippi River.[47] After the Revolution, the fortunes of most eastern tribes declined precipitously. In the north, the destruction of traditional hunting, fishing, and trading territories caused overwhelming poverty and disease.[48] After the War of 1812, where most Great Lakes tribes had sided with the British, United States dealings with the defeated tribes became ever harsher. In the south, American military campaigns waged by Andrew Jackson and others ravaged several tribes.[49] In all areas, the pressures of often illegal American settlement in Indian country created conflict and destabilization of tribal communities. The United States tended to ignore tribal pleas to maintain the treaty-guaranteed reservation boundaries.

By the 1830s, American Indian policy concentrated on the forced removal of Indian peoples. President Jackson pushed through Congress the Indian Removal Act of 1830.[50] The United States then renegotiated old treaties of military alliance in favor of new treaties of land cession and Indian removal, whereby entire Indian nations agreed to move west beyond the Mississippi River. Even the Cherokee Nation, which had won an important victory in the Supreme Court,[51] could not avoid the renegotiation of its foundational Treaty of Hopewell, resulting in the Trail of Tears.[52]

---

[46]   David H. Getches, Charles F. Wilkinson, Robert A. Williams, Jr., and Matthew L.M. Fletcher, Cases and Materials on Federal Indian Law 94 (6th ed. 2011).

[47]   1 Francis Paul Prucha, The Great Father: The United States Government and American Indians 214–469 (1784) (describing the removal of the eastern Indians).

[48]   Matthew L.M. Fletcher, The Eagle Returns: The Legal History of the Grand Traverse Band of Ottawa and Chippewa Indians 2–33 (2012); Mary Lethert Wingard, North Country: The Making of Minnesota (2010).

[49]   Anthony F.C. Wallace, The Long, Bitter Trail: Andrew Jackson and the Indians (1993).

[50]   An Act: To provide for an exchange of lands with the Indians residing in any of the states or territories, and for their removal west of the river Mississippi, 4 Stat. 411–12 (1830).

[51]   Worcester v. Georgia, 31 U.S. 515 (1832).

[52]   Rennard Strickland, Fire and the Spirits—Cherokee Law From Clan to Court 65–67 (1975).

Reservation Era

The American policy of removal of the eastern Indians gave way to the reservation-based policy of dealing with the western tribes, a period dominating the latter half of the 19th century.

Once again, militarily powerful Indian communities confronted the United States, forcing the negotiation of several treaties purportedly guaranteeing that large tracts of land would remain tribal lands forever. For example, the 1851 treaty of Fort Laramie between the Lakota, Nakota, and Dakota Indians, the Cheyenne Indians, other tribal nations, and the United States reserved almost all of the Dakota Territory and parts of three other states to the tribal nations.[53] Treaties reserved vast amounts of land for tribes such as the Crow Nation, the confederated tribes at the Flathead, Colville, and Yakima reservations, and elsewhere.[54] As it had in the east, however, the establishment of the reservations quickly led to hardship for the Indian communities. The declining fortunes of Indian nations, along with the demand for Indian lands, encouraged the United States to seek additional treaty concessions from tribes. Indian tribes on the verge of starvation and threatened with being overwhelmed by the non-Indian intruders on their lands had little choice but to comply.

Allotment Era

As the treaty period came to a close, American Indian law and policy became geared toward breaking up some of the larger tribal reservations for purposes of American settlement, while expanding their efforts to "civilize" Indian people. This period in American Indian law and policy is often referred to as the allotment era.[55] The allotment era formally began in 1887 but the Interior Department had been exposing Indian nations to allotment since at least the 1850s. Congress ended the allotment era in 1934.

Allotment refers to the division of large tribal reservations into smaller parcels, with individual parcels of typically 160 or 80 acres "allotted" to Indian heads of households, and the rest of the reservation land being put on the open market as "surplus" lands. The tribal allotments would be owned in trust by the federal government for a period that ranged from five to 25 years, depending on the tribal-specific implementing statute. At the end of the trust period, the government would issue a patent to the Indian

---

[53] Francis Paul Prucha, American Indian Treaties: The History of a Political Anomaly 237–40 (1994).

[54] Id. at 235–60.

[55] See generally D.S. Otis, The Dawes Act and the Allotment of Indian Lands (1973).

landholder, who then acquired full title to the land. But at that point, the land became taxable by state and local governments. Often, as soon as the land reverted to Indians, it would be lost one way or another—through tax foreclosures, theft, fraud, or any number of other devices.

While allotment of Indian lands had been tried in the east as far back as the late 18th century, at Cherokee in the early 19th century, and also in the Old Northwest in the 1850s, it was not the prime focus of American policy until Congress passed the General Allotment Act (also known as the Dawes Act) in 1887.[56] In the next few decades, Congress enacted numerous statutes intending to implement allotment on various tribal reservations.

The allotment statutes often violated express treaty provisions. In the case *Lone Wolf v. Hitchcock*,[57] the leaders of Kiowa, Comanche, and Apache tribes that had signed the Treaty of Medicine Lodge alleged that the United States had used deception to acquire the consent of the community to allotment and in any event had violated the treaty. The Supreme Court held that the United States had plenary power over Indian affairs and therefore had authority to unilaterally abrogate Indian treaties. The Court also held that the political question doctrine would foreclose most challenges to Congressional Indian affairs legislation.

Merrill Gates, Chairman of the United States Board of Indian Commissioners, referred to the allotment policy in 1901 as "a mighty pulverizing engine to break up the tribal mass."[58] President Theodore Roosevelt borrowed the phrase in his first annual message to Congress.[59] Unfortunately for Indian people, allotment was a terribly effective method in reducing the tribal land base. From 1887 when Congress adopted this policy until 1934 when it ended the policy, two-thirds of tribal land holdings moved into non-Indian ownership.[60]

The allotment era, more so than any other era in federal Indian policy, contributed to the severe doctrinal and jurisdictional

---

[56] Act of Feb. 8, 1887, c. 119, § 1, 24 Stat. 388, codified as amended at 25 U.S.C. §§ 331 et seq., repealed, Pub.L. 106–462, Title I, § 106(a)(1), Nov. 7, 2000, 114 Stat. 2007.

[57] 187 U.S. 553 (1903). See generally Angela R. Riley, The Apex of Congress' Plenary Power over Indian Affairs: The Story of Lone Wolf v. Hitchcock, Indian Law Stories 189 (Carole Goldberg, Kevin K. Washburn, and Philip P. Frickey, eds. 2011).

[58] Kenneth H. Bobroff, Retelling Allotment: Indian Property and the Myth of Common Ownership, 54 Vand. L. Rev. 1559, 1610 (2001).

[59] See id. at 1610 n. 272.

[60] Stacy L. Leeds, Borrowing from Blackacre: Expanding Tribal Land Bases through the Creation of Future Interests and Joint Tenancies, 80 N.D. L. Rev. 827, 831–32 (2004).

complexity in Indian country cases. The division of Indian reservations into smaller parcels, with some of the parcels being owned by Indians in fee simple, some owned by non-Indians in fee simple, and some held in trust as reservation land created the jurisdictional problem of "checkerboarding," with some parcels being under tribal and federal jurisdiction, and others being under state and local jurisdiction.[61] Finally, allotment created the incredible problem of "fractionated heirships."[62] In some remarkable cases, several thousand heirs have an undivided interest in a small amount of acreage. Since no one person can control the land, the United States often has de facto control of the land, leasing it to ranchers or farmers and collecting rents for the Indian owners.[63] In recent decades, the United States has taken substantial efforts to deal with this serious problem.

Assimilation

During the reservation and allotment period, the United States attempted to assimilate Indian people into the American mainstream. American policy of this era included attempts to "civilize" American Indians by educating Indian children in the American style, forcing Indian households into farming, and eliminating the communal ownership of tribal lands in favor of individual property ownership.[64]

As the Supreme Court noted, "The objectives of allotment were simple and clear cut: to extinguish tribal sovereignty, erase reservation boundaries, and force assimilation of Indians into the society at large."[65] President Grant's "Peace Policy" initiated many of these assimilative programs. "President Grant and Commissioner Parker hoped to place Indians on reservations where they could be

---

[61] Seymour v. Superintendent, 368 U.S. 351, 358 (1962); DeCoteau v. District Court, 420 U.S. 425, 466–67 (1975) (Douglas, J., dissenting). See generally Leonard A. Carlson, Federal Policy and Indian Land: Economic Interests and the Sale of Indian Allotments, 1900–1934, 57 Ag. Hist. 33 (1983); Carl G. Hakansson, Allotment at Pine Ridge Reservation: Its Consequences and Alternative Remedies, 73 N.D. L. Rev. 231 (1997).

[62] Brian Sawers, Tribal Land Corporations: Using Incorporation to Combat Fractionation, 88 Neb. L. Rev. 385 (2009); Jessica A. Shoemaker, Like Snow in the Springtime: Allotment, Fractionation, and the Indian Land Tenure Problem, 2003 Wis. L. Rev. 729. E.g., Covelo Indian Community v. Watt, 551 F. Supp. 366, 375 (D. D.C. 1982).

[63] See generally Cobell v. Norton, 240 F.3d 1081 (D.C. Cir. 2001).

[64] Frederick E. Hoxie, A Final Promise: The Campaign to Assimilate the Indians, 1880–1920 (1984); Amelia V. Katanski, Learning to Write "Indian": The Boarding School Experience and American Indian Literature (2005).

[65] County of Yakima v. Yakima Indian Nation, 502 U.S. 251, 254 (1992). See generally Frederick E. Hoxie, A Final Promise: The Campaign to Assimilate the Indians, 1880–1920 (1984); Francis Paul Prucha, American Indian Policy in Crisis: Christian Reformers and the Indians, 1865–1900 (1976).

taught the methods of modern agriculture and be economically independent."[66] Modern commentators have harshly criticized this program of "civilization": "This policy focused on assimilating the Indians and otherwise transforming them from 'savages' into 'civilized' men. This process took the form of converting Indians to Christianity and providing Western education to Indian children, with the federal government expending considerable sums on building boarding schools and hiring teachers."[67]

Through statute and treaty, Congress enacted numerous measures by which Indians could discard their "uncivilized" lives and become American citizens. Prior to 1924, Indians could become American citizens, for example, "through a treaty provision; through the granting of an allotment; through issuance of a patent in fee simple by the Secretary; by 'adopting the habits of civilized life'; by minor status; by birth; through service in the American military upon judicial application, by marriage, and pursuant to specific acts of Congress." In 1924, Congress enacted the Indian Citizenship Act, providing for citizenship of the remaining non-citizen American Indians.[68]

The Indian New Deal

In 1928, Congress received the Meriam Report, which provided the first detailed and comprehensive overview of the state of American Indian nations and people.[69] The Report offered significant empirical evidence that the allotment and assimilation policies of the federal government were failures. Indian people were the poorest and worst educated people in the United States. The Report found that the allotment acts had done little more than dispossess Indian people of their lands. The Roosevelt Administration Interior Department, led by Interior Department Secretary Harold Ickes, Indian Affairs Commissioner John Collier, and Nathan Margold and Felix S. Cohen in the Solicitor's Office, now-legendary leaders and reformers in the field of modern Indian law and policy, proposed legislation that would dramatically depart from the policies of the allotment era and their diminishment of tribal governmental authority.

---

[66]   Wisconsin v. Stockbridge-Munsee Community, 366 F. Supp. 2d 698, 714 (E.D. Wis. 2004), aff'd, 554 F.3d 657 (7th Cir. 2009).

[67]   Robert B. Porter, The Demise of the Ongwehoweh and the Rise of the Native Americans: Redressing the Genocidal Act of Forcing American Citizenship upon Indigenous Peoples, 15 Harv. Black Letter L.J. 107, 113 (1999) (footnotes omitted).

[68]   Act of June 2, 1924, 43 Stat. 253 (codified at 8 U.S.C. § 1401(b) (1994)).

[69]   Report of the Institute for Government Research, The Problems of Indian Administration (1928).

In 1934, Congress passed the Indian Reorganization Act (IRA).[70] The IRA ended the allotment era by prohibiting further allotment of Indian reservations and taking action to maintain what was left of the tribal land base.[71] Congress granted authority to the Secretary of Interior to repurchase lands lost during the allotment era and hold that land in trust for Indian tribes and individual Indians.[72]

The IRA, as its name suggested, allowed Indian tribes to reorganize their tribal governments into more modern structures, as well as allowing for federally charted corporations with which to conduct business operations.[73] For the first time, omnibus Congressional legislation aimed at Indian affairs allowed for tribes to opt out of the legislation. As Assistant Interior Solicitor and co-author of the original draft of the IRA, Felix Cohen drafted a comprehensive legal memorandum for local Bureau officials advising tribes how to reorganize, which included an outline of powers that Cohen suggested could be included in a tribal constitution.[74] Most of these constitutions remain in force, and initially provided for Secretarial oversight of day-to-day tribal government operations (although those provisions are no longer extant). The IRA remains the foundational federal legislation in modern Indian affairs.

Termination Era

Despite the recent enactment and success of the IRA, by the late 1940s members of Congress engaged in anti-Communist Cold War rhetoric pushed for the repeal of the Act and the termination of the federal-tribal relationship.[75] In 1953, Congress passed House Concurrent Resolution 108, calling for the eventual termination of services and programs to tribal governments. Congress then began the process of choosing individual Indian tribes and terminating them. Congress targeted tribes mostly in California, Oregon, Utah, Oklahoma, and Wisconsin for termination, a process that consisted of cutting off federal appropriations, disbanding tribal government,

---

[70]　Wheeler-Howard Act, Act of June 18, 1934, 48 Stat. 984, codified at 25 U.S.C. §§ 5101 et seq.

[71]　25 U.S.C. § 5101.

[72]　25 U.S.C. § 5108.

[73]　25 U.S.C. §§ 5123, 5124.

[74]　Felix S. Cohen, On the Drafting of Tribal Constitutions (David E. Wilkins, ed. 2006).

[75]　Charles F. Wilkinson & Eric R. Biggs, The Evolution of the Termination Policy, 5 Am. Indian L. Rev. 139 (1977).

and privatizing tribal businesses.[76] President Kennedy informally put the practice on hold and by 1973 Congress had formally ended the termination era by restoring the Menominee Tribe to full status as a federally recognized tribe.[77] Not all terminated tribes have been restored, however.

During the Termination era, Congress enacted several statutes that served the process of termination. In 1953, Congress enacted a statute commonly known as Public Law 280 that extended state criminal and civil adjudicatory jurisdiction into Indian country in several states, most notably in California, without tribal consent.[78] Other states had the option of accepting jurisdiction over Indian country.

Under the Kennedy and Johnson Administrations, termination proponents lost momentum as the federal government became engaged in the War on Poverty. Congress continued its paternalistic and assimilationist bent, however, and in 1968, Congress passed the Indian Civil Rights Act,[79] also known as the Indian Bill of Rights, which required tribal governments to comply with many federal constitutional rights.

Self-Determination Era

President Johnson's 1968 Message to Congress on Goals and Programs for the American Indians, titled The Forgotten American, proposed a new goal of ending the debate about termination and stressed self-determination.[80] Among other things, that message called for enactment of the Indian Civil Rights Act to provide for tribal consent before extension of state jurisdiction under Public Law 280, as Congress did later that year. Also, in conjunction with that message, President Johnson established the National Council on Indian Opportunity ("NCIO"), chaired by the Vice President and consisting of seven cabinet-level officials and six Indian leaders (later funded by Congress and expanded by President Nixon to include the Attorney General and two more tribal leaders). The

---

[76] For a list of termination acts, see David H. Getches, Charles F. Wilkinson, Robert A. Williams, Jr., Matthew L.M. Fletcher, and Kristen A. Carpenter, Cases and Materials on Federal Indian Law 235 (7th ed. 2017).

[77] Pub.L. 93–197, Dec. 22, 1973, 87 Stat 770.

[78] Aug. 15, 1953, c. 505, § 2, 67 Stat. 588, codified in relevant part at 18 U.S.C. § 1162. See also 28 U.S.C. § 1360(a) (parallel civil provision).

[79] Pub. L. 90–284, Title II, § 201, 82 Stat. 77 (1968), codified at 25 U.S.C. §§ 1301 et seq.

[80] 4 Week Comp. Pres. Docs. 438 (1968).

NCIO made a number of policy proposals that provided the basis for President Nixon's Special Message to Congress.[81]

In 1970, President Nixon's message to Congress announced a fundamental shift in federal Indian policy—self-determination.[82] The Message renounced the termination policy, established that adherence to the federal trust responsibility would guide federal Indian policy, and proposed a structure to dramatically reduce federal control over tribes—by recognizing greatly increased tribal authority to manage affairs on their reservations as a replacement for federal bureaucratic control.

The Nixon Administration and later Administrations proposed and oversaw the adoption of numerous Self-Determination Acts and Self-Governance Acts in which Congress finally fulfilled the original promise of the IRA to allow Indian tribes to take over federal Indian affairs programs.[83] Congress also took steps to encourage tribal economic development in the enactment of statutes such as the Indian Finance Act of 1974,[84] the Indian Tribal Government Tax Status Act of 1982,[85] and the Indian Gaming Regulatory Act of 1988.[86] Congress enacted legislation supporting tribal law enforcement, the development of tribal courts, and perhaps the most controversial Indian affairs statute in the era, the Indian Child Welfare Act,[87] requiring the transfer of state court cases involving Indian child custody to tribal courts. Congressional Indian affairs legislation did not, however, include a major reworking or change in the IRA that would have created certainty or even predictability in tribal government jurisdiction and authority.

During this period, and most especially in three monumental decisions in 1978, the Supreme Court played an increasingly important role in federal Indian law.[88] In *Oliphant v. Suquamish*

---

[81] Thomas A. Britten, The National Council on Indian Opportunity: Quiet Champion of Self-Determination 264 (2014).

[82] Message from the President of the United States Transmitting Recommendations for Indian Policy, H.R. Doc. No. 363, 91st Cong., 2d. Sess. (1970); 116 Cong. Rec. 23258.

[83] See generally Philip S. Deloria, The Era of Indian Self-Determination: An Overview, in Indian Self-Rule: First-Hand Accounts of Indian-White Relations from Roosevelt to Reagan 191 (Kenneth R. Philp, ed. 1986).

[84] Pub. L. 93–262, § 2, Apr. 12, 1974, 88 Stat. 77, 25 U.S.C. §§ 1451 et seq.

[85] Pub. L. 97–473, Title II, § 202(a), Jan. 14, 1983, 96 Stat. 2608, codified as amended at 26 U.S.C. § 7871.

[86] Pub. L. 100–497, 102 Stat. 2467, codified at 25 U.S.C. §§ 2701 et seq.

[87] Pub. L. 95–608, § 2, Nov. 8, 1978, 92 Stat. 3069, codified at 25 U.S.C. §§ 1901 et seq.

[88] See generally Philip P. Frickey, (Native) American Exceptionalism in Federal Public Law, 119 Harv. L. Rev. 431, 436 (2005); David H. Getches, Beyond Indian Law: The Rehnquist Court's Pursuit of States' Rights, Color-Blind Justice and Mainstream Values, 86 Minn. L. Rev. 267, 361 (2001); David H. Getches, Conquering

Indian Tribe,[89] the Court held that Indian tribes do not have the authority to prosecute non-Indians for crimes committed in Indian country.[90] A few days after *Oliphant*, the Court recognized in *United States v. Wheeler*[91] that Indian tribes have inherent authority to punish members for crimes committed in Indian country. Finally, in *Santa Clara Pueblo v. Martinez*,[92] perhaps the most far-reaching decision of the three, the Court held that Indian tribes retain immunity from suit in federal courts absent their consent. In the same case, the Court recognized that tribes retain inherent authority to decide all internal legal and political questions, such as membership, domestic relations, and tribal governance.

The Supreme Court's common law rulings in recent decades have contributed to the dynamic changes in federal Indian law. In 1981's *Montana v. United States*,[93] the Court held that Indian tribes have limited civil jurisdiction over nonmembers on non-Indian fee land within the reservation, subject to two heavily litigated exceptions.[94] In *California v. Cabazon Band of Mission Indians*,[95] the Court held that states cannot regulate the high-stakes bingo operations of California tribes.[96] In *Cotton Petroleum Corp. v. New Mexico*,[97] and in *Sherrill v. Oneida Indian Nation*,[98] the Court held that states have relatively expansive taxation and regulation rights in Indian country.

§ 1.3   A Demographic Introduction to Indian Country

A first step in the study of Indian law is to gain some understanding of the state of Indian tribes, Indian individuals, and

---

the Cultural Frontier: The New Subjectivism of the Supreme Court in Indian Law, 84 Cal. L. Rev. 1573, 1576 (1996).

[89]   435 U.S. 191 (1978).

[90]   The Supreme Court extended that holding to all nonmembers in Duro v. Reina, 495 U.S. 676 (1990).

[91]   435 U.S. 313 (1978).

[92]   436 U.S. 49 (1978).

[93]   450 U.S. 544 (1981).

[94]   Douglas B. L. Endreson, Reconciling the Sovereignty of Indian Tribes in Civil Matters with the Montana Line of Cases, 55 Villanova L. Rev. 863 (2010); Sarah Karakoff, Tribal Civil Judicial Jurisdiction Over Nonmembers: A Practical Guide For Judges, 81 U. Colo. L. Rev. 1187 (2010).

[95]   480 U.S. 202 (1987).

[96]   Congress enacted the Indian Gaming Regulatory Act the next year. Pub. L. 100–497, Oct. 17, 1988, 102 Stat. 2467, codified at 25 U.S.C. §§ 2701 et seq.

[97]   490 U.S. 163 (1989).

[98]   544 U.S. 197 (2005).

Indian lands and resources. Overgeneralization is inevitable, for American Indians are a wildly heterogeneous group of peoples. The differences are many: landed and landless tribes; large and small tribes; eastern and western tribes; "federally recognized," "non-federally recognized," and terminated tribes; reservation and urban Indians; traditional and more assimilated Indians; and special situations with their own distinct legal histories, such as the tribes of Oklahoma and Natives of Alaska and Hawaii.

Reservations vary greatly in size and geography. The Navajo reservation consists of more than 17 million acres of high, grazing and red rock land in Arizona, New Mexico, and Utah—an area larger than West Virginia. In North and South Dakota, the four big Sioux reservations amount to about 5 million acres of mostly prairie. In contrast, the smallest reservation is less than 100 acres, and a few small reservations have no residents at all. Most reservations are west of the one-hundredth meridian, a north-south line running through the center of Nebraska. Consequently, high numbers of Indian law cases are heard by the Eighth, Ninth, and Tenth Circuit Courts of Appeal.

In the 2010 Census, the annual population estimate for the American Indian population alone was 2.9 million and in combination with another race the total was 5.1 million. Today approximately half of the Indian population lives on or adjacent to a reservation. Partly as a result of relocation programs of the termination era of the 1950s and 1960s that moved Indians from reservations to the cities, the other half lives in urban areas and almost three-fourths of that urban population lives in metropolitan areas of one million or more inhabitants.

In 2008, the Census Bureau reported that 24 percent of all Indians (approximately 800,000) were living below the poverty level (based on a 1998–2000 average). However, that figure is down from 1990, when 31 percent of all Indians were below the poverty level. As of 2000, the unemployment rate on reservations was 13 percent compared to 6.3 percent for the overall U.S. average. However, unemployment rates vary dramatically between reservations. The Kickapoo reservation in Texas reported a 70 percent unemployment rate, the Navajo Nation's unemployment rate was 25 percent, and the Cherokee Nation's unemployment rate was below the national average at 5.8 percent.

According to the BIA's latest figures released in 2005, Indian tribes and individuals own approximately 56 million acres of land, an increase of approximately 4 million acres since 1980. This figure includes 45.7 million acres of tribal trust land and 10.1 million acres of individual trust allotments. Alaska Natives hold another 44 million acres as a result of the Alaska Native Claims Settlement Act of 1971. In all, American Indians groups hold about 4.2 percent of the land in the United States.

Chapter 2

THE ORIGINS OF FEDERAL INDIAN LAW

Analysis

The foundational principles of federal Indian law arrived early in the Supreme Court's Indian law jurisprudence. This chapter parses the so-called Marshall Trilogy of cases that brought us the working rules for federal, state, and tribal government interaction. These cases were of enormous import to the United States and to the American political elite, raising and deciding questions impacting the massive financial investment in land speculation and states' rights under the federal government leading up to the Civil War.

§ 2.1   The Doctrine of Discovery

The Doctrine of Discovery is an early federal common law set of principles, now thoroughly repudiated as a legitimate doctrine, governing land transactions between Indian nations and outsiders. The "doctrine" holds that Indian people do not hold their lands in fee simple absolute, but instead only hold a right to occupy their land—a so-called "Indian title." The "discovering" sovereign and its successors own a preemption right that bars Indian people and Indian nations from selling their lands to anyone except the sovereign. This theory dominates the imagination of legal scholars and Indian affairs policy makers even today, but never had firm historical or practical basis.

Early United States' Indian affairs policies were consistent with the Doctrine of Discovery. After the Framing of the Constitution, the First Congress enacted the first Trade and Intercourse Act, and reauthorized them for several decades.[1] **See § 3.1.** These early statutes provided for direct regulation and control

---

[1]   Trade and Intercourse Act, Act of July 22, 1790, ch. 33, 1 Stat. 137 (1790); Act of March 30, 1802, ch. 13, 2 Stat. 139 (1802); Act of June 30, 1834, ch. 161, 4 Stat. 729 (1834), codified as amended at 25 U.S.C. §§ 177, 261–265; 18 U.S.C. § 1152.

by the federal government over all aspects of trade with Indians, including comprehensive regulation of intercourse with Indians and tribes. At least on paper, Congress exercised strict control over Indian commercial transactions for over two centuries.

The leading theory legally supporting the appropriation of Indian lands by non-Indian people and governments remains the "Doctrine of Discovery."[2] This theory assumes that Indigenous peoples did not own land and resources in the same manner as European nations and their colonial subjects. Indian people merely occupied or possessed the land, taking resources from the land as needed. The designation of this kind of land ownership is original Indian title, or aboriginal title, or Indian title, or a permutation of those phrases. Since the theory assumes Indian people do not own land, the land was free for the taking by European forces. The first European nation that arrived in a particular area occupied by Indigenous peoples acquired "discovery" rights to the land exclusive as to all other nations. European governments with discovery rights could clear title to the land by either purchasing the occupancy rights of the Indian people from them, or by conquering the Indians by military force. A later permutation under American law was that the taking of Indian title did not require the payment of just compensation under the Takings Clause of the United States Constitution.[3] **See § 4.1.**

The English Crown, as noted in **§ 2.3**, asserted plenary control over intercourse with Indian nations and Indian people. As the Doctrine of Discovery provided, the national government with discovery rights could regulate the method by which the lands of the Indian peoples were acquired. The English, for the considerable part, chose acquisition rather than conquest.[4]

Johnson v. McIntosh

In 1823, the Supreme Court decided *Johnson v. McIntosh*.[5] The case involved Indian land sales by the Illinois and Piankeshaw Indian nations to individual purchasers in 1773 and 1775 that conflicted with an after-acquired purchaser from the United States in 1818, and cemented the Doctrine of Discovery in American law.

---

[2]   See generally Robert A. Williams, Jr., The American Indian in Western Legal Thought 308–23 (1990); Robert J. Miller, The Doctrine of Discovery in American Indian Law, 42 Idaho L. Rev. 1 (2005).

[3]   Tee-Hit-Ton Indians v. United States, 348 U.S. 272 (1955).

[4]   Stuart Banner, How the Indians Lost Their Land: Law and Power on the Frontier 10–111 (2005).

[5]   21 U.S. 543 (1832). The court report spells "McIntosh" as "M'Intosh," which was not William McIntosh's preferred spelling.

The case arose from complicated, collusive, and still misunderstood facts. Drawing from the statement of the case provided by the Supreme Court's official reporter, we learn that the Illinois chiefs sold two parcels of land to individuals at a British military post on July 5, 1773 for $24,000 in American dollars.[6] Further, we learn that on October 18, 1775, Piankeshaw chiefs sold two parcels of land to individuals at a different British military post for $31,000.[7] The lands were located in the southern part of what is now Indiana and Illinois. None of the original purchasers ever occupied the land in question.[8] The sole party claiming occupancy was McIntosh, who had purchased 11,560 acres from the United States in 1818.[9] The United States apparently acquired its interest in this land from the State of Virginia, which had claimed the territory prior to the Revolution, and then turned over its claim to the area to the federal government in 1783.[10] At least portions of land in the various transactions overlapped. How much overlapping land is difficult to ascertain because the Indian and the non-Indian purchasers described the lands in culturally different ways. Regardless, Johnson, representing the original purchasers, and McIntosh, the 1818 purchaser, conflicted over ownership, and the Supreme Court reviewed the matter.

The Holding and Reasoning

The Supreme Court held that the Indian nations had no authority to alienate lands because they did not own the land; and that the Indian nations could only alienate their occupancy or possessory rights to the sovereign, not to individuals. In other words, neither the 1773 nor the 1775 sales were valid. McIntosh prevailed because he had acquired the land from the United States, and the United States had acquired the land by virtue of the Doctrine of Discovery.

In *Johnson*, Chief Justice Marshall introduced the Doctrine of Discovery as a formal matter into federal common law. The Court first held that discovery gave rights to the discovering nation over all other European governments: "This principle was, that discovery gave title to the government by whose subjects, or by whose authority, it was made, against all other European governments, which title might be consummated by possession."[11]

---

6 Id. at 550–54.

7 Id. at 555–58.

8 Id. at 560, 561–62.

9 Id. at 560.

10 Id. at 559.

11 Id. at 573.

Indian governments did not enjoy the discovery right.[12] Chief Justice Marshall explained that Indians retained rights in the lands they occupied, but that those rights had been limited post-Discovery. Specifically, the discovering nation acquired superior title to the lands held by Indigenous peoples.[13] Indian title amounted to the right to continue occupying and enjoying the land, subject to the will of the discoverer; Indian nations could not sell the land to anyone except the discovering nation.[14] The federal government, according to the chief justice, held the preemption right, the right to extinguish Indian title via purchase or conquest, but also *title* to the Indian lands.[15]

The chief justice supposed that Indians would assimilate under the governance of the United States as "conqueror."[16] He reasoned that conquering nations did not eradicate those they had conquered, but would allow conquered people to join the ranks of the victorious nation. He presumed that conquered people would not be "wantonly oppressed" by the government, setting the stage for the federal trust responsibility toward Indian nations and Indian people. **See § 5.2.**

---

[12] Id. ("The exclusion of all other Europeans, necessarily gave to the nation making the discovery the sole right of acquiring the soil from the natives, and establishing settlements upon it. It was a right with which no Europeans could interfere. It was a right which all asserted for themselves, and to the assertion of which, by others, all assented.").

[13] Id. at 574 ("In the establishment of these relations, the rights of the original inhabitants were, in no instance, entirely disregarded; but were necessarily, to a considerable extent, impaired.").

[14] Id. ("They were admitted to be the rightful occupants of the soil, with a legal as well as just claim to retain possession of it, and to use it according to their own discretion; but their rights to complete sovereignty, as independent nations, were necessarily diminished, and their power to dispose of the soil at their own will, to whomsoever they pleased, was denied by the original fundamental principle, that discovery gave exclusive title to those who made it.").

[15] Id. at 587 ("The United States, then, have unequivocally acceded to that great and broad rule by which its civilized inhabitants now hold this country. They hold, and assert in themselves, the title by which it was acquired. They maintain, as all others have maintained, that discovery gave an exclusive right to extinguish the Indian title of occupancy, either by purchase or by conquest; and gave also a right to such a degree of sovereignty, as the circumstances of the people would allow them to exercise.").

[16] Id. at 589 ("The title by conquest is acquired and maintained by force. The conqueror prescribes its limits. Humanity, however, acting on public opinion, has established, as a general rule, that the conquered shall not be wantonly oppressed, and that their condition shall remain as eligible as is compatible with the objects of the conquest. Most usually, they are incorporated with the victorious nation, and become subjects or citizens of the government with which they are connected. The new and old members of the society mingle with each other; the distinction between them is gradually lost, and they make one people. Where this incorporation is practicable, humanity demands, and a wise policy requires, that the rights of the conquered to property should remain unimpaired; that the new subjects should be governed as equitably as the old, and that confidence in their security should gradually banish the painful sense of being separated from their ancient connexions, and united by force to strangers.").

Even as Chief Justice Marshall adopted these rules, he mocked the doctrine itself, stating that it was an "extravagant . . . pretension" for Euro-Americans to follow a rule that they may take significant property rights from indigenous peoples through discovery.[17]

How the Native Sellers Understood the Transactions

Recently, Dr. Patricia Seed has uncovered a map drawn by the Piankeshaw Indians in 1775, a map that tells a very different story than the ones told by the parties and the Supreme Court.[18] The map details the 1775 purchase by the Wabash Company from the Indians' point of view and knowledge, showing that they engaged in "pricking holes into the buckskin and employing indigenous symbols. . . ."[19] The map shows the rivers and the drainage basin between the Mississippi and Ohio Rivers, but "indicates the positions of the rivers schematically."[20] In other words, rather than show straight boundary lines cutting across the rivers, the Piankeshaw mapmakers drew the rivers in relatively straight lines only loosely based on the latitudinal and longitudinal lines. The Piankeshaw map shows "[d]istances along the rivers . . . as the time it would take to travel from one Indian village to another. . . ."[21] Information detailing the rivers as part of a system, not as included in arbitrary boundary lines, was far more important to the Indian people who drew them.

The Piankeshaw people apparently understood whatever transaction to have occurred between themselves as involving various rivers or river systems, not north-south, east-west boundary lines that cut across the rivers unnaturally. The Piankeshaw map indicates that perhaps no meeting of the minds ever occurred between the company and the Indian nation.

Fletcher v. Peck

Johnson had arisen from the ashes of an earlier case, *Fletcher v. Peck*, decided in 1810.[22] *Fletcher* adjudicated the rights of land speculators who had acquired their interests in the Yazoo land fraud, in which all but one Georgia legislator had been bribed to enact bills to grant 35 million acres of land to these speculators for

---

[17] Id. at 591.

[18] Patricia Seed, Oxford Map Companion: One Hundred Sources in World History 122–23 (2014).

[19] Id. at 122.

[20] Id.

[21] Id.

[22] 10 U.S. 87 (1810).

a couple pennies an acre.[23] Much of the land at issue included lands
owned and occupied by Indian tribes, including the Cherokee
Nation.[24] "An outraged Georgia electorate repealed the grants,
signaling their contempt for their predecessors by ordering all
records of the grants excised from the state's public records and the
original act of sale publicly burned."[25]

The *Fletcher* Court, citing the Contracts Clause, invalidated
the repeal of the land grant act,[26] but with great reluctance, partly
because the nascent Marshall Court had not yet reached a place
where it felt comfortable invalidating acts of state legislatures.[27]
After *Fletcher*, the Yazoo land speculators flocked to D.C. to petition
Congress for compensation settlement in exchange for quieting of
their interests in the lands.[28] The petitioners in *Johnson* had
analogous land claims in the Indiana Territory and sought
compensation from Congress as well, but were unsuccessful.[29] They
turned to federal court litigation in an effort to improve their
chances of receiving compensation for their interests in the same
manner as the Yazoo fraud beneficiaries.[30]

The outcome of the litigation—rejection of the claim on the
basis that the federal government retained the fee simple title in
accordance with the Doctrine of Discovery[31]—generated fodder for
debate over whether the federal government or the states held the
title, even though Chief Justice Marshall made it clear that the
federal government alone retained such rights.[32] Moreover, as

---

[23]   Horace H. Hagan, Fletcher v. Peck, 16 Geo. L. J. 1, 8 (1927) ("two cents an acre").

[24]   Robert J. Miller, The Doctrine of Discovery in American Indian Law, 42 Idaho L. Rev. 1, 60 (2005). Hagan asserts that the Indian tribes in Georgia "were more than a match for the State of Georgia alone. . . ." Horace H. Hagan, Fletcher v. Peck, 16 Geo. L. J. 1, 8 (1927).

[25]   Lindsay G. Robertson, Conquest by Law: How the Discovery of America Dispossessed Indigenous Peoples of Their Lands 30 (2005).

[26]   Fletcher v. Peck, 10 U.S. 87, 137 (1810).

[27]   Fletcher v. Peck, 10 U.S. 87, 130 (1810).

[28]   Lindsay G. Robertson, Conquest by Law: How the Discovery of America Dispossessed Indigenous Peoples of Their Lands 30–35 (2005).

[29]   Id. at 36–44.

[30]   Id. at 43 ("The question of the validity of the Illinois and Wabash land purchases would now finally become a judicial question.").

[31]   Johnson v. McIntosh, 21 U.S. 543, 573 (1823).

[32]   Compare Report of the Select Committee of the House of Representatives (March 3, 1827), reprinted in 2 Southern Rev. 541, 552 (1828) ("These decisions of the Supreme Court accord with what we have stated, excepted that they do not directly determine, whether the right of extinguishing Indian occupancy belongs to the United States or to the State. We are unable to form an idea of a sovereign State, which has not the power of legislating upon all matters within its jurisdiction."), with Johnson v. McIntosh, 21 U.S. 543, 586 (1823) ("The ceded territory was occupied by numerous and warlike tribes of Indians; but *the exclusive right of the United States to*

Professor Robertson argued, the chief justice had to return to *Johnson* in *Worcester v. Georgia*, **see § 2.2**, in order to stamp out the ambiguity over whether the federal government retained fee title to Indians lands or a preemption right, a critical question in the politics of Indian removal.[33]

Chief Justice Marshall's characterization of Indian people in 1823 "as a dependent, and in some respects as a distinct people, occupying a country claimed by Great Britain, and yet too powerful and brave not to be dreaded as formidable enemies . . ."[34] would later shape the question of federal power in Indian affairs.

§ 2.2   *The Cherokee Cases*

The Cherokee Cases—*Cherokee Nation v. Georgia*[35] and *Worcester v. Georgia*[36]—form the remaining two cases of the so-called Marshall Trilogy of foundational Indian law decisions. These opinions establish Indian nations as a politically separate political communities within the United States, and also confirm federal supremacy in Indian affairs nationally.

The Cherokee Nation and *Georgia v. Tassels*

The holding in *Cherokee Nation v. Georgia* is as simple as it narrow—Indian tribes are not "foreign State[s]" as envisioned in Article III, section 2, paragraph 1 of the Constitution.[37] It is the Court's dictum that Indian tribes are "domestic dependent nations" and its role in the tragic story of the Cherokee Nation that gives the decision its importance.

Chief Justice Marshall, writing for only one other Justice, wrote the lead opinion.[38] Justices Johnson and Baldwin concurred in the outcome, writing opinions weighed against Indian interests.[39] At the chief justice's informal request,[40] Justice Thompson wrote a dissent in which Justice Story concurred.[41] It was unusual for the

---

extinguish their title, and to grant the soil, has never, we believe, been doubted.") (emphasis added).

[33]   Lindsay G. Robertson, Conquest by Law: How the Discovery of America Dispossessed Indigenous Peoples of Their Lands 133 (2005).

[34]   Johnson v. McIntosh, 21 U.S. 543, 596 (1823).

[35]   30 U.S. 1 (1831).

[36]   31 U.S. 515 (1832).

[37]   30 U.S. 1, 20 (1831) (Marshall, C.J.).

[38]   Id. at 15 (Marshall, C.J.).

[39]   Id. at 20 (Johnson, J., concurring); id. at 31 (Baldwin, J., concurring).

[40]   Francis S. Stites, John Marshall: Defender of the Constitution 162 (1981).

[41]   Cherokee Nation v. Georgia, 30 U.S. 1, 50 (1831) (Thompson, J., dissenting).

Marshall Court to render such a fragmented decision,[42] evidence that the Marshall Court had begun to split apart as the Chief Justice aged and that the question of state authority in Indian Country was a contentious one.

The impetus for the case was the derogation by the State of Georgia of the Cherokee Nation—a community with written laws and a functioning government,[43] a sitting delegation in Congress,[44] a treaty relationship with the United States,[45] and a surplus of food[46]—through a progressive series of intentionally provocative state laws. The United States, at one time, had promised the State of Georgia to negotiate with the Cherokee Nation and eventually remove the tribe to the west, and had from Georgia's point of view failed to fulfill its promise.[47] Hoping to encourage the United States to act on its promise, the State declared Cherokee territory to be "Cherokee County," purporting to open its lands to state citizens for settlement.[48] The laws barred Indians from testifying in court, and further required non-Indians living in Cherokee Indian country to obtain a license from the state.[49] The laws asserted the primacy of state law in Indian country, and declared all Indian laws null and void.

The Execution of Corn Tassels

However, before the Cherokee Nation brought suit, another case arose out of Cherokee Indian country that reached the Supreme Court, a case ultimately captioned *State v. Tassels*.[50] The state court convicted Corn Tassel, or George Tassels, an Indian

---

[42]   David P. Currie, The Constitution in the Supreme Court: The First Hundred Years 195–96 (1985).

[43]   Cherokee Nation v. Georgia, 30 U.S. 1, 75 (1831) (Thompson, J., dissenting) ("The laws of Georgia set out in the bill, if carried fully into operation, go the length of abrogating all the laws of the Cherokees, abolishing their government, and entirely subverting their national character.").

[44]   Joseph C. Burke, The Cherokee Cases: A Study in Law, Politics, and Morality, 21 Stan. L. Rev. 500, 505 (1969).

[45]   Treaty with the Cherokee, 7 Stat. 18 (1785), reprinted in 2 Indian Affairs: Laws and Treaties 8 (Charles J. Kappler 1904); Treaty with the Cherokee, 7 Stat. 39 (1791), reprinted in 2 Indian Affairs: Laws and Treaties 29 (Charles J. Kappler 1904).

[46]   David M. Wishart, Evidence of Surplus Production in the Cherokee Nation Prior to Removal, 55 J. Econ. Hist. 120 (1995).

[47]   Rennard Strickland, The Tribal Struggle for Indian Sovereignty: The Story of the Cherokee Cases, in Indian Law Stories 61, 65 (Carole Goldberg et al., eds. 2011).

[48]   Id.

[49]   Id.

[50]   Georgia v. Tassels, 1 Dud. 229, 229 (Ga. 1830); Tim Alan Garrison, The Legal Ideology of Removal: The Southern Judiciary and the Sovereignty of Native American Nations 111–15 (2002).

man, of murder and sentenced him to death. "The state court decision, allegedly written by William H. Crawford, completely vindicated Georgia's sovereign right to govern the Indians and denounced Northern fanatics for making the Cherokee question a party issue."[51]

Tassel sought a writ of habeas corpus from federal courts, and the Supreme Court issued a stay.[52] Georgia, expressing utter contempt for the Court, executed the man two days later.[53] The Georgia legislature then passed a resolution asserting that the United States Supreme Court did not possess authority to review the decisions of Georgia state courts, and even barred state officials from executing federal law.[54]

After the Corn Tassel debacle, the Cherokee Nation wanted to speed up resolution of its dispute with Georgia, and avoid litigating in Georgia's courts. The tribe decided to invoke the Supreme Court's original jurisdiction under Article III, Section 2 of the Constitution, which provides in relevant part, "In all cases affecting ambassadors, other public ministers and consuls, and those in which a state shall be party, the Supreme Court shall have original jurisdiction." In short, "states" may invoke the Court's original jurisdiction. Unfortunately for the Cherokee Nation, choosing to sue Georgia directly in Supreme Court allowed the Court to avoid the merits of the tribal claims by focusing instead on the Court's original jurisdiction power.

Cherokee Nation v. Georgia

In *Cherokee Nation*, the Supreme Court fractured badly, with the six Justices authoring four separate opinions. Four Justices agreed that Indian tribes were "nations," but four also agreed that tribal nations could not invoke the Court's original jurisdiction. Chief Justice Marshall's lead opinion, joined only by Justice M'Lean, concluded that the Court had no jurisdiction to hear the merits of the Cherokee Nation's claims. Two concurring Justices, Johnson and Baldwin, wrote separately and also concluded that the Court could not hear the matter. Justice Thompson, joined by Justice Story, dissented, concluding that Indian nations were entities authorized by the Constitution to bring suit against States under the Court's original jurisdiction. Justice Duvall, who was deaf, did not participate that Term.

---

[51] Joseph C. Burke, The Cherokee Cases: A Study in Law, Politics, and Morality, 21 Stan. L. Rev. 500, 512 (1969).

[52] 1 Charles Warren, The Supreme Court in United States History 733 (rev. ed. 1926).

[53] Id. at 734.

[54] Id. at 733–34.

In the lead opinion, Chief Justice Marshall began by holding that Indian tribes were "states" (but not States of the Union) as envisioned by the Constitution,[55] a holding contested by the Justices concurring in the result.[56] The two dissenting Justices joined the Chief Justice in holding that Indian tribes are "nations," but they would have held that tribal nations could invoke the Court's original jurisdiction.

A majority agreed that Indian tribes were "nations," and had been treated as such by the United States and its European forebears. Chief Justice Marshall wrote that the United States had entered into treaties with Indian nations under the Treaty Power of the Constitution, and Congress had legislated in light of Indian nationhood.[57] Indian nations governed themselves, made war with each other and the United States, and acted like any other national sovereign.[58]

In oft-quoted words, the chief justice then answered in the negative the question whether this Indian tribe could be considered a "foreign State."[59] Indian nations were not "States" of the Union, either; Indian nations were "domestic dependent nations."[60] Chief Justice Marshall's justifications were wanting. Drawing from *Johnson v. McIntosh*, see § 2.1, the Chief Justice reasoned that since the United States held superior title to Indian lands under the Doctrine of Discovery, Indian nations could not be foreign nations.[61] Of course, the Cherokee Nation's lands were vested to them by treaty, and could not any longer be considered original Indian title subject to defeasance at the will of the United States. Chief Justice Marshall then emphasized another questionable rationale, given the relative strength of the Cherokee Nation at the time; that Indian nations were mere wards of the federal government, dependent on the government for their very existence.[62]

---

[55]   Cherokee Nation v. Georgia, 30 U.S. 1, 16 (1832) (Marshall, C.J.).

[56]   Id. at 25 (Johnson, J., concurring) ("Must every petty kraal of Indians, designating themselves a tribe or nation, and having a few hundred acres of land to hunt on exclusively, be recognized as a state?"); id. at 40 (Baldwin, J., concurring) ("[T]he Cherokees were then dependants, having given up all their affairs to the regulation and management of congress, and that all the regulations of congress, over Indian affairs were then in force over an immense territory, under a solemn pledge to the inhabitants, that whenever their population and circumstances would admit they should form constitutions and become free, sovereign and independent states on equal footing with the old component members of the confederation. . . .").

[57]   Id. at 16 (Marshall, C.J.).

[58]   Id. (Marshall, C.J.).

[59]   Id. at 17 (Marshall, C.J.).

[60]   Id. (Marshall, C.J.).

[61]   Id. (Marshall, C.J.).

[62]   Id. (Marshall, C.J.).

The Chief Justice's strongest argument was that the Cherokee Nation had agreed to divest itself of its external sovereignty by entering into treaties under which it agreed to come under the protection of the United States.[63] By coming under the protection of the federal government, the Cherokee Nation could no longer enter into alliances with other nations and would defend the United States as a military and political partner. Similarly, the United States would defend the Cherokee Nation from threats to the tribe's sovereignty and borders. The internal sovereignty of the Cherokee Nation would remain untouched. While a nation does not automatically give up its status as a nation by agreeing to come under the protection of a superior sovereign, it was reasonable for the Supreme Court to conclude that an Indian nation located wholly within the United States' borders was not a foreign nation.

Because the Cherokee Nation attempted to invoke the Supreme Court's original jurisdiction under Article III, Section 2 of the Constitution, the Court concluded that only States or foreign nations—not "domestic" nations—had standing to bring suit.

Justices Johnson and Baldwin wrote stinging concurrences arguing that Indians and Indian tribes were too degraded and insignificant to meet the international law definition of "nation" at all, and agreeing that Indian tribes were dependent.[64] Justice Thompson, joined by Justice Story, later added a dissent that argued for finding that Indian tribes such as the Cherokee Nation are foreign nations, whether understood to be so by the Founders or not.[65] Applying international law principles, the dissent argued that the Cherokee Nation did not lose its status as a foreign nation by virtue of agreeing to be dependent on the United States for military protection.

While *Johnson v. McIntosh* concerned states' rights in a tangential manner, states' rights were the leading issue in the Cherokee cases. Southern states used the issue with the Cherokee Nation as a reason to confront the federal government and the Supreme Court. Yet, not knowing the immediate future, Chief Justice Marshall wrote that the 1832 Term in which the *Worcester* case was decided would focus more on the decisions of some Southern states to enact "nullification laws" by which the states asserted the authority to nullify federal tariffs and the

---

[63] Id. at 17–18 (Marshall, C.J.).

[64] Id. at 23–27 (Johnson, J., concurring); id. at 48–51 (Baldwin, J., concurring).

[65] Id. at 50–53 (Thompson, J., dissenting).

Congressional debate over whether to reauthorize the Bank of the United States.[66]

Worcester v. Georgia

Instead of the nullification laws or the Bank of the United States being the question by which the Court would make a critical statement about federalism, the case to do so—by sheer accident of timing—was *Worcester v. Georgia*.[67] In *Worcester*, the Supreme Court finally addressed the merits of the Cherokee Nation's claims, and held that the Supremacy Clause precluded the State of Georgia from interfering with federal treaty rights held by the Cherokee Nation.

The Supreme Court voted 5–1 to declare unenforceable the laws of Georgia purporting to invalidate the entire Cherokee Nation in *Worcester v. Georgia*.[68] Though Chief Justice Marshall's wife Polly had passed during the previous recess and his health wavered, he delivered an opinion that one commentator declared was "one of the most powerful he ever delivered."[69] Justice Story wrote to his wife, "Thanks be to God, . . . the Court can wash their hands clean of the iniquity of oppressing the Indians and disregarding their rights."[70] Justice M'Lean offered a concurring opinion and concurred in the chief justice's opinion as well.[71] Justice Baldwin dissented but refused to allow his dissent to be published.[72]

The *Worcester* reasoning drew heavily from Justice Thompson's dissent, abandoning the "domestic dependent nations" characterization of Indian nations in favor of recognizing Indian nations as "distinct, independent political communities." The decision is a Supremacy Clause decision, holding that state laws interfering or conflicting with federal laws are void.

The core of the majority opinion relied upon the enactment of the First Congress of the trade and intercourse acts.[73] He focused on what we now call the original public understanding of the status of

---

[66]   David Loth, Chief Justice: John Marshall and the Growth of the Republic 357 (1949);Richard P. Longaker, Andrew Jackson and the Judiciary, 71 Pol. Sci. Q. 341, 348 (1956).

[67]   31 U.S. 515 (1832).

[68]   31 U.S. 515, 596 (1832).

[69]   Jean Edward Smith, John Marshall: Definer of a Nation 518 (1996).

[70]   Francis S. Stites, John Marshall: Defender of the Constitution 164 (1981).

[71]   Worcester v. Georgia, 31 U.S. 515, 563 (1832) (M'Lean, J., concurring).

[72]   Id. at 561. Justice Baldwin did write a substantial dissent, but due to his antagonism directed at the Supreme Court's reporter, Richard Peters, Jr., and what appears to be severe mental illness, he refused to allow it to be published. Lindsay G. Robertson, Justice Henry Baldwin's "Lost Opinion" in Worcester v. Georgia, 24 J. S.Ct. Hist. 50 (1999).

[73]   Worcester v. Georgia, 31 U.S. 515, 557–58 (1832).

Indian tribes as nations, encapsulated by Congress in those early statutes. Like Justice Thompson's *Cherokee Nation* dissent, the Chief Justice described Indian nations as entities capable of treating with the United States, and as governments with plenary authority over their own lands. The opinion included very powerful language analogizing Indian nations to foreign powers:

> The Indian nations had always been considered as distinct, independent political communities, retaining their original natural rights, as the undisputed possessors of the soil, from time immemorial; with the single exception of that imposed by irresistible power, which excluded them from intercourse with any other European potentate than the first discoverer of the coast of the particular region claimed: and this was a restriction which those European potentates imposed on themselves, as well as on the Indians. The very term "nation," so generally applied to them, means "a people distinct from others."[74]

In a final iteration of the Court's challenge to the State of Georgia and all the Southern States threatening nullification of federal law, Chief Justice Marshall threw down the gauntlet by making absolutely clear that state law does not apply in Indian Country:

> The Cherokee nation, then, is a distinct community, occupying its own territory, with boundaries accurately described, in which the laws of Georgia can have no force, and which the citizens of Georgia have no right to enter, but with the assent of the Cherokees themselves, or in conformity with treaties, and with the acts of congress. The whole intercourse between the United States and this nation, is by our constitution and laws, vested in the government of the United States.[75]

There had not been a stronger statement of respect for the legal authority of Indian tribes—and there have been few statements of the kind since.

Of course, the political reality of the day foreclosed a future in the American Southeast for the bulk of the Cherokee Nation, which the federal government, under President Jackson and others, forced to undergo the genocidal Trail of Tears.[76] Justice Breyer dedicated a

---

[74]   Id. at 559.

[75]   Id. at 561.

[76]   Theda Perdue & Michael D. Green, The Cherokee Nation and the Trail of Tears (2007); Rennard Strickland & William M. Strickland, A Tale of Two Marshalls: Reflections on Indian Law and Policy, the Cherokee Cases, and the Cruel Irony of Supreme Court Victories, 47 Okla. L. Rev. 111, 122–26 (1994); Ronald N. Satz, The

chapter of his book, *Making Our Democracy Work: A Judge's View*, to the Cherokee Nation's story. His takeaway was that the Supreme Court's decision in *Worcester* highlighted the limitations of the Court's power in the early 19th century. As a result, "[D]uring the next half century the Court, perhaps aware of its limitations, did not meaningfully test its power of judicial review."[77]

Even so, the so-called Marshall Trilogy serves as a critical source of foundational principles that continue to guide federal Indian law.

§ 2.3   Federal Control over Indian Affairs

Congress asserts—and the Supreme Court recognizes—a plenary power in Indian affairs.[78] The Executive branch also enjoys this plenary power as well, since Congress long ago delegated expansive authority to the President and the Interior Department.[79] This power has been used for great good and for great harm to Indian people and to Indian tribes.

The Precursor—The British Proclamation of 1763

European national primacy in Indian affairs long predated the American Republic. In 1763, in part as a response to the widespread war waged by Indian military forces led by the Ottawa *ogema* Pontiac,[80] the Crown issued a proclamation prohibiting anyone from purchasing Indian lands west of a boundary line set at the Allegheny Mountains—the infamous Norman Yoke.[81] The Proclamation of 1763 and its subsequent arbitrary enforcement and alteration became one of the flashpoints of the American Revolution.[82] After the Battle of Yorktown diminished the necessary war powers of the Continental Congress, the interrelated questions

---

Cherokee Trail of Tears: A Sesquicentennial Perspective, 73 Ga. Hist. Q. 431 (1989); Carl J. Vipperman, The Bungled Treaty of New Echota: The Failure of Cherokee Removal, 1836–1838, 73 Ga. Hist. Q. 540 (1989).

[77]   Stephen Breyer, Making Our Democracy Work: A Judge's View 33 (2010).

[78]   United States v. Lara, 541 U.S. 193, 200 (2004); Washington v. Confederated Bands and Tribes of the Yakima Indian Nation, 439 U.S. 463, 470 (1979); United States v. Kagama, 118 U.S. 375 (1886).

[79]   25 U.S.C. §§ 2, 9.

[80]   Robert A. Williams, Jr., The American Indian in Western Legal Thought 232 (1990); Robert N. Clinton, The Dormant Indian Commerce Clause, 27 Conn. L. Rev. 1055, 1092 (1994).

[81]   See generally Robert A. Williams, Jr., The American Indian in Western Legal Thought 232–86 (1990); Robert N. Clinton, The Proclamation of 1763: Colonial Prelude to Two Centuries of Federal-State Conflict over the Management of Indian Affairs, 69 B. U. L. Rev. 329 (1989).

[82]   Robert A. Williams, Jr., The American Indian in Western Legal Thought 232 (1990). Cf. Peter Onuf, Toward Federalism: Virginia, Congress, and the Western Lands, 34 Wm. & Mary Q. 3d Series 353, 363 (1977).

of the western boundaries, state western land claims, and the expansion of the nation—all of which had its origins in British Imperial policy and also which implicated the nation's Indian affairs—created an additional outlet for the exercise of national authority.[83] Another related major concern relevant to this Article that drove the states together is the question of the western lands and the expansion of the United States. Before the states could trust the national government in regards to their interests, they had to trust each other.[84] And before they could trust each other, they had to rely upon a national government. The disputes that the states had with each other—the landed states represented by Virginia and the landless states represented by Maryland—in addition to the claims of the United States, held up the ratification of the Articles for years.[85]

The Origins of Federal Indian Affairs Power

National authority derived from the people's sovereignty during the time of the national period originated in the necessities of the Revolutionary War and, in some respects, the important questions that continued unanswered after the conclusion of major combat operations. The Founders believed that there could have been other necessities that created national power in the national period. For example, Alexander Hamilton and others sought to create a national debt for which no individual state would take responsibility, but would have to be dealt with on a national level.[86] Under this theory, which came to partial fruition in the Articles and in the Constitution, the states would be bound together by the necessity of paying off a national debt.[87] There were at least two other independent "necessities" that brought the colonies together as a nation prior to the ratification of the Articles that are relevant to this Article—the relationship of Indian tribes to the United States and the states and the related question of the western lands.

Many of the first treaties between the nascent nation and Indian tribes were treaties of military alliance or non-intervention

---

[83]   See generally Peter Onuf, Toward Federalism: Virginia, Congress, and the Western Lands, 34 Wm. & Mary Q. 3d Series 353 (1977); Peter Onuf, From Colony to Territory: Changing Concepts of Statehood in Revolutionary America, 97 Pol. Sci. Q. 447, 449 (1982).

[84]   "Maryland . . . held back [its ratification of the Articles of Confederation] to secure settlement of the public lands which was eventually made. That State gave its assent [the final state to do so] in March, 1871." Samuel Freeman Miller, Lectures on the Constitution of the United States 42 (1893). See generally Merrill Jensen, The Cession of the Old Northwest, 23 Mississippi Valley Hist. Rev. 27 (1936).

[85]   Id. at 32–47.

[86]   Merrill Jensen, The Creation of the National Domain, 1781–1784, 26 Miss. Valley Hist. Rev. 323, 366–68 (1939).

[87]   Id.

and cooperation.[88] In the Treaty of Fort Pitt with the Delawares, for example, "it was agreed that all past offenses were to be mutually forgiven, peace was established, and in case of war each party was to assist the other."[89] In general, however, the Continental Congress was mostly unsuccessful in treating with Indian nations during the Revolution to the extent that they could not reach the goals of reaching alliances or guaranteeing neutrality.[90] According to Walter Mohr, there were significant reasons why the Indians sided with the British, including the fact that "the Americans were desirous, mainly, of depriving the Indians of their lands."[91] Ultimately, the tribal assaults on American towns did little to influence the outcome of the war.[92] In the South, especially, American military victories against the Indian tribes were substantial.[93]

This exercise of necessary national authority by the Continental Congress served as the leading focal point of what could now be referred to as the Indian affairs power, although, to be sure, the attempt to treat with and then the fighting against Indian tribes also are examples of the exercise of the foreign affairs power. According to John Ranney, "Probably the most persistent of the active factors promoting co-operation in America was military necessity. . . . [E]ach of the early attempts at union was a direct consequences of some military threat . . . [from, for example] the Indians. . . ."[94] The exercise of this national authority by the Continental Congress is part of the origin of the Indian affairs power, a power that the national sovereign appeared to inherit from the King.[95] After the Revolution ended, the necessity of dealing with the Indian tribes remained. Perhaps this is where the Indian Affairs Power made its clearest, independent debut. No one had forgotten the near-successful war waged by Pontiac in 1763[96]—and the possibility of another offensive. According to Walter Mohr, "The Indians are not mentioned in the treaty of 1783, yet they were a very influential factor in the negotiations."[97] John Marshall recalled

---

[88]   Walter H. Mohr, Federal Indian Relations 1774–1788, at 37–91 (1933).

[89]   Id. at 73; see also Treaty of Fort Pitt, 7 Stat. 13 (Sept. 17, 1778).

[90]   Walter H. Mohr, Federal Indian Relations 1774–1788, at 87–88 (1933).

[91]   Id. at 40.

[92]   Id. at 87.

[93]   Id. at 60.

[94]   John C. Ranney, The Bases of American Federalism, 3 Wm. & Mary Q. (3d Series) 1, 14 (1946).

[95]   Jack N. Rakove, Taking the Prerogative out of the Presidency: An Originalist Perspective, 37 Pres. Stud. Q. 85, 92 (2007) (discussing authorities that made this claim).

[96]   See generally Robert A. Williams, Jr., The American Indian in Western Legal Thought 236–39 (1990).

[97]   Walter H. Mohr, Federal Indian Relations 1774–1788, at 93 (1933).

decades later in a private letter to Justice Story how the American leadership continued to fear an Indian offensive that could all but drive the nascent American nation into the sea.[98] If anything, immediately after the hostilities with Britain ceased, perhaps the necessity increased, given that some powerful Indian tribes that had historically sided with the British were either concerned that the Americans would soon move against them or were continuing to agitate against the Continental Congress with British support.[99] In addition, even the economic interests of New York and Pennsylvania in tapping into the Indian fur trade required union.[100]

Articles of Confederation

The draft language of Article IX, clause four, of the Articles of Confederation indicates that the intent of the Framers—at one point—was to vest the entire Indian affairs power in the United States, not the states.[101] However, the Articles of Confederation apparently preserved the rights of state legislatures, making ambiguous that original intent:

> The United States in Congress assembled shall also have the sole and exclusive right and power of . . . regulating the trade and managing all affairs with the Indians, not members of any of the States, provided that the legislative right of any State within its own limits be not infringed or violated. . . .[102]

The debates of the framers of the Articles of Confederation in the Indian affairs context were disjointed and inconclusive.[103] It appears that the final provision ratified in 1781 consisted of the squeezing together a combination the nationalists' proposed language and the anti-federalists' proposed language—without serious consideration of the impact it would have on the meaning of

---

[98]   Richard C. Brown, Illustrious Americans: John Marshall 213 (1968) ("The Indians were a fierce and dangerous enemy whose love of war made them sometimes the aggressors, whose numbers and habits made them formidable, and whose cruel system of warfare seemed to justify every endeavor to remove them to a distance from civilized settlements.") (quoting 1828 letter from Chief Justice Marshall to Justice Story).

[99]   See generally Walter H. Mohr, Federal Indian Relations 1774–1788, at 118–21 (1933).

[100]   John C. Ranney, The Bases of American Federalism, 3 Wm. & Mary Q. (3d Series) 1, 15 (1946) (quoting William Grayson of the Virginia Convention, 3 The Debates in the Several State Conventions on the Adoption of the Federal Constitution 278 (Jonathan Elliott, 2nd ed. 1896)).

[101]   Oneida Indian Nation v. New York, 860 F.2d 1145, 1155–57 (2d Cir. 1988), cert. denied, 493 U.S. 871 (1989).

[102]   Articles of Confederation art. IX, § 4.

[103]   Robert N. Clinton, The Dormant Indian Commerce Clause, 27 Conn. L. Rev. 1055, 1139–47 (1994).

the final provision. As noted by James Madison, Article IX, paragraph 4 was "obscure and contradictory."[104]

The Constitution

By the time of the framing of the Constitution, the drafters moved away from vesting any reserved authority in the states. The intent, as Professor Robert Clinton showed in his comprehensive historical research, was to divest the states of any and all Indian affairs power.[105] But where the Constitution reserves exclusive authority to the United States, it did not use the comprehensive language that would vest the exclusive national power with Congress. Herein rests one of the biggest puzzles of federal Indian law—why didn't the Founders keep language similar to the Articles of Confederation, language that would have appeared to vest exclusive Indian Affairs Power in Congress?

Instead, the Founders vested Congress with the power to regulate commerce with the Indian tribes. By negative implication, it would appear Congress does not have the authority to exercise the entire national Indian affairs power that it had under the Articles, subject to the proviso. While Congress has extensive authority in this vein, there is reasonable skepticism that Congress's authority as derived from the Indian Commerce Clause alone is plenary. But the story of federal power over Indian affairs remains incomplete.

The Contours of Federal Plenary Power

The plenary character of Congressional power could once described as all but "absolute,"[106] with the Supreme Court refusing for about a century to hear any challenges to Indian affairs legislation or exercises of regulatory discretion under the political question doctrine.[107] However, that characterization is not accurate, with the Court, on rare occasions, striking down Indian affairs

---

[104] The Federalist No. 42, at 284–85 (J. Cooke, ed. 1961).

[105] Robert N. Clinton, There Is No Federal Supremacy Clause for Indian Tribes, 34 Ariz. St. L.J. 113, 149 (2003). See also Richard D. Pomp, The Unfulfilled Promise of the Indian Commerce Clause and State Taxation, 63 The Tax Lawyer 897 (2010).

[106] Mashunkashey v. Mashunkashey, 134 P.2d 976, 979 (Okla. 1942).

[107] E.g., Tee-Hit-Ton Indians v. United States, 348 U.S. 272, 281 (1955); United States v. Alcea Band of Tillamooks, 329 U.S. 40, 46 (1946); Northwestern Bands of Shoshone Indians v. United States, 324 U.S. 335, 339 (1945); Lone Wolf v. Hitchcock, 187 U.S. 553, 566 (1903); Cherokee Nation v. Hitchcock, 187 U.S. 294, 306–08 (1902); United States v. Kagama, 118 U.S. 375, 383 (1886); Beecher v. Wetherby, 95 U.S. 517, 525 (1877); United States v. 43 Gallons of Whiskey, 93 U.S. 188, 197 (1876); Holden v. Joy, 84 U.S. 211, 247 (1872); The Cherokee Tobacco, 78 U.S. 616, 621 (1870); Marsh v. Brooks, 49 U.S. 223, 228 (1850); United States v. Rogers, 45 U.S. 567, 572 (1845); Mitchel v. United States, 34 U.S. 711, 740 (1835).

regulation in the modern era.[108] Congressional plenary power is nothing more than the power necessary to govern Indian affairs.

Three main theories have served to provide sources for this plenary Indian Affairs Power. *First*, the express grant of authority in Article I is the Indian Commerce Clause, providing Congress with the sole and presumably exclusive authority to regulate commerce with the "Indian tribes."[109] The Supreme Court long has accepted the Indian Commerce Clause as the source of Congressional plenary power,[110] despite some reservations.[111] The Supreme Court also has identified the Treaty Clause, the War Power, and the Property Clause, for example, as other sources of the Indian Affairs Power.[112]

Second, the federal government has acquired authority in Indian affairs in various treaties with Indian tribes.[113] In general, Indian nations traded much of their external sovereignty in exchange for federal government protection of their internal sovereignty. For example, the Cherokee Nation agreed to the divestiture of its external sovereignty in exchange for the right to remain in the southeastern United States free from the interference of the states and their citizens.[114]

Third, the Supreme Court theorized that preconstitutional federal authority as described in *United States v. Curtiss-Wright Export Corp.*[115] authorized federal power. The Court had once implied that such a power could exist in *United States v. Kagama*,[116] and then over a century later in *United States v. Lara*,[117] the Court asserted it explicitly. In *Kagama*, the Court recognized that Congress had authority to enact criminal laws in Indian Country—the Major Crimes Act[118]—under an amalgamation

---

[108] E.g., Hodel v. Irving, 481 U.S. 704 (1987) (striking down portions of the Indian Land Consolidation Act).

[109] Const. Art. I, § 8, cl. 3.

[110] United States v. Lara, 541 U.S. 193, 200 (2004); Cotton Petroleum Corp. v. New Mexico, 490 US. 163, 192 (1989); Washington v. Confederated Bands and Tribes of the Yakima Nation, 439 U.S. 463, 470 (1979).

[111] United States v. Kagama, 118 U.S. 375, 378–79 (1886); Adoptive Couple v. Baby Girl, 133 S.Ct. 2552, 2566–71 (2013) (Thomas, J., concurring); United States v. Lara, 541 U.S. 193, 215 (2004) (Thomas, J., concurring in the result).

[112] United States v. Lara, 541 U.S. 193, 200–01 (2004).

[113] Cf. Missouri v. Holland, 252 U.S. 416 (1920).

[114] Treaty of Hopewell, arts. III & IV, 7 Stat. 18, 19 (1785).

[115] 299 U.S. 304 (1936).

[116] 118 U.S. 375 (1886).

[117] 541 U.S. 193 (2004).

[118] Act of Mar. 3, 1885, ch. 341, 23 Stat. 385, codified as amended at 18 U.S.C. § 1153.

of implied authorities that focused on Indian "dependence."[119] The Court suggested that this power rested in the federal government as a matter of constitutional pragmatism. **See § 3.7**.

What was a certainty, however—at least at the time of the ratification of the Constitution—was that federal authority in Indian affairs (whatever its scope) was sole and exclusive of state authority.[120] History shows with certainty that one of the greater weakness of the national government under the Articles of Confederation of the non-exclusive character of the Indian Affairs Power.[121] The Court has long interpreted the Indian Commerce Clause as excluding the authority of states to enter the field of Indian affairs, unless Congress consents. **See § 5.6**. And yet, for decades, Indian activists and scholars decried federal plenary power in Indian affairs because of it was the source of deeply destructive federal Indian law and policy.[122] Beginning especially in the mid-1980s, Indian law specialists and scholars became divided over the scope and legitimacy of federal plenary power in Indian affairs.[123] While plenary power once created untold hardships for Indian people, Congress had lately begun using its plenary power, in most

---

[119] United States v. Kagama, 118 U.S. 375, 384–85 (1886).

[120] Seminole Tribe of Florida v. Florida, 517 U.S. 44, 62 (1996); Oneida County, N.Y. v. Oneida Indian Nation of N.Y., 470 U.S. 226, 234 (1985); Cayuga Indian Nation v. Cuomo, 565 F. Supp. 1297, 1307–08 (W.D. N.Y. 1983); Mohegan Tribe v. State of Connecticut, 528 F. Supp. 1359, 1368–69 (D. Conn. 1982); Akhil Reed Amar, America's Constitution: A Biography 107–08 (2005).

[121] County of Oneida, N.Y. v. Oneida Indian Nation of N.Y., 470 U.S. 226, 234 n. 4 (1985); Robert J. Miller, The Doctrine of Discovery in American Indian Law, 42 Idaho L. Rev. 1, 49 (2005).

[122] E.g., Russel Lawrence Barsh & James Youngblood Henderson, The Road: Indian Tribes and Political Liberty 112–34 (1980); Vine Deloria, Jr. & Clifford M. Lytle, American Indians, American Justice 40–45 (1983).

[123] Compare Robert Laurence, Learning to Live with the Plenary Power of Congress over the Indian Nations, 30 Ariz. L. Rev. 413 (1988); Robert Laurence, On Eurocentric Myopia, the Designated Hitter Rule, and "The Actual State of Things", 30 Ariz. L. Rev. 459 (1988); with Milner S. Ball, Constitution, Court, Indian Tribes, 1987 Am. B. Found. Research J. 1 (arguing that Congress does not have plenary power to legislate in the field of Indian affairs); Robert N. Clinton, There Is No Federal Supremacy Clause for Indian Tribes, 34 Ariz. St. L.J. 113 (2003) (same); Richard B. Collins, Indian Consent to American Government, 31 Ariz. L. Rev. 365 (1989); Steven Paul McSloy, Back to the Future: Native American Sovereignty in the 21st Century, 20 N.Y.U. Rev. L. & Soc. Change 217 (1993); Robert A. Williams, Jr., Learning Not to Live with Eurocentric Myopia: A Reply to Professor Laurence, 30 Ariz. L. Rev. 439 (1988); Robert A. Williams, The Algebra of Federal Indian Law: The Hard Trail of Decolonizing and Americanizing the White Man's Indian Jurisprudence, 1986 Wis. L. Rev. 219 (raising the first sophisticated modern attack on the plenary powers of the federal government in Indian affairs).

instances, to enact statutes for the benefit of Indian tribes and Indian people.[124]

Undermining the theoretical foundations of federal plenary power might serve to limit federal authority over Indian affairs, but it might also destroy much of what Indian people and tribes relied upon as their best hopes for a remedy. As Justice Blackmun worried in an analogous context, should the Court hold that the federal government's Indian Affairs Power is constricted, much of Title 25 of the United States Code could lose its footing and come crashing down.[125] Statutes such as the Indian Child Welfare Act,[126] the Indian Civil Rights Act,[127] or even the various Indian self-determination acts[128]—statutes that did not obviously implicate Indian commerce—appeared to be at risk if Indian law scholars were successful in persuading the Court to limit federal plenary power.

---

[124] See generally Charles Wilkinson, Blood Struggle: The Rise of Modern Indian Nations (2005); Matthew L.M. Fletcher, The Supreme Court and Federal Indian Policy, 85 Neb. L. Rev. 121, 140–54 (2006).

[125] Morton v. Mancari, 417 U.S. 535, 552–53 (1974).

[126] 25 U.S.C. §§ 1901 et seq.

[127] 25 U.S.C. §§ 1301 et seq.

[128] E.g., Indian Self-Determination and Educational Assistance Act, 25 U.S.C. §§ 5301 et seq.; Native American Housing Assistance and Self-Determination Act, 25 U.S.C. §§ 4101 et seq.

Chapter 3

CENTURIES OF SHIFTING AMERICAN INDIAN LAW AND POLICY

Analysis

§ 3.1   The Trade and Intercourse Acts

The Trade and Intercourse Acts, a series of statutes now codified as amended in various places in Titles 18 and 25 of the United States Code, served as the first broad statement of federal Indian law and policy. The Acts, prohibiting any land transactions with Indian tribes without Congressional approval, regulated all commerce with Indians and Indian tribes, and provided for the punishment of non-Indians that committed crimes in Indian Country. The Acts, also known as the Non-Intercourse Act(s), provided the legal basis for many of the Indian land claims in the northeastern United States and elsewhere.

An important precursor to the Trade and Intercourse Acts was the British Royal Proclamation of 1763, **see § 2.3**, which prohibited American colonists from purchasing Indian lands or engaging in

41

any kind of commerce with Indians and Indian tribes without the consent of the King or his delegates. The Proclamation contributed a great deal to the animosity between the Americans and the British that led to the American Revolution. The Declaration of Independence is rife with complaints about British Indian affairs policy. The United States' first take on Indian affairs, Article IX of the Articles of Confederation, nevertheless maintained the primacy of the national government in Indian affairs, but was undermined by a proviso that allowed the states to legislate in the field anyway. **See § 2.3.** The Constitution's Indian Commerce Clause offered a clearer provision providing for exclusive Congressional authority in Indian affairs.

In 1790, the First Congress enacted the first Trade and Intercourse Act, implementing its Indian affairs authority contained in the Commerce Clause. The statute provided for federal regulation of all commerce and other "intercourse" with Indians and Indian tribes; a ban on land purchases without federal consent; and the provision of punishment for non-Indians who committed crimes against Indians in Indian Country.[1]

The rule that only the federal government may authorize the alienation or sale of Indian lands extended enormous federal power over tribal lands. Typically, owners of private property in the Western legal tradition have the presumptive authority to sell their own lands, but federal law made an exception of Indians and Indian tribes. The federal government's exclusive authority in this area allowed the United States to dictate the terms upon which the acquisition of Indian lands would occur. As Indian tribes ceded lands to the United States through treaty provisions, the United States would then control the first alienation of the lands to American citizens and business entities and use that power to generate significant federal revenue. Over time, the Supreme Court's view of federal authority in this field expanded to allow Congress to alienate Indian lands *without* tribal consent at all, usually by abrogating Indian treaties. **See §§ 3.5, 3.6.**

In 1834, Congress passed a final Trade and Intercourse Act restructuring federal Indian policy.[2] The 1834 Trade and Intercourse Act is one of the most important statutes in Indian affairs history.[3] Portions of section 12 are now codified as amended in 25 U.S.C. § 177, barring trade and intercourse by private citizens

---

[1]   Act of July 22, 1790, 1 Stat. 137, 138.

[2]   Act of June 30, 1834, 4 Stat. 729, 730, partially codified as amended at 25 U.S.C. §§ 177, 261–65; 18 U.S.C. § 1152.

[3]   Francis Paul Prucha, American Indian Policy in the Formative Years: The Indian Trade and Intercourse Acts, 1790–1834, at 250–51 (1962).

with Indians and tribes. The remainder of the 1834 Act codified Indian trade regulations and Indian country criminal law.[4]

§ 3.2   Indian Removal

Congress's enactment of the Indian Removal Act of 1830[5] was the statutory culmination of a long-standing American goal of moving the Indians west—at first, west of the Appalachian Mountains; later, after the Louisiana Purchase in 1803, west of the Mississippi River. Several factors motivated the American policy, including the paternalistic goal of civilizing the Indians and the resolving the simmering crisis over slavery and states' rights, but the most important factor was the desire for Indian lands.

The statute provided that the President should negotiate land cession treaties with Indian tribes, authorizing the government to offer lands west of the Mississippi River in exchange for eastern lands.[6] The Act did not authorize the President to use force in order to compel the tribes to cede land, but the government did on occasion use military force to compel tribal leaders to "consent" to a removal treaty, or to physically compel removal. For example, President Jackson's administration negotiated the Treaty of Dancing Rabbit Creek with the Choctaw nation in September of 1830.[7] Treaty negotiators threatened tribes with refusing to prevent the states from encroaching on their lands and promising that the tribe would become all but extinct unless they signed the treaty— "the choice to either cede or submit to state law."[8]

The story of the Cherokee Nation, subjected to the Trail of Tears, is most well known. In 1832, the Supreme Court decided *Worcester v. Georgia*, a ruling that protected tribal treaty rights and held that "the laws of Georgia can have no force" in Cherokee Indian Country.[9] **See § 2.2**. The *Worcester* decision gave some hope to the southeastern Indian tribes that removal was not inevitable. But that small shred of hope dissipated after the Jackson Administration embarked on a course leading to the Trail of Tears.

The legal document driving the removal of the people of the Cherokee Nation was the 1835 Treaty of New Echota.[10] The treaty

---

[4]   Id. at 261–66. 25 U.S.C. §§ 261 et seq. (Indian trader statutes); 18 U.S.C. § 1152 (Indian Country Crimes Act).

[5]   Act of May 28, 1830, 4 Stat. 411.

[6]   Act of May 28, 1830, § 2, 4 Stat. 412.

[7]   7 Stat. 333.

[8]   Lindsay G. Robertson, Conquest by Law: How the Discovery of America Dispossessed Indigenous Peoples of Their Lands 137 (2005).

[9]   31 U.S. 515, 561 (1832).

[10]   7 Stat. 478.

guaranteed lands in fee to the Cherokee people in what is now Oklahoma that "never be embraced within the boundaries of any State or Territory."[11] The treaty is a prototypical removal treaty. Despite a vigorous debate as to the validity of the negotiations, the Senate ratified the treaty by one vote in March 1836.[12] Over 15,000 of the remaining Cherokees petitioned Congress to stop removal, but to no avail.[13] Secretary of War Lewis Cass sent the American army to Cherokee territory and directed the army to force the Cherokees to move—and to use force if they resisted. In 1838, General Winfield Scott ordered his troops to round up the Cherokees into concentration camps before forcing the Indian people to march west. "All told, about 4,000 died during the course of capture and detention in temporary stockades, and the removal itself."[14]

§ 3.3   The Reservation System and the Rise of the Federal Bureaucracy

Indian removal to the west kick-started the establishment of the reservation system and the establishment of a federal administrative apparatus to govern Indian country. Most Indian reservations are and were located west of the Mississippi River, though there are many in the eastern portions of the United States.

Early Indian reservations arose from negotiated terms often, but not always, memorialized in treaties with the United States and Indian nations. Charles F. Wilkinson referred to the reservation system as a form of "measured separatism."[15] Indian reservations would allow for Indian nations to retain a limited form of independence and self-governance, preserving a place for Indigenous culture and language, all the while protected and supported by the federal government. Many Indian treaties provided for direct material and financial from the federal government to Indian nations and Indian people, and set aside specific lands for exclusive Indian use, occupation, and ownership.

In later decades, Congress and occasionally the President via Executive Order could establish an Indian reservation. In the

---

[11]   Id.

[12]   Rennard Strickland & William M. Strickland, A Tale of Two Marshalls: Reflections on Indian Law and Policy, the Cherokee Cases, and the Cruel Ironies of Supreme Court Victories, 47 Okla.L.Rev. 111, 123 (1994).

[13]   Id. at 124–25.

[14]   Grant Foreman, Indian Removal: The Emigration of the Five Civilized Tribes 312 n. (1970).

[15]   Charles F. Wilkinson, American Indians, Time, and the Law 14–19 (1987).

modern era, the Interior Secretary may also declare the establishment of an Indian reservation.[16]

§ 3.4   The Bureau of Indian Affairs

The Bureau of Indian Affairs is the federal agency charged with administering most of the United States' Indian affairs programs. It is part of the Interior Department.

Prior to the establishment of a Commissioner of Indian Affairs in 1832,[17] the federal officers administering Indian affairs did not have a firm place in the highest echelons of the federal government; that is, Indian affairs had no centralized structure originating in Washington, D.C.[18] The Indian affairs agency operated out of the War Department (now the Defense Department). In 1824, the Secretary of War believed that it was imminent that Congress would legislate to establish a centralized federal Indian agency and created the Bureau of Indian Affairs (BIA) by an act of administrative fiat.[19] War Secretary Calhoun effectively established the BIA in a letter to Thomas McKenney, whom he appointed to handle Indian affairs "accounting functions" and other Indian affairs work.[20]

The 1832 statute authorized the appointment of a Commissioner nominated by the President and confirmed by the Senate to direct and manage Indian affairs.[21] But the 1832 Act did not provide legal authority for the BIA. An 1834 Act reorganized the BIA structure of certain Indian agents who reported to certain area superintendents, who in turn reported to the Commissioner.[22] It was not the comprehensive establishment of a federal subagency but instead a mere restructuring of what was already in place. Felix Cohen identified the 1834 statute as the "organic act" of the Bureau of Indian Affairs, though he cited to the 1832 Report from the Office of Indian Affairs for that proposition.[23]

Even so, it could be said that the 1824 administrative action to create the Bureau of Indian Affairs, along with the 1832 and 1834 Acts of Congress modifying and supplementing the BIA, constitute

---

[16]   25 U.S.C. § 5110.

[17]   Act of July 9, 1832, 4 Stat. 564.

[18]   See generally Curtis E. Jackson & Marcia Galli, A History of the Bureau of Indian Affairs and Its Activities Among Indians 1–43 (1977).

[19]   Id. at 42.

[20]   Id. at 43–44.

[21]   Act of July 9, 1832, 4 Stat. 564.

[22]   Act of June 30, 1834, 4 Stat. 735.

[23]   Felix S. Cohen, Handbook of Federal Indian Law 10 (1942 ed.) (citing Report of the Commissioner of Indian Affairs 1 (1832)).

the organic laws of the Bureau. In 1849, Congress transferred the Bureau to the Interior Department.[24] In 1977, Congress eliminated the Commissioner of Indian Affairs and promoted the head of the federal Indian bureaus (Indian Affairs and Indian Education) to Assistant Secretary status within the Department of Interior.

For much of its existence, the Bureau of Indian Affairs has been a mixed bag for tribal interests. At many points in its history, the Bureau has been a source in incredible torment for Indian people and Indian nations. Corruption, incompetence, and capriciousness are hallmarks of the Bureau's history. The BIA and its officers dominated Indian reservation governance, often through the control of Indian trust assets, treaty annuities, and other funds. At other times, however, BIA officials took extraordinary action in efforts to assist Indian nations.

In 2000, at the ceremony commemorating the 175th anniversary of the founding the Bureau, Assistant Secretary for Indian Affairs Kevin Gover formally apologized to Indian people and Indian nations on behalf of the Bureau of Indian Affairs.[25]

Assistant Secretary Gover's apology came in the early stages of a long-running class action lawsuit brought by individual American Indians seeking an accounting by the Interior and Treaty Departments of assets held by the government in individual Indian money accounts, *Cobell v. Babbitt* (later concluding several Interior Secretaries as *Cobell v. Jewell*). The *Cobell* suit encapsulated wide-ranging incompetence of the federal government in administering the federal trust duties assigned to it by Congress, and the government's forceful resistance to acknowledging the accountability for its failures. In 2009, Congress ratified a settlement between the federal government and the plaintiff class for $3.4 Billion. **See § 5.2.**

§ 3.5   The End of the Treaty Era

In 1871, Congress passed a statute that purported to eliminate the authority of the President and the Senate to negotiate and ratify treaties with Indian tribes.[26] The United States continued to

---

[24]   Act of March 3, 1849, § 5, 9 Stat. 395.

[25]   146 Cong. Rec. E1453–03 (Sept. 8, 2000). Mr. Gover's remarks are also published in the American Indian Law Review. Kevin Gover, Remarks at the Ceremony Acknowledging the 175th Anniversary of the Establishment of the Bureau of Indian Affairs, 25 Am. Indian L. Rev. 161 (2000–2001).

[26]   The statute appeared in an 1871 appropriations bill relating to the Yankton Sioux Reservation. George William Rice, 25 U.S.C. § 71: The End of Indian Sovereignty or a Self-Limitation of Contractual Ability?, 5 Am. Indian L. Rev. 239, 240 (1977).

recognize as valid any treaty rights effective on that date.[27] As one commentator noted: "From the standpoint of the Indian nations, it made little difference what manner of ratification and procedure was incumbent upon the representative of the United States who dealt with them. There was no change in the legal effect of such agreements. . . ."[28] From that point, the United States continued to negotiate with Indian tribes, but the resulting agreements would have to be adopted by Congress as legislation.[29]

Importantly, the statute preserved extant Indian treaties and treaty provisions: "[N]o obligation of any treaty lawfully made and ratified with any such Indian nation or tribe prior to March 3, 1871, shall be hereby invalidated or impaired. . . ."[30] Indian treaties remain valid unless later abrogated by an Act of Congress or agreement with an Indian nation.[31]

The statute came about when Members of the House of Representatives expressed institutional jealousy over the lack of House input in Indian affairs.[32] Typically, the House's role was merely to approve appropriations in simple legislation to implement Indian treaties.[33] Decades later, one commentator would argue that at least some Congressmen opposed the authority of the Office of Indian Affairs, and sought greater control over Indian affairs.[34]

It is far from obvious that Congress has the power to legislate as to prohibit the President and the Senate from entering into treaties with Indian nations, a power left to the exclusive control of the President and the Senate. A vehicle to challenge the constitutionality of the statute has never been before the Supreme Court, and perhaps never will, but at least one sitting Supreme Court Justice doubts its constitutionality.[35] However, as a statement of federal Indian policy, the statute has been effective in foreclosing new, formal Indian treaties since its enactment.

---

[27]   16 Stat. 566, codified at 25 U.S.C. § 71.

[28]   George William Rice, 25 U.S.C. § 71: The End of Indian Sovereignty or a Self-Limitation of Contractual Ability?, 5 Am. Indian L. Rev. 239, 247 (1977).

[29]   Antoine v. Washington, 420 U.S. 194, 203–204 (1975).

[30]   25 U.S.C. § 71.

[31]   Cf. United States v. Lara, 541 U.S. 193, 201 (2004).

[32]   George William Rice, 25 U.S.C. § 71: The End of Indian Sovereignty or a Self-Limitation of Contractual Ability?, 5 Am. Indian L. Rev. 239, 240 (1977).

[33]   Id.

[34]   1 Laurence Frederick Schmeckebier, The Office of Indian Affairs: Its History, Activities and Organization 56 (1927).

[35]   United States v. Lara, 541 U.S. 193, 218 (2004) (Thomas, J., concurring in the judgment).

§ 3.6   Allotment and Assimilation

The establishment of Indian reservations allowed the federal government to undertake a series of wide ranging experiments in Indian affairs in the latter half of the 19th century designed to undermine measured separatism. Most notably, the Interior Department and then Congress embarked on a program of allotment of Indian reservation lands to individual Indians intending to break up the communal land ownership systems of many Indian nations guaranteed by treaty. The United States also embarked on social programs, often delivered through Indian education programs, designed to assimilate Indian people into the melting pot of American citizenry. The overriding theory of allotment and assimilation was that of the vanishing Indian.[36] Federal Indian affairs was designed to either hasten or ease the end of American Indian cultures in the United States.

Allotment: "Pulverizing" the Tribal Land Mass

As the treaty period came to a close, American Indian law and policy became geared toward breaking up some of the larger tribal reservations for purposes of American settlement, while expanding efforts to "civilize" Indian people. This period in American Indian law and policy is often referred to as the allotment era.[37]

Allotment refers to the division of large tribal reservations into smaller parcels, with individual parcels of typically 160 or 80 acres "allotted" to Indian heads of households, and the rest of the reservation land being put on the open market as "surplus" lands. The tribal allotments would be owned in trust by the federal government for a period that ranged from five to 25 years, depending on the tribal-specific implementing statute. At the end of the trust period, the government would issue a patent to the Indian landholder, who then acquired full title to the land. But at that point, the land became taxable by state and local governments. Often, as soon as the land reverted to Indians, it would be lost one way or another—often through tax foreclosures, theft, fraud, or any number of shady dealings.[38] The point of the trust period was to allow the Indians to learn the ways of land ownership, which meant that they needed to learn how to exploit the land as an economic tool, either through farming or ranching. But often the land that the government allotted to Indians was the worst land in the

---

[36]   See generally Kathryn E. Fort, The Vanishing Indian Returns: Tribes, Popular Originalism, and the Supreme Court, 57 St. Louis U. L. J. 297 (2013).

[37]   See generally Judith Royster, The Legacy of Allotment, 27 Ariz. St. L.J. 1 (1997).

[38]   Kenneth H. Bobroff, Retelling Allotment: Indian Property Rights and the Myth of Common Ownership, 54 Vand. L. Rev. 1559, 1561–62 (2001).

reservation, with the best lands being made available to non-Indians as surplus. Even where Indian people were able to maintain ownership of the land (or to maintain its trust status), the land was unusable.

While allotment of Indian lands had been tried in the east as far back as the late 18th century, at Cherokee in the early 19th century,[39] and also in the Midwest in the 1850s,[40] it was not the declared focus of American policy until Congress passed the General Allotment Act (also known as the Dawes Act) in 1887.[41] In the next few decades, Congress enacted numerous statutes intending to implement allotment on various tribal reservations, usually driven by non-Indians with eyes on good lands owned by Indian nations.[42]

The allotment statutes often violated express treaty provisions. In the case *Lone Wolf v. Hitchcock*,[43] the leaders of Kiowa, Comanche, and Apache tribes that had signed the Treaty of Medicine Creek alleged that the United States had used deception to acquire the consent of the community to allotment and in any event had violated the treaty.[44] The Supreme Court held that the United States had plenary power over Indian affairs and therefore had authority to unilaterally abrogate Indian treaties.[45] See § 3.7.

Allotment was enormously effective in destroying the tribal land base. From 1887 when Congress adopted this policy until 1934 when it ended the policy, tribal land holdings declined from over 135 million acres to less than 50 million acres.[46]

The allotment era, more so than any other era in federal Indian policy, contributed to the extreme doctrinal and jurisdictional complexity of federal Indian law. The division of Indian reservations into smaller parcels, with some of the parcels being owned by Indians in fee simple, some owned by non-Indians in fee simple, and some held in trust as reservation land created a jurisdictional morass referred to as "checkerboarding," with some parcels being under tribal and federal jurisdiction, and others being under state

---

[39] Francis Paul Prucha, American Indian Treaties: The History of a Political Anomaly 173, 233 (1994).

[40] Id. at 241–42.

[41] Act of Feb. 8, 1887, 24 Stat. 388.

[42] D.S. Otis, The Dawes Act and the Allotment of Indian Lands 141 (Francis Paul Prucha, ed. 1973).

[43] 187 U.S. 553 (1887).

[44] Id. at 558.

[45] Id. at 565–67.

[46] Carrie E. Garrow, Government Law and Policy and the Indian Child Welfare Act 86 N.Y. St. B.J. 10, 12 (March/April 2014) (citing Vine Deloria, Jr. & Clifford M. Lytle, American Indians, American Justice 10 (1984)).

and local jurisdiction.[47] Each allotment implementation act allowed for unique circumstances to develop, often arising under the differing provisions relating to the end of the trust period. In most places, the trust period ended when it expired, but in places like Minnesota, the trust period ended when the local Indian agent made a determination that one of the potential Indian owners was "competent."[48] And under some federal statutes, an Indian agent had authority to alienate trust patents if he determined that one of the Indian owners was "incompetent."[49] Of course, the definition of "competence" varied by each individual Indian agent.[50]

Finally, allotment created the excruciating problem of "fractionated heirships."[51] Because most Indian people (even today) do not execute valid wills, the land of an Indian decedent would pass to the Indian's heirs as joint tenants in common. And when those heirs began to pass (again, without wills), the next generation of children would receive an interest in common as well. In some remarkable cases, several thousand heirs have an interest in a small amount of acreage. Since no one person can control the land, the United States often has de facto control of the land, leasing it to ranchers or farmers and collecting rents for the Indian owners.

Indian Education: "Kill the Indian"[52]

The first efforts by non-Indians to formally educate American Indians—by the Jesuits in Florida during the 16th century—were attempts to " 'Christianize' and 'civilize' the heathen."[53] President Washington articulated a policy favoring the acculturation or assimilation of American Indians, a policy less costly than declaring

---

[47] Solem v. Bartlett, 465 U.S. 463, 471–72 (1984); Ann E. Tweedy, Unjustifiable Expectations: Laying to Rest the Ghosts of Allotment-Era Settlers, 36 Seattle U. L. Rev. 129, 13031 (2012).

[48] Edward Michael Peterson, Jr., That So-Called Warranty Deed: Clouded Land Titles on the White Earth Indian Reservation in Minnesota, 59 N.D. L. Rev. 159, 165–68 (1983).

[49] E.g., 25 U.S.C. § 378.

[50] Cf. generally Janet McDonnell, Competency Commissions and Indian Land Policy, 1913–1920, S.D. Hist. 21 (1980).

[51] See generally Kenneth H. Bobroff, Retelling Allotment: Indian Property Rights and the Myth of Common Ownership, 54 Vand. L. Rev. 1559, 16–17 (2001); G. William Rice, The Indian Reorganization Act, the Declaration on the Rights of Indigenous Peoples, and a Proposed Carcieri "Fix": Updating the Trust Land Acquisition Process, 45 Idaho L. Rev. 575, 578 (2009).

[52] The materials in this subsection are derived from an amicus brief drafted and filed by the Michigan State University Indigenous Law and Policy Center. Brief of Amici Curiae American Indian Studies Professors Dr. Suzanne L. Cross and Dr. K. Tsianina Lomawaima, A.A. v. Needville Independent School District, 611 F.3d 248 (5th Cir. 2009) (No. 09–20091), https://turtletalk.files.wordpress.com/2009/06/needville-historian-amicus-brief.pdf.

[53] Indian Education: A National Tragedy—A National Challenge, S. Rep. 91–501, 91st Cong., 1st Sess., at 140–41 (Nov. 3, 1969).

war on them.[54] Consequently, affairs between Indian tribes and American governments memorialized in Indian treaties often have revolved around the education of Indian children.[55] During the era of federal Indian law and policy in which the United States and Indian tribes engaged in treaty negotiations, tribal treaty negotiators often negotiated for treaty language requiring the federal government to provide funds for the education of American Indian children. Over 150 Indian treaties included provisions relating to Indian education. In 1819, Congress established a fund— later known as the "civilization fund"—usually distributed to missionary societies for the purpose of transforming American Indians from "hunters to agriculturalists."[56]

Tribal treaty negotiators who hoped to provide for their children a means to learn English as a second language or to learn mathematics did not realize that they had inadvertently negotiated for the kidnapping of their children by American government and military officials, the abuse of their children by educators and missionaries, and the ruinous undermining of their cultures and religions. Captain Richard H. Pratt, superintendent of the famed Carlisle Indian School from 1879 to 1904, is best known for his infamous statement that embodies American Indian education policy in the late 19th century: "A great general has said that the only good Indian is a dead one. . . . In a sense, I agree with the sentiment, but only in this: that all the Indian there is in the race should be dead. *Kill the Indian in him, to save the man.*"[57] Meanwhile, "[i]n 1892 and 1904, federal regulations outlawed the practice of tribal religions entirely, and punished Indian practitioners by either confinement in agency prisons or by withholding rations."[58] Federal authorities also contracted with non-Indian religious groups to operate Indian schools in efforts to stamp out American Indian culture and religion.[59] The intent of American policymakers and educators may not have been to harm Indian people, but ostensibly to assist American Indians to survive

---

[54]   Id. at 142; Scott Laderman, "It Is Cheaper and Better to Teach a Young Indian Than to Fight an Old One": Thaddeaus Pound and the Logic of Assimilation, 26:3 Am. Indian Culture & Res. J. 85 (2002).

[55]   Indian Education: A National Tragedy—A National Challenge, S. Rep. 91–501, at 142 (Nov. 3, 1969).

[56]   Id. at 143.

[57]   Richard H. Pratt, The Advantages of Mingling Indians with Whites (1892), reprinted in Americanizing the American Indians: Writings by the "Friends of the Indian" 1880–1900, at 260, 260–61 (Francis Paul Prucha ed. 1973) (emphasis added).

[58]   Senator Daniel K. Inouye, Discrimination and Native American Religious Rights, 23 U. West L.A. L. Rev. 3, 12–13 (1992).

[59]   Jill E. Martin, Constitutional Rights and Indian Rites: An Uneasy Balance, 3:2 Western Leg. Hist. 245, 248 (Summer/Fall 1990).

inevitable colonization by Americans. Nevertheless, the end result was the near-destruction of tribal culture and religion across the United States, often through the forced imposition of non-Indian religion upon American Indian students. "The history of the 'lost generation' of Native American children, shuffled off to BIA boarding schools, is itself a history of violence, intimidation, and repression."[60]

Federal Indian policy of the late-19th century moved into a new period of "civilizing" Indian children through coercive and destructive education, usually at federal and church-operated boarding houses located away from the children's homes and communities. In 1880, the Board of Indian Commissioners wrote in their annual report, "As a savage we cannot tolerate him [the Indian] any more than as a half-civilized parasite, wanderer, or vagabond. The only alternative left is to fit him by education for civilized life."[61] Using the limited funds Congress provided in accordance with treaty terms, and then greater appropriations beginning in 1870, federal bureaucrats intensified the brutal process of "civilizing" Indian children through education. "The federal government correctly assumed that the young are the life blood of a culture and that the molding and transformation of the children and their values might prove an effective way of destroying Indian heritage at its roots."[62] Despite reducing the number of Indian schools operated by church societies in the 1880s, non-Indian religion remained the dominant feature of American Indian education at the Bureau of Indian Affairs' schools.[63] On-reservation federal officials directed money appropriated by Congress to fulfill treaty obligations to church-run Indian schools, usually over tribal objections.[64] "Though the schools were run by the federal government, Christianity was mandatory. . . . 'For most secular as well as missionary educators, 'civilization' was inconceivable if not grounded in Christian—especially Protestant—values. . . .' "[65]

---

[60]   Barbara Perry, Silent Victims: Hate Crimes Against Native Americans 32 (2008).

[61]   Board of Indian Commissioners, Annual Report of the Board of Indian Commissioners (1880), reprinted in Americanizing the American Indians: Writings by the "Friends of the Indian" 1880–1900, at 193, 194 (Francis Paul Prucha ed. 1973).

[62]   John W. Ragsdale, Jr., The Movement to Assimilate the American Indians: A Jurisprudential Study, 57 UMKC L. Rev. 399, 409 (1989).

[63]   Jill E. Martin, Constitutional Rights and Indian Rites: An Uneasy Balance, 3:2 Western Leg. Hist. 245, 250–51 (Summer/Fall 1990).

[64]   Id. at 251–52.

[65]   Amelia V. Katanski, Learning to Write "Indian": The Boarding-School Experience and American Indian Literature 33 (2005).

American policymakers harshly criticized the lifestyles of tribal Indians in the late 19th century and sought to eliminate any trace of Indian culture and religion in Indian children. In 1889, General Thomas J. Morgan, Commissioner of Indian Affairs, recommended that Indian children being educated in grammar schools should be structured in such as a way as to eliminate "the irregularities of camp life, which is the type of all tribal life, [to force Indian youth to] give way to the methodical regularity of daily routine."[66] Morgan also recommended that the United States withhold rations, use Indian police, and send United States soldiers to compel Indian children to attend school,[67] a recommendation endorsed by Congress explicitly in 1893.[68] Indian parents who opposed the taking of their children to these schools faced criminal prosecution and possible incarceration.[69]

Federal Indian affairs agents were obsessed with removing Indian children from their cultural roots. It typically began with literal kidnappings of Indian children, spurred on by rhetorical arguments from policymakers that the only way to effectively civilize Indians was to remove them forcibly from their homes and their cultures, "tak[ing] them in their infancy and plac[ing] them in fostering schools; surrounding them with an atmosphere of civilization, maturing them in all that is good, and developing them into men and women instead of allowing them to grow up as barbarians and savages."[70] A federal Indian agent at the Hopi Indian community described hunting down Indian children who had escaped to caves or cellars, sometimes defended by their parents, who would have to be restrained by force to prevent the kidnapping of their children.[71]

The Bureau of Indian Affairs developed and operated a large number of off-reservation boarding schools throughout Indian Country by the turn of the 20th century, using Captain Richard Pratt's Carlisle Indian School as a model.[72] Pratt introduced an

---

[66] Thomas J. Morgan, Supplemental Report on Indian Education (1889), reprinted in Americanizing the American Indians: Writings by the "Friends of the Indian" 1880–1900, at 221, 231 (Francis Paul Prucha ed. 1973).

[67] Thomas J. Morgan, Compulsory Education (1892), reprinted in Americanizing the American Indians: Writings by the "Friends of the Indian" 1880–1900, at 252, 255–56 (Francis Paul Prucha ed. 1973).

[68] Indian Education: A National Tragedy—A National Challenge, S. Rep. 91–501, 91st Cong., 1st Sess., at 151 (Nov. 3, 1969) (citing 25 U.S.C. § 283).

[69] Id.

[70] Thomas J. Morgan, A Plea for the Papoose (n.d.), reprinted in Americanizing the American Indians: Writings by the "Friends of the Indian" 1880–1900, at 239, 243 (Francis Paul Prucha ed. 1973).

[71] Leo Crane, Indians of the Enchanted Desert 172–73 (1972).

[72] Sally J. McBeth, The Primer and the Hoe, Nat. Hist., Aug. 1984, at 4, 6.

"outing system" for Indian children, placing Indian children in non-Indian homes far from the reservation in the summer so that they never returned home during their eight-year tenure in his boarding school.[73] The strict regimen of military-style discipline pervaded federal boarding schools well into the 1960s.[74] Pratt introduced the notion that this form of education was necessary to "kill the Indian" and "save the man."[75]

Federal policy designed to eradicate American Indian culture and religion continued well into the 20th century. In 1928, Lewis Meriam of the Institute for Government Research, later the Brookings Institute, published a massive report of his investigation of American Indian affairs. The report concluded that American Indian education policy was an utter failure, doing egregious harm to Indian people by undermining their cultures and religions.[76] Even as late as 1952, federal bureaucrats still sent American Indian children to federal boarding schools far from their homes: "Navajo children in Oregon, Northwest Indians in Oklahoma."[77] Well into the 1960s, many non-Indian educators refused to incorporate American Indian history into their curricula on the theory that "their culture was going to be lost anyway and they would be better off in the long run if they knew less of it."[78] Of note, Indian school instructors believed that Indian children would either chose a life of "total 'Indianness'—whatever that is—and complete assimilation into the dominant society."[79] This confusion is consistent with a deep misunderstanding of what it means to be an American Indian person in the modern era: Indian people coexist as fully functional American citizens while at the same time retaining significant connections to traditional tribal culture and religion.

§ 3.7 The Expansion of Federal Plenary Power

By the end of the 19th century, federal assertions of power expanded dramatically, with Congress aggressively legislating to upset internal tribal prerogatives on criminal law and property,

---

[73] Indian Education: A National Tragedy—A National Challenge, S. Rep. 91–501, 91st Cong., 1st Sess., at 148 (Nov. 3, 1969); K. Tsianina Lomawaima, They Called It Prairie Light: The Story of Chilocco Indian School 5 (1994).

[74] Indian Education: A National Tragedy—A National Challenge, S. Rep. 91–501, at 69–70 (Nov. 3, 1969).

[75] Carrie E. Garrow, Government Law and Policy and the Indian Child Welfare Act 86 N.Y. St. B.J. 10, 12 (March/April 2014).

[76] Lewis Meriam, The Problem of Indian Administration 11 (1928). See also Indian Education: A National Tragedy—A National Challenge, S. Rep. 91–501, at 12–13, 152–56 (Nov. 3, 1969).

[77] Id. at 14.

[78] Id. at 26.

[79] Id. at 61–62.

most especially. Federal plenary power pervaded everything from the external sovereignty of Indian nations down to the day to day lives of reservation Indians. Congress passed the Major Crimes Act in 1885 and the General Allotment Act in 1887. Both statutes involved significant federal interventions into tribal governance. Meanwhile, the Bureau of Indian Affairs asserted greater and greater authority, formally and informally, over reservation governance, often without express Congressional authorization. The United States Supreme Court rejected Indian challenges to federal power, holding that federal Indian affairs policies were analogous to political questions not subject to judicial review.[80]

In general terms, the Marshall Trilogy of foundational Indian law cases established that federal power in Indian affairs is plenary and exclusive. **See §§ 2.1, 2.2.** But the Supreme Court did not address the outer contours of federal power until the 1880s.

Ex parte Kan-Gi-Shun-Ca (Crow Dog)

The first critical Supreme Court decision exploring the limits of federal plenary power arose out of the murder of Sin-ta-ge-le-Scka (Spotted Tail) by Kan-gi-shun-ca (Crow Dog) in the Dakota Territory.[81] The Supreme Court held in *Ex parte Crow Dog* that federal criminal law does not apply to Indian country criminal acts between reservation Indians.[82]

In accordance with the tribal custom of the time, the representatives of the two families and other tribal leaders met for several days to discuss punishment.[83] The Anglo-American notion of indictment, trial by jury, and punishment was foreign to this tribal community.[84] The tribe decided to punish Crow Dog in a manner that took the victim's and perpetrator's families' interests into consideration, as well as the community itself. Crow Dog, as he could have been under American law, was not executed or jailed. The community decided to punish Crow Dog by requiring him to pay compensation of $600, eight horses, and a blanket to the

---

[80] The leading scholarly papers on federal power in Indian affairs are Sarah H. Cleveland, Powers Inherent in Sovereignty: Indians, Aliens, Territories, and the Nineteenth Century Origins of Plenary Power over Foreign Affairs, 81 Tex. L. Rev. 1, 25–81 (2002), and Nell Jessup Newton, Federal Power over Indians: Its Sources, Scope, and Limitations, 132 U. Pa. L. Rev. 195 (1984).

[81] See generally Sidney Harring, Crow Dog's Case: American Indian Sovereignty, Tribal Law and United States Law in the Nineteenth Century (1994).

[82] 109 U.S. 556 (1883).

[83] B.J. Jones, Tribal Courts: Protectors of the Native Paradigm of Justice, 10 St. Thomas L. Rev. 87, 90 (1997).

[84] See generally Kevin K. Washburn, American Indians, Crime, and the Law, 104 Mich. L. Rev. 709 (2006); Kevin K. Washburn, Federal Criminal Law and Tribal Self-Determination, 84 N.C. L. Rev. 779 (2006).

victim's family.[85] Non-Indians, fueled by local Indian agents, were enraged by what they viewed as a lack of punishment.[86] The local United States Attorney initiated a criminal prosecution and procured a conviction and death sentence against Crow Dog, ultimately vacated by the Supreme Court in *Ex parte Crow Dog*.[87] See § 7.4.

A federal statute extended federal criminal jurisdiction over "any place within [the United States'] sole and exclusive jurisdiction. . . ."[88] However, a related statutes barred federal jurisdiction over Indian country crimes committed by one Indian against another.[89] The federal government argued that the 1868 Treaty of Fort Laramie and an 1877 enactment impliedly repealed the earlier federal statutes and authorized the prosecution.[90] The 1868 treaty contained a provision commonly called the "bad men clause."[91] One portion of the bad men clause read:

> If bad men among the Indians shall commit a wrong or depredation upon the person or property of any one, white, black, or Indian, subject to the authority of the United States and at peace therewith, the Indians herein named solemnly agree that they will, upon proof made to their agent and notice by him, deliver up the wrong-doer to the United States, to be tried and punished according to its laws.[92]

Though a superficial reading of the plain language of this provision suggests that the federal government did have jurisdiction over Indian-on-Indian crimes, the provision actually means crimes by Indians against Indians of other Indian nations; hence, the reference to Indians "at peace" with the United States. Interpreting a similar provision contained in the 1868 Treaty of Fort Sumpter, the Navajo Nation Supreme Court pointed out that the language there arose directly from conflicts with the Comanche Nation.[93] As

---

[85] Sidney Harring, Crow Dog's Case: American Indian Sovereignty, Tribal Law and United States Law in the Nineteenth Century 199 (1994).

[86] B.J. Jones, Tribal Courts: Protectors of the Native Paradigm of Justice, 10 St. Thomas L. Rev. 87, 90 (1997).

[87] 109 U.S. 556 (1883).

[88] Id. at 560 (citing Rev. Stat. § 2145).

[89] Id. at 570 (citing Rev. Stat. § 2146).

[90] Id. at 562–70.

[91] See generally James D. Leach, "Bad Men Among the Whites" Claims after Richard v. United States, 43 N.M. L. Rev. 533, 534–35 (2013); Note, A Bad Man is Hard to Find, 127 Harv. L. Rev. 2521 (2014).

[92] Treaty with the Sioux Indians, art. 1, para. 3, April 29, 1868, 15 Stat. 635.

[93] Means v. District Court of Chinle Judicial District, 2 Am. Tribal L. 439, 448 (Navajo Nation Supreme Court 1999).

such, the "bad men" clause was not intended, it appears, to include crimes involving solely Indians from the same reservation, or to affect internal tribal justice.

The government in *Crow Dog* further argued that an 1877 statute implementing amendments to the 1868 treaty authorized the federal prosecution.[94] That provision stated: "And congress shall, by appropriate legislation, secure to them an orderly government; they shall be subject to the laws of the United States, and each individual shall be protected in his rights of property, person, and life."[95] The government argued that the general federal obligation to secure peace on the reservation expressed in the statute authorized the prosecution.

The Court disagreed with the government on both points. It held that a federal death sentence should not be the result of an implied repeal of a federal statute expressly disclaiming jurisdiction over the crime at issue.[96] Then, in oft-quoted language noted for its paternalistic ethnocentrism, the Court pointed out the unfairness of allowing federal criminal jurisdiction over an Indian-on-Indian crime through an implied repeal:

> It is a case where, against an express exception in the law itself, that law, by argument and inference only, is sought to be extended over aliens and strangers; over the members of a community, separated by race, by tradition, by the instincts of a free though savage life, from the authority and power which seeks to impose upon them the restraints of an external and unknown code, and to subject them to the responsibilities of civil conduct, according to rules and penalties of which they could have no previous warning; which judges them by a standard made by others, and not for them, which takes no account of the conditions which should except them from its exactions, and makes no allowance for their inability to understand it. It tries them not by their peers, nor by the customs of their people, nor the law of their land, but by superiors of a different race, according to the law of a social state of which they have an imperfect conception, and which is opposed to the traditions of their history, to the habits of their lives, to the strongest prejudices of their savage

---

[94]   Ex parte Crow Dog, 109 U.S. 556, 568 (1883).

[95]   Id.

[96]   Id. at 570–71. See also id. at 571 ("It is a case involving the judgment of a court of special and limited jurisdiction, not to be assumed without clear warrant of law. It is a case of life and death.").

nature; one which measures the red man's revenge by the maxims of the white man's morality.[97]

The Court also held that the 1877 statute could not be construed to extend federal criminal jurisdiction over Indians, who were "wards" of the federal government, and not American citizens over which such a law might apply:

> The pledge to secure to these people, with whom the United States was contracting as a distinct political body, an orderly government, by appropriate legislation thereafter to be framed and enacted, necessarily implies, having regard to all the circumstances attending the transaction, that among the arts of civilized life, which it was the very purpose of all these arrangements to introduce and naturalize among them, was the highest and best of all,—that of self-government, the regulation by themselves of their own domestic affairs, the maintenance of order and peace among their own members by the administration of their own laws and customs. They were nevertheless to be subject to the laws of the United States, not in the sense of citizens, but, as they had always been, as wards, subject to a guardian; not as individuals, constituted members of the political community of the United States, with a voice in the selection of representatives and the framing of the laws, but as a dependent community who were in a state of pupilage, advancing from the condition of a savage tribe to that of a people who, through the discipline of labor, and by education, it was hoped might become a self-supporting and self-governed society.[98]

The Court added for good measure that since the federal government had not previously attempted to prosecute Indians for crimes against other Indians in Indian country.[99] Several decades had passed since the enactment of Revised Statutes §§ 2145 and 2146 without a federal prosecution.[100]

Importantly, the Supreme Court applied the clear statement rule that authorizes extension of federal law into the internal affairs of Indian nations only where Congress clearly expressed its intent to do so:

---

[97]   Id.

[98]   Id. at 568–69.

[99]   Id.

[100] Id.

To give to the clauses in the treaty of 1868 and the agreement of 1877 effect, so as to uphold the jurisdiction exercised in this case, would be to reverse in this instance the general policy of the government towards the Indians, as declared in many statutes and treaties, and recognized in many decisions of this court, from the beginning to the present time. *To justify such a departure, in such a case, requires a clear expression of the intention of congress,* and that we have not been able to find.[101]

The clear statement rule is further addressed in § 5.6.

United States v. Kagama

In *United States v. Kagama,*[102] Supreme Court located Congressional power to regulate internal tribal affairs in the relationship between Indian nations and the United States, which the Court characterized as "wards of the nation" and "pupils."[103] Notably, the Court rejected the federal government's claim that the Indian Commerce Clause supplied federal power to enact criminal laws for Indian country. Instead, the Court relied on the federal government's trust obligation to ensure law and order in Indian country as the source of authority.

As detailed in § 7.4, Congress's reaction to the *Ex parte Crow Dog* decision was swift and decisive. Congress extended federal criminal jurisdiction to seven specified felony acts in 1885.[104] The first federal indictments for murder under the 1885 Act arose, according to the Supreme Court, on the Hoopa Valley Indian Reservation in northern California.[105] The federal government had established the Hoopa Reservation by executive action in 1864.[106] The Hupa reservation surrounded the Trinity River just before it combines with the Klamath River. The Yurok reservation begins at that collision. A small town on the modern Yurok Reservation called

---

[101] Id. at 572 (emphasis added).

[102] 118 U.S. 375 (1886).

[103] Id. at 382. Justice Miller's opinion states these phases appear in Cherokee Nation v. Georgia, 30 U.S. 1 (1831), and Worcester v. Georgia, 31 U.S. 515 (1832). He was mistaken—"wards of the nation" appears nowhere in either opinion. However, Chief Justice Marshall's lead opinion in Cherokee Nation asserts that Indian people "are in a state of pupilage." Cherokee Nation v. Georgia, 30 U.S. 1, 17 (1831).

[104] Act of March 3, 1885, § 9, 23 Stat. 385.

[105] United States v. Kagama, 118 U.S. 375, 375 (1886).

[106] Sidney L. Harring, The Distorted History that Gave Rise to the "So Called" Plenary Power Doctrine: The Story of United States v. Kagama, in Indian Law Stories 149, 153 (Carole Goldberg, Kevin K. Washburn, and Philip P. Frickey, eds. 2011). See also Karuk Tribe v. Ammon, 209 F.3d 1366, 1370 (Fed. Cir. 2000), cert. denied, 532 U.S. 941 (2001); Parravano v. Babbitt, 70 F.3d 539, 542 (9th Cir. 1995).

Weitchpec is there. The Yurok reservation follows the river down to the sea.

The Supreme Court affirmed the federal government's authority to prosecute Kagama. The Court first distinguished the *Kagama* geographic facts from the *Crow Dog* facts—the Hoopa Valley Indian Reservation was located within a State of the Union (not a territory).[107]

The Court then searched systematically in the Constitution for a source of authority permitting Congress to enact the Major Crimes Act. The Court began with the Indians Not Taxed Clauses, first of Article I and then of the Fourteenth Amendment.[108] The Court read these provisions literally and suggested that there could be Indians taxed by states: [And] "if there were such within a state as were taxed to support the government, they should be counted for representation, and in the computation for direct taxes levied by the United States."[109] But the Court concluded that neither Clause "shed much light on the power of congress over the Indians in their existence as tribes distinct from the ordinary citizens of a state or territory."[110]

The Court then turned its attention to the Indian Commerce Clause, which the United States had suggested was the strongest source of Congressional authority. The Court, again reading the Constitution literally, rejected that claim: "[W]e are not able to see in either of these clauses of the constitution and its amendments any delegation of power to enact a code of criminal law for the punishment of the worst class of crimes known to civilized life when committed by Indians. . . ."[111] In short, the Court stated that there was no express provision in the Constitution allowing Congress to enact a general criminal code for Indians.

The government further argued that the Indian Commerce Clause should be interpreted more broadly than the rest of the Commerce Clause apparently because of the special status of Indian nations. The Court, drawing upon and perhaps attempting to reinterpret *Cherokee Nation v. Georgia*, asserted that Indian nations were neither States nor nations under the Constitution.[112] Refusing to reference Indian nations at all, and apparently dismissing tribal sovereignty altogether, the Court pointed out:

---

[107] United States v. Kagama, 118 U.S. 375, 378 (1886).

[108] Id.

[109] Id.

[110] Id.

[111] Id. at 379.

[112] Id. (citing 30 U.S. 1, 20 (1831)).

But these Indians are within the geographical limits of the United States. The soil and the people within these limits are under the political control of the government of the United States, or of the states of the Union. There exists within the broad domain of sovereignty but these two. There may be cities, counties, and other organized bodies, with limited legislative functions, but they are all derived from, or exist in, subordination to one or the other of these. The territorial governments owe all their powers to the statutes of the United States conferring on them the powers which they exercise, and which are liable to be withdrawn, modified, or repealed at any time by congress.[113]

For the *Kagama* Court, there was only federal and state sovereignty. States and their political subdivisions drew sovereignty from the people as states. The United States and its political territories drew sovereignty from the people as the federal government. The Court suggested that in a later case, it would decide whether States had authority to enact criminal codes for Indians: "What authority the state governments may have to enact criminal laws for the Indians will be presently considered."[114]

Surprisingly, the Court then suggested that Congress's authority to regulate territories could derive from the Territory and Property Clause of the Constitution, but also from the fact that the United States owned that land exclusively as to States:

But this power of congress to organize territorial governments, and make laws for their inhabitants, arises, not so much from the clause in the constitution in regard to disposing of and making rules and regulations concerning the territory and other property of the United States, as from the ownership of the country in which the territories are, and the right of exclusive sovereignty which must exist in the national government, and can be found nowhere else.[115]

The import of this remarkable turn would become apparent when the Court later located Congressional power in what we now call the federal trust responsibility.

Next, the Court addressed the ownership of reservation lands, relying in large part on the federal policy of non-intercourse with Indians and Indian nations. The Court noted that the Hoopa

---

[113] Id. at 379–80.

[114] Id. at 380.

[115] Id.

reservation was located in California, which the United States originally had acquired in the Treaty of Guadalupe Hildago.[116] Then the Court mentioned the Doctrine of Discovery and the federal policy prohibiting land transactions with Indian tribes.[117] These factors laid a framework for the Court to suggest later that all Indian lands were owned by the United States.

At this point, the Court acknowledged a form of limited sovereignty of Indian nations over internal affairs that foreclosed the application of federal or state laws:

> [Indians] were, and always have been, regarded as having a semi-independent position when they preserved their tribal relations; not as states, not as nations, not as possessed of the full attributes of sovereignty, but as a separate people, with the power of regulating their internal and social relations, and thus far not brought under the laws of the Union or of the state within whose limits they resided.[118]

The Court suggested that the 1871 statute ending the treaty period had been a federal statement of policy altering the choice to deal with Indian nations with simple legislation rather than through the treaty process.[119] That Congress chose to regulate Indian affairs through legislation also had import for the Court.

The Court then finally reached the issue, whether Congress was authorized to provide for criminal jurisdiction over crimes committed by Indians against other Indians in Indian country, and the Court concluded that Congress did:

> These Indian tribes *are* the wards of the nation. They are communities *dependent* on the United States,—dependent largely for their daily food; dependent for their political rights. They owe no allegiance to the states, and receive from them no protection. Because of the local ill feeling, the people of the states where they are found are often their deadliest enemies. From their very weakness and helplessness, so largely due to the course of dealing of the federal government with them, and the treaties in which it has been promised, there arises the duty of protection, and with it the power.

---

[116] Id. at 381.

[117] Id.

[118] Id. at 381–82.

[119] Id. at 382 ("But, after an experience of a hundred years of the treaty-making system of government, congress has determined upon a new departure,—to govern them by acts of congress. This is seen in the act of March 3, 1871. . . .").

* * *

> The power of the general government over these remnants
> of a race once powerful, now weak and diminished in
> numbers, is necessary to their protection, as well as to the
> safety of those among whom they dwell.[120]

The "duty of protection" language recalls Justice Thompson's
dissent in *Cherokee Nation* and Chief Justice Marshall's opinion in
Worcester v. Georgia. **See § 2.2**. Through the treaty process, Indian
nations agreed to divest themselves of external sovereignty but not
their plenary power over the internal affairs of Indian nations.

But through the Major Crimes Act, Congress had asserted
power over the internal affairs of Indian nations. The Court
concluded that Congress could do so because it viewed Indians as
dependent on the federal government from everything between
"political rights" to "daily food." It was true that Indian nations,
including the Indians of the Klamath River, could become
dependent on the United States for rations—after all, the federal
government often had threatened to halt rations to Indian nations
as a means of governing Indian country. Moreover, the Court
suggested, the threats from state governments and their citizens
further supported Congressional action. The "local ill feeling" from
non-Indians near Indian reservations had repeatedly generated
enormously bloody conflicts in California.[121] These wars
dramatically affected the Yurok people in the 1850s and 1860s.[122]
However, those bloody clashes did not reach the Hoopa Reservation
until the United States military brought them to the Hoopa Valley
in the 1860s.[123] In short, the perceived dependence of and threats to
Indian people all arose directly from federal actions. Congress's
effort to bring law and order to Indian country in the form of the
Major Crimes Act was ironic then and now given the large-scale
disruption and bloodshed initiated by federal actors.

The Court's final justifications for its conclusion that Congress
had inherent authority to enact the Major Crimes Act involved the
exclusive character of federal Indian affairs law and policy. The

---

[120] Id. at 383–84, 385 (emphasis in original).

[121] See generally Steve Talbot, California Indians, Genocide of, in 1
Encyclopedia of American Indian History 230–231 (Bruce E. Johansen and Barry M.
Pritzker, eds., 2007); Byron Nelson, Jr., Our Home Forever: The Hupa Indians of
Northern California 37–113 (1994).

[122] Sidney L. Harring, The Distorted History that Gave Rise to the "So Called"
Plenary Power Doctrine: The Story of United States v. Kagama, in Indian Law
Stories 149, 158 (Carole Goldberg, Kevin K. Washburn, and Philip P. Frickey, eds.
2011).

[123] Byron Nelson, Jr., Our Home Forever: The Hupa Indians of Northern
California 79–91 (1994).

Court noted that Congress had always been the political entity that had asserted authority over Indian affairs, and that states were not so authorized:

> [Exclusive Congressional authority] has always been recognized by the executive, and by congress, and by this court, whenever the question has arisen. . . . It must exist in [the federal government] government, because it never has existed anywhere else; because the theater of its exercise is within the geographical limits of the United States; because it has never been denied; and because it alone can enforce its laws on all the tribes.[124]

The Court's conclusion that nothing in the Constitution expressly authorized the enactment of the Major Crimes Act is almost certainly wrong. Federal courts routinely cited the *Kagama* Court's theory of guardianship over Indians as the core of federal power in Indian affairs.[125] In recent decades, however, the Supreme Court recognizes federal authority to enact a general federal criminal law without reference to *Kagama*. For example, in *Negonsott v. Samuels*.[126] the Court asserted without discussion that "Congress has plenary authority to alter [Indian country criminal] jurisdictional guideposts,"[127] without reference to *Kagama*.

Some lower courts suggest that the holding in *Kagama* that the Indian Commerce Clause does not authorize Congress to enact criminal laws (and presumably other Indian affairs statutes reaching beyond the narrow scope of Indian commercial relations) is no longer good law. At least one federal circuit has recognized that the Indian Commerce Clause alone authorizes the Major Crimes Act.[128] Moreover, the Sixth Circuit, in dicta, has suggested that *Kagama*'s description of Congressional power over Indian affairs "appears no longer to be an accurate statement of the law."[129] However, the Supreme Court has not expressly retreated from *Kagama*.

---

[124] United States v. Kagama, 118 U.S. 375, 383, 384–85 (1886).

[125] E.g., Petition of Carmen, 165 F. Supp. 942, 948–949 (N.D. Cal. 1958), aff'd, 270 F.2d 809 (9th Cir. 1959) (per curiam), cert. denied, 361 U.S. 934 (1960).

[126] 507 U.S. 99 (1993).

[127] Id. at 103. See also United States v. Antelope, 430 U.S. 641, 648 (1978) ("Congress has undoubted constitutional power to prescribe a criminal code applicable in Indian country.").

[128] E.g., United States v. Lomayaoma, 86 F.3d 142, 145 (9th Cir.).

[129] United States v. Doherty, 126 F.3d 769, 778 n.2 (6th Cir. 1997), cert. denied, 524 U.S. 917 (1998).

United States v. Sandoval

In the exercise of its Indian affairs powers, Congress also possesses the power to determine which groups of people are subject to plenary power. In 1913, the Supreme Court decided *United States v. Sandoval*.[130]

The legal question concerned whether Pueblo lands were Indian country for purposes of federal jurisdiction. That question allowed the Court to answer a different question altogether; namely, whether Congress had authority to over the Pueblo Indians, who the Court had previously held were outside of the protection of Congress in *United States v. Joseph*, a case involving Indians of the Taos Pueblo.[131] The New Mexico territorial court had also concluded that Pueblo lands were *not* Indian country in another case involving the Taos Pueblo.[132]

In reaching the conclusion that Congress had authority to regulate the Santa Clara Pueblo, thereby rendering Pueblo lands "Indian country", the *Sandoval* Court argued that Pueblo Indians were not civilized: "Always living in separate and isolated communities, adhering to primitive modes of life, largely influenced by superstition and fetishism, and chiefly governed according to the crude customs inherited from their ancestors, they are essentially a simple, uninformed, and inferior people."[133] This was a remarkable conclusion, given that the Supreme Court decades earlier had argued that Pueblo Indians had nothing in common with other Indians, and had reached a pinnacle of civilization.[134] The New Mexico territorial court even more bluntly concluded that all courts had reached the conclusion that Pueblo Indians were not "wards" of the federal government.[135]

The *Sandoval* Court brushed those precedents aside, especially *Joseph*, and concluded that the federal liquor statute was more "comprehensive" than the statutes under review in earlier cases.[136]

---

[130] 231 U.S. 28 (1913).

[131] 94 U.S. 614 (1876).

[132] United States v. Mares, 88 P. 1128 (N.M. Terr. 1907).

[133] United States v. Sandoval, 231 U.S. 28, 39 (1913).

[134] United States v. Joseph, 94 U.S. 614, 617 (1876).

[135] United States v. Mares, 88 P. 1128, 1128 (N.M. Terr. 1907) (citing United States v. Varela, 1 N. M. 593 (1874); United States v. Santistevan, 1 N. M. 583 (1874); Pueblo Indian Tax Case, 76 P. 307 (N.M. Terr. 1904); United States v. Joseph, 94 U.S. 619 (1876); Ex parte Crow Dog, 109 U.S. 556 (1883); United States v. Richie, 58 U.S. 525, 538 (1854)).

[136] United States v. Sandoval, 231 U.S. 28, 48–49 (1913).

Felix Cohen would harshly criticize the *Sandoval* Court for its inconsistency and ethnocentrism.[137]

The chief flaw with this series of opinions that occasionally recurs in Indian law jurisprudence is to mistake the racial status of Indian people with their political status. As one commentator noted, "The fundamental error in the opinion, one that is repeated to this day, is to think of Indians as a race and not a nation. It is easy to do it you just pluck one Indian at a time."[138]

Lone Wolf v. Hitchcock

The Supreme Court's deference to Congressional plenary power over Indian affairs reached its peak in *Lone Wolf v. Hitchcock*.[139] The Supreme Court held that the United States had plenary power over Indian affairs and therefore had authority to unilaterally abrogate Indian treaties. The Court also held that the political question doctrine would foreclose most challenges to Congressional Indian affairs legislation.

Lone Wolf should be discussed in light of the Supreme Court's earlier decisions in three cases involving the Cherokee Nation of Oklahoma, *Thomas v. Gay*,[140] *Stephens v. Cherokee Nation*,[141] and *Cherokee Nation v. Hitchcock*.[142] In *Thomas*, the Supreme Court affirmed that Congress may through simple legislation abrogate an Indian treaty, even without tribal consent.[143] The latter two cases involved Congressional Acts passed in the 1890s asserting control over the tribal citizenship authority of the so-called Five Civilized Tribes for purposes of administering the allotment of their reservations.[144] The Supreme Court upheld the authority of Congress to allow appeals from the citizenship decisions to a federal court in *Stephens*, relying in part on *Thomas*.[145]

In 1902, the Supreme Court in *Cherokee Nation v. Hitchcock* characterized the statute affirmed in *Stephens* as one "wherein the United States practically assumed the full control over the

---

[137] Felix Cohen, Field Theory and Judicial Logic, 59 Yale L.J. 238, 263 (1950).

[138] Gerald Torres, Who Is an Indian? The Story of United States v. Sandoval, in Indian Law Stories 109, 132 (Carole Goldberg, Kevin K. Washburn, and Philip P. Frickey eds., 2011).

[139] 187 U.S. 553 (1903).

[140] 169 U.S. 264 (1898).

[141] 174 U.S. 445 (1899).

[142] 187 U.S. 294 (1902).

[143] Thomas v. Gay, 169 U.S. 264, 271 (1898) ("It is well settled that an act of congress may supersede a prior treaty, and that any questions that may arise are beyond the sphere of judicial cognizance, and must be met by the political department of the government.").

[144] Stephens v. Cherokee Nation, 174 U.S. 445, 476 (1899).

[145] Id. at 483–84 (citing Thomas v. Gay, 169 U.S. 264, 271 (1898)).

Cherokees, as well as the other nations constituting the five civilized tribes, and took upon itself the determination of membership in the tribes for the purpose of adjusting their rights in the tribal properties."[146] There, the federal government began leasing Cherokee lands under the statute over the Nation's objections. The Court asserted, "The plenary power of control by Congress over the Indian tribes and its undoubted power to legislate, as it had done through the act of 1898, directly for the protection of the tribal property, was in [*Stephens*] reaffirmed."[147] Presaging *Lone Wolf*, the Court held that the federal taking of tribally-owned property was no taking at all, so long as the asset remained in federal hands in another form.[148]

The very next month, the Supreme Court broadly reaffirmed the plenary power principles established in these three cases in *Lone Wolf v. Hitchcock*.[149] *Lone Wolf* arose out a fantastical set of facts involving the federal government's appropriation of a treaty-guaranteed Indian reservation for allotment purposes.[150]

In 1867, the Kiowa and Comanche nations executed a treaty with the United States called the Treaty of Medicine Lodge.[151] Plains Apache people later joined the treaty. The treaty reduced the tribes' landholdings from 90 million acres to 2.9 million acres.[152] Importantly, though, the treaty "set apart" the reservation "for the absolute and undisturbed use and occupation" of the signatory nations.[153] The treaty also included a provision allowing individual Indians to select land for agricultural purposes; however, unlike typical allotment provisions, this section provided for the continued communal tribal ownership of that land.[154]

---

[146] Cherokee Nation v. Hitchcock, 187 U.S. 294, 295 (1902).

[147] Id. at 306.

[148] Id. at 307–08.

[149] 187 U.S. 553 (1903).

[150] See generally Angela R. Riley, The Apex of Congress' Plenary Power over Indian Affairs: The Story of Lone Wolf v. Hitchcock, Indian Law Stories 189 (Carole Goldberg, Kevin K. Washburn, and Philip P. Frickey eds., 2011).

[151] 15 Stat. 581 (1867).

[152] Angela R. Riley, The Apex of Congress' Plenary Power over Indian Affairs: The Story of Lone Wolf v. Hitchcock, Indian Law Stories 189, 195 (Carole Goldberg, Kevin K. Washburn, and Philip P. Frickey eds., 2011).

[153] Treaty of Medicine Creek, art. 2, 15 Stat. 581 (1867).

[154] Id., art. 6. Angela R. Riley, The Apex of Congress' Plenary Power over Indian Affairs: The Story of Lone Wolf v. Hitchcock, Indian Law Stories 189, 195–96 (Carole Goldberg, Kevin K. Washburn, and Philip P. Frickey eds., 2011).

Article 12 of the treaty provided for additional land cessions by the parties, but only if three-fourths of the adult male Indians consented.[155]

In 1887, Congress passed the General Allotment Act.[156] **See § 3.6**. In accordance with the shift in federal policy, the federal government established the Jerome Commission in 1892 to negotiate allotment and land cessions with the Kiowa, Comanche, and Plains Apache nations.[157] The Indian nations refused to reopen the 1867 treaty. Lone Wolf the Younger, adopted son of the legendary tribal leader Lone Wolf the Elder, spoke against the efforts by the Commission to amend the treaty.[158] The Commission eventually presented the terms of allotment: 160 acre allotments for every member of the nations, sale of two million acres of land, a per capita distribution of funds derived from the government's purchase of land, and a federal trust account established in the tribes' name to be held by the United States.[159]

The proposal also allowed non-Indians to receive allotments.[160] Along with the Commission itself, these non-Indians set about to procure signatures to meet the three-fourths requirement set out in the 1867 treaty.[161] At least some of the non-Indians procuring signatures did so in an "unscrupulous" manner, leading many Indians to further distrust the Commission.[162] Soon, even those Indians who had signed the proposal began to oppose the Commission, and attempted to withdraw their signatures.[163] The Commission left the reservation with enough signatures for the Indian agent to certify it had met the three-fourths requirement.[164]

Lone Wolf's challenge reached the Supreme Court in 1903.[165] The Attorney General argued that the 1871 statute ending the treaty era and the 1886 decision in *United States v. Kagama* had

---

[155] Lone Wolf v. Hitchcock, 187 U.S. 553, 564 (1903) (quoting Treaty of Medicine Creek, art. 12, 15 Stat. 581 (1867)) (bracket in original).

[156] 24 Stat. 388 (1887), codified as amended at 25 U.S.C. §§ 331 et seq., repealed, Pub.L. 106–462, Title I, § 106(a)(1), Nov. 7, 2000, 114 Stat. 2007.

[157] Angela R. Riley, The Apex of Congress' Plenary Power over Indian Affairs: The Story of Lone Wolf v. Hitchcock, Indian Law Stories 189, 202 (Carole Goldberg, Kevin K. Washburn, and Philip P. Frickey eds., 2011).

[158] Id. at 202–03.

[159] Id. at 203.

[160] Id. at 204.

[161] Id.

[162] Id. at 204–05.

[163] Id. at 205.

[164] Id.

[165] Lone Wolf v. Hitchcock, 187 U.S. 553 (1903).

dramatically altered the way Congress regulated Indian affairs.[166] For the government, Indian people were "absolutely incapable of protecting [themselves]. . . ."[167]

The Supreme Court, per Justice White, agreed with the Attorney General on the federal government's broad prerogatives rather than the Interior's Secretary's factual defense. The Court determined that the issue here was not a government taking of private property, but mere administration of tribal property.[168] The Court concluded that Congressional plenary power arising from the federal "guardianship" over Indians had authorized Congress to alter treaty arrangements: "Congress possessed a paramount power over the property of the Indians, by reason of its exercise of guardianship over their interests, and that such authority might be implied, even though opposed to the strict letter of a treaty with the Indians."[169]

The Court disclaimed much of its authority to review Congressional Indian affairs enactments by squarely placing plenary power in the hands of Congress as a political branch, all but labeling Indian affairs as an unreviewable political question: "Plenary authority over the tribal relations of the Indians has been exercised by Congress from the beginning, and the power has always been deemed a political one, not subject to be controlled by the judicial department of the government."[170]

Moreover, the Court would presume that Congress was acting in "perfect good faith" toward Indian people, further justifying a hands-off approach to judicial review of Indian affairs enactments amending Indian treaties: "When, therefore, treaties were entered into between the United States and a tribe of Indians it was never doubted that the power to abrogate existed in Congress, and that in a contingency such power might be availed of from considerations of governmental policy, particularly if consistent with perfect good faith towards the Indians."[171]

The Court relied on *Kagama* to reaffirm its view shared by the Attorney General that Indians were wards of the federal

---

[166] Angela R. Riley, The Apex of Congress' Plenary Power over Indian Affairs: The Story of Lone Wolf v. Hitchcock, Indian Law Stories 189, 221 (Carole Goldberg, Kevin K. Washburn, and Philip P. Frickey eds., 2011).

[167] Id. (quoting Appellees Brief at 16, Lone Wolf v. Hitchcock, 187 U.S. 553 (1903) (No. 275)).

[168] Lone Wolf v. Hitchcock, 187 U.S. 553, 565 (1903) (describing the issue as "a controversy between Indians and the government respecting the power of Congress to administer the property of the Indians").

[169] Id.

[170] Id. at 565.

[171] Id. at 566.

government guardian. The Court referenced a hypothetical time when Indian nations would be "emancipated" from the "protection" of the United States.[172]

In perhaps one of the more notorious statements of the guardianship era of federal plenary power, the Court concluded that the federal guardian's policy choices relating to Indian property simply were not subject to judicial review:

> Indeed, the controversy which this case presents is concluded by the decision in *Cherokee Nation v. Hitchcock*, . . . decided at this term, where it was held that full administrative power was possessed by Congress over Indian tribal property. In effect, the action of Congress now complained of was but an exercise of such power, a mere change in the form of investment of Indian tribal property, the property of those who, as we have held, were in substantial effect the wards of the government. We must presume that Congress acted in perfect good faith in the dealings with the Indians of which complaint is made, and that the legislative branch of the government exercised its best judgment in the premises. In any event, as Congress possessed full power in the matter, the judiciary cannot question or inquire into the motives which prompted the enactment of this legislation. If injury was occasioned, which we do not wish to be understood as implying, by the use made by Congress of its power, relief must be sought by an appeal to that body for redress, and not to the courts. The legislation in question was constitutional, and the demurrer to the bill was therefore rightly sustained.[173]

This statement, that Indian affairs was under the sole jurisdiction of Congress so much that the Supreme Court would not engage in judicial review, amounts to a vacature of the federal judiciary's role in Indian affairs. Moreover, the conclusion that allotment was not a taking of property but a change only in the "investment" of Indian assets effectively removed the Fifth Amendment's Taking Clause analysis from the government's allotment of Indian trust property. *Lone Wolf* granted Congress authority to break up Indian reservations through allotment without bothering to make efforts to acquire Indian consent.[174]

---

[172] Id. at 567.

[173] Id. at 568.

[174] Angela R. Riley, The Apex of Congress' Plenary Power over Indian Affairs: The Story of Lone Wolf v. Hitchcock, Indian Law Stories 189, 221 (Carole Goldberg, Kevin K. Washburn, and Philip P. Frickey eds., 2011).

The Supreme Court eventually retreated from the guardianship model adopted in *Lone Wolf* and contemporaneous cases, but not for many decades. The Supreme Court began to understand Congress's enactments in relation to Indians and tribes in light of a general trust relationship. Federal waivers of federal immunity from suit works a dramatic change in the Court's analysis of Congressional Indian affairs enactments. In *United States v. Sioux Nation*,[175] the Supreme Court distinguished *Lone Wolf* in Indian property takings cases because Congress had expressly waived federal immunity from suit to allow the Sioux Nation to sue to recover damages for the taking of the Black Hills.[176]

But the damage done to American Indian property rights by allotment has never been undone, or compensated.

§ 3.8   Indian Citizenship

The foundational principles of federal Indian law have directly affected American Indian citizenship, voting rights, and political rights throughout American history. It is now well established that American Indians are American citizens entitled to all of the privileges and immunities enjoyed by all American citizens. But the United States did not grant citizenship to most American Indians until 1924, and some states still did not allow American Indians to vote as late as mid-20th century.

Federal and state law relating to American Indian citizenship and voting rights derives directly from two foundational principles—Congressional plenary and exclusive authority to deal in Indian affairs. From the Framing, the United States Constitution set aside Indian people for purposes of apportionment as "Indians not taxed."[177] Indians were not "free Persons," nor were they slaves (that is, "all other Persons"). In *Dred Scott v. Sandford*,[178] where the Supreme Court held that African-Americans could not be American citizens, and therefore had no right to bring a suit, the Court addressed American Indian citizenship as well. The Court contrasted American Indians with African-Americans, relying on this language to conclude that Indians could theoretically obtain

---

[175] 448 U.S. 371 (1980).

[176] Id. at 414.

[177] U.S. Const. Art. I, § 2, ¶ 3 ("Representatives and direct Taxes shall be apportioned among the several States which may be included within this Union, according to their respective Numbers, which shall be determined by adding to the whole Number of free Persons, including those bound to Service for a Term of Years, and excluding Indians not taxed, three fifths of all other Persons.").

[178] 60 U.S. 393 (1857).

citizenship and voting rights through an Act of Congress, but that African-Americans could not.[179]

The Fourteenth Amendment did little to alter the tribal-federal relationship and Indian citizenship. Historians conclude that the Fourteenth Amendment was "defined to mean that *tribal* Indians are not taxable as long as they remain subject to the jurisdiction of their tribe in any degree and hold tribal allegiance in any degree."[180] The Fourteenth Amendment was a continuation of the "Indians Not Taxed" Clause exclusion of tribal Indians from those that had abandoned their tribal relations.

Prior to the adoption of the Fourteenth Amendment, Congress debated the Civil Rights Act of 1866.[181] From these debates and from the text of the Act, we hear Senator Trumbull asserting, "Our dealings with the Indians are with them as foreigners, as separate nations. We deal with them by treaty and not by law. . . ."[182]

So, Congress's continuing presumption was that Indian people were not American citizens—and could not be—because of their own political relationship with their own Indian tribes. Senator Howard objected to the inclusion of the "Indians Not Taxed" clause in Section 1 of the Amendment because it was unnecessary: "I hope that the amendment [adding the "Indians not taxed clause"] to the amendment will not be adopted. Indians born within the limits of the United States and who maintain their tribal relations are not in the sense of this amendment born subject to the jurisdiction of the United States. They are regarded, and always have been in our legislation and jurisprudence, as being quasi-foreign nations."[183]

Elk v. Wilkins

The Supreme Court confirmed that after Reconstruction, which extended citizenship to freed slaves, Indian people's status as noncitizens remained unchanged. Congress employed the same "Indians Not Taxed" language from Article I of the Constitution in

---

[179] Id. at 403–04.

[180] George Beck, The Fourteenth Amendment as Related to Tribal Indians: Section I, "Subject to the Jurisdiction Thereof" and Section II, "Excluding Indians Not Taxed", 28 Am. Indian Culture & Research J. 37, 37 (2004) (emphasis in original).

[181] 14 Stat. 27 (1866).

[182] George Beck, The Fourteenth Amendment as Related to Tribal Indians: Section I, "Subject to the Jurisdiction Thereof" and Section II, "Excluding Indians Not Taxed", 28 Am. Indian Culture & Research J. 37, 38 (2004) (quoting Cong. Globe, 39th Cong., 1st Sess., at 498 (Jan. 30, 1866)).

[183] Id. at 44 (quoting Cong. Globe, 39th Cong., 1st Sess., at 2890 (1866)).

the Fourteenth Amendment as well.[184] In *Elk v. Wilkins*,[185] the Court held that American Indians born in Indian country may not acquire citizenship upon their birth under the Fourteenth Amendment. In other words, American Indians could only acquire citizenship through an Act of Congress.

No one knows for sure what tribe John Elk was born into, but it is apparent he moved away from reservation life to live in Omaha as a white man; in the words of the Supreme Court, he "voluntarily separate[ed] himself from his tribe and taking up his residence among white citizens. . . ."[186] In describing the status of American Indians, Justice Gray points out numerous justifications for excluding American Indians from the polls that courts and policymakers would rely upon for another nine decades, including loyalty to an Indian nation, status as a ward of the United States, and immunity from state taxes.[187]

The Court concluded that American Indians could not be born as American citizens, nor could they become naturalized citizens absent of Act of Congress.[188]

The Court also distinguished cases such as the *Standing Bear* decision on grounds that even non-citizens are entitled to bring petitions for writs of habeas corpus.[189] That statement may have come to a surprise by members of Indian nations held in military prisons or Indian reservations by force.

Justice Harlan dissented on the grounds that at the Framing, there must have been Indians "not members of any tribe" counted for purposes of representation under Article I of the Constitution.[190] As no Act of Congress expressly granted these Indians citizenship, no Act appeared to be necessary. Even so, Justice Harlan would have held that the 1866 Civil Rights Act extending citizenship "reached Indians not in tribal relations."[191] Quoting from the legislative history of the Fourteenth Amendment, Justice Harlan suggested that Congress meant to include, for example, "wild

---

[184] U.S. Const. Amend. 14, § 2 ("Representatives shall be apportioned among the several states according to their respective numbers, counting the whole number of persons in each state, excluding Indians not taxed.").

[185] 112 U.S. 94 (1884).

[186] Id. at 99.

[187] Id. at 99–100.

[188] Id. at 101–02.

[189] Id. at 108.

[190] Id. at 112 (Harlan, J., dissenting).

[191] Id.

roaming Indians" as the people meeting the "Indians not taxed" label.[192]

During the latter half of the 19th century and the early 20th century, Congress provided avenues for Indian people to acquire federal citizenship (state citizenship was a different matter) in various Indian treaties and federal statutes. Usually, Congress tied citizenship to the "civilized" status of American Indian individuals, often tied to the relinquishment of tribal membership and treaty rights, expressions of loyalty to the United States, and acceptance of Christianity and an agrarian livelihood. The *Elk* Court helpfully listed and described numerous Indian treaties providing for federal citizenship of the citizens of the signatory Indian nations.[193]

In 1924, Congress extended American citizenship to all American Indians by statute.[194]

State Constitutions and State Law

American Indian citizenship under state law was perhaps even more complicated than under federal law. Some states authorized Indians to vote even before the Reconstruction, such as Michigan, but imposed vague obligations on Indians based on the "civilized" character of an Indian, whether the Indian was a ward of the federal government, or whether the Indian had renounced tribal status or treaty rights.

For many decades that followed, states typically concluded that Indian people were "wards" of the United States or "uncivilized"—in both instances legally incapable of voting. By the early 20th century, the remaining states that resisted allowing Indians to vote concluded that reservation Indians were not residents of the state in which the reservation was located. In 1962, the New Mexico Supreme Court held that Navajo Nation members are entitled to vote in state elections,[195] the last state to recognize voting rights for American Indians, rejecting the residence claim.

§ 3.9   The Indian Reorganization Act

The Indian Reorganization Act (IRA), also known as the Wheeler-Howard Act or the Indian New Deal,[196] established a structure and process by which Indian nations could establish a

---

[192] Id. at 114 (quoting Sen. Trumbull, Cong. Globe, 1st Sess., 39th Cong. 528).

[193] Elk v. Wilkins, 112 U.S. 94, 100–07 (1884).

[194] Indian Citizenship Act of 1924, 43 Stat. 253, codified as amended at 8 U.S.C. § 1401.

[195] Montoya v. Bolack, 372 P.2d 387 (N.M. 1962).

[196] Act of June 18, 1934, c. 576, 48 Stat. 984, codified as amended at 25 U.S.C. §§ 5101 et seq.

constitutional representative governments if they so choose. The statute also provided for Indian nations to charter federal corporations for economic development purposes. The IRA formally ended allotment in practice and as policy. The IRA authorized the Interior Secretary to acquire land in trust for Indian nations and individual Indians. The IRA remains the foundational organic statute governing Indian affairs to this day.

In 1928, Congress received the Meriam Report, which provided the first detailed and comprehensive overview of the state of American Indian nations and people. The formal title of the report was "The Problem of Indian Administration." The Institute for Government Research, later known as the Brookings Foundation, completed the report with the funding of the Rockefeller Foundation at the request of Interior Secretary Herbert Work. The Report offered wide ranging empirical evidence that the allotment and assimilation policies of the federal government were massive failures. Indian people were the poorest and worst educated people in the United States.[197] The Report found that federal policy, most notably the allotment acts, had done little more than dispossess Indian people of their lands.[198] While the Report's factual findings were invaluable, its recommendations, which included assimilation-style educational programs,[199] were mostly ignored.

The IRA also formally ended the allotment era by prohibiting further allotment of Indian reservations.[200] Congress also authorized the Interior Secretary to take action to maintain what was left of the tribal land base.[201] Congress granted authority to the Secretary to re-acquire some of the lands lost during the allotment era and hold that land in trust for Indian tribes and individual Indians,[202] but had never adequately funded the program, forcing tribes to purchase land themselves. The IRA also put into place an Indian preference in employment mandate for the Bureau of Indian Affairs.[203] While the Bureau resisted this requirement for decades, by the end of the century the vast majority of Bureau employees were members of federally recognized Indian tribes.

The IRA, as its name suggested, allowed Indian tribes to reorganize their tribal governments into more modern structures,

---

[197] Institute for Government Research, The Problem of Indian Administration: Summary of Findings and Recommendations 1–6 (1928).

[198] Id. at 6–8.

[199] Id. at 21–23.

[200] 25 U.S.C. § 5101.

[201] 25 U.S.C. §§ 5102, 5103.

[202] 25 U.S.C. § 5108.

[203] 25 U.S.C. §§ 5116 et seq.

but only if the tribes agreed to adopt the provisions of the IRA.[204] For the first time, plenary Congressional legislation aimed at Indian affairs allowed for tribes to opt out of the legislation. Of the approximately 250 tribes for which the Interior Secretary held elections, two-thirds of the tribes voted to approve the IRA and reorganize.[205] However, some observers have argued that local Bureau officials threatened to cut off federal appropriations if tribal voters did not approve the IRA, leaving the notion of tribal consent in some communities questionable at best.[206]

Another controversy with tribal government reorganization revolves around the form that tribal governments take. Many tribal governments that had operated under a traditional government structure more suited to a tribe's culture adopted governing documents envisioned by Bureau officials to transform Indian tribes into American municipal governments.[207] As Assistant Interior Solicitor and co-author of the IRA, Felix Cohen had drafted a comprehensive legal memorandum for local Bureau officials advising tribes how to reorganize, which included an outline of powers that Cohen suggested could be included in a tribal constitution.[208] It appears that many local federal officials misread the memorandum and forced tribes to adopt a "model" constitution based on the outline.[209] These constitutions, many of which are still in use, often provided for a limited separation of powers; no tribal courts; and a list of enumerated tribal council powers.[210] Additionally, these constitutions usually required approval by the Secretary of Interior or his designee (the local Bureau official) of any amendments to the tribe's constitution and provisions that required the Secretary to approve every single resolution or ordinance enacted by a tribal council before it was valid.[211] In some instances, the Bureau forced tribes to adopt artificial membership

---

[204] 25 U.S.C. § 5123.

[205] See generally Theodore H. Haas, Ten Years of Tribal Government Under I.R.A. 13–34 (1947).

[206] But see Felix S. Cohen, The Erosion of Indian Rights, 1950–1953: A Case Study in Bureaucracy, 62 Yale L.J. 348, 348–49 (1953).

[207] Vine Deloria, Jr. & Clifford Lytle, The Nations Within: The Past and Future of American Indian Sovereignty 70 (1984).

[208] Felix S. Cohen, On the Drafting of Tribal Constitutions (David E. Wilkins, ed. 2006).

[209] See id. at xxviii.

[210] See generally Matthew L.M. Fletcher, American Indian Tribal Law 143–79 (2011).

[211] Vine Deloria, Jr. & Clifford Lytle, The Nations Within: The Past and Future of American Indian Sovereignty 142–43 (1984).

criteria as a means to limit tribal membership, and therefore tribal appropriations.[212]

Despite these concerns, the IRA was an enormous success for most Indian tribes. It was the first time that Congress had taken action to formally recognize *and support* the authority of tribal communities to make their own laws and be governed by them. The IRA remains the foundational federal legislation in Indian affairs.

§ 3.10 Termination

Despite the recent enactment and success of the IRA, by the late-1940s members of Congress engaged in anti-Communist Cold War rhetoric pushed for the repeal of the Act and the termination of the federal-tribal relationship.[213] In 1953, Congress passed House Concurrent Resolution 108, calling for the eventual termination of services and programs to tribal governments.[214] Congress then began the process of choosing individual Indian tribes and terminating them. Congress targeted tribes mostly in California, Oregon, Utah, Oklahoma, and Wisconsin for termination, which consisted of cutting off federal appropriations, disbanding tribal government, and privatizing tribal businesses. Termination was utterly devastating to tribal communities. President Kennedy informally put the practice on hold and by 1973 Congress had formally ended the termination era by restoring the Menominee Tribe to full status as a federally recognized tribe.[215] Not all terminated tribes have been restored, however.

During the Termination era, Congress enacted several statutes that served the process of termination. In 1953, Congress enacted a statute commonly known as Public Law 280 that extended state criminal and civil adjudicatory jurisdiction into Indian Country in several states, most notably in California, without tribal consent. Other states had the option of accepting jurisdiction over Indian Country. Public Law 280 remains valid law, although Congress added a tribal consent provision in 1968 to any future requests by states to acquire jurisdiction. **See § 7.4.**

In 1968, Congress passed the Indian Civil Rights Act, also known as the Indian Bill of Rights, which required tribal

---

[212] E.g., Snowden v. Saginaw Chippewa Indian Tribe of Mich., 32 Indian L. Rep. 6047, 6048–49 (Saginaw Chippewa Indian Tribe Appellate Court 2005) (linking modern tribal membership disputes to federal government meddling in the tribal constitutional ratification process in the 1930s).

[213] Kenneth R. Philp, Termination Revisited: American Indians on the Trail of Self-Determination, 1933–1953, at 68–69 (1999).

[214] H. Con. Res. 108, 67 Stat. B122 (Aug. 1, 1953).

[215] Charles F. Wilkinson, Blood Struggle 57–86 (2005).

governments to comply with many federal constitutional rights. **See § 6.4.** Democratic Senator Sam Ervin, an ardent foe of civil rights legislation aimed at desegregating the South and providing equal protection and due process to African-Americans, sponsored the bill.[216] He held hearings for several years as chair of the powerful Subcommittee on Constitutional Rights aimed at documenting civil rights violations by tribal governments. It is now apparent that Sen. Ervin's motivation in sponsoring the bill was to continue the assimilation of Indian communities and to undermine the civil rights program of his own party at the same time.[217]

During this period, the Supreme Court's few decisions in Indian law cases tended to support and affirm the authority of tribal governments and tribal courts. In 1959, the Court decided *Williams v. Lee*,[218] holding that Arizona state courts do not have jurisdiction over civil suits brought against reservation Indians for incidents arising in Indian Country. **See § 6.7.** This seemingly innocuous decision was later heralded by Charles Wilkinson as the beginning of the modern era of federal Indian law.[219]

§ 3.11   *Menominee Tribe v. United States*

Another under-heralded case, *Menominee Tribe v. United States*,[220] is a watershed in federal Indian law. The decision helped to put an end to the termination era, limited the reach of Public Law 280, and applied the clear statement rule to hold that an Act of Congress does not abrogate tribal authority or Indian rights absent a clear expression of intent by Congress to do so.

In *Menominee Tribe*, the Supreme Court held that Congress had not abrogated the treaty rights of the Tribe in the Menominee Termination Act of 1954.[221] The Court abrogated a contrary result reached by the Wisconsin Supreme Court, which had affirmed the conviction of tribal members for violation of state hunting and fishing laws and regulations.[222] After the Wisconsin Supreme Court issued its opinion and the United States Supreme Court denied certiorari, the Menominee Nation brought suit against the United States seeking compensation for the taking of its members' treaty rights.[223] Though a deeply-split panel of the United States Court of

---

[216] Angela R. Riley, Indians and Guns, 100 Geo. L.J. 1675, 1704–06 (2012).

[217] Id.

[218] 358 U.S. 217 (1959).

[219] Charles F. Wilkinson, American Indians, Time, and the Law 1 (1987).

[220] 391 U.S. 404 (1968).

[221] Id. at 412–13.

[222] State v. Sanapaw, 124 N.W.2d 41 (Wis. 1963), cert. denied, 377 U.S. 991 (1964).

[223] Menominee Tribe v. United States, 388 F.2d 998, 1000 (Ct. Cl. 1967).

Claims held the United States was not liable for Wisconsin's interference with Menominee treaty rights,[224] the government altered its position before the Supreme Court. The posture of the case before the Supreme Court was unusual in that the Tribe and the United States both agreed that the Tribe's treaty rights remained extant, with the State of Wisconsin as *amicus curiae* the only entity arguing for abrogation.

In 1854, the Tribe and the federal government agreed to the Treaty of Wolf River in which the Tribe ceded much of its property interests to the government in exchange for a reservation of Indian lands in an area stocked with game and fish for the express purpose of allowing the Indians to maintain their means of sustenance and ways of life—"for a home, to be held as Indian lands are held."[225] However, in 1954, Congress enacted a termination act intending to disband the tribal government.[226] The Act wiped out the tribe's business activities.[227] The termination act also held that the laws of Wisconsin would apply to the tribal corporation and the tribal members.[228] Worse, the former reservation constituted the entirety of Menominee County, and the State of Wisconsin refused to support the new county, leaving all state taxes to be paid by the new tribal corporation, Menominee Enterprises, Inc.[229] The corporation, controlled largely by non-Menominee business people, mismanaged the community horribly.[230] Moreover, the State began to enforce its hunting and fishing laws against tribal members, culminating in the Wisconsin case holding that the termination act had abrogated the treaty.[231]

The Court, per Justice Douglas, held that since the termination act never mentioned treaty rights, Congress could not have intended to abrogate those rights.[232] The Court reasoned that since ambiguities in treaties and statutes must be interpreted for the benefit of Indian tribes, the termination act's silence was dispositive: "We decline to construe the Termination Act as a backhanded way a abrogating the hunting and fishing rights of

---

[224] Id. at 1009–10.

[225] Treaty of Wolf River, art. 2, 10 Stat. 1064 (1854).

[226] Act of June 17, 1954, c. 303, § 1, 68 Stat. 250.

[227] Nancy Oestreich Lurie, Menominee Termination: From Reservation to Colony, 31:3 Hum. Org. 257, 262 (1972).

[228] Id.

[229] Id. at 263.

[230] See generally id. at 263–67.

[231] State v. Sanapaw, 124 N.W.2d 41 (Wis. 1963), cert. denied, 377 U.S. 991 (1964).

[232] Menominee Tribe of Indians v. United States, 391 U.S. 404, 410 (1968).

these Indians."[233] Moreover, the Court noted that the year before Congress passed the termination act, Congress had enacted Public Law 280, which included a provision that protected certain treaty rights even after a state acquired jurisdiction over Indian lands.[234] Since Congress knew how to abrogate treaty rights, but chose not to do so in the termination act, the treaty rights remained viable.[235]

§ 3.12 Indian Self-Determination

Federal Indian policy underwent enormous change beginning in the 1960s and concentrated in the 1970s. The 1960s saw the quiet end of the Termination Era and the 1970s saw the rise of the Self-Determination Era. "Self-determination" constitutes the strongest expression of Congressional and Executive branch support for the development of tribal governments, reservation economies, and Indian people, as well as recognition of the importance of tribal sovereignty. While express federal policy continues to favor tribal self-determination, the 1990s and the first decade of 21st century offered a glimpse of what may be the next era of federal Indian policy as Congress continued to pare down federal spending in Indian affairs.

Winding Down the Termination Era

The termination era, **see § 3.10**, is over, but has no obvious end point. Congress did not immediately repeal House Concurrent Resolution 108, but by the mid-1960s, it was no longer the policy of Congress to seek to end the trust relationship.

Congress never addressed many of the consequences of the termination era, including the massive loss of tribal lands and other assets and the destruction of developing tribal governments. Congress did act in a piecemeal manner in the early 1970s to restore pockets of Indian lands that had been taken during the Termination Era.[236] After tribes that had been terminated petitioned for restoration as federally recognized tribes, Congress began to enact "restoration acts," in which. The first restoration act, the Menominee Restoration Act in 1973,[237] served as a powerful rejection of the termination policy.[238] These restoration acts also came in case-by-case fashion, with Congress apparently requiring

---

[233] Id. at 412.

[234] Id. at 410–11.

[235] Id.

[236] Michael C. Walch, Terminating the Indian Termination Policy, 35 Stan. L. Rev. 1181, 1192–94 (1983).

[237] Pub. L. 93–197, Dec. 22, 1973, 87 Stat. 770.

[238] See generally Charles F. Wilkinson, Blood Struggle: The Rise of Modern Indian Nations 177–205 (2005).

the petitioning terminated tribe to prove continuing tribal status before agreeing to restore the tribe through the administrative acknowledgment process.[239] Some tribes have never been restored, while some tribes' restorations are ongoing in the first decade of the 21st century.

Indian Self-Determination

President Johnson's 1968 Message to Congress on Goals and Programs for the American, titled "The Forgotten American," proposed a new goal of ending the debate about termination and stressed self-determination.[240] Among other things, that message called for enactment of the Indian Civil Rights Act to provide for tribal consent before extension of state jurisdiction under Public Law 280, as Congress did later that year.[241]

Also, in conjunction with that message, President Johnson established the National Council on Indian Opportunity ("NCIO"), chaired by the Vice President and consisting of seven cabinet-level officials and six Indian leaders (later funded by Congress and expanded by Nixon to include the Attorney General and two more tribal leaders).[242] The NCIO made a number of policy proposals that provided the basis for President Nixon's Special Message to Congress.[243]

In 1970, President Nixon's message to Congress furthered the fundamental shift in federal Indian policy to self-determination.[244] President Nixon expressly repudiated the termination policy.[245] The Nixon Message renounced the termination policy, established that adherence to the federal trust responsibility would guide federal Indian policy, and proposed a structure to dramatically reduce federal control over tribes—by recognizing greatly increased tribal authority to manage affairs on their reservations as a replacement for federal bureaucratic control.[246]

---

[239] Michael C. Walch, Terminating the Indian Termination Policy, 35 Stan. L. Rev. 1181, 1209 n. 171 (1983).

[240] 4 Week Comp. Pres. Docs. 438 (1968).

[241] Cohen's Handbook of Federal Law § 1.07, at 97 (2012 ed.).

[242] Id. at 96.

[243] Thomas A. Britten, The National Council on Indian Opportunity: Quiet Champion of Self-Determination 264 (2014).

[244] Message from the President of the United States Transmitting Recommendations for Indian Policy, H.R. Doc. No. 363, 91st Cong., 2d. Sess. (1970); 116 Cong. Rec. 23258.

[245] Wenona T. Singel, The First Federalists, 62 Drake L. Rev. 775, 812–813 (2014).

[246] Samuel R. Cook, Ronald Reagan's Indian Policy in Retrospect: Economic Crisis and Political Irony, 24:1 Policy Studies J. 11, 12–13 (1996).

The Nixon Administration and later Administrations proposed and oversaw the adoption of numerous Self-Determination Acts and Self-Governance Acts in which Congress finally fulfilled the original promise of the Indian Reorganization Act to allow Indian tribes to take over federal Indian affairs programs.[247]

Congress also took steps to encourage tribal economic development in the enactment of statutes such as the Indian Finance Act of 1974;[248] the Indian Tribal Government Tax Status Act of 1982;[249] and the Indian Gaming Regulatory Act of 1988.[250] Congress enacted legislation supporting tribal law enforcement, the development of tribal courts, and perhaps the most controversial Indian affairs statute in the era, the Indian Child Welfare Act,[251] requiring the transfer of state-court cases involving Indian child custody to tribal courts. Federal Indian affairs legislation did not, however, include a major reworking or change in the IRA that would have comprehensively regulated tribal government jurisdiction and authority over nonmembers.

Some commentators argue that the self-determination era has morphed into an era of "nation-building," where Indian nations, for the first time, have begun to take the lead in governing Indian lands.[252]

Indian Civil Rights

In 1968, after years of intermittent hearings, Congress enacted the Indian Civil Rights Act, purporting to extend the protections of the Bill of Rights to Indian people.[253] **See § 6.4.** In 1896, the Supreme Court in *Talton v. Mayes* had held that the Constitution

---

[247] Philip S. Deloria, The Era of Indian Self-Determination: An Overview, in Indian Self-Rule: First-Hand Accounts of Indian-White Relations from Roosevelt to Reagan 191 (Kenneth R. Philp ed., 1986); Michael Gross, Indian Self-Determination and Tribal Sovereignty: An Analysis of Recent Federal Policy, 56 Tex. L. Rev. 1195 (1978).

[248] Pub. L. 93–262, § 2, Apr. 12, 1974, 88 Stat. 77, codified at 25 U.S.C. §§ 1451 et seq.

[249] Pub. L. 97–473, Title II, § 202(a), Jan. 14, 1983, 96 Stat. 2608, codified as amended at 26 U.S.C. § 7871.

[250] Pub. L. 100–497, 102 Stat. 2467, codified at 25 U.S.C. §§ 2701 et seq.

[251] Pub. L. 95–608, § 2, Nov. 8, 1978, 92 Stat. 3069, codified at 25 U.S.C. §§ 1901 et seq.

[252] See generally David H. Getches, Charles F. Wilkinson, Robert A. Williams, Jr., Matthew L.M. Fletcher, and Kristen A. Carpenter, Cases and Materials on Federal Indian Law 273–76 (7th ed. 2017); Harvard Project on American Indian Economic Development, The State of Native Nations: Conditions under U.S. Policies of Self-Determination (2008); Rebuilding Native Nations: Strategies for Governance and Development (Miriam Jorgensen, ed. 2007).

[253] Pub. L. 90–284, Title II, § 201, Apr. 11, 1968, 82 Stat. 77, codified as amended at 25 U.S.C. §§ 1301 et seq.

did not apply to Indian tribes.[254] **See § 6.3**. Senator Sam Ervin of North Carolina, an ardent segregationist and opponent of President Johnson's "Great Society" legislative package, pushed for Indian civil rights legislation for years.[255] The Act forwarded a slate of American constitutional rights protections that would thereafter apply to tribal governments and people under their jurisdiction. Tribal and federal opposition to the bill forced a few modifications to the general bill of constitutional rights, such as the elimination of an establishment clause, the right to counsel for indigent defendants, and the right to a grand jury indictment.

Tribal Economic Development & Indian Gaming

Beginning with a provision in the Indian Reorganization Act that authorized Indian tribes to create special federal corporations for the purposes of engaging in business activities,[256] the United States has long encouraged Indian nations to exploit business opportunities as a means to generate revenue to pay for government services. Because most Indian nations are located in areas where there is no ready tax base (and because the Supreme Court has steadily limited tribal taxation authority over nonmembers),[257] most tribal governments have no other option but to develop their business opportunities, such as they are.[258]

Federal support for Indian nations during the early decades of the self-determination era focused less on federal appropriations and more on improving tribal economic opportunities. In 1974, Congress passed the Indian Finance Act and, in 1985, the Indian Tribal Government Tax Status Act, to grease the wheels for tribal economic development, but these measures were underfunded and far short of what was required to allow most tribes to generate significant government revenues. Enterprising—and desperate—Indian tribes, as early as the 1950s and expanding into the 1970s, began to license or even open their own gaming enterprises, usually

---

[254] 163 U.S. 376 (1896).

[255] For a biography of Sen. Ervin, see Karl E. Campbell, Senator Sam Ervin, Last of the Founding Fathers (2007).

[256] 25 U.S.C. § 5124.

[257] Michigan v. Bay Mills Indian Community, 134 S.Ct. 2024, 20445 (2014) (quoting Matthew L.M. Fletcher, In Pursuit of Tribal Economic Development as a Substitute for Reservation Tax Revenue, 80 N. D. L. Rev. 759, 774 (2004), and citing Robert A. Williams, Jr., Small Steps on the Long Road to Self-Sufficiency for Indian Nations: The Indian Tribal Governmental Tax Status Act of 1982, 22 Harv. J. Legis. 335, 385 (1985)).

[258] See generally Robert J. Miller, Reservation "Capitalism": Economic Development in Indian Country (2012).

high stakes bingo facilities, with an eye to expanding to Vegas-style casino gaming.[259]

The advent of Indian gaming has changed tribal-federal-state relations far beyond any policy of Congress or the Executive branch. The federal government under the Carter and Reagan administrations saw that gaming could generate significant government revenues, moving tribes toward self-sufficiency. Like President Nixon before him, President Reagan sought to encourage Indian tribes to engage in creative means of generating governmental revenue. In his 1983 federal Indian policy statement, he said, "It is important to the concept of self-government that tribes reduce their dependence on Federal funds by providing a greater percentage of the cost of their self-government."[260] This was part and parcel of President Reagan's goal of reducing the size of government by eliminating the need for federal appropriations.

Shortly after President Reagan issued his policy statement, the Interior Secretary issued a statement opposing any federal legislation that would expose Indian gaming operations to state regulation. In particular, the statement noted:

> A number of Indian tribes have begun to engage in bingo and similar gambling operations on their reservations for the very purpose enunciated in the President's Message. Given the often limited resources which tribes have for revenue-producing activities, it is believed that this kind of revenue-producing possibility should be protected and enhanced.[261]

The Department of Interior, the Indian Health Service, and the Small Business Administration had quietly been offering construction funds, sanitation services, and loan guarantees to Indian tribes for the purpose of constructing high stakes bingo halls to tribes in New York, Florida, and California since at least the late 1970s. Some Indian tribes may have engaged in high stakes bingo or other forms of gaming since the late 1960s. The 1983 statements from President Reagan and the Department of Interior allowed the subtle encouragement of Indian gaming to flower into overt support.

By the time the challenges from states and others to Indian gaming reached the Supreme Court in 1987's *California v. Cabazon Band of Mission Indians*,[262] the federal government had provided so much support to Indian bingo operations that the Court was hard-

---

[259] G. William Rice, Tribal Governmental Gaming Law 1–71 (2006).

[260] President Ronald Reagan, Statement on Indian Policy (Jan. 24, 1983).

[261] United States Department of Interior Statement (March 2, 1983).

[262] 480 U.S. 202 (1987).

pressed to find a compelling reason to deny tribes access to gaming. In 1988, Congress provided a federal legislative underpinning for Indian gaming, allowing high stakes bingo games without state regulation, but required Indian tribes to enter into a formal compacting arrangement with the states before they could begin Vegas-style gaming, such as slot machines and poker. **See Chapter 9**.

Indian Culture and Education

Federal Indian policy since 1960 has seen dramatic reversal of long-standing policies seeking either directly or indirectly to assimilate Indian people into the larger American society. Beginning with the rejection of the Termination Era in the 1960s, Congress began to expand federal programs in Indian education, Indian child welfare, Indian health care, and tribal cultural property. Some of these programs have been successful, while the success of others is blocked by lack of funding or political machinations.

In education, federal legislation intending to improve Indian educational opportunity has not been very successful, in large part due to failure of Congress to appropriate sufficient funding. While President Bill Clinton acknowledged a federal duty in Indian education and stated the Executive branch's policy of seeking to cooperate with Indian tribes to improve Indian educational achievement,[263] progress has been slow.[264] In higher education, Congress's support of tribal community colleges through the Tribally Controlled College or University Assistance Act[265] has been excellent, although federal appropriations per student have dropped over 50 percent.

In 1978, Congress enacted the Indian Child Welfare Act.[266] **See § 8.8**. This statute mandates that any state court case involving an adoption or other action that could lead to the termination of parental rights of an Indian child must be transferred to tribal court unless narrow exceptions are met. State courts must provide notice to Indian tribes with an interest in the child and offer them a chance to intervene, and due process protections for Indian families.

---

[263] Exec. Order No. 13096, American Indian and Alaska Native Education, 34 Weekly Comp. Pres. Doc. 1580 (Aug. 10, 1998).

[264] See generally Raymond Cross, American Indian Education: The Terror of History and the Nation's Debt to the Indian Peoples, 21 U. Ark. Little Rock L. Rev. 941 (1999).

[265] Pub. L. 95–471, Oct. 17, 1978, 92 Stat. 1325, codified as amended at 25 U.S.C. §§ 1801 et seq.

[266] Pub. L. 95–608, Nov. 8, 1978, 92 Stat. 3069, codified at 25 U.S.C. §§ 1901 et seq.

In 1976, Congress enacted the Indian Health Care Improvement Act,[267] designed to expand health care services to both urban and reservation Indians under the administration of the Indian Health Service (IHS). The work of the IHS has been exemplary, with mortality rates and infant mortality rates of Indian people declining in significant numbers, but Indian people still have the worst health of any demographic in the United States. According to the United States Civil Rights Commission, "persistent discrimination and neglect continue to deprive Native Americans of a health system sufficient to provide health care equivalent to that provided to the vast majority of Americans."[268]

Congress has taken several steps to prevent the continuing loss of tribal cultural property and languages, most notably with the American Indian Religious Freedom Act.[269] The Act states that it is the policy of the federal government not to interfere with Indian religious practices and sacred sites located on federal or tribal lands. President Clinton later issued an Executive Order requiring federal agencies to consult with Indian tribes before engaging in activities that might interfere with tribal religious practices.[270]

In 1990, Congress passed the Native American Graves Protection and Repatriation Act,[271] requiring federal agencies and museums to conduct an inventory of Indian remains and sacred objects in their possession. If an Indian tribe could prove that it was the origin of the remains or objects, then the agency or museum was obligated to repatriate them.[272] But like many Congressional initiatives in Indian affairs since 1960, this statute is limited in its application and subject to circumvention by scientists who have convinced federal courts to interpret the statute narrowly, as in the case of The Old One, or Kennewick Man,[273] and by state entities, as in the Jim Thorpe case.[274] Still, many tribes are successful at enforcing the statute.[275]

---

[267] Pub. L. 94–437, Sept. 30, 1976, 90 Stat. 1400, codified as amended at 25 U.S.C. §§ 1601 et seq.

[268] United States Commission on Civil Rights, Broken Promises: Evaluating the Native American Health Care System 6 (Sept. 2004).

[269] Pub. L. 95–341, Aug. 11, 1978, 92 Stat. 469, codified at 42 U.S.C. § 1996.

[270] Exec. Order No. 13007, 61 Fed. Reg. 26771 (May 24, 1996).

[271] Pub. L. 101–601, Nov. 16, 1990, 104 Stat. 3048, codified as amended at 25 U.S.C. §§ 3001 et seq.

[272] 25 U.S.C. § 3005.

[273] Bonnichsen v. United States, 367 F.3d 864 (9th Cir. 2004).

[274] Thorpe v. Borough of Jim Thorpe, 770 F.3d 255 (3rd Cir. 2014).

[275] E.g., Eric Hemenway, Finding Our Way Home, in Accomplishing NAGPRA: Perspectives on the Intent, Impact, and Future of the Native American Graves Protection and Repatriation Act 83 (Sangita Chari & Jaime M.N. LaVallee, eds. 2013).

§ 3.13   *Morton v. Mancari*

Morton v. Mancari is a landmark case that established the political status classification in relation to federal actions taken in accordance with the federal government's trust relationship with Indian nations. In short, so long as the federal government acts in accordance with its trust duties, the judiciary will not treat the action as a race-based action that may trigger strict scrutiny under the Fifth Amendment's equal protection component. Instead, the judiciary will uphold the action so long as it is rationally related to the trust relationship.

Morton v. Mancari arose when a group of non-Indian Bureau of Indian Affairs employees challenged a Bureau regulation that granted preference in employment promotion decisions to qualified American Indians.[276] To be eligible for the preference, a qualified American Indian "must be one-fourth or more degree Indian blood and be a member of a federally-recognized tribe."[277] The Court held that the preference was not a violation of the Fifth Amendment due process clause that prohibits invidious discrimination.[278] First, the Court noted that the preference was not "racial" in character, but instead "an employment criterion reasonably designed to further the cause of Indian self-government and to make the BIA more responsive to the needs of its constituent groups."[279] The Court analogized the criterion to "the constitutional requirement that a United States Senator, when elected, be 'an Inhabitant of that State for which he shall be chosen,' or that a member of a city council reside within the city governed by the council."[280] The Court focused on the fact that the criterion benefited certain Indians not because of their racial characteristics but because they were "members of quasi-sovereign tribal entities whose lives and activities are governed by the BIA in a unique fashion."[281] As such, the Court applied its rational basis test for determining the constitutionality of the practice.[282]

Footnote 24 of Justice Blackmun's opinion in *Morton v. Mancari* may become the most important footnote in 21st century Constitutional litigation involving federal and state statutes relating to Indian tribes and individual Indians. It was this footnote in which the Court first articulated a theory that federal statutory

---

[276]   Morton v. Mancari, 417 U.S. 535, 539 (1974).

[277]   Id. at 553 n. 24 (quoting 44 BIAM 335, 3.1).

[278]   Id. at 553–55.

[279]   Id. at 554.

[280]   Id. (quoting Const. Art. I, § 3, cl. 3).

[281]   Id.

[282]   Id.

or regulatory preferences favoring Indians should not be analyzed under the rubric of the strict scrutiny analysis applied to laws that apply specifically to racial minorities.[283] Instead, footnote 24 theorized that federal statutes relating to Indian tribes that are reasonably related to the federal government's trust relationship with Indian tribes and individual Indians are classifications based on the political status of these groups, not their racial characteristics: "The preference is not directed towards a 'racial' group consisting of 'Indians'; instead, it applies only to members of 'federally recognized' tribes. This operates to exclude many individuals who are racially to be classified as 'Indians.' In this sense, the preference is political rather than racial in nature."[284] Unfortunately, footnote 24 is a superficially theorized aspect of the *Mancari* decision and, arguably, would be mere dictum if the Court had not relied upon this formulation of the political relationship between the federal government and Indian tribes and individual Indians in later cases.[285]

Later Supreme Court decisions have relied upon *Mancari* for the proposition that the Fifth and Fourteenth Amendments do not require courts to apply strict scrutiny to federal and state statutes that apply only to American Indians. These statutes can be divided into statutes that benefit Indian tribes and those that do not. For example, the first case that reached the Court in which a claimant made the strict scrutiny argument was *Fisher v. District Court*.[286] That case involved a child custody dispute between Indian parents that had been originally adjudicated in tribal court.[287] The foster parents initiated adoption proceedings in Montana state court, to which the mother objected.[288] The Court held that the tribal court had exclusive jurisdiction and the state court could not adjudicate the child's adoption.[289] The foster parents had argued that the denial of access to state courts amounted to discriminatory treatment, but the Court, citing *Mancari* and without significant

---

[283] Id. at 553 n. 24.

[284] Id.

[285] E.g., Washington v. Washington State Commercial Passenger Fishing Vessel Ass'n, 443 U.S. 658, 673 n. 20 (1979); Washington v. Confederated Bands and Tribes of the Yakima Indian Nation, 439 U.S. 463, 500–501 (1979); Moe v. Confederated Salish & Kootenai Tribes, 425 U.S. 463, 479–80 (1976); United States v. Antelope, 430 U.S. 641, 645–46 (1977); Fisher v. District Court, 424 U.S. 382, 391 (1976) (per curiam). Cf. Delaware Tribal Business Committee v. Weeks, 430 U.S. 73, 84–85 (1977) (applying *Mancari* for the proposition that Acts of Congress related to Indian affairs would be held to the rational basis test).

[286] 424 U.S. 382 (1976) (per curiam).

[287] Id. at 383.

[288] Id. at 383–84.

[289] Id. at 390.

discussion, rejected the claim.[290] A year later, in *United States v. Antelope*,[291] the Court held that the application of a federal enclave murder statute to tribal members did not constitute race discrimination.[292] Two Coeur d'Alene Indians had been convicted of felony murder under federal law for the murder of an Indian woman in Indian Country, a first degree murder.[293] Had they been classified as non-Indians, they would have been prosecuted under Idaho law, which had no felony murder statute.[294] In order to establish first degree murder in Idaho, the prosecutors would have had to prove premeditation and deliberation, elements of the crime that federal prosecutors did not have to prove.[295] The Court, per Chief Justice Burger, engaged in slightly more analysis than it did in the *Fisher* case, but not much more. The Court noted that the Indian Commerce Clause explicitly allows Congress to enact legislation relating to Indians and that the history of federal-tribal relations supported that position.[296] Subsequently, three times since *Antelope*, the Court has rejected claims that Indian law had benefited Indians and Indian tribes; twice in the tax arena[297] and once in the treaty fishing rights arena.[298] None of these cases analyzed the question further, holding that *Mancari* was dispositive.

Tribal membership in a federally recognized tribe remains the foundation of the *Mancari* doctrine. The doctrine also applies to intertribal relations as well; for example, the practice of contracting preferences by one tribe favoring itself over another tribe, or so-called tribal preference.[299]

§ 3.14   Federal Programs and Self-Determination

The rise of tribal self-determination did not end federal programs benefitting American Indians, but reductions in federal resources partially resulting from the greater emphasis on tribes have restricted expensive federal programming. Two Supreme

---

[290] Id. at 390–91 (citing Mancari, 417 U.S. at 551–55).

[291] 430 U.S. 641 (1977).

[292] Id. at 645–46.

[293] Id. at 642–43.

[294] Id. at 644.

[295] Id.

[296] Id. at 645.

[297] Washington v. Confederated Bands and Tribes of the Yakima Indian Nation, 439 U.S. 463, 500–501 (1979); Moe v. Confederated Salish & Kootenai Tribes, 425 U.S. 463, 479–80 (1976).

[298] Washington v. Washington State Commercial Passenger Fishing Vessel Ass'n, 443 U.S. 658, 673 n. 20 (1979).

[299] EEOC v. Peabody Western Coal, 773 F.3d 977, 988 (9th Cir. 2014).

Court decisions provided guidelines for federal authority to cut American Indian programs.

Morton v. Ruiz

In 1974, the Supreme Court decided *Morton v. Ruiz*,[300] which held that the Bureau of Indian Affairs acted arbitrarily and capriciously in denying general assistance benefits to tribal members living off-reservation.[301] Under the Snyder Act,[302] which provides broad authorization for federal agencies to provide governmental services to Indians, Congress appropriated funds for services designated for Indians "throughout the United States. . . ."[303] The Bureau of Indian Affairs denied general assistance to tribal members who lived near, but not on, the Tohono O'odham Nation's reservation.[304] The government argued that only Alaska and Oklahoma Indians were eligible for federal services if they lived off-reservation.[305] But Indian affairs officials had routinely made representations to Congress that federal appropriations would benefit Indians "near" a reservation as well.[306] Finally, the Court noted that the Bureau of Indian Affairs did not publish its policy barring federal benefits to off-reservation Indians, making its reliance upon the policy fundamentally unfair.[307] In short, unless the government made clear changes to its policy, the Court would treat appropriations as benefitting Indians "on or near" the reservation.[308]

Lincoln v. Vigil

The Supreme Court's decision in *Lincoln v. Vigil*,[309] made 19 years later, revealed far greater deference to the government's choices as to government services eligibility. There, the Indian Health Service had chosen to cancel a program designed to assist disabled Indian children in the southwest in favor of a national program.[310] The program had been funded by the Service through lump-sum Congressional appropriations, which the Court held committed the continuation of the program to agency discretion.[311]

---

[300] 415 U.S. 199 (1974).

[301] Id. at 231.

[302] 25 U.S.C. § 13.

[303] Morton v. Ruiz, 415 U.S. 199, 208 (1974).

[304] Id. at 204–05.

[305] Id. at 212–13.

[306] Id. at 214–29.

[307] Id. at 234–35.

[308] Id. at 238.

[309] 508 U.S. 182 (1993).

[310] Id. at 184.

[311] Id. at 192–94.

The Court specifically rejected the claim that the general federal trust relationship barred the Service from cutting the program.[312]

§ 3.15   638 and Self-Governance Contracting: *The Contract Support Costs Cases*

Under the Indian Self-Determination and Education Assistance Act of 1975 and its amendments (ISDEAA), the Bureau of Indian Affairs and Indian tribes have shared the administration of Indian affairs programs and services in a unique contracting process.[313] The Interior Department must contract with Indian tribes, at their request, to "plan, conduct, and administer" federal Indian affairs programs otherwise administered by the Interior, Health and Human Services, or Housing and Urban Development Departments.[314]

The federal agency must also cover "contract support costs."[315] ISDEAA defines contract support costs to include costs that tribal contractor must pay as an incident to the operation of the federal contract that the federal agency would not have incurred.[316]

In *Cherokee Nation v. Leavitt*,[317] Indian tribes had sued the federal government for the failure to pay contract support costs.[318] The government's claim was that Congress never appropriated funds expressly designed to cover contract support costs, relieving the agencies from paying those costs to the tribal contractors.[319] The Court was not persuaded to defer to the agency's choices to spend federal money on its own overhead, such as the Indian Health Service's Washington, D.C. office.[320] The Court placed the onus on the federal agency to seek relief or assistance from Congress, not by denying the tribal contractors funds normally available to other federal contractors.[321]

---

[312] Id. at 194–95.

[313] Pub. L. 93–638, Jan. 4, 1975, 88 Stat. 2203, codified as amended at 25 U.S.C. § 5301. See also Indian Self-Determination and Education Assistance Act Amendments of 1988, Pub. L. 100–472, Title I, § 209, Oct. 5, 1988, 102 Stat. 2285 (establishing tribal self-governance demonstration project); Indian Self-Determination Act Amendments of 1994, Pub. L. 103–413, October 25, 1994, 108 Stat. 4250 (making tribal self-governance project permanent), codified at 25 U.S.C. § 5631.

[314] 25 U.S.C. § 5321(a)(1) (Interior and Health and Human Services); cf. 25 U.S.C. § 4145a (housing).

[315] 25 U.S.C. § 5325(a)(2).

[316] Cherokee Nation of Oklahoma v. Leavitt, 543 U.S. 631, 635 (2005).

[317] 543 U.S. 631 (2005).

[318] Id. at 635.

[319] Id.

[320] Id. at 641–42.

[321] Id. at 642–43.

The Supreme Court held in a sequel, *Salazar v. Ramah Navajo Chapter*,[322] that the government remains liable for unpaid contract support costs despite the continuing failure of Congress to appropriate adequate funds to pay the costs to tribes.[323] The Court again reminded the government that Congress is the appropriate place for the agencies to seek relief, not funds mandated for tribal use.[324]

---

[322] 567 U.S. 182 (2012).

[323] Id. at 192–93.

[324] Id. at 200.

Chapter 4

INDIAN PROPERTY INTERESTS

Analysis

There are many forms of property that permeate American Indian affairs that are unique to Indian nations and people. Possibly because of a combination of differing cultural understandings of property interests and non-Indian dominance of property structures post-contact coupled with cultural imperialism and ethnocentrism, Indian property interests have often not been on firm footing under American law. This chapter begins with the doctrine of Indian title, cemented into American law by in the early years of the United States, but complex American Indian property regimes long predate the imposition of American property concepts.

§ 4.1   Indian Title

Indian title, also known as original Indian title, aboriginal title, or other derivative names, under federal Indian law is a right of Indian nations to possess and occupy lands. Indian title may also be known as unrecognized title, in contrast to vested or recognized title. **See § 4.2.** Indian title may only be alienated by an Indian nation to the federal government, either through purchase or conquest. Indian title still meant that Indian nations and individual Indians retained significant possessory rights over the land. Indian people could farm, extract resources, and improve the land as any landowner could. The Supreme Court's decision in *Johnson v. McIntosh*, **see § 2.1**, originally noted the contours of Indian title.

There are few—and perhaps no—parcels of land upon which Indian title has not been extinguished,[1] although there may be specific aboriginal rights that remain extant. For example, some Indian nations in the southwest remain on unceded lands, but those lands are preserved by treaty or statute. The last Indian title decisions reached by the Supreme Court came in the mid-20th century. However, some tribal and Indian claimants continue to bring claims that a specific aspect of Indian title, such as a hunting or fishing right, remains.[2]

From the vantage point of Indian nations and Indian people, Indian title suffered from enormous defects. The United States could extinguish Indian title at will, and the federal government often treated Indian people living on unceded territory as squatters. On occasion, the United States would not even seek tribal consent to extinguishment of Indian title, and simply turned Indian lands and resources over to third parties.[3]

However, tribal efforts to prevent the alienation of their lands protected by Indian title usually failed, though Congress intermittently would enact jurisdictional statutes to allow specific tribes to bring suit to seek compensation for the loss of Indian title; ultimately, Congress enacted a total of 134 such statutes before 1946.[4] **See § 4.6**. That year, Congress enacted the Indian Claims Commission Act to allow Indian nations to sue for loss of Indian title.[5] **See § 4.6**.

Tee-Hit-Ton Indians v. United States

In *Tee-Hit-Ton Indians v. United States*,[6] the Supreme Court held that the Fifth Amendment did not require the federal government to compensate Alaska Natives for the taking of timber on Indian lands held under the doctrine of Indian title.[7]

To resolve the question whether Congress had vested property rights in Alaska Natives, the Supreme Court granted certiorari in

---

[1]   Walter R. Echo-Hawk, In the Courts of the Conqueror: The 10 Worst Indian Law Cases Ever Decided 365 (2010).

[2]   E.g., Native Village of Eyak v. Blank, 688 F.3d 619 (9th Cir. 2012) (holding that a tribe may assert rights under original title); Agua Caliente Band of Cahuilla Indians v. Coachella Valley Water District, No. EDCV 13–883–JGB, 2015 WL 1600065 (C.D. Cal., Mar. 20, 2015) (rejecting aboriginal water rights claim).

[3]   David E. Wilkins, Hollow Justice: A History of Indigenous Claims in the United States 1–7 (2013).

[4]   Id. at 10–12.

[5]   Indian Claims Commission Act of 1946, 60 Stat. 1049, codified at 25 U.S.C. §§ 70 et seq.

[6]   348 U.S. 272 (1955) (citations omitted).

[7]   Id. at 290–91.

the *Tee-Hit-Ton* matter.[8] The Court would clarify what constitutes recognition or vesting of Indian property rights, and then whether takings of Indian title are compensable, holding that neither the Alaska Organic Act of 1884,[9] nor the act establishing Alaska civil government,[10] vested a compensate property right in Alaska Natives.[11] For recognition or vesting, the Court noted that "there must be the definite intention by congressional action or authority to accord legal rights, not merely permissive occupation."[12]

Once the Court concluded that Congress had not vested property rights in Alaska Natives, the Court then addressed whether takings of Indian title are compensable. The Court's earliest precedent was *Johnson v. McIntosh*,[13] which had held that only the national sovereign could extinguish Indian title, "either by purchase or conquest."[14] *Johnson*, at least arguably, assumes that Indian title is compensable by reference to "purchase." The Court's later precedents did little to deviate from that interpretation. The Court cited to some cases had held that Indian nations could not prevent the United States from extinguishing Indian title,[15] ignoring others that had held otherwise,[16] but none had answered the question of compensation. One precedent established that establishment of "Indian title based on aboriginal possession" raises "political, not justiciable issues."[17] These precedents collectively could have led the Court in *Tee-Hit-Ton* to hold that Congress can take Indian title, even without tribal consent, but that the taking is compensable; what the compensation will be could have been held to be a non-justiciable political question.

Instead, the Court rejected the compensation claim altogether. Rather than offer legal analysis, the Court offered a superficial history lesson riddled with deeply unfortunate historical

---

[8]　　Tee-Hit-Ton Indians v. United States, 348 U.S. 272, 276 (1955).

[9]　　Act of May 17, 1884, 23 Stat. 24.

[10]　　Act of June 6, 1900, 31 Stat. 321.

[11]　　Tee-Hit-Ton Indians v. United States, 348 U.S. 272, 278–79 (1955).

[12]　　Id.

[13]　　21 U.S. 543 (1823).

[14]　　Id. at 587.

[15]　　E.g., Buttz v. Northern Pacific Railroad Co., 119 U.S. 55 (1886) (rejecting claims to possession of Dakota lands); Beecher v. Wetherby, 95 U.S. 517 (1877) (rejecting claims to possession of Menominee timber); Martin v. Waddell's Lessee, 41 U.S. 367 (1842) (rejecting claims to possession of lands in New Jersey); Clark v. Smith, 38 U.S. 195 (1839) (rejecting claims to possession of Chickasaw lands).

[16]　　E.g., United States ex rel. Hualapai Indians of Arizona v. Santa Fe Pacific Railroad, 314 U.S. 339 (1941).

[17]　　United States ex rel. Hualapai Indians of Arizona v. Santa Fe Pacific Railroad, 314 U.S. 339, 347 (1941).

assumptions that simply were not true now or at the time of the decision:

> Every American schoolboy knows that the savage tribes of this continent were deprived of their ancestral ranges by force and that, even when the Indians ceded millions of acres by treaty in return for blankets, food and trinkets, it was not a sale but the conquerors' will that deprived them of their land.[18]

The Court further suggested without evidence that the growth of the United States could have been impeded if government takings of Indian title were compensable by law, as opposed to voluntary Congressional "contributions" to Indian nations.[19]

Eventually, the Tee-Hit-Ton clan and other Tlingit and Haida Alaska Natives would be the beneficiaries of a federal statute authorizing compensation for the loss of their homelands.[20] **See § 13.1**.

Indian nations continue to bring suits alleging a violation of Indian title (more recently, these suits use the phrase "aboriginal title"). They are difficult suits for tribal interests to win. In *Native Village of Eyak v. Blank*,[21] for example, a split Ninth Circuit en banc panel held (7–4) against the subsistence fishing claims of several Native Alaskan villages in the outer continent shelf, finding that the villages failed to prove exclusive use of claimed areas. The majority stated that a claim to aboriginal title fails unless a tribal group meets two requirements to prove aboriginal rights— "continuous use and occupancy" and "exclusivity."[22] On the question of exclusivity, the majority rejected the Villages' argument that there was sufficient evidence of exclusivity.[23]

However, in *Pueblo of Jemez v. United States*,[24] the Tenth Circuit revived a Quiet Title Act claim for aboriginal title against the federal government. The court first went into a detailed history of aboriginal title and how that doctrine relates to the New Mexico Pueblos. Of critical importance were the 1848 Treaty of Guadalupe Hildago and the Supreme Court's 1941 decision in *United States v. Santa Fe Pacific Railroad Co.*[25] The 1848 treaty extended the

---

[18]   Tee-Hit-Ton Indians v. United States, 348 U.S. 272, 289 (1955).

[19]   Id. at 290–91.

[20]   Walter R. Echo-Hawk, In the Courts of the Conqueror: The 10 Worst Indian Law Cases Ever Decided 390 (2010).

[21]   688 F.3d 619 (9th Cir. 2012) (en banc) (per curiam).

[22]   Id. at 622 (citations omitted).

[23]   Id. at 624–25.

[24]   790 F.3d 1143 (10th Cir. 2015).

[25]   314 U.S. 339 (1941).

aboriginal title ("Indian title") analysis to the New Mexico territory.[26] *Santa Fe Pacific* confirmed that the New Mexico Pueblos aboriginal title survived a century of federal government interventions.[27]

Ultimately, the court held that a federal government surveyor's determination in 1860 that the relevant lands were "vacant," and the following transfer of the land to a non-Indian did not serve to abrogate aboriginal title.[28]

§ 4.2   Recognized or Vested Property Rights

Recognized or vested Indian property rights, sometimes known as recognized title, arise when a federal action acknowledges Indian property rights to land and resources. Often, the recognition of property rights comes through ratified treaty, federal statute, or other official federal act. Recognized Indian property rights taken by the United States are subject the Fifth Amendment's Takings and Just Compensation Clause.

Congressional taking of recognized or vested Indian and tribal property is subject to the Takings and Just Compensation Clause of the Fifth Amendment. The Supreme Court stated in *United States v. Klamath and Moadoc Tribes*,[29] that the federal government's Indian affairs powers do not empower the government to take Indian and tribal property for its own or other purposes without the payment of just compensation.[30]

Similarly, in *United States v. Creek Nation*,[31] the Court held the United States liable for the taking of Creek lands reserved by treaty, stating that guardianship does not allow for mere confiscation of tribal vested title.[32]

Numerous lower court decisions have acknowledged the Supreme Court's holdings.[33] The sheer number of cases in which the

---

[26]   Pueblo of Jemez v. United States, 790 F.3d 1143, 1156 (10th Cir. 2015).

[27]   Id. at 1160–61.

[28]   Id. at 1163.

[29]   304 U.S. 119 (1938).

[30]   Id. at 123.

[31]   295 U.S. 103 (1935).

[32]   Id. at 109–110 (emphasis added) (citations omitted).

[33]   E.g., Lower Brule Sioux Tribe v. State of South Dakota, 711 F.2d 809, 824 n.20 (8th Cir. 1983), cert. denied, 464 U.S. 1042 (1984); Lac Courte Oreilles Band of Lake Superior Chippewa Indians v. Voigt, 700 F.2d 341, 351–352 (7th Cir. 1983), cert. denied, Besadny v. Lac Courte Oreilles Band of Lake Superior Chippewa Indians, 464 U.S. 805 (1983); Swim v. Bergland, 696 F.2d 712, 717 (9th Cir. 1983); United States v. Southern Pacific Transp. Co., 543 F.2d 676, 686 (9th Cir. 1976); United States v. State of Washington, 520 F.2d 676, 693 (9th Cir. 1975), cert. denied, 423 U.S. 1086 (1976); United States v. Peterson, 121 F. Supp. 2d 1309, 1318 n.12 (D. Mont. 2000).

Supreme Court addressed the federal taking of Indian and tribal property without compensation demonstrates that the Court's deference to the government's status as a "guardian" to its Indian "wards" did not allow for confiscation of Indian and tribal property.[34] It also suggests that the United States *did* routinely confiscate Indian and tribal property in the early 20th century.

Shoshone Tribe of Indians I and *II*

In *Shoshone Tribe of Indians of Wind River Reservation in Wyoming v. United States (Shoshone I)*,[35] the Supreme Court held that the United States vested an undivided property interest in the Wind River Reservation, and that the inclusion of the Northern Arapaho Tribe constituted a compensable taking of that interest.[36]

The Shoshone Tribe's title to the reservation—more than 3 million acres large—was vested in treaties executed in 1863 and 1868.[37] Like many treaties establishing reservations, the 1868 treaty utilized "set aside" or "set apart" language to denote the exclusive beneficial interest of the tribe and its members.[38] The treaty also provided that the Shoshone tribe could admit "other friendly tribes or individual Indians as from time to time they may be willing, with the consent of the United States, to admit amongst them. . . ."[39]

Eventually, the United States settled the Northern Arapaho Tribe, foes of the Shoshone Tribe, on the Wind River Reservation between 1870 and 1878, without the consent of the Shoshone Tribe.[40] Though perhaps even the Arapaho Tribe had not expected to be settled permanently on the Wind River Reservation (at least according to the Court's opinion), by 1878 "nearly the whole tribe was on the scene."[41] The Commissioner of Indian Affairs and Congress presumed for many years that the government's

---

[34] E.g., Chippewa Indians of Minnesota v. United States, 301 U.S. 358, 375–376 (1937); Shoshone Tribe of Indians of Wind River Reservation in Wyoming v. United States, 299 U.S. 476, 497 (1937); United States v. Creek Nation, 295 U.S. 103, 109–110 (1935); Yankton Sioux Tribe of Indians v. United States, 272 U.S. 351, 359 (1926); Lane v. Pueblo of Santa Rosa, 249 U.S. 110, 113 (1919); Choate v. Trapp, 224 U.S. 665, 678 (1912); Jones v. Meehan, 175 U.S. 1, 32 (1899).

[35] 299 U.S. 476 (1937).

[36] Id. at 496–98.

[37] Treaty between the United States of America and the Eastern Bands of Shoshonee Indians, 18 Stat. 685 (July 2, 1863); Treaty between the United States of America and the eastern band of Shoshonees and the Bannack tribe of Indians, 15 Stat. 673 (July 3, 1868).

[38] 18 Stat. at 674.

[39] Id.

[40] Shoshone Tribe of Indians of Wind River Reservation in Wyoming v. United States, 299 U.S. 476, 486–87 (1937).

[41] Id. at 488.

settlement of the Northern Arapaho Tribe on the Wind River Reservation without the Eastern Shoshone Tribe's consent was lawful.[42] In 1891, the Commissioner declared that the Arapaho Tribe enjoyed equal claim to the reservation.[43]

Congress authorized the Eastern Shoshone Tribe, through a jurisdictional act, to sue the United States for compensation for the loss of an undivided half of its reservation in 1927.[44] The Court of Claims awarded $793,821.49 to the tribe under a theory of trespass.[45] However, that court held that the date at which the Shoshone Tribe could be compensated for trespass was 1891, when the Commissioner made his declaration,[46] and not 1878, when the government first made the Arapaho settlement permanent, or perhaps an earlier date. The Supreme Court reversed this holding, and remanded for a new factual determination on damages.[47]

Still, the Court refused to describe the United States' settlement of another tribe on the Wind River Reservation as equivalent to the exercise of the power of eminent domain, a taking of a property right subject to compensation.[48] The Congressional jurisdictional act was sufficient to allow the judiciary to award damages for the taking, and was apparently necessary because, for the Court, the federal government's power to take tribal interests in reservation land was not an exercise of eminent domain.[49] According to the Court, the United States owned the land: "Title in the strict sense was always in the United States, though the Shoshones had the treaty right of occupancy with all its beneficial incidents."[50]

Even so, the tribal "right of occupancy" was a vested property right compensable under the Fifth Amendment.[51] Takings compensable under the Fifth Amendment are subject to an award of interest.[52] Rejecting the claim by the government that Indian property rights were somehow different, the Court roundly held that the government's powers in Indian affairs remained subject to

---

[42]   Id. at 489–90.

[43]   Id. at 491–92.

[44]   Act of March 3, 1927, 44 Stat. 1349.

[45]   Shoshone Tribe of Indians of Wind River Reservation in Wyoming v. United States, 82 Ct. Cl. 23, 94 (1935), rev'd, 299 U.S. 476 (1937).

[46]   Id. at 45–46.

[47]   Shoshone Tribe of Indians of Wind River Reservation in Wyoming v. United States, 299 U.S. 476, 494–98 (1937).

[48]   Id. at 492–94.

[49]   Id. at 493.

[50]   Id. at 496.

[51]   Id. at 497.

[52]   Id.

the Fifth Amendment's takings and just compensation clause, stating, "Spoliation is not management."[53]

On remand, the Court of Claims reset the damage amount to $4,408,444.23, including interest.[54] The court also included the value of the timber taken off the reservation during the period. On appeal, the Shoshone Tribe would have to contend with the views of the Supreme Court and the United States Attorney General that Indian tribes only received a vested interest in property rights expressly granted to the tribes, which would have excluded mineral, timber, and other rights.[55]

In *United States v. Shoshone Tribe of Indians (Shoshone II)*,[56] the Supreme Court affirmed the $4.4 million judgment against the United States for the taking of the Wind River Reservation, and affirmed that the compensation included the taking of timber from the reservation.[57] The main dispute before the Court in *Shoshone II* involved whether the tribe's vested property rights to the reservation included mineral and timber resources.[58]

The Court focused on the language of the 1868 treaty that provided for the "absolute and undisturbed use and occupation of the Shoshonee Indians. . . ."[59] The Court read that language in light of the purpose of the treaty, which was to "grant[ ] and assure[ ] to the tribe peaceable and unqualified possession of the land in perpetuity."[60] Clarifying somewhat the Court's statements about the ownership of reservation land, the Court held that minerals and timber forms a constituent part of the property rights vested to the tribe.[61] The Court further noted that the tribal and federal parties to the 1868 treaty knew about the timber and mineral resources, but the federal government did not reserve to itself the rights to those resources.[62] Drawing upon the rules of construction of Indian treaty language, the Court concluded that the 1868 treaty reserved

---

[53]   Id. at 497–98 (citations omitted).

[54]   Shoshone Tribe of Indians of Wind River Reservation in Wyoming v. United States, 85 Ct. Cl. 331, 381 (1937), aff'd, 304 U.S. 111 (1938).

[55]   E.g., United States v. Cook, 86 U.S. 591 (1873), cited in David H. Getches, Daniel M. Rosenfelt, and Charles F. Wilkinson, Federal Indian Law: Cases and Materials 542 (1979).

[56]   304 U.S. 111 (1938).

[57]   Id. at 112.

[58]   Id. at 113.

[59]   Id. at 116.

[60]   Id.

[61]   Id.

[62]   Id. at 117.

to the tribe all the property rights of the reservation, presumably excepting the "naked fee" referenced earlier.[63]

The Court further elaborated that the "set apart" language of the 1868 treaty squarely places the beneficial ownership of reserved lands in tribal hands: "Subject to the conditions imposed by the treaty, the Shoshone Tribe had the right that has always been understood to belong to Indians, undisturbed possessors of the soil from time immemorial."[64] The purposes of the establishment of the reservation included the establishment of a true homeland for the tribe, with the only restriction placed on the tribe's ownership being the federal government's right to govern certain aspects of the alienation of the land.[65]

Presumably, the "naked fee" title remaining with the United States after the establishment of the reservation amounts to nothing more than the federal government's prohibition on purchase of Indian lands without federal approval.[66]

The Court would return again and again to questions about what specific treaty terms reserved to Indian nations.

Montana v. United States

The Supreme Court's decision in *Montana v. United States*,[67] mostly known for establishing what would become known as a general rule on tribal authority over nonmembers, **see § 8.1**, also interpreted the scope of the Crow Tribe's reservation of property rights under the First and Second Treaties of Fort Laramie.[68] The Court's primary holding was that the United States retained ownership of riverbed of the Big Horn River even after the treaties, and that the State of Montana acquired ownership when it entered the Union in 1889.[69]

Rather than apply the canon of construing Indian treaties, the Court read the Crow treaties narrowly. Recall that the 1851 treaty expressly reserved "the privilege of hunting, fishing, or passing over any of the tracts of country. . . ."[70] The 1868 treaty established the tribe's reservation, and expressly "set apart [the reservation] for the

---

[63]   Id.

[64]   Id. at 117.

[65]   Id. at 117–18.

[66]   25 U.S.C. § 177.

[67]   450 U.S. 544 (1981).

[68]   First Treaty of Fort Laramie, 11 Stat. 749 (Sept. 17, 1851); Second Treaty of Fort Laramie, 15 Stat. 649 (May 7, 1868).

[69]   Montana v. United States, 450 U.S. 544, 553–57 (1981).

[70]   First Treaty of Fort Laramie, art. 5, 11 Stat. 749 (Sept. 17, 1851).

absolute and undisturbed use and occupation" of the tribe.[71] That treaty also prohibited persons "to pass over, settle upon, or reside in the territory described in this article for the use of said Indians. . . ."[72] The Court held that the "set apart" language and the power to exclude persons from the reservation "simply begs the question of the precise extent of the conveyed lands to which this exclusivity attaches."[73] The *Montana* majority pointed out that the Crow treaties never expressly mentioned the riverbed, and therefore could not have been considered a grant of the riverbed from the government to the tribe.[74]

Two decades later, in *Idaho v. United States*,[75] a case involving the submerged lands under Lake Coeur d'Alene, the Supreme Court restated the test as a two-part determination: "We ask whether Congress intended to include land under navigable waters within the federal reservation and, if so, whether Congress intended to defeat the future State's title to the submerged lands."[76] In that case, the state conceded that the tribe had expressly requested access to the lake for fishing purposes, ostensibly distinguishing the *Montana* fact pattern.[77] Reviewing the history of federal government and tribal negotiations over the status of the reservation, the Court concluded that Congress recognized that the reservation included the submerged lands.[78]

Hodel v. Irving and *Babbitt v. Youpee*—The Indian Land Consolidation Act

In *Hodel v. Irving*[79] and *Babbitt v. Youpee*,[80] the Supreme Court reaffirmed that Congress may not take vested Indian property without compensation, even where the property interests arguably were tiny, and even where the taking was done in the interest of preserving and enhancing tribal land holdings.

In *Irving*, the Supreme Court struck down Section 207 of the Indian Land Consolidation Act,[81] which purported to escheat tribal members' interests in reservation or trust land to the tribe if the

---

[71]　Second Treaty of Fort Laramie, art. 2, 15 Stat. 649, 650 (May 7, 1868).

[72]　Id.

[73]　Montana v. United States, 450 U.S. 544, 554–55 (1981).

[74]　Id. at 554.

[75]　533 U.S. 262 (2001).

[76]　Id. at 273 (citations omitted).

[77]　Id. at 274.

[78]　Id. at 280–81.

[79]　481 U.S. 704 (1987).

[80]　519 U.S. 234 (1997).

[81]　Pub. L. 97–459, Jan. 12, 1983, 96 Stat. 2515, formerly codified at 25 U.S.C. § 2206.

value of the property right earned less than $100 the year before and constituted less than two percent of the total acreage of the overall parcel.[82] Congress offered no compensation for the escheatment to the tribal member property owners, ultimately a fatal flaw.

Congress enacted the statute intending to alleviate the problem of fractionated heirships on Indian lands.[83] "Fractionated heirships" arise over the course of several generations where Indian land owners fail to properly probate their estates. Even in the late 19th century, the federal government was aware that allotted lands could be subject to this pernicious property ownership problem where a growing number of people own undivided interests in a parcel of land.[84]

The *Irving* Court described the problem as "extraordinary."[85] The Court, however, rejected the government's argument that the escheatment was a *de minimis* taking not subject to the Fifth Amendment's just-compensation mandate.[86] The Court concluded that the statute's abrogation of the descent and devise of this class of property was a taking implicating the Just Compensation Clause.[87]

Babbitt v. Youpee,[88] decided nearly a decade later, is a sequel to *Irving*. In *Youpee*, Congress had amended Section 207 of the Indian Land Consolidation Act in 1984 to limit the escheatment provision to interests in Indian land only upon the death of the owner with the interest.[89]

The Court held that the statute as amended again constituted a taking mandating just compensation under the Fifth Amendment.[90]

---

[82]   Id. at 709 (quoting Section 207, as enacted in 1983).

[83]   See generally Kenneth H. Bobroff, Retelling Allotment: Indian Property Rights and the Myth of Common Ownership, 54 Vand. L. Rev. 1559, 1616 (2001); Jessica A. Shoemaker, Comment, Like Snow in the Spring: Allotment, Fractionation, and the Indian Land Tenure Problem, 2003 Wis. L. Rev. 729, 729.

[84]   Ann. Rep. of the Commissioner of the Office of Indian Affairs to the Secretary of the Interior 193 (1892).

[85]   Hodel v. Irving, 481 U.S. 704, 714 (1987).

[86]   Id.

[87]   Id. at 718.

[88]   519 U.S. 234 (1997).

[89]   Pub. L. 98–608, Oct. 30, 1984, 98 Stat. 3173.

[90]   Babbitt v. Youpee, 519 U.S. 234, 243–244 (1997).

§ 4.3   Trust Property

Trust property includes lands and other assets owned in trust by the United States for the benefit of Indian nations or individual Indians. Trust property is immune from state taxation and regulation.[91] The United States' owes an enhanced trust duty to safeguard tribal trust property and assets. For details on the acquisition of trust lands, **see § 7.3**.

Trust land parcels are the equivalent of reservation lands, and may be declared a new reservation by the Interior Secretary. In *United States v. John*,[92] the Supreme Court held that trust lands owned by the Interior Secretary are "Indian country" as that term is used and defined by federal criminal statutes.[93] There, a citizen of the Mississippi Band of Choctaw Indians argued, along with the State of Mississippi, that his federal prosecution under the Major Crimes Act[94] was invalid on the basis that the federal government had no authority to prosecute crimes arising on trust lands.[95] The Court held that land acquired by the United States and declared to be held in trust by the federal government for the benefit of an Indian nation was "Indian country."[96]

Similarly, the Supreme Court held in *Oklahoma Tax Commission v. Citizen Band Potawatomi Indian Tribe* that a state may not tax a tribal member's income arising in Indian country, which includes trust lands.[97]

§ 4.4   Executive Order Reservation Lands

Several Indian reservations originated in Presidential actions known as Executive orders. On occasion, treaties or federal statutes authorized the President to declare a reservation by Executive order. These Executive orders create vested or recognized title in the reservation lands. In other occasions, no federal enactment authorized the creation of a reservation by that method. In such circumstances, the Executive order may be revoked, and the reservation disestablished, at the whim of the President without just compensation. However, Congress may expressly or impliedly ratify the creation of the reservation, or acquiesce in its creation. In those instances, the Executive order reservation is entitled to

---

[91]   25 U.S.C. § 5108.

[92]   437 U.S. 634 (1978).

[93]   18 U.S.C. § 1151 defines "Indian country" for federal criminal and civil purposes.

[94]   18 U.S.C. § 1153.

[95]   United States v. John, 437 U.S. 634, 649–50 (1978).

[96]   Id. at 649.

[97]   498 U.S. 505, 511 (1991).

recognition, and the taking of that reservation is subject to a takings analysis.

Sioux Tribe of Indians v. United States

In *Sioux Tribe of Indians v. United States*,[98] the Supreme Court concluded that the termination of a reservation created by Executive order is a not a compensable taking if the understanding of Congress and the Executive branch was that the creating of the reservation did not create a "compensable interest."[99]

The *Handbook of Federal Indian Law* reported that the Attorney General in 1924 suggested that Indians and tribes could have a compensable interest in Executive order reservations.[100] In matching opinions, Attorney General Stone argued that the Interior Secretary's decision to allow the taking of mineral interests from Executive order reservations under a federal statute that did not mention Indian lands was improper.[101] The Attorney General's reasoning was that Executive orders creating Indian reservations at least provided a right of occupancy to the Indians, and that the judiciary had effectively recognized that a government taking of the right of occupancy was compensable.[102] The Supreme Court would reject that view in the 1940s and 1950s.[103] See § 4.1.

In 1919, Congress prohibited the withdrawal of lands from the public domain by the President for the creation of Indian reservations.[104]

§ 4.5　　Restricted Fee Lands

Restricted fee lands usually arise from tribal land acquisitions from funds acquired through a federal-tribal land-claims settlement account or other trust account. Examples also include land retained or reacquired in fee by Indian Pueblos in New Mexico with land grants successfully recognized by the Spanish, Mexican, and American governments.

---

[98] 316 U.S. 317 (1942).

[99] Id. at 331.

[100] Felix S. Cohen, Handbook of Federal Indian Law 299 (1941) (quoting).

[101] 34 U.S. Op. Atty. Gen. 171, 181 (May 12, 1924) (addressing the President); 34 U.S. Op. Atty. Gen. 181, 192 (May 27, 1924) (addressing the Interior Secretary).

[102] 34 U.S. Op. Atty. Gen. 171, 176–77 (May 12, 1924); 34 U.S. Op. Atty. Gen. 181, 187 (May 27, 1924).

[103] Attorney General Stone's opinions on the mineral estate did not survive judicial review, either. Note, Tribal Property Interests in Executive-Order Reservations: A Compensable Indian Rights, 69 Yale L. J. 627, 632 & n. 28 (1960) (citing an unpublished federal district court decision).

[104] Act of June 30, 1919, 41 Stat. 34, codified at 43 U.S.C. § 150.

Typically, these lands are acquired under land claims settlement statutes like the Seneca Nation Settlement Act of 1990,[105] and are Indian country under 25 U.S.C. § 1151(b). Section 1774f provided that tribal lands purchased with settlement funds would be taken off state and local tax rolls and held in "restricted fee status" by the Nation. In *Citizens against Casino Gambling in Erie County v. Hogen*,[106] the court held that such lands met the definition of Indian country in § 1151.[107] The court first found that the settlement act demonstrated Congressional intent to set aside the land for Indian purposes: "Congress's application of the Nonintercourse Act to land purchased with SNSA [Seneca Nation Settlement Act of 1990] funds is a sufficient statement of its intent that the land be used by the SNI [Seneca Nation of Indians] for Indian purposes."[108] Similarly, the settlement act demonstrated Congress's intention to keep the land under federal superintendence: "In the instant case, Congress affirmatively imposed the Nonintercourse Act's restrictions against alienation on land purchased with SNSA funds. [S]ubjecting land to the Nonintercourse Act's restrictions sufficiently demonstrates federal superintendence over the land."[109]

Cases recognizing that fee lands held by Indian Pueblos under land grants recognized by Spanish, Mexican, and American governments are restricted fee lands include *United States v. Arrieta*.[110]

§ 4.6   Land Claims

Indian land claims have been a controversial part of federal Indian law and policy for centuries. Individual Indians and Indian nations have brought claims arising under treaties and federal statutes seeking return of illegally taken land or money damages or specific relief. This section surveys the major types of claims and the history behind them.

---

[105] Pub. L. 101–504, Nov. 3, 1990, 104 Stat. 1292, codified at 25 U.S.C. §§ 1774 et seq.

[106] No. 07–CV–0451S, 2008 WL 2746566 (W.D.N.Y., July 8, 2008).

[107] Id. at *38–51.

[108] Id. at *41.

[109] Id. at *48. See also Citizens Against Casino Gambling in Erie County v. Chaudhuri, 802 F.3d 267 (2d Cir.2015).

[110] 436 F.3d 1246, 1249 (10th Cir. 2006). See also Pub. L. 109–133, Dec. 20, 2005, 119 Stat. 2573, codified at 25 U.S.C. § 331 note (confirming tribal and federal criminal jurisdiction over Pueblo restricted fee lands). Thanks to Dan Rey-Bear for providing these authorities.

Jurisdictional Acts

Prior to the enactment of the Indian Claims Commission Act of 1946 and the Indian Tucker Act in 1949, Indians and tribes were forced to seek special jurisdictional statutes from Congress authorizing suit against the government for money damages, often arising from claims for breach of treaty rights.[111] The tribes rarely benefitted from these special jurisdictional statutes.[112] Less than 30 percent of Indian claims under these jurisdictional statutes resulted in recovery of any money damages at all.[113] Indian nations recovered about 1 percent the amount they claimed was owed to them.[114] Many of these claims were not land claims but provide the background on the legal backdrop upon which tribes brought land claims later.

Indian Claims Commission Act

In 1946, Congress enacted the Indian Claims Commission Act (ICCA).[115] Section 2 of the ICCA authorized Indian tribes to bring claims against the United States occurring before August 14, 1946.[116]

The ICCA was intended to stop the Congressional practice of adopting piecemeal jurisdictional acts to allow for tribal claims to proceed in federal court: "The 'chief purpose of the [ICCA was] to dispose of the Indian claims problem with finality.' "[117] The process of obtaining jurisdictional acts was unfair and costly, and often amounted to nothing.[118]

The statute was designed to allow the widest variety of tribal claims.[119] The Act authorized and instructed the Indian Claims Commission to consider Indian claims in a new light, allowing the

---

[111] Samuel J. Flickinger, The American Indian, 20 Fed. Law. 212, 214 (1960).

[112] Id. at 214–15.

[113] Nancy Oestreich Lurie, The Indian Claims Commission Act, 311 Annals of the American Academy of Political and Social Science 56, 58 (1957). See also Robert W. Barker, The Indian Claims Commission—The Conscience of the Nation in Its Dealings with the Original American, 20 Fed. Law. 240, 241 (1960); Richard B. Collins & Karla D. Miller, A People Without Law, 5 Indigenous L. J. 83, 113 (2006).

[114] Russel Lawrence Barsh, Indian Land Claims Policy in the United States, 58 N.D. L. Rev. 7, 10–11 (1982).

[115] Pub. L. 79–726, August 13, 1946, 60 Stat. 1049, codified at 25 U.S.C. §§ 70 et seq.

[116] 25 U.S.C. § 70a.

[117] United States v. Dann, 470 U.S. 39, 45 (1985). See also Robert W. Barker, The Indian Claims Commission—The Conscience of the Nation in Its Dealings with the Original American, 20 Fed. Law. 240, 241–42 (1960).

[118] Russel Lawrence Barsh, Indian Land Claims Policy in the United States, 58 N.D. L. Rev. 7, 11–12 (1982).

[119] Otoe and Missouria Tribe of Indians v. United States, 131 Ct. Cl. 593, 602, 131 F. Supp. 265, 271 (1955), cert. denied, 350 U.S. 848 (1955).

Commission to reform the treaty terms to conform to Indian understandings of the meaning of the treaty provisions, similar to how courts utilize the canons of construing Indian treaties in the modern era.[120]

However, the Act effectively prohibited claims demanding the return of Indian lands, though nothing in the statute expressly prohibited recovery of land.[121] Section 2 referred to "payments made by the United States on the claim. . . ."[122] Section 19 used the term "amount" to refer to "relief"[123] and section 22 referred to "sums" to be appropriated by Congress to pay out judgments.[124] The Taos Pueblo may be the only tribe that succeeded in bringing a claim to recover land—its sacred Blue Lake—and even that required a multi-year period of lobbying Congress.[125]

Further supporting the notion that the ICCA was not intended to restore the tribal land base, and adding an important dimension to how the tribal claims would be litigated, the Act allowed Indian nations to hire their own counsel, and that counsel could be compensated up to 10 percent of the total award.[126] The 10 percent take certainly encouraged counsel to seek the highest dollar value for tribal claims, but strongly discouraged attorneys to bring claims for land recovery.

The Commission valued Indian land sales from the fair market value of the land at the time of the transaction. Congress also provided the United States with a chance to prove "offsets," federal money already spent on the Indian nation for numerous purposes that would be charged against the ultimate damages award.[127] From the point of view of many (but certainly not all) Indian and tribal claimants, restrictions on the ability of Indian nations to recover their land rendered the ICCA process a nullity. Even for successful Indian and tribal claimants, the judgment funds were

---

[120] Ralph A. Barney, Some Legal Problems under the Indian Claims Commission Act, 20 Fed. Law. 235, 238 (1960).

[121] Sandra C. Danforth, Repaying Historical Debts: The Indian Claims Commission, 49 N.D. L. Rev. 359, 390–91 (1973).

[122] 70 U.S.C. § 70a.

[123] 25 U.S.C. § 70r.

[124] 25 U.S.C. § 70u.

[125] R.C. Gordon-McCutcheon, The Taos Indians and the Battle for Blue Lake (1991). At least one other tribe refused to accept the Commission's monetary damages conclusions, preferring to seek land recovery instead. Sandra C. Danforth, Repaying Historical Debts: The Indian Claims Commission, 49 N.D. L. Rev. 359, 393 (1973) (referencing the Pit River Tribe).

[126] 25 U.S.C. § 70n.

[127] 70 U.S.C. § 70a.

insufficient to allow the claimants to restore their historic land bases.[128]

Congress intended the Commission to be concluded with its business in a few short years.[129] Indian nations had five years to file a claim.[130] In five years, 852 claims were filed.[131] Congress was forced to repeatedly extend the Commission's deadline but many claims never reached resolution.[132] Eventually, Congress terminated the Commission and transferred remaining claims to the Court of Federal Claims in 1978.[133]

United States v. Sioux Nation

The leading case arising out of the Indian Claims Commission is *United States v. Sioux Nation of Indians*.[134] The case arose out of the United States' forced breakup of the Great Sioux Reservation, established by treaty in 1868 and covering the Dakotas and parts of several other states, through a series of treaty amendments and post-treaty "agreements." Ultimately, the Supreme Court a multi-million dollar judgment in favor of the Sioux tribes for the taking of their Black Hills homelands, a judgment the tribes have so far refused to collect upon, instead demanding the return of the land.

The collected Sioux nations, which included the Lakota, the Dakota, and Nakota nations, sought compensation for the government's taking of the Black Hills in the latter part of the 19th century. The 1868 Treaty of Fort Laramie established the Great Sioux Reservation, which included the Black Hills in what is now western South Dakota, setting aside the lands "for the absolute and undisturbed use and occupation of the Indians. . . ."[135] Moreover, Article IV of the treaty made it virtually impossible to amend the treaty (at least on paper), providing that the treaty could not be amended unless approved of by "at least three fourths of all the

---

[128] Robert W. Barker, The Indian Claims Commission—The Conscience of the Nation in Its Dealings with the Original American, 20 Fed. Law. 240, 243 (1960).

[129] 25 U.S.C. § 70v (providing for the termination of the Commission).

[130] 25 U.S.C. § 70k.

[131] Thomas Le Duc, The Work of the Indian Claims Commission under the Act of 1946, 26 Pac. Hist. Rev. 1, 2 (1957).

[132] David H. Getches, Charles F. Wilkinson, Robert A. Williams, Jr., Matthew L.M. Fletcher, and Kristen A. Carpenter, Cases and Materials on Federal Indian Law 309 (7th ed. 2017).

[133] Id.

[134] 448 U.S. 371 (1980). To be sure, the decision discussed here is not technically a review of an Indian Claims Commission report, but the result of a 1978 jurisdictional act authorizing further review of the Black Hills claim. Pub. L. 95–243, March 13, 1978, 92 Stat. 153. Congress reinstated the claim after the Court of Claims ruled the claim was barred by res judicata. United States v. Sioux Nation, 519 F.2d 1298, 1306 (Ct. Cl.), cert. denied, 423 U.S. 1016 (1975).

[135] Fort Laramie Treaty of April 29, 1868, art. 2, 15 Stat. 635.

adult male Indians."[136] An important feature of the treaty was that the United States promised to provide the Indians with subsistence rations and materials necessary "to assist the Sioux in becoming civilized farmers. . . ."[137] The Indian nations faced mass starvation.[138]

After failing to persuade the Indians to consent to the cession of the Black Hills in accordance with the 1868 treaty amendment procedure, Congress abrogated the treaty with simple legislation in 1877.[139] The government's payment to the tribes under the 1877 Act for the Black Hills—"subsistence rations"—was nothing close to the value of the land.[140]

After several false starts, the Indian Claims Commission held in 1974 that the 1877 Act constituted a taking to which the tribes were entitled to just compensation, an outcome the Court of Claims affirmed.[141] The court held that the plaintiffs were entitled to an award of interest at the rate of 5 percent per year on a principal of $17.1 million dating back to 1877.[142]

The Supreme Court adopted the legal standard from the Court of Claims in *Three Affiliated Tribes of the Fort Berthold Reservation v. United States*.[143] There, the court distinguished between disputes that arose where the federal government acted as a trustee to Indian or tribal property interests, and when the government acted as a sovereign in the exercise of eminent domain powers.[144]

In *Sioux Nation*, the Supreme Court rejected the government's claims that its taking of the Black Hills was not subject to the Fort Berthold test, holding, "But the court must also be cognizant that 'this power to control and manage [is] not absolute. While extending to all appropriate measures for protecting and advancing the tribe, it [is] subject to limitations inhering in . . . a guardianship and to pertinent constitutional restrictions.' "[145]

---

[136] Id. at art. 4, 15 Stat. 635.

[137] United States v. Sioux Nation, 448 U.S. 371, 375 (1980).

[138] John P. LaVelle, Rescuing Paha Sapa: Achieving Environmental Justice by Restoring the Great Grasslands and Returning the Sacred Black Hills to the Great Sioux Nation, 5 Great Plains Natural Resources J. 40, 50–52 (2001) (footnotes omitted).

[139] Id. at 382–83.

[140] Id. at 386.

[141] Sioux Nation of Indians v. United States, 601 F.2d 1157 (1979), aff'd, 448 U.S. 371 (1980).

[142] United States v. Sioux Nation, 448 U.S. 371, 390 (1980).

[143] 390 F.2d 686 (1968).

[144] Id. at 691.

[145] United States v. Sioux Nation, 448 U.S. 371, 415 (1980) (quoting United States v. Creek Nation, 295 U.S. 103, 109–11 (1935)).

The Sioux tribal nations have continued to refuse the judgment award, which is now more than $1 billion.[146]

United States v. Dann

The payment of a monetary judgment by the federal government to an Indian Claims Commission claimant extinguishes the tribal title claim.[147] In *United States v. Dann*,[148] the Supreme Court held that the certification of a federal judgment award by the General Accounting Office and the deposit of the funds in a United States Treasury Department trust account constituted "payment" under the ICCA, and the underlying tribal property interests had been extinguished.

Dann involved the property rights claims of two sisters, Mary and Carrie Dann, members of what the Supreme Court called an "autonomous band" of the Western Shoshone Tribe.[149] The sisters were ranchers who grazed livestock on more than 5000 acres of land they argued had never been ceded to the United States.[150] They had argued that they retained aboriginal title to the lands, and the United States claimed that an earlier Indian Claims Commission judgment involving one band of the Western Shoshone, the Te-Moak Tribe, had extinguished the title.[151] The Dann sisters were not citizens of the Te-Moak Tribe, and the tribe later argued that they had not intended to extinguish title to all Western Shoshone lands. In 1979, the government paid out the judgment by depositing funds into a Treasury Department trust account.[152]

The Supreme Court held that the dual roles played by the federal government both as defendant in the claims suit and as the bank account holder, or trustee, to the tribe's trust account effectively invoked the finality of judgment provision of the ICCA and extinguished title.[153]

This apparent conflict of interest all too often interferes with the federal government's proper administration of its trust

---

[146] Maria Streshhinsky, Saying No to $1 Billion: Why the impoverished Sioux Nation won't take federal money, The Atlantic, Feb. 9, 2011.

[147] 25 U.S.C. § 70(a).

[148] 470 U.S. 39 (1985).

[149] Id. at 43.

[150] Id.

[151] Temoak Band of Western Shoshone Indians v. United States, 593 F.2d 994 (Ct. Cl. 1979).

[152] United States v. Dann, 470 U.S. 39, 44 (1985).

[153] Id. at 49–50.

relationship with Indian nations.[154] **See § 5.2.** Here, the government *qua* judgment debtor had a vested interest in quickly and efficiently extinguishing title to Western Shoshone lands, in conflict with the government *qua* trustee and its obligation to preserve tribal self-determination.

§ 4.7 Non-Intercourse Act Claims

The Non-Intercourse Act,[155] one of the first federal Indian affairs statutes enacted by Congress,[156] formed the legal basis of several large land claims brought by Indian nations in the eastern part of the United States beginning in the 1960s. The Act prohibited land transactions with Indians and Indian nations without the consent of the United States. Because several states in the east had purchased land from Indian nations after the enactment of the statute without authorization, the tribal claimants argued that those transactions were void ab initio, and sought equitable and monetary relief.

Jurisdictional Barriers to Land Claims

Indian nations had not been able to bring land claims under the Non-Intercourse Act—or other statutes or theories—for two main reasons: jurisdiction and legal capacity. Jurisdictionally, Indian nations were in a bind because federal courts usually rejected land claims for failure to allege a federal claim, and state courts rejected land claims because the claims were federal. In 1966, Congress enacted a statute that was intended to allow Indian nations to bring suit in federal court with the same status as the United States so long as there was a federal cause of action.[157]

Oneida I

In *Oneida Indian Nation of New York v. Oneida County, New York (Oneida I)*,[158] the Supreme Court held that Indian nations may bring trespass actions to recover rents due on lands allegedly taken in violation of the Non-Intercourse Act under 28 U.S.C. §§ 1331 and 1362.

Oneida I arose out of a test case brought by the Oneida Indian Nation of New York, the Oneida Indian Nation of Wisconsin, and the Oneida of the Thames Band Council, against New York State

---

[154] See generally Ann C. Juliano, Conflicted Justice: The Department of Justice's Conflict of Interest in Representing Native American Tribes, 37 Ga. L. Rev. 1307 (2003).

[155] 25 U.S.C. § 177.

[156] Act of July 20, 1790, ch. 33, § 4, 1 Stat. 137.

[157] 28 U.S.C. § 1362.

[158] 414 U.S. 661 (1974).

involving a 1795 land sale in Madison and Oneida Counties.[159] The historical background of the land transaction is critically important. During the Revolutionary War, the six Haudenosaunee (Iroquois) Nations split apart, with the Oneidas and Tuscaroras departing from the other nations and fought on the American side.[160] In the 1784 Treaty of Fort Stanwix with the Six Iroquois Nations, the Oneida and Tuscarora Nations' lands were secured: "The Oneida and Tuscarora Nations shall be secured in possession of the lands on which they are settled."[161] The State of New York then proceeded to "systematically defraud the Oneidas out of their entire territory over the next fifty years despite the solemn assurances of federal treaties and laws."[162]

The Supreme Court held that a right to possession conferred by federal law, such as a treaty or other law, creates a federal question.[163] The Court held that Indian tribal claims to lands always originated in federal law from before the Founding of the Republic.[164] The Court also noted that it had previously decided numerous cases involving Indian claims to land.[165] Importantly, the Court did not rely exclusively upon § 1362, but instead on both §§ 1331 and 1362.[166]

Oneida II

In *Oneida County, N.Y. v. Oneida Indian Nation of New York (Oneida II)*,[167] the Supreme Court held that the Oneida Indian Nation could maintain a federal common law cause of action and that the Non-Intercourse Act did not preempt tribal land claims.

On remand from the Supreme Court in *Oneida I*, the federal district court held a trial on the test case, which sought back rent and trespass damages for 100,000 acres in Madison and Oneida Counties.[168] In 1795, according the court's findings of fact, the State

---

[159] George C. Shattuck, The Oneida Land Claims: A Legal History 27 (1991).

[160] Arlinda F. Locklear, The Oneida Land Claims: A Legal Overview, in Iroquois Land Claims 141, 145–46 (Christopher Vecsey & William A. Starna, eds. 1988).

[161] Id. at 146 (quoting Treaty of Fort Stanwix, Article 2, 7 Stat. 15 (Oct. 22, 1784)).

[162] Id. at 147.

[163] Oneida Indian Nation of New York v. Oneida County, N.Y., 414 U.S. 661, 666–67 (1974).

[164] Id. at 667.

[165] Id. at 667–72.

[166] Id. at 667.

[167] 470 U.S. 226 (1985).

[168] Arlinda F. Locklear, The Oneida Land Claims: A Legal Overview, in Iroquois Land Claims 141, 147 (Christopher Vecsey & William A. Starna, eds. 1988); George C. Shattuck, The Oneida Land Claims: A Legal History 27 (1991).

and the federal government conflicted over whether the Non-Intercourse Act barred the State from purchasing Indian lands.[169] Over the objections of the United States, a small group of Oneida Indians armed with "powers of attorney" purportedly sold 100,000 acres to the State in a deal consummated in Albany, New York, far from the Oneida homeland.[170] No United States treaty commissioner participated.[171]

Similarly, as a matter of law, the court held that the transaction violated the Non-Intercourse Act.[172] Borrowing from previous Non-Intercourse Act claims, the court adopted four elements a tribe must show in order to establish a prima facie case:

> 1) [The plaintiff] is or represents an Indian "tribe" within the meaning of the Act; 2) the parcels of land at issue herein are covered by the Act as tribal land; 3) the United States has never consented to the alienation of the tribal land; 4) the trust relationship between the United States and the tribe, which is established by coverage of the Act, has never been terminated or abandoned.[173]

The tribe had no trouble making the requisite showing on the four questions.

The court also held that land transactions conducted in violation of the Act were void, even if the underlying transaction was unfair or fraudulent on the purchaser. [174] Of course this means even if an Indian nation was adequately paid for the land it sold to an improper purchaser in violation of the Non-Intercourse Act, the transaction was still void in its inception.

The court concluded that the plaintiffs had proven their case and ordered Madison and Oneida Counties to pay damages for the two years claimed by the plaintiffs.[175] The Second Circuit affirmed.[176]

The Supreme Court also affirmed, 5–4. The Court first reaffirmed there was a federal common law cause of action for

---

[169] Oneida Indian Nation of New York State v. Oneida County, 434 F. Supp. 527, 524 (N.D. N.Y. 1977), aff'd, 719 F.2d 525 (2d Cir. 1983), aff'd, 470 U.S. 226 (1985).

[170] Id. at 535.

[171] Id.

[172] Id. at 537–41.

[173] Id. at 537–38 (quoting Mashpee Tribe v. New Seabury Corp., 427 F.Supp. 899, 902 (D. Mass. 1977)).

[174] Id. at 541.

[175] Id. at 548.

[176] Oneida Indian Nation of New York State v. Oneida County, 719 F.2d 525 (2d Cir. 1983), aff'd, 470 U.S. 226 (1985).

Indian nations to bring a possessory action against the counties.[177] The Court did not reach the alternative argument that the Non-Intercourse Act authorized the suit.[178]

The Court then rejected the counties' claim that the Non-Intercourse Act actually preempted the common law cause of action.[179] While the Non-Intercourse Act may have spoken as to the rights to land in question, the Court held that the Act "not speak directly to the question of remedies for unlawful conveyances of Indian land."[180] The Court compared the Act to 25 U.S.C. § 194, a 19th century statute that placed a burden of proof on "white person[s]" defending land claims by Indians, and concluded that Congress did not normally statutorily provide for remedies in Indian lands statutes.[181] Moreover, as the Court noted in *Oneida I*, the Court had previously addressed several Indian land claims without finding preemption by the Non-Intercourse Act.[182]

The Court then addressed a panoply of defenses raised by the counties. The first defense was that that the Oneida claim was barred by the state statute of limitations. Usually, when a federal statute of limitations is not present, the court would borrow the state's statute of limitations. The Supreme Court rejected that claim on the grounds that federal policy did not support the application of state statutes of limitations to Indian claims.[183] The Court noted that Congress had only adopted a statute of limitations for federal claims brought by the United States on behalf of Indian nations in 28 U.S.C. § 2415, and for the first time established a six-year limitation on tribal tort and contract claims in a 1982 statute, the Indian Claims Limitation Act.[184] **See § 4.8**. No federal statute of limitations applied to Non-Intercourse Act claims, and "[i]t would be a violation of Congress' will were we to hold that a state statute of limitations period should be borrowed in these circumstances."[185]

The Court also rejected the laches defense, that too much time had passed since the transactions, because the counties abandoned the defense before the Second Circuit.[186] Of note, the Court added

---

[177] Oneida County, N.Y. v. Oneida Indian Nation of New York, 470 U.S. 226, 233–36 (1985).

[178] Id. at 233.

[179] Id. at 236–40.

[180] Id. at 237.

[181] Id. at 239.

[182] Id. at 239–40.

[183] Id. at 240–44.

[184] Id. at 241–44.

[185] Id. at 244.

[186] Id. at 244–45.

that laches and other equitable defenses were inappropriate defenses to Indian land claims.[187]

Similarly, the Court next rejected the third defense, abatement, which would have provided that the cause of action in the relevant version of the Non-Intercourse Act, the 1793 provision, expired when that statute expired (and was replaced with an identical provision) in 1796.[188]

The Court also rejected the fourth defense, that the United States had ratified the 1795 transaction in the treaties of 1798 and 1802.[189] In those treaties, the tribe stated it would "quit claim" lands from "the last purchase" and to "land heretofore ceded," without specific reference to the 1795 transaction.[190] The Court applied the canons of construction to reach the conclusion that neither treaty provision demonstrated "a plain and unambiguous intent to extinguish Indian title."[191]

Finally, the Court rejected the counties' justiciability argument, premised on the view that Indian affairs are the sole province of Congress.[192]

Congressional Land Claims Settlements

Following the filing of the Oneida test case, several other eastern Indian nations brought suit against states, local governments, and others alleging Non-Intercourse Act violations.[193] Many, but not all, of these claims resulted in settlement agreements between the tribal parties, states, and the federal government ratified by an Act of Congress. Frequently, the stated purpose of the settlement acts was to protect the property rights of non-Indian landowners, whose titles to land may have been clouded by the land claims.

In 1972, the Passamaquoddy Tribe sued the United States seeking an order from the federal court requiring the government to bring suit against the State of Maine alleging violations of Indian title.[194] The suit resulted in an unusual federal court order requiring the Department of Justice to file a "protective complaint" on behalf of the Passamaquoddy and Penobscot tribes before a

---

[187] Id. at 244 n. 16.

[188] Id. at 245–46.

[189] Id. at 246–48.

[190] Id. at 247 n. 19 (quoting).

[191] Id. at 248.

[192] Id. at 248–50.

[193] Tim Vollman, A Survey of Eastern Indian Land Claims, 1970–1979, 31 Me. L. Rev. 5, 8–12 (1979).

[194] Id. at 8.

statute of limitations period expired,[195] which then resulted in the de facto federal recognition of the tribes by the United States.[196]

In 1980, Congress enacted the Maine Indian Claims Settlement Act,[197] which concluded the land claims of the Passamaquoddy, Penobscot, and Houton Band of Maliseet Indians.[198] The Act ratified an agreement between the United States as the tribes' trustee and the State of Maine.[199] Congress found that the Maine Indian land claims involved novel and complex issues and might not be resolved for up to fifteen years, and specifically reference a cloud on the titles of non-Indian property owners.[200] The Act provided a federal fund for the tribes to draw upon in purchasing lands to help restore the tribal land base.[201] Controversially, the Act provided for state civil and criminal jurisdiction over Indian lands in Maine.[202] However, the tribes may retain jurisdiction under the Indian Child Welfare Act.[203]

In 1975, the Narragansett Tribe of Rhode Island sued the State of Rhode Island and private property owners under the Non-Intercourse Act.[204] The Narragansetts were not a federally recognized tribe when they brought the suit, and fairly quickly reached a settlement with the state in 1978.[205] Though the United States had not participated in the negotiations, the tribe and the state agreed that the United States should expend $3.5 million to conclude the settlement.[206] Ultimately, the Interior Solicitor agreed, and recommended that Congress ratify the settlement and appropriate the funds.[207]

In 1978, Congress enacted the Rhode Island Indian Claims Settlement Act.[208] Like the Maine settlement statute that would

---

[195] Joint Tribal Council of the Passamaquoddy Tribe v. Morton, 388 F. Supp. 649 (D. Me.), aff'd, 528 F.2d 370 (1st Cir. 1975).

[196] Tim Vollman, A Survey of Eastern Indian Land Claims, 1970–1979, 31 Me. L. Rev. 5, 9–10 (1979).

[197] Pub. L. 96–420, Oct. 10, 1980, 94 Stat. 1785, codified at 25 U.S.C. §§ 1721 et seq.

[198] 25 U.S.C. § 1721(1).

[199] H. Rep. 96–1353, at 13 (Sept. 19, 1980).

[200] Id. at 13–14.

[201] 25 U.S.C. § 1724.

[202] 25 U.S.C. § 1725(a).

[203] 25 U.S.C. § 1727.

[204] Tim Vollman, A Survey of Eastern Indian Land Claims, 1970–1979, 31 Me. L. Rev. 5, 10 (1979).

[205] Id. at 13–14.

[206] Id.

[207] Id. at 14.

[208] Pub. L. 95–395, Sept. 30, 1978, 92 Stat. 813, codified at 25 U.S.C. §§ 1701 et seq.

follow it, this statute arose out of settlement negotiations.[209] Again, Congress noted the cloud on the titles of non-Indian landowners.[210] Also, the settlement act provided for state jurisdiction over Indian lands.[211] The Narragansett Tribe would later win federal recognition as an Indian tribe under the federal administrative acknowledgment process.[212]

In 1976, the Mashpee Tribe sued landowners on Cape Cod in the Town of Mashpee.[213] The tribe's claim went to trial and was defeated on the ground that the tribe could not prove that it was a tribe under the Non-Intercourse Act.[214] That decision has been subject to rigorous scholarly attack.[215] Judge Skinner allowed numerous expert witnesses to testify that the Mashpee claimants constituted a tribe, but became frustrated by the lack of consensus on the definition.[216] Trial witness Vine Deloria, Jr.'s definition—"As I use it and understand other people using it, it means a group of people living pretty much in the same place who know who their relatives are"[217]—may have been indicative of the lack of clarity on the question. The jury came back with a verdict that Judge Skinner used to dismiss the claim: "After forty days of testimony, the jury came up with the following 'irrational' decision: The Mashpee were not a Tribe in 1790, were a Tribe in 1834 and 1842, but again were not a Tribe in 1869 and 1870."[218]

The Massachusetts Indian Land Claims Settlement Act,[219] as with prior settlement acts, arose out of negotiation between the parties.[220] The statute effectively conferred federal recognition on the Wampanoag Tribal Council of Gay Head, Inc.[221] However, a separate tribal group split apart during the approval of the

---

[209] H. Rep. 95–1453, at 6 (Aug. 8, 1978).

[210] Id.

[211] 25 U.S.C. § 1708(a).

[212] Final Determination for Federal Acknowledgement of Narragansett Indian Tribe of Rhode Island, 48 Fed.Reg. 6177 (1983).

[213] Tim Vollman, A Survey of Eastern Indian Land Claims, 1970–1979, 31 Me. L. Rev. 5, 10–11 (1979).

[214] Mashpee Tribe v. Town of Mashpee, 447 F. Supp. 940 (D. Mass. 1978).

[215] Gerald Torres & Kathryn Milun, Translating Yonnondio by Precedent and Evidence: The Mashpee Indian Case, 1990 Duke Law Journal 625 (1990).

[216] Id. at 634.

[217] James Clifford, Identity in Mashpee, in The Predicament of Culture: Twentieth-Century Ethnography, Literature, and Art 323 (1988).

[218] Gerald Torres & Kathryn Milun, Translating Yonnondio by Precedent and Evidence: The Mashpee Indian Case, 1990 Duke Law Journal 625, 635–36 (1990) (citation omitted).

[219] Pub. L. 100–95, Aug. 18, 1987, 101 Stat. 704, codified at 25 U.S.C. §§ 1771 et seq.

[220] H. Rep. 99–918, at 3 (Sept. 26, 1986).

[221] 25 U.S.C. § 1771f.

settlement,[222] and was later administratively recognized by the United States. As with prior acts, the statute provided specific processes for the purchase of lands with the settlement funds.[223] And again the federal statute allowed for state jurisdiction over the settlement lands.[224]

Congress also enacted settlement acts to conclude the land claims brought by the Mashantucket Pequot Tribal Nation,[225] the Seneca Nation of Indians,[226] and the Mohegan Tribe.[227] However, for the most part, the land claims brought by the New York Haudenosaunee tribes did not reach settlement.

Many of the so-called Eastern land claims began with a petition from the tribe to the Department of Interior seeking a decision to pursue land claims as the trustee of Indian assets.[228] The timing of these petitions is critical, given that in 1966 Congress had established a six-year statute of limitations on these claims. In 1972, 1977, and finally in 1982, as the claims were to expire, the Interior Solicitor and the Justice Department concluded that the United States could be liable for the expiration of million-dollar Indian land claims, and sought to quickly file suits or to legislatively extend the statute of limitations. **See § 4.8.**

City of Sherrill v. Oneida Indian Nation and Its Progeny

In 2005, the Supreme Court held in *City of Sherrill v. Oneida Indian Nation of New York*,[229] an Indian taxation case, that various equitable defenses, primarily laches, or what Professor Kathryn Fort refers to as "The New Laches,"[230] may be applied by federal courts to tribal claims brought under the Non-Intercourse Act.

In the case, the Oneida Nation purchased land in fee that had been ancient tribal land within the borders of its reservation.[231] The

---

[222]　H. Rep. 99–918, at 3–4 (Sept. 26, 1986).

[223]　25 U.S.C. §§ 1771c, 1771d.

[224]　25 U.S.C. § 1771e.

[225]　Pub. L. 98–134, Oct. 18, 1983, 97 Stat. 851, codified at 25 U.S.C. §§ 1751 et seq.

[226]　Pub. L. 101–503, Nov. 3, 1990, 104 Stat. 1292, codified at 25 U.S.C. §§ 1774 et seq.

[227]　Pub. L. 103–377, Oct. 19, 1994, 108 Stat. 3501, codified at 25 U.S.C. §§ 1775 et seq.

[228]　Tim Vollman, A Survey of Eastern Indian Land Claims, 1970–1979, 31 Me. L. Rev. 5, 9 (1979) (Passamoquoddy); id. at 11 (Oneida, Cayuga, St. Regis Mohawk, Catawba).

[229]　544 U.S. 197 (2004).

[230]　Kathryn E. Fort, The New Laches: Creating Title Where None Existed, 16 Geo. Mason L. Rev. 357 (2009).

[231]　City of Sherrill, N.Y. v. Oneida Indian Nation of New York, 544 U.S. 197, 202 (2005).

Nation sought immunity from local regulation and taxes on the land.[232] The Court rejected the claim, holding that too much time had passed since the Nation controlled the land and that the checker-boarded jurisdictional pattern that would have resulted from the immunities would undermine the settled regulatory framework.[233]

The Supreme Court applied a new form of equitable defense merging laches, acquiescence, and impossibility, to defeat the tribe's claim to a tax immunity.[234]

The Court relied on the case of *Felix v. Patrick*,[235] in which the Court had held that an *individual* Indian's land claim was invalid because of laches. The Court ignored a somewhat more recent case that was directly on point, *Ewert v. Bluejacket*,[236] which had held that equitable defenses do not apply to *tribal* claims.

In *Oneida II*, the Court upheld lower court decisions finding liability on the part of the counties and the State of New York against various defenses,[237] but explicitly left open the question of whether laches might serve to bar the land claims.[238] In response to the dissent from Justice Stevens arguing that the land claims should be dismissed on the basis of laches,[239] Justice Powell, writing for the majority, stated, "[I]t is questionable whether laches properly could be applied."[240]

Over the next several years, however, the Second Circuit applied the Sherrill reasoning to dismiss all but one of the remaining land claims of the Haudenosaunee nations in New York.[241] These land claims arose from transactions more than 200 years old. Haudenosaunee land claims had been successful on the merits in the lower courts, resulting in multiple judgments totaling millions of dollars. In dismissing the post-Sherrill claims, however,

---

[232] Id. at 211.

[233] Id. at 214.

[234] Id. at 217.

[235] 145 U.S. 317 (1892).

[236] 259 U.S. 129 (1922).

[237] Oneida County, N.Y. v. Oneida Indian Nation of New York, 470 U.S. 226, 236 (1985).

[238] Id. at 244.

[239] Id. at 258 (Stevens, J., dissenting).

[240] Id. at 244 n. 16.

[241] Cayuga Indian Nation v. Pataki, 413 F.3d 266 (2d Cir. 2005), cert. denied, 547 U.S. 1128 (2006); Oneida Indian Nation v. County of Oneida, 617 F.3d 114 (2d Cir. 2010), cert. denied, 565 U.S. 970 (2011); Onondaga Nation v. State of New York, 500 F. App'x 87 (2d Cir. 2012), cert. denied, 134 S.Ct. 419 (2013). See also Stockbridge-Munsee Community v. State of New York, 756 F.3d 163 (2d Cir. 2014), cert. denied, 135 S.Ct. 1492 (2015); Shinnecock Indian Nation v. State of New York, 628 Fed.Appx. 54 (2d Cir., Oct. 27, 2015), cert. denied, 136 S.Ct. 2512 (2016).

the Second Circuit used a theory that the disruption inherent in the claims must foreclose the claims on their face.

One land claim survived before a *Sherrill* defense—*Canadian St. Regis Band of Mohawk Indians v. State of New York*.[242] The Hogansburg Triangle area of the land claim did not disrupt non-Indian governance because the area was inhabited mostly by tribal members.[243]

Recently, the Oneida Indian Nation of New York entered into a massive agreement with the State of New York, and Madison and Oneida Counties, to conclude decades of vituperative litigation over land claims, property taxes, gaming, and other disputes.[244] Similarly, the St. Regis Mohawk Tribe entered into agreement with the State of New York and St. Lawrence County concluding land claims and resolving jurisdictional, taxation, and regulatory problems.[245]

§ 4.8   Historical Barriers to Indian Land Claims

The number of Indian land claims discussed in this chapter belies the incredible difficulties Indian nations have faced—and continue to face—in raising their claims to land in the courts. This chapter has already discussed jurisdictional, policy, and common law barriers. We now turn to other historical barriers, such as access to counsel and government records, and questions on the legal capacity of Indians to sue and to testify.

Justice Blackmun's wrote in *South Carolina v. Catawba Indian Tribe, Inc.*,[246] reconstructing an element of the legislative history behind the continuing extensions of the statute of limitations for land claims in the 1970s, that "Members of Congress emphasized repeatedly that Indian land claims were difficult to research, that Indians historically had lacked adequate legal assistance and administrative resources, and that the United States had not played its proper role in bringing suits on the Indians' behalf."[247]

---

[242] Nos. 5:82–CV–0783, 5:82–CV–1114, 5:89–CV–0829 (LEK/TWD), 2013 WL 3992830 (N.D. N.Y., July 23, 2013).

[243] Id. at *15–20.

[244] Memorandum Decision and Order, State of New York v. Jewell, No. 6:08–CV–0644 (LEK/DEP) (N.D. N.Y., March 4, 2014), https://turtletalk.files.wordpress.com/2014/03/341-order-dismissing-case.pdf.

[245] Memorandum of Understanding between the County of St. Lawrence, the Saint Regis Mohawk Tribe, and the State of New York (May 28, 2014), http://www.srmt-nsn.gov/_uploads/site_files/NYS–SRMT–SLC_MOU_Signed_5–28–14.pdf.

[246] 476 U.S. 498 (1986).

[247] Id. at 519 n. 6 (1986) (Blackmun, J., dissenting).

Often, tribes did not have resources or understanding of the legal system sufficient to bring successful claims, nor did their prospective attorneys.[248] The problem of hiring attorneys to bring complex suits against the federal government plagued Indian nations throughout the 19th and 20th centuries.[249]

While some states barred Indian nations from suing or Indian people from testifying, Indians and tribes did have the capacity to sue in more jurisdictions than is usually assumed.[250] But that assumption drove many Indians and tribes to not file suits to press their claims.[251]

In 1982, Congress enacted the Indian Claims Limitation Act of 1982.[252] Congress enacted the statute, in part, due to concerns that the United States faced massive liability for failure to prosecute tribal land claims.[253]

The statute provides a process by which an Indian nation may petition the Attorney General to investigate land claims, requiring the Department of Justice to decide whether to proceed with the claim. If the government declines, and publishes the rejection in the Federal Registration, the tribe has a year to file its own claim.

Though federal law requires the United States attorney to represent Indians in all suits at law and equity,[254] in 1978, the United States Attorney General Griffin Bell explicitly stated that he would not bring any land claims suits on behalf of Indian tribes or individual Indians because of the harm to the current landowners, who he claimed to be "innocent."[255]

Since the United States has only rarely chosen to decide at all, § 2415 land claims are effectively stalled forever.

---

[248] Richard B. Collins & Karla D. Miller, A People Without Law, 5 Indigenous L. J. 83, 85 (2006).

[249] Nancy Oestereich Lurie, The Indian Claims Commission Act, 311 Annals 56, 57 (1957).

[250] Id. at 117.

[251] Id.

[252] 28 U.S.C. § 2415.

[253] H.R. Rep. No. 97–954, at 6 (1982). See also Covelo Indian Community v. Watt, 551 F. Supp. 366 (D.D.C. 1982), aff'd, Nos. 82–2377, 82–2417, 1982 U.S. App. LEXIS 23138 (D.C. Cir. Dec. 21, 1982).

[254] 25 U.S.C. § 175.

[255] Letter from Griffin B. Bell, Attorney General, to Cecil B. Andrus, Secretary of Interior, reprinted at S. Rep. 96–569, at 12 (1980).

Chapter 5

THE FEDERAL-TRIBAL RELATIONSHIP

Analysis

The relationship between the United States and Indian nations and tribal citizens is unique, but usually described by courts and policymakers through the metaphor of a trust relationship. The relationship began with the earliest treaties between the United States and Indian nations, starting in 1778, and perhaps even earlier as the United States is a successor to hundreds of other treaties between other European nations and Indian nations. The earliest Supreme Court cases, following early treaty language, described the relationship in terms of a protectorate, with the superior sovereign agreeing to protect the inferior sovereigns. The tribes agreed to relinquish external sovereign authority, such as the power to enter into treaties with states or other foreign nations. Internal tribal sovereignty would remain extant.

However, the Supreme Court began to use the metaphor of a guardianship, a metaphor that quickly infiltrated American Indian affairs political discussion and rhetoric. Under this metaphor, the United States served as a "guardian" to its Indian "wards," akin to children who were incompetent to determine their own affairs. The guardian-ward metaphor still infuses much of Indian affairs policy and judicial decisionmaking. Eventually, by the 1970s, the federal government thoroughly rejected the old metaphors in favor of a trust relationship.

The trust relationship is both metaphorical and actual, as the United States owns and partially controls billions in tribal and individual Indian assets.

§ 5.1   Federal Recognition of Indian Nations

Indian tribes become federally recognized usually in one of three ways—an Act of Congress, federal administrative action, or by judicial decree.[1] Annually, the Secretary of the Interior must publish in the Federal Register a list of federally recognized tribes.[2]

Federal recognition as an Indian tribe is a necessary status for Indian nations to benefit from the federal trust responsibility. **See** § 5.2. There are currently 567 federally recognized tribes.[3] Indian nations with extant treaty relationships usually enjoyed federal recognition first, followed by tribes subject to Acts of Congress or Executive orders later ratified by Congress. Over 200 Alaska Native nations that remained under a cloud of uncertain recognition until 1993, when Assistant Interior Secretary Ada Deer formally published a list of 226 Alaska Native tribes recognized by the Interior Department.[4]

Prior to the 1960s, Indian tribes earned or acquired federal recognition on a case-by-case basis, usually through action by the Department of the Interior.[5] In the 19th century, the Supreme Court established that federal recognition decisions likely are not justiciable under the political question doctrine.[6] However, in *United States v. Sandoval*,[7] the Supreme Court placed a minimal limit on Congressional power to recognize Indian tribes by holding that Congress may not "arbitrarily" call any group except "distinctly Indian communities" a tribe.[8] Still, "even though modern law may not treat tribal existence purely as a political question, as such, it is clear that most courts give great deference to congressional and executive determinations of tribal status."[9]

The federal government first articulated standards on what would become known as federal recognition after the enactment of

---

[1]   Pub. L. 103–454, § 103(3), Nov. 2, 1994, 108 Stat. 4791.

[2]   25 U.S.C. § 5131.

[3]   Indian Entities Recognized and Eligible to Receive Services from the United States Bureau of Indian Affairs, 82 Fed. Reg. 4915 (Jan. 17, 2017).

[4]   David S. Case, Commentary on Sovereignty: The Other Alaska Native Claim, 25 J. Land Resources & Envtl. L. 149, 152–53 (2005).

[5]   United States General Accounting Office, Indian Issues—Improvements Needs in Tribal Recognition 3 (Nov. 2001).

[6]   United States v. Holliday, 70 U.S. 407, 419 (1865).

[7]   231 U.S. 28 (1913).

[8]   Id. at 46.

[9]   Masayesva v. Zah, 792 F. Supp. 1178, 1183–1185 (D. Ariz. 1992).

the Indian Reorganization Act in 1934,[10] which required the Secretary of the Interior to hold elections to allow tribes to opt in or reject the statute's provisions.[11] Still called the "Cohen criteria," after Felix S. Cohen, an architect of the IRA,[12] they are reprinted in the original edition of the *Handbook of Federal Indian Law*:

(1)   That the group has had treaty relations with the United States.

(2)   That the group has been denominated a tribe by act of Congress or Executive Order.

(3)   That the group has been treated as having collective rights in tribal lands or funds, even though not expressly designated a tribe.

(4)   That the group has been treated as a tribe or band by other Indian tribes.

(5)   That the group has exercised political authority over its members, through a tribal council or other governmental forms.

Other factors considered, though not conclusive, are the existence of special appropriation items of the group and the social solidarity of the group.[13]

Interior promulgated updated regulations in 1994[14] and then again in 2015.[15] Courts review federal recognition decisions made under the administrative recognition process under an arbitrary and capricious standard.[16]

The administrative process is so fraught that many tribes successfully earning federal recognition did so by directly petitioning Congress. Examples of Congressional recognition of Indian nations include the Pascua Yaqui Tribe of Arizona;[17]

---

[10]   Act of June 18, 1934, 48 Stat. 984, codified as amended at 25 U.S.C. §§ 52021 et seq.

[11]   25 U.S.C. § 5123.

[12]   59 Fed. Reg. 9280, 9283 (Feb. 25, 1994).

[13]   Felix S. Cohen, Handbook of Federal Indian Law 271 (1941).

[14]   Procedures for Establishing that an American Indian Group Exists as an Indian Tribe, 59 Fed. Reg. 9293 (Feb. 25, 1994).

[15]   Federal Acknowledgment of American Indian Tribes, 80 Fed. Reg. 37,862 (July 1, 2015), codified at 25 C.F.R. Part 83.

[16]   5 U.S.C. § 706(2)(A). E.g., Muwekma Ohlone Tribe v. Salazar, 708 F.3d 209, 220–223 (D.C. Cir. 2013); Samish Indian Nation v. United States, 419 F.3d 1355, 1369 (Fed. Cir. 2005); Cherokee Nation of Oklahoma v. Norton, 389 F.3d 1074, 1087 (10th Cir. 2004), cert. denied sub nom., Delaware Tribe of Indians v. Cherokee Nation of Oklahoma, 546 U.S. 812 (2005).

[17]   Pub. L. 95–375, Sept. 18, 1978, 92 Stat. 712.

Pokagon Band of Potawatomi Indians;[18] Little Traverse Bay Bands of Odawa Indians;[19] and the Little River Band of Ottawa Indians.[20] Moreover, following the end of the termination era, Congress began to restore to federal recognition many of the tribes it had previously terminated.[21]

The modern federal acknowledgment process, coupled with the authority granted to the Interior Department in the Indian Reorganization Act, have come together on occasion to allow the United States to interfere dramatically in the internal governance of Indian tribes. Under federal law, if an Indian tribe reorganizes in accordance with the Indian Reorganization Act, the Secretary of Interior must first approve the tribe's proposed constitution.[22] For tribes recently recognized or reorganized, this requirement allows the federal government to decide elemental questions of tribal law that should be decided by the tribe alone. Tribes should have exclusive authority over internal tribal matters such as membership requirements. Depending on an administration's political leanings, this approval requirement can do enormous damage to Indian tribes by creating artificial and arbitrary tribal membership requirements.

§ 5.2   Federal Trust Responsibility

The federal government's trust responsibility to Indian nations and Indian people constitutes a foundational basis for federal-tribal relations in the modern era. The scope of the federal trust responsibility largely is defined and controlled by statutes creating a federal trust obligation to individual Indians and Indian tribes that often can be enforced against the United States, sometimes incurring enormous liability on the United States. The United States also retains and recognizes a general trust obligation to Indians and tribes that justifies federal Indian affairs legislation and programs.

The relationship of Indian tribes to the United States is founded on "the settled doctrine of the law of nations" that when a stronger sovereign assumes authority over a weaker sovereign, the

---

[18] Restoration of Federal Services to the Pokagon Band of Potawatomi Indians, Pub. L. 103–323, Sept. 21, 1994, 108 Stat. 2152.

[19] Little Traverse Bay Bands of Odawa Indians and the Little River Band of Ottawa Indians Act, Pub. L. 103–324, Sept. 21, 1994, 108 Stat. 2156.

[20] Id.

[21] E.g., United Auburn Indian, Pub. L. 103–434, § 202, Oct. 31, 1994, 108 Stat. 4533. See generally Charles F. Wilkinson & Eric R. Biggs, The Evolution of the Termination Policy, 5 Am. Indian L. Rev. 139 (1977); Michael C. Walch, Note, Terminating the Indian Termination Policy, 35 Stanford L. Rev. 1181 (1983).

[22] 25 U.S.C. § 5123(a)(2), (d).

stronger one assumes a duty of protection for the weaker one, which does not surrender its right to self-government.[23]

Federal trust obligations arose in the formation of the relationship between the United States and Indian tribes. "Protection" was a term of art under international law that the Supreme Court in *Worcester v. Georgia*[24] interpreted in the context of treaties with Indian tribes to encapsulate the federal obligation to the tribes. "Protection" meant then and now that the United States agreed to a legal duty of preserving Indian and tribal property and autonomy to the maximum extent allowable in the national interest. In *Worcester*, the foundational Supreme Court case on federal Indian law, Chief Justice Marshall wrote that the concept of protection required the United States to prevent trespass against Indian lands and to protect reservation Indians from violence by outsiders: *"The Cherokees acknowledge themselves to be under the protection of the United States, and of no other power. Protection does not imply the destruction of the protected."*[25]

The *Worcester* Court, using the language of political partnership continued:

> The Indian nations were, from their situation, necessarily dependent on some foreign potentate for the supply of their essential wants, and for their protection from lawless and injurious intrusions into their country. That power was naturally termed their protector. . . . *This relation was that of a nation claiming and receiving the protection of one more powerful: not that of individuals abandoning their national character, and submitting as subjects to the laws of a master."*[26]

"Protection" is best characterized as the external relationship between unequal sovereigns. In exchange, Indian nations agreed to turn over their exterior sovereignty—that is, the right to enter into treaties with foreign powers—to the United States. As Father Francis Paul Prucha, the leading historian on Indian treaties declared, "In such treaties the Indians agreed to submission to the United States *in their external political affairs."*[27]

---

[23] Worcester v. Georgia, 31 U.S. 515, 551–56, 560–61 (1832); see also United States v. Candelaria, 271 U.S. 432, 442 (1926) (Congress "was but continuing the policy which prior governments had deemed essential to the protection of such Indians.").

[24] 31 U.S. 515 (1832).

[25] Id. at 551–52 (emphasis added).

[26] Id. at 555 (emphasis added).

[27] Francis Paul Prucha, American Indian Treaties: The History of a Political Anomaly 6 (1994) (emphasis added).

The federal trust obligation is sacred to Indian nations, as sacred as the treaties where the trust relationship originates.[28] The federal obligation to protect tribal interests is limited only by "the overriding interests of the National Government as when the tribes seek to engage in foreign relations, alienate their lands to non-Indians without federal consent, or prosecute non-Indians in tribal courts which do not accord the full protections of the Bill of Rights."[29] The United States undertook duties to Indian tribes through recognizing their status as being under the "protection" of the federal government.

Numerous court cases have recognized Congress's general obligation of "protection" first recognized in Indian treaties to all tribes and all instances of federal legislation intending to implement federal duties. The protection theory of Indian treaties finds its way into numerous court decisions. For example, the Puget Sound and Great Lakes Indian nations relied upon the United States to protect its fishing areas.[30] The so-called "bad men" clause of several 1860s treaties in which the United States and Indian nations divided up their law and order obligations has its root in the protection theory.[31]

Guardian-Ward Relationship

During the 19th and early 20th centuries, the United States frequently described the federal-tribal relationship as akin to a guardianship, with the United States acting as a guarding to its tribal and Indian wards. During this period, federal plenary power over Indian affairs reached its apex, with Congress and the Executive branch interfering with internal tribal affairs and Indian property interests to an unprecedented extent, and the Supreme Court rarely interfering in the policy choices of the United States. See § 3.7. The guardianship theory of federal-tribal affairs is no longer the dominant political view of the United States.

In the Cherokee cases, Chief Justice Marshall, writing for himself and one other Justice, initially referred to the relationship between Indians and the United States as "resembl[ing] that of a

---

[28] See generally Robert A. Williams, Jr., Linking Arms Together: American Indian Treaty Visions of Law and Peace, 1600–1800 (1997).

[29] Washington v. Confederated Tribes of the Colville Indian Reservation, 447 U.S. 134, 153–54 (1980).

[30] Washington v. Washington State Commercial Passenger Fishing Vessel Assn., 443 U.S. 658, 667 (1979); United States v. Michigan, 471 F. Supp. 192, 206 (W.D. Mich. 1979), modified, 653 F.2d 277 (6th Cir.), cert. denied, 454 U.S. 1124 (1981); United States v. Washington, 384 F. Supp. 312, 401 (W.D. Wash. 1974), aff'd, 520 F.2d 676 (9th Cir. 1975), cert. denied, 423 U.S. 1086 (1976).

[31] E.g., Tsosie v. United States, 825 F.2d 393, 399 (10th Cir. 1987).

ward to his guardian."[32] But a year later, backed by a 5–1 majority of the Court, he wrote that "Indian nations [were] distinct political communities, having territorial boundaries, within which their authority is exclusive, and having a right to all the lands within those boundaries, which is not only acknowledged, but guarantied by the United States."[33] In short, Congress's obligations related to the external sovereignty of Indian nations.

As the fortunes of Indians and tribes declined throughout the rest of the 19th century and early 20th century,[34] Congress and the Supreme Court asserted greater authority over the internal sovereignty of Indian nations as well.[35] The Supreme Court adopted a position extremely deferential to Congressional judgment on Indian affairs legislation closely aligned with the political question doctrine that was firmly rooted in the guardian-ward model of Indian affairs.[36] In short, applying a guardianship model of Indian affairs, the Supreme Court would decline to review Congressional enactments in Indian affairs—even where they effectuated a taking of Indian and tribal property, for example—so long as Congress acted in "good faith."[37]

Congress began its slow retreat from the guardianship model in 1934 when it enacted the Indian Reorganization Act.[38] The Act, for the first time in Indian affairs history, sought tribal consent to the statute's operating provisions.[39] While Congress continued to vacillate on Indian affairs through the middle part of the 20th century, by 1975 the United States recognized "the obligation of the United States to respond to the strong expression of the Indian people for self-determination by assuring maximum Indian participation in the direction of . . . Federal services to Indian communities. . . ."[40] The United States has remained committed to

---

[32]   Cherokee Nation v. Georgia, 30 U.S. 1, 17 (1831) (Marshall, C.J., lead opinion).

[33]   Worcester v. Georgia, 31 U.S. 515, 557 (1832).

[34]   See generally Angie Debo, A History of the Indians of the United States 284–331 (1970).

[35]   E.g., Major Crimes Act, Act of March 3, 1885, 23 Stat. 385 (extending federal criminal jurisdiction to on-reservation crimes between Indians); General Allotment Act, Feb. 8, 1887, 24 Stat. 388 (authorizing the Secretary of Interior to subdivide Indian reservations and alienate "surplus" lands).

[36]   E.g., Lone Wolf v. Hitchcock, 187 U.S. 553, 565 (1903); United States v. Kagama, 118 U.S. 375, 384 (1886).

[37]   Lone Wolf v. Hitchcock, 187 U.S. 553, 565–66 (1903).

[38]   Act of June 18, 1934, 48 Stat. 984, codified as amended at 25 U.S.C. §§ 5101 et seq.

[39]   25 U.S.C. § 5123(a)(1).

[40]   25 U.S.C. § 5131(a).

tribal self-determination, and continues to recognize that its obligations to Indians and tribes is in the nature of a trust.[41]

Similarly, the Supreme Court significantly retreated from analyzing the federal obligations to Indians and tribes using the guardianship model. In the 1970s, the Court acknowledged that would apply a form of judicial review of Congressional Indian affairs enactments that asked if the law had a rational basis in relation to Congress's obligations to Indians and tribes under the Fifth Amendment's Due Process or Takings Clauses.[42] No longer does the Court defer to federal executive and legislative actions to the extent it did under the guardianship model, for better or worse.

The Supreme Court also moved toward applying the principles of common law trust doctrine to Congress's enactments in relation to Indians and tribes. Congress's waiver of federal immunity from suit works a dramatic change in the Court's analysis of Congressional Indian affairs enactments. In *United States v. Sioux Nation*,[43] the Supreme Court distinguished *Lone Wolf* in Indian property takings cases because Congress had expressly waived federal immunity from suit to allow the Sioux Nation to sue to recover damages for the taking of the Black Hills.[44] Likewise, in *United States v. Mitchell*,[45] involving Congressional waivers of immunity such as the Indian Tucker Act,[46] the Court recognized that the federal government's control over tribal resources may give rise to a fiduciary duty arising out of common law trust principles that mandates compensation in the event of a breach of duty.[47]

The cases show that the Supreme Court has rejected the *Lone Wolf*-era political question analysis completely, recognized general Congressional waivers of federal immunity from suits to recover damages for the taking of Indian and tribal property, and acknowledged that Congress's legislative authority in Indian affairs is restricted by the Constitution. As such, the Supreme Court has

---

[41] E.g., Tribal Self-Governance Act, 25 U.S.C. § 5366(b); American Indian trust Fund Management Reform Act, 25 U.S.C. § 4041(1)–(3); Native American Housing Assistance and Self-Determination Act, 25 U.S.C. § 4101(3)–(4).

[42] E.g., Morton v. Mancari, 417 U.S. 535, 555 (1974); Delaware Tribal Business Committee v. Weeks, 430 U.S. 73, 85 (1977).

[43] 448 U.S. 371 (1980).

[44] Id. at 414.

[45] 463 U.S. 206 (1983).

[46] 28 U.S.C. § 1505.

[47] 463 U.S. 206, 225–26 (1983).

acknowledged "the undisputed existence of a general trust relationship between the United States and the Indian people."[48]

General Trust Relationship

The modern understanding of the relationship between Indian nations and the United States that began with "protection" is often referred to as the general trust relationship.[49] The general trust relationship simply obligates and authorizes the federal government to protect tribal and Indian property rights, preserve and enhance tribal self-governance, guarantee law and order in Indian country, and provide government services to Indian people. The modern Congress usually states explicit recognition of its general trust relationship when passing legislation designed for Indians and tribes.[50] "Nearly every piece of modern legislation dealing with Indian tribes contains a statement reaffirming the trust relationship between tribes and the federal government."[51]

The general trust relationship imposes upon the United States a duty to safeguard the property rights of individual Indians and Indian tribes, imposing upon the federal government the highest fiduciary duty. In *Seminole Nation v. United States*,[52] the Supreme Court expressed that it would hold the United States to the "most exacting fiduciary standards" when administering tribal assets:

> In carrying out its treaty obligations with the Indian tribes the Government is something more than a mere contracting party. Under a humane and self imposed policy which has found expression in many acts of Congress and numerous decisions of this Court, it has charged itself with moral obligations of the highest responsibility and trust. Its conduct, as disclosed in the acts of those who represent it in dealings with the Indians, should therefore be judged by the most exacting fiduciary standards.[53]

---

[48]   United States v. Mitchell, 463 U.S. 206, 225 (1983); see also United States v. Jicarilla Apache Nation, 564 U.S. 162, 176 (2011); United States v. White Mountain Apache Tribe, 537 U.S. 465, 475 n. 3 (2003).

[49]   Felix S. Cohen, Handbook of Federal Indian Law xi, xiii (1941).

[50]   E.g., Indian Child Welfare Act, 25 U.S.C. § 1901(2)–(3); Indian Self-Determination and Education Assistance Act, 25 U.S.C. § 5301(a); id., 25 U.S.C. § 5301(b); Tribal Law and Order Act, Pub. L. 111–211, § 202(a), July 29, 2010, 124 Stat. 2258; Native American Housing Assistance and Self-Determination Act, 25 U.S.C. § 4101(2)–(4).

[51]   Cohen's Handbook of Federal Indian Law § 5.04[4][a], at 420–421 (2005 ed.), quoted in United States v. Jicarilla Apache Nation, 564 U.S. 162, 192–93 (2011) (Sotomayor, J., dissenting).

[52]   316 U.S. 286 (1942).

[53]   Id. at 297 (footnote omitted).

The United States has enacted legislation designed to protect tribal and Indian property rights since at least the First Congress, which passed the first version of the Non-Intercourse Act in the Trade and Intercourse Act of 1790.[54] **See § 3.1**. More modern enactments allow the Interior Secretary to acquire land in trust for the benefit of Indians and tribes.[55] Reservation and trust land may not be alienated from an Indian or Indian nation without the consent of the federal government, and is generally immune from state and local regulation and taxation.[56]

Another important aspect of the general trust relationship is that it imposes upon the federal government a duty to preserve tribal self-governance and autonomy. Professor Charles F. Wilkinson likened the treaty relationship that originated the general trust relationship as a kind of "measured separatism."[57] At the core of measured separatism is the protection for individual Indians and tribal governments from interference by state and local governments, and private persons and entities as well. It is probably the most critical aspect of the "protection" the federal government agreed to provide Indians and tribes in treaties and statutes. A necessary corollary to the federal duty to protect tribal autonomy requires the United States to safeguard and support tribal governments.

The duty to preserve tribal autonomy is an ancient one. In *Worcester v. Georgia*,[58] the Court described how treaties established the autonomy of tribes.[59] In treaty times, Indian nations contracted with the United States to remain outside of state authority and control.[60] The very fact that the President and the Senate engaged in treaty-making with Indian nations is recognition of the sovereignty and right to self-governance of all Indian tribes. The Supreme Court also has recognized that Indian nations' right to

---

[54]   An Act to regulate trade and intercourse with the Indian tribes, July 22, 1790, 1 Stat. 137, now codified as amended at 25 U.S.C. §§ 177, 261–265; 18 U.S.C. § 1152. The protective purpose of the Act is clear: "The Indian Nonintercourse Act, 25 U.S.C. § 177, has been perhaps the most significant congressional enactment regarding Indian lands. The Act's overriding purpose is the protection of Indian lands." United States for and on behalf of Santa Ana Indian Pueblo v. University of New Mexico, 731 F.2d 703, 706 (10th Cir.) (citation omitted), cert. denied, 469 U.S. 853 (1984).

[55]   25 U.S.C. § 5108.

[56]   E.g., 25 U.S.C. § 5108 ("Title to any lands or rights acquired pursuant to this Act . . . shall be taken in the name of the United States in trust for the Indian tribe or individual Indian for which the land is acquired, and such lands or rights shall be exempt from State and local taxation.").

[57]   Charles F. Wilkinson, American Indians, Time, and the Law 14 (1987).

[58]   31 U.S. 515 (1831).

[59]   Id. at 595.

[60]   E.g., DeCoteau v. District Court, 420 U.S. 425, 431 (1975).

self-governance predates the establishment of the American Republic, and does not require recognition through the treaty process.[61] Alaska Native tribes, for example, have no treaty with the United States, but still retain the right to self-government, and the federal government is obligated to protect it.[62]

Since the announcement of the self-determination era by Presidents Johnson and Nixon, the United States has engaged in a complicated Indian affairs policy that provides greater governmental authority for tribal governments while maintaining the general trust relationship.[63] The Nixon Administration and later Administrations proposed and oversaw the adoption of numerous statutes in which Congress finally allowed Indian tribes to take over federal Indian affairs programs.[64] The 1975 Indian Self-Determination and Education Assistance Act[65] is the core statute of this era. The Congressional statement of policy accompanying the statute is the clearest statement supporting tribal autonomy the United States could have expressed:

> The Congress declares its commitment to the maintenance of the Federal Government's unique and continuing relationship with, and responsibility to, individual Indian tribes and to the Indian people as a whole through the establishment of a meaningful Indian self-determination policy that will permit an orderly transition from the Federal domination of programs for, and services to, Indians to effective and meaningful participation by the Indian people in the planning, conduct, and administration of those programs and services. In accordance with this policy, the United States is committed to supporting and assisting Indian tribes in the development of strong and stable governments, capable of administering quality programs and developing the economies of their respective communities.[66]

---

[61] E.g., NLRB v. Pueblo of San Juan, 276 F.3d 1186, 1192 (10th Cir. 2002); Poodry v. Tonawanda Band of Seneca Indians, 85 F.3d 874, 880–81 (2d Cir.), cert. denied, 519 U.S. 1041 (1996); John v. Baker, 982 P.2d 738, 751 (Alaska 1999).

[62] Cf. Alaska Pacific Fisheries v. United States, 248 U.S. 78, 88–89 (1918).

[63] Stephen Cornell & Joseph P. Kalt, American Indian Self-Determination: The Political Economy of a Policy that Works, HKS Faculty Research Working Paper Series RWP10–043, John F. Kennedy School of Government, Harvard University, at 17 (Nov. 2010).

[64] See generally Philip S. Deloria, The Era of Indian Self-Determination: An Overview, in Indian Self-Rule: First-Hand Accounts of Indian-White Relations from Roosevelt to Reagan 191 (Kenneth R. Philp, ed. 1986).

[65] Pub. L. 93–638, Jan. 4, 1975, 88 Stat. 2203, codified as amended at 25 U.S.C. §§ 5301 et seq.

[66] 25 U.S.C. § 5301.

Finally, the general trust relationship obligates and authorizes the United States to enact a wide variety of statutes designed to provide governmental services to Indian people at least equal to those provided to other American citizens by their states. The federal government's trust obligation to provide services deriving from its original treaty obligations now takes form in the multitude of statutes detailing federal services provision to Indians and tribes. The courts read these statutes and the public policy behind them broadly in light of the trust responsibility.[67]

The federal government's obligation to provide several additional services, including education, health care, housing, and public safety, is discussed below.

Education

In numerous instances, Indian leaders negotiated for the provision of education of their children.[68] Some early reservation schools educated a generation of Indian leaders that negotiated a second round of treaties, continuing to negotiate for education resources in the treaty process.[69] From the earliest Indian law decisions, the Supreme Court recognized that the United States had undertaken an obligation to provide educational services to Indian people.[70] "Over 110 Indian treaties stipulated that the federal government shall provide an education to the members of the signatory tribes."[71]

Congress's enactment of the Indian Self-Determination and Education Assistance Act,[72] was designed to reverse federal control over Indian lives, allowing Indian tribes to "gain[ ] greater control over the primary and secondary education of their children."[73] The Act authorized Indian tribe to contract with the federal government to provide their own educational services, formerly administered by the United States.[74] In places, the tribal control over Indian

---

[67] Morton v. Ruiz, 415 U.S. 199, 236 (1974).

[68] E.g., Treaty with the Makah, art. 11, Jan. 31, 1855, 12 Stat. 939.

[69] E.g., James M. McClurken, Augustin Hamlin, Jr.: Ottawa Identity and the Politics of Persistence, in Being and Becoming Indian: Biographical Studies of North American Frontiers 82 (James A. Clifton ed. 1989).

[70] E.g., United States v. Shoshone Tribe of Indians of Wind River Reservation in Wyoming, 304 U.S. 111, 114–14 (1938).

[71] Raymond L. Cross, American Indian Education: The Terror of History and the Nation's Debt to the Indian Peoples, 21 U. Ark. Little Rock L. Rev. 941, 950 (1998/1999).

[72] Pub. L. 93–638, Jan. 4, 1975, 88 Stat. 2203.

[73] Harvard Project on American Indian Economic Development, The State of Native Nations: Conditions under U.S. Policies of Self-Determination 199 (2008).

[74] 25 U.S.C. § 5321.

education has been a dramatic improvement over federal administration.

Health Care

One of the largest federal agencies providing services to American Indians is the Indian Health Service. The federal duty to provide health care to Indian people originates in many Indian treaties.[75]

The provision of health care services to Indian people began in the earliest decades of the American Republic. It appears that the federal government's early motivation was a cynical one—to prevent the spread of contagious diseases like smallpox from Indian people to non-Indians.[76]

The Snyder Act of 1921[77] serves as the original national incarnation of the federal government's authorization and obligation to provide health care services. Then, the United States instructed health care programs to be administered by the Bureau of Indian Affairs.[78] In 1955, Congress transferred primary federal responsibility for Indian health care administration to the Indian Health Service.[79]

The Indian Health Care Improvement Act of 1976 now governs the provision of health care services to Indian people.[80] Congress found that "Federal health services to maintain and improve the health of the Indians are consonant with and required by the

---

[75] E.g., Treaty with the Makah, art. 11, Jan. 31, 1855, 12 Stat. 939; United States v. Michigan, 471 F. Supp. 192, 234 (W.D. 1979), modified, 653 F.2d 277 (6th Cir.), cert. denied, 454 U.S. 1124 (1981).

[76] Betty Pfefferbaum, Rennard Strickland, Everett R. Rhoades and Rose L. Pfefferbaum, Learning How to Heal: An Analysis of the History, Policy, and Framework of Indian Health Care, 20 Am. Indian L. Rev. 366, 368–69 (1995/1996); Indian Health Care Improvement Act, Hearings before the Subcommittee on Health and the Environment of the House Committee on Interstate and Foreign Commerce, 94th Cong., 2d Sess. 65 (1976) (Statement of Everett R. Rhoades, M.D., President, Assn. of American Indian Physicians).

[77] Pub. L. 67–85, Nov. 21, 1921, 42 Stat. 208, codified at 25 U.S.C. § 13.

[78] Koral E. Fusselman, Note, Native American Health Care: Is the Indian Health Care Reauthorization and Improvement Act of 2009 Enough to Address Persistent Health Problems within the Native American Community?, 18 Wash. & Lee J. Civil Rts. & Soc. Just. 389, 395 (2012).

[79] Transfer Act, Pub. L. 83–568, § 1, 68 Stat. 674 (1954). See also Betty Pfefferbaum, Rennard Strickland, Everett R. Rhoades and Rose L. Pfefferbaum, Learning How to Heal: An Analysis of the History, Policy, and Framework of Indian Health Care, 20 Am. Indian L. Rev. 366, 382 (1995/1996).

[80] Pub. L. 94–437, 90 Stat. 1400, codified in part at 25 U.S.C. §§ 1601 et seq. Later amendments are discussed in Koral E. Fusselman, Note, Native American Health Care: Is the Indian Health Care Reauthorization and Improvement Act of 2009 Enough to Address Persistent Health Problems within the Native American Community?, 18 Wash. & Lee J. Civil Rts. & Soc. Just. 389, 397–401 (2012).

Federal Government's historical and unique legal relationship with, and resulting responsibility to, the American Indian people."[81]

Housing

The general trust relationship also requires the federal government to provide adequate housing to Indian people. Several Indian treaties provide for housing and shelter.[82] In 1996, Congress enacted the Native American Housing Assistance and Self-Determination Act.[83]

Public Safety

The federal government's obligation to provide for law and order in Indian country dates back to the earliest treaties and Congressional enactments. President Washington's policy statements articulated an early recognition of the United States' obligation to ensure law and order in Indian country.[84]

Some early treaties recognized inherent tribal sovereignty to prosecute all persons within Indian country, and provided that the United States would protect reservation boundaries.[85] Other treaties provided for the sharing of jurisdiction over lawbreakers.[86] Importantly, some treaties include the so-called "bad men" clause, similarly dividing jurisdiction over lawbreakers between the federal government and tribes.[87]

The United States quickly provided for federal statutory authorization for the exercise of criminal jurisdiction in Indian country. The first Trade and Intercourse Act made it a federal crime to "go into any town, settlement, or territory belonging to any

[81]   25 U.S.C. § 3302(7).

[82]   See generally Virginia Davis, A Discovery of Sorts: Reexamining the Origins of the Federal Indian Housing Obligation, 18 Harv. Black Letter L. J. 211 (2002).

[83]   Pub. L. 104–330, Oct. 26, 1996, 110 Stat. 4017, codified at 25 U.S.C. §§ 4101 et seq.

[84]   Seventh Annual Address of President George Washington, 1 Messages and Papers of the Presidents, 1789–1897, at 181, 185 (James D. Richardson, ed., 1897).

[85]   E.g., Treaty with the Delawares, art. 4, Sept. 17, 1778, 7 Stat. 13; Treaty of Hopewell, art. 5, Nov. 28, 1785, 7 Stat. 18; id. art. 9; Treaty with the Choctaw, art. 4, Jan 3, 1786, 7 Stat. 21; Treaty with the Chickasaw, art. 4, Jan. 10, 1786, 7 Stat. 24; Treaty with the Shawnees, art. 7, Jan. 31, 1786, 7 Stat. 26; Treaty of Greenville, art. VI, Aug. 3, 1795, 7 Stat. 49.

[86]   E.g., Treaty with the Sauk and Foxes, art. 4, Nov. 3, 1804, 7 Stat. 84; Treaty with the Florida Tribes of Indians, art. 4, Sept. 18, 1823, 7 Stat. 224; Treaty with the Kansa, art. 10, June 3, 1825, 7 Stat. 244; Treaty with the Ponca, art. 4, June 9, 1825, 7 Stat. 247; Treaty with the Sioune Oglala Tribes, art. 4, July 5, 1825, 7 Stat. 252.

[87]   E.g., Treaty with the Sioux, art. 1, April 29, 1868, 15 Stat. 635; Treaty with the Crows, art. 1, May 7, 1868, 15 Stat. 649; Treaty with the Navajo, art. 1, June 1, 1868, 15 Stat. 667.

nation or tribe of Indians, and ... commit any crime upon, or trespass, against, the person or property of any Indian. ..."[88] Congress continued to expand federal criminal jurisdiction through the enactment of the final Trade and Intercourse Act in 1834.[89] Congress later enacted the Major Crimes Act[90] and other relevant statutes to govern criminal law enforcement. **See § 7.4.**

Despite the early federalization of Indian country law enforcement, Congress did not expressly acknowledge its trust obligation to provide for public safety to Indians and tribes until 2010. Then, Congress passed the Tribal Law and Order Act and affirmed its trust obligation.[91] Section 202 of the Act reads: "Congress finds that ... (1) the United States has distinct legal, treaty, and trust obligations to provide for the public safety of Indian country. ..."[92] The Justice Department had recognized a trust obligation some years before.[93]

The judiciary has accepted the general trust relationship as a justification for the federalization of Indian country criminal jurisdiction.[94]

Federal Liability for Breach of Trust

The judiciary will enforce specific federal trust duties, often imposing significant liability on the United States for breach of trust. The legal test for Indian nations to successfully seek money damages or other relief against the federal government is stringent, however. First, the tribal plaintiff must demonstrate that a federal statute has created an explicit federal duty or obligation, and that that duty or obligation was breached. Second, the tribal plaintiff must show that the statute mandates compensation for its violation.

Mitchell I and *II*

United States v. Mitchell I[95] and *II*[96] arose from the timber-rich Quinault Reservation in the State of Washington near the Pacific

---

[88]   Act of July 22, 1790, 1 Stat. 137 (1790).

[89]   Act of June 30, 1834, ch. 161, § 25, 4 Stat. 729, codified as amended at 18 U.S.C. § 1152 (now known as the Indian Country Crimes Act).

[90]   Act of March 3, 1885, 23 Stat. 385, codified as amended at 18 U.S.C. § 1153.

[91]   Pub. L. 111–211, § 201, July 29, 2010, 124 Stat. 2258.

[92]   Id.

[93]   Janet Reno, The Tribal-Federal Partnership, Nation to Nation (Dep't of Justice, Office of Tribal Justice), Aug. 1996, at 1.

[94]   E.g., United States v. Wadena, 152 F.3d 831, 847 (8th Cir. 1998); LaPier v. McCormick, 986 F.2d 303, 305 (9th Cir. 1993). Cf. United States v. Antelope, 430 U.S. 641, 669 (1977) ("Congress has undoubted constitutional power to prescribe a criminal code applicable in Indian country. . . .").

[95]   United States v. Mitchell, 445 U.S. 535 (1980) (Mitchell I).

[96]   United States v. Mitchell, 463 U.S. 206 (1983) (Mitchell II).

coast, and the federal government's consent to the substantial deforestation of the reservation on behalf of private interests. In 1971, Helen Mitchell and more than 500 Quinault Indians sued the United States "for what were alleged to be flagrant and pervasive waste and mismanagement in federal handling of timber sales on the Quinault Reservation."[97] At the time of the creation of the reservation, 98 percent of reservation was covered in forests too thick to allow tribal members access.[98] In 1905, despite the thick forests, the government began the allotment process.[99] Federal legislation authorized the Interior Department to sell timber from allotted lands, with the government administering that process.[100] Decades later, much of the Quinault Reservation had been deforested, generating untold wealth, but with little benefit to tribal members.

The Mitchell plaintiffs sued in the Court of Claims to recover damages for the loss of the timber wealth and the misadministration of the logging enterprises.[101] The Mitchell plaintiffs sued under a theory that the government's actions constituted a compensable breach of duty owed them by the government under the General Allotment Act of 1887.[102] Section 1 of the Act authorized the Executive branch to allot each reservation, while Section 5 established that the United States would retain title to each allotted parcel for 25 years after the initial allotment.[103]

Federal control over reservation resources without accountability to the Indian nations and people was pervasive at that time. The federal guardianship theory of Indian affairs dominated the era, and the Interior Department was used to acquiring pro forma consent from Indian people without offering adequate advice or consultation.

In *Mitchell I*, the Supreme Court held that the General Allotment Act did not unambiguously create a fiduciary duty relating to the federal management of the allotted lands. The Court first noted that the federal statute must be unambiguous when

---

[97] Richard W. Hughes, Can the Trustee Be Sued for Its Breach: the Sad Saga of United States v. Mitchell, 26 S.D. L. Rev. 447, 447 (1981).

[98] Id. at 448–49 (citing Quinault Allottee Assn. v. United States, 485 F.2d 1391, 1393 (Ct. Cl. 1973), cert. denied, 416 U.S. 961 (1974)).

[99] Richard W. Hughes, Can the Trustee Be Sued for Its Breach: the Sad Saga of United States v. Mitchell, 26 S.D. L. Rev. 447, 449 (1981).

[100] 25 U.S.C. §§ 406–407.

[101] Mitchell v. United States, 591 F.2d 1300 (Ct. Cl. 1979), rev'd, 445 U.S. 535 (1980).

[102] 24 Stat. 388, codified at 25 U.S.C. §§ 331 et seq., repealed Pub. L. 106–462, Title I, § 106(a)(1), Nov. 7, 2000, 114 Stat. 2007.

[103] United States v. Mitchell, 445 U.S. 535, 540–41 (1980).

establishing a federal trust duty.[104] Ironically, the Court held that the Indian allottee was in control of the timber resources on his or her allotment.[105] The Court then held that the legislative history of the allotment act confirmed that the intent of the statute was to place control in an allotment's resources with Indian people.[106] Of course, none of this was realistic.

The Court remanded for consideration by the lower court whether "other statutes might provide a basis for liability,"[107] leading to *Mitchell II*. And so in 1983, the Supreme Court held in *Mitchell II* that the government did retain control over Quinault allotment timber and imposed liability on the government for breach of trust.[108] The Court held that federal timber management statutes and regulations unambiguously created a fiduciary duty, the breach of which created a compensable claim against the government by the beneficiaries. The Court characterized the government's role in managing the timber resources of the Quinault Reservation as "pervasive."[109] As noted earlier, the Quinault plaintiffs pointed out that the government controlled all aspects of the timber sales.

The Court's reasoning initially focused on the law, rather than the practice. In this instance, the law and practice conformed to each other. First, the Court found that "Indians had no right to sell timber on reservation land ..." until 1910, when Congress expressly authorized the sale of timber.[110] The Court then focused on the practice and history, and determined that the Department of Interior asserted nigh-absolute control over timber sales.[111]

Returning to the law, the Court pointed out that later federal statutes required the Interior Secretary to take on even "stricter duties ... with respect to timber management...."[112] In 1934, as part of the Indian Reorganization Act, Congress "expressly directed that the Interior Department manage Indian forest resources 'on the principle of sustained-yield management.'"[113] Related regulations provided for a sustained yield and long-term

---

[104] United States v. Mitchell, 445 U.S. 535, 542 (1980).

[105] Id. at 542–43.

[106] Id. at 543.

[107] Gregory C. Sisk, Litigation with the Federal Government § 4.07(b), at 283 (4th ed. 2006).

[108] United States v. Mitchell, 463 U.S. 206, 226 (1983).

[109] Id. at 219.

[110] Id. (citing Act of June 25, 1910, ch. 431, §§ 7–8, 36 Stat. 855, 857, codified as amended, 25 U.S.C. §§ 406–407).

[111] Id. at 220.

[112] Id.

[113] Id. at 221 (discussing 25 U.S.C. § 466, now codified at 25 U.S.C. § 5109).

preservation of the timber resource.[114] In 1964, Congress again imposed timber management rules on the Interior Department, requiring the Secretary to manage timber resources for the highest benefit possible for present and future Indian generations.[115]

Three years previously, the Supreme Court had interpreted these timber resource management rules in *White Mountain Apache Tribe v. Bracker*.[116] **See § 8.5.** The *Mitchell II* Court referred to that case to reach the conclusion that the Interior Department " 'exercises literally daily supervision over the harvesting and management of tribal timber.' . . . Virtually every stage of the process is under federal control."[117]

This control over tribal and Indian resources, for the Court, created a fiduciary duty, the breach of which was compensable in the form of money damages. The facts of this case presented the Court with the elements of a common law trust—a trustee, a beneficiary, and a trust corpus.[118] The general trust relationship further cemented the government's obligations as a trustee to tribal and Indian resources.[119]

Once the Court concluded that a fiduciary duty existed, the Court drew from the common law of trusts to determine whether a breach of the duty was compensable. The government's view— raised here and elsewhere—was that breaches of trust were not compensable under a guardian-ward theory of governance. The Court rejected that notion, finding that the establishment of a fiduciary duty required the application of common law trust principles, which allowed for compensation.[120]

United States v. White Mountain Apache Tribe

In *United States v. White Mountain Apache Tribe*,[121] the Supreme Court held that the United States was liable for failing to manage assets held in trust, Fort Apache, for the benefit of the tribe in accordance with a federal statutory mandate.

In 1960, a federal statute addressed the status of the Fort Apache Military Reservation,[122] which had been established by the

---

[114] Id.

[115] Id. at 222.

[116] White Mountain Apache Tribe v. Bracker, 448 U.S. 134 (1980).

[117] United States v. Mitchell, 463 U.S. 206, 222 (1983) (quoting White Mountain Apache Tribe v. Bracker, 448 U.S. 136, 147 (1980)).

[118] Id. at 224–25.

[119] Id. at 225 (citations omitted).

[120] Id. at 226.

[121] 537 U.S. 465 (2003).

[122] Pub. L. 86–392, Mar. 16, 1960, 74 Stat. 8 (1960).

American military in the 1870s within Apache territory.[123] The Fort Apache military post served as a means of control over the White Mountain Apache people for about six decades, 1870 until 1922.[124] The military also oversaw the mass dispossession of Indian lands and resources during this period.[125] In 1923, the fort became a Bureau of Indian Affairs boarding school named after President Theodore Roosevelt, and the school engaged in abusive efforts to destroy Apache culture.[126]

In the 1960 statute placed the land and buildings in trust for the benefit of the tribe until the Interior Secretary ceased using the property for administrative or school purposes.[127] The government continued using the property but by 1998, the fort was listed as one of the 100 most endangered national monuments.[128] The tribe commissioned an engineering study in 1993 that determined it would cost $14 million to rehabilitate the property.[129]

The Supreme Court held that the government's occupation and use of the fort created a fiduciary duty.[130] The government argued that the 1960 statute did not establish a compensable fiduciary duty, but the Court again drew upon the common law of trusts to conclude that the United States was obliged to prevent spoilage of the property.[131]

Navajo I and II

Decided on the same day as *White Mountain Apache, United States v. Navajo Nation (Navajo I)*[132] reached an opposite conclusion, holding that the Indian Mineral Leasing Act[133] did not create a compensable fiduciary duty.

The Navajo Nation reservation contains vast natural resource wealth that has been exploited to great profit, but relatively little of that profit has inured to the people of the Navajo Nation.

The United States later enacted the Indian Mineral Leasing Act of 1938.[134] The Act authorized Indian tribes, with Secretarial

---

[123] John R. Welch & Ramon Riley, Reclaiming Land and Spirit in the Western Apache Homeland, 25:1 Am. Indian Q. 5, 5 (2001).
[124] Id. at 7.
[125] Id. at 6–7.
[126] Id. at 7–8.
[127] Pub. L. 86–392, Mar. 16, 1960, 74 Stat. 8 (1960).
[128] United States v. White Mountain Apache Tribe, 537 U.S. 465, 469 (2003).
[129] Id.
[130] Id. at 475.
[131] Id. at 475–76.
[132] 537 U.S. 488 (2003).
[133] Act of May 11, 1938, 52 Stat. 347, codified at 25 U.S.C. § 396a.
[134] Act of May 11, 1938, 52 Stat. 347, codified at 25 U.S.C. § 396a.

approval, to lease unallotted tribal lands for mineral extraction purposes. The statute was designed to bring clarity to the leasing of Indian lands and to incorporate the public policy favoring tribal self-determination established in the 1934 Indian Reorganization Act.[135] Though the statute allowed for tribes to enter into leases with business partners, the Interior Secretary retained final approval authority.

The Navajo Nation entered into a lease with Peabody Coal Company in 1964, with royalties of 20 to 37 1/2 cents per ton going to the tribe.[136] Despite the 1938 Act's policy favoring tribal self-determination, the federal government controlled all aspects of the leasing negotiation and administration.[137] The royalties provided for in 1964 lease that the government negotiated were a "pittance," but allowed for renegotiation in 20 years.[138] In 1984, the Interior Department did reopen the lease, and preliminarily approved a royalty rate increase to 20 percent, a much higher figure.[139] Peabody appealed the decision to an administrative panel, which was set to approve the higher royalty rate.[140]

Then, Peabody Coal hired a personal friend of the Interior Secretary, Donald Hodel, to approach the Secretary.[141] The tribe received no notice of this meeting, and did not learn about the meeting for many years.[142] After the meeting, using language culled from a Peabody Coal memorandum, Interior Secretary Hodel ordered the reconsideration of the decision.[143] Peabody Coal then offered to accept a 12 1/2 percent royalty rate, which was far less than federal government studies showed was fair.[144] The Navajo Nation faced severe economic pressure and felt forced to accept the reduced royalty rate.[145] The Interior Department did not mention to the Navajo Nation anything about the visit from Peabody's lobbyist or the fact that Peabody Coal lawyers had written the memorandum that effectively became the decision of the Interior Department.[146]

---

[135] Peter F. Carroll, Note, Drumming Out the Intent of the Indian Mineral Leasing Act of 1938, 7 Pub. Land & Res. L. Rev. 135, 137–38 (1986).

[136] Brief for Respondent at 2, United States v. Navajo Nation, 537 U.S. 488 (2003) (No. 01–1375), 2002 WL 31323741.

[137] Id.

[138] Id.

[139] Id.

[140] Id.

[141] Id. at 7–9.

[142] Id. at 7.

[143] Id. at 8–9.

[144] Id. at 10–11.

[145] Id. at 11.

[146] Brief of Amicus Curiae National Congress of American Indians at 2–3, United States v. Navajo Nation, 537 U.S. 488 (2003) (No. 01–1375).

As the Navajo Nation would argue in its brief, the reopening of the negotiations and the delay in the negotiations violated express mandates in the regulations.[147]

In 1993, the Navajo Nation sued for breach of trust. The Federal Circuit eventually held that the United States liable for an amount estimated to be about $600 million.[148]

The Supreme Court reversed, holding that the Indian Mineral Leasing Act of 1938 did not create a compensable fiduciary duty.[149] The Court first noted that the 1938 Act merely requires Secretarial approval of negotiated leases, not a "comprehensive managerial role" equivalent to the sale of Indian timber in *Mitchell II*.[150] The Court simply ignored the tribe's claim that the Interior Department controlled all aspects of Indian mineral leasing, and relied on the statutory text alone.

Moreover, the Court rejected the tribe's claim that the 12 1/2 percent royalty rate was a violation of a compensable trust duty, pointing to federal regulations that merely required the Interior Secretary not to approve leases with a less than 10 percent royalty rate.[151] Finally, the Court noted that nothing required the Navajo Nation to accept the new lease, and that the Interior Secretary's actions were minimal.[152]

In *United States v. Navajo Nation (Navajo II)*,[153] the Supreme Court again rejected a claim to liability for the Peabody Coal lease. On remand, the Federal Circuit had held that the Navajo-Hopi Rehabilitation Act of 1950[154] and the Surface Mining Control and Reclamation Act of 1977[155] established a compensable fiduciary duty that the government violated in approving the Peabody Coal lease.[156]

The Court first held that the lease at issue—which was set for ten years in accordance with the Indian Mineral Leasing Act—was

---

[147] Brief on the Merits for the Respondent, United States v. Navajo Nation, 537 U.S. 488 (2003) (No. 01–1375).

[148] Transcript of Oral Argument of Paul E. Frye on Behalf of the Respondent at 30, United States v. Navajo Nation, 537 U.S. 488 (No. 01–1375).

[149] United States v. Navajo Nation, 537 U.S. 488, 493 (2003).

[150] Id. at 507.

[151] Id. at 510 (citing 25 C.F.R. § 211.15(c) (1985)).

[152] Id. at 512.

[153] 556 U.S. 287 (2009).

[154] Act of April 19, 1950, 64 Stat. 46, codified at 25 U.S.C. §§ 631 et seq.

[155] Pub. L. 95–87, Aug. 3, 1977, 91 Stat. 523, codified as amended at 30 U.S.C. §§ 1201 et seq.

[156] Navajo Nation v. United States, 501 F.3d 1327, 1346 (Fed. Cir. 2007), rev'd 556 U.S. 287 (2009).

not governed at all by the Navajo-Hopi Rehabilitation Act, which allows for 25 year leases extendable to 50 years.[157] The Court then held that the original 1964 lease could not have been governed by the Surface Mining Control and Reclamation Act because the lease predated the Act by 13 years.[158]

Most damaging to tribal interests, however, was the Court's holding that comprehensive federal control over Indian leasing did not give rise to a compensable fiduciary duty.[159] The Court had held in *Navajo I* that the Indian Mineral Leasing Act did not mandate comprehensive federal control, and ignored the tribe's claim that the Interior Department still retained control over leasing on the reservation in line with the control exercised by the government over timber resources in *Mitchell II*. In *Navajo II*, the Court acknowledged that the Interior Department may have exercised control, but there was no statute creating a trust duty.[160]

Cobell

The long-running *Cobell* class action suit involved the single greatest series of breaches of trust and fiduciary duties by the United States in relation to Indian assets.[161] The suit resulted in a $3.4 billion settlement arranged by the Obama Administration and the class plaintiffs, the largest admission of federal liability in history.

The suit involved the administration of Individual Indian Money (IIM) accounts by the Interior and Treasury Departments.[162] IIM accounts were created by the federal government in its administration of Indian lands that had been allotted during the allotment era but which had not yet been fee-patented, meaning that the lands remained under the federal government's trust.[163] Indian allottees and their heirs often do not retain control over their allotments, allowing the Interior Department to administer the lands.[164] The allotments often yield rents from leases and other commercial arrangements paid to the United States as trustee of the allotments, and that money is deposited into IIM accounts.[165] There were many thousands of IIM account holders, and the federal government simply was not competent to administer the trust: the

---

[157] United States v. Navajo Nation, 556 U.S. 287, 297–98 (2009).

[158] Id. at 300.

[159] Id. at 301–02.

[160] Id. at 302.

[161] See generally Cobell v. Norton, 240 F.3d 1081 (D.C. Cir. 2001).

[162] Id. at 1088.

[163] Id. at 1087.

[164] Id. at 1088.

[165] Id. at 1088–89.

federal courts held that the government did not know with precision how many IIM accounts there were, nor did the government know what the value of a given account was.

The *Cobell* class plaintiffs originally sought an accounting and later expanded their claims to include a requirement that the federal government establish a proper system to administer the IIM accounts.

The *Cobell* litigation continued on for years. Then on July 12, 2005, Judge Lamberth delivered a scathing condemnation of Interior while issuing another injunction in the case, this one requiring Interior to give notice to all past or present IIM account holders that "any information related to the IIM Trust lands or other IIM Trust assets that current and former IIM Trust account holders receive from the Department of the Interior may be unreliable." The notice went on to warn IIM Trust account holders to "keep in mind the questionable reliability of IIM Trust information received from Interior in making any decisions affecting their trust assets."[166]

In July 2006, the D.C. Circuit Court of Appeals took the extraordinary step of removing him as presiding judge in the *Cobell* litigation.[167]

The new judge, Hon. James Robertson, quickly held a 10-day bench trial in October 2007. In the order that followed, Judge Robertson concluded that the accounting ordered by the court could not be concluded.[168] However, the court concluded that "a remedy must be found for the Department's unrepaired, and irreparable, breach of its fiduciary duty over the last century. And it does mean that the time has come to bring this suit to a close."[169]

Despite these words, the judiciary did not resolve the case—the parties and Congress did.[170] The Obama Administration quickly moved to settle the litigation. The D.C. Circuit explained the broad terms of the settlement as such:

> First, an amended complaint would be filed setting forth two classes:

---

[166]   Cobell v. Norton, 229 F.R.D. 5 (D. D.C. 2005).

[167]   Cobell v. Kempthorne, 455 F.3d 317, 335–36 (D.C. Cir. 2006).

[168]   Cobell v. Kempthorne, 532 F. Supp. 2d 37, 103 (D. D.C. 2008) ("What has been determined to this point is that the Department of the Interior has not-and cannot-remedy the breach of its fiduciary duty to account for the IIM trust.").

[169]   Id.

[170]   Claims Resolution Act of 2010, Pub. L. 111–291, Dec. 8, 2010, 124 Stat. 3064.

(1) the Historical Accounting Class, consisting of individual beneficiaries who had an IIM account (with at least one cash transaction) between October 25, 1994 (the date on which the 1994 Act became law) and September 30, 2009 (the "record date" of the parties' agreement), and

(2) the Trust Administration Class, consisting of the beneficiaries who had IIM accounts between 1985 and the date of the proposed amended complaint as well as individuals who, as of September 30, 2009, "had a recorded or other demonstrable ownership interest in land held in trust or restricted status, regardless of the existence of an IIM [a]ccount and regardless of the proceeds, if any, generated from the [l]and".

The settlement envisioned that the Historical Accounting Class would be certified pursuant to [FRCP] Rule 23(b)(1)(A) and 23(b)(2), in the alternative, with no individual right to opt out of the class; the Trust Administration Class would be certified pursuant to Rule 23(b)(3) with an opt-out right.

Second, the Secretaries of Interior and Treasury would deposit $1.412 billion into a settlement fund. From this fund, each member of the Historical Accounting Class would receive $1,000, in exchange for the release of the Secretary of Interior's "obligation to perform a historical accounting of [the class member's] IIM Account or any individual Indian trust asset". The Trust Administration Class members would receive a baseline payment of $500 plus an additional pro rata share of the remaining settlement funds in accordance with an agreed-upon compensation formula. The Trust Administration Class payment would release the Secretary from liability arising out of any past mismanagement of IIM accounts and trust properties. The scope of that release would not be unlimited: for example, claims for payment of existing account balances, breach-of-trust claims arising after September 30, 2009, and water-rights claims would fall outside of its scope.

Third, in addition to the class and compensation structure, the proposed settlement provided for:

(1) establishment of a $1.9 billion Trust Land Consolidation Fund for the Secretary to acquire fractional interests in trust lands;

(2) establishment of an Indian Education Scholarship Fund;

(3) potential tax-exempt status, at the election of Congress, for funds received by the class members;

(4) reasonable attorneys' fees, expenses, and costs for class counsel, to be awarded at the discretion of the district court,

(5) incentive payments for the class representatives, to be awarded at the discretion of the district court.

The proposal also stated that the class settlement agreement was contingent upon the enactment of legislation by Congress to authorize certain aspects of the settlement.[171]

On June 20, 2011, Judge Thomas F. Hogan granted a motion for final approval of the *Cobell* settlement. Some allotment holders chose to opt out of the settlement, to the extent they could.

The Conflicted Federal Trustee—*Nevada* and *Jicarilla*

One of the biggest challenges facing Indian and tribal interests and the United States is the reality that the federal government's trust obligations to Indians and tribes may conflict with other federal obligations. In general, the Supreme Court has repeatedly ratified the federal government's decisions in conflict situations where the government has spurned its trust duties in favor of other government prerogatives.

The leading case finding no impropriety in the federal government's conflicts of interest is *Nevada v. United States*.[172] The decision is part of a long-running series of cases and disputes over the Pyramid Lake and Truckee River waters.[173] The river flows into the lake, which serves as the homeland of the Paiute Indian Tribe.[174] Congress eventually authorized the Bureau of Reclamation to utilize Truckee and Carson River water to irrigate desert lands for agricultural and other purposes.[175]

Before the project took hold, the United States brought an action against private landowners with water rights on the two

---

[171] Cobell v. Salazar, 679 F.3d 909, 914–15 (D.C. Cir.), cert. denied sub nom., Craven v. Cobell, 133 S.Ct. 543 (2012).

[172] 463 U.S. 110 (1983).

[173] Ann Carey Juliano, A Step Backward in the Government's Representation of Tribes: The Story of Nevada v. United States, in Indian Law Stories 297, 298–303 (Carole E. Goldberg, Kevin K. Washburn, & Philip P. Frickey, eds. 2011).

[174] Id. at 298–99.

[175] Id. at 300.

rivers to clear title for the reclamation project and the Paiute Indian Tribe in 1913.[176] The first important federal conflicts of interest arose in the drafting of the complaint on behalf of the tribe. First, federal attorneys purposefully sought only irrigation rights to the rivers and did not include fishing rights.[177] Second, government attorneys never considered that the quantity of water would be an issue because at the time of the suit, the water supply was more than adequate for both the tribe and the federal reclamation project.[178] Later, after decades of litigation, the federal government reached a settlement with the private landowners that allowed for some irrigation-related water rights for the tribe.[179]

Decades after the conclusion of the original Orr Ditch litigation, the United States brought suit on behalf of the Pyramid Lake Paiute Tribe for water to provide for the maintenance of a fishery in the river and lake.[180] The Interior Department had simply chosen to supply water to non-tribal interests without providing a written justification for the decision, in violation of its trust duties to the tribe. Shortly thereafter, the United States sued to enforce the tribal right to a fishery in the Truckee River.[181]

The Supreme Court eventually heard the matter, and held that the doctrine of res judicata controlled the matter to defeat the government's claims in its role as trustee for the tribe.[182] The government could have brought a fishery claim in 1913, but it chose not to, and that claim was therefore barred in 1973.[183]

The trickier aspect of the decision was whether the tribe was barred by the same res judicata-based judgment. The Court held that the United States represented the tribe's interest in the original Orr Ditch settlement, and therefore the tribe was also barred from asserting new water rights.[184] The Ninth Circuit had held that the government's representation of the tribe in 1913 clouded by its conflict of interest violated its trust duties to the tribe.[185] That court concluded that the government could not legally

---

[176] Id.

[177] Id. at 301.

[178] Id.

[179] Id. at 301–02.

[180] Id. at 302–03. See also Nevada v. United States, 463 U.S. 110, 113 (1983).

[181] Ann Carey Juliano, A Step Backward in the Government's Representation of Tribes: The Story of Nevada v. United States, in Indian Law Stories 297, 307–11 (Carole E. Goldberg, Kevin K. Washburn, & Philip P. Frickey, eds. 2011).

[182] Nevada v. United States, 463 U.S. 110, 128–34 (1983).

[183] Id. at 134.

[184] Id. at 134–44.

[185] United States v. Truckee-Carson Irrigation District, 649 F.2d 1286, 1310 (9th Cir. 1981), rev'd 463 U.S. 110 (1983).

have represented the tribe's interests in 1913, and therefore the tribe's fisheries claim was not barred.[186]

The Supreme Court disagreed, holding that common law trust principles cannot control in a circumstance where Congress has imposed a specific duty on the government that conflicts with the general trust relationship.[187] The outcome of this holding is that the United States categorically denies that a conflict of interest exists involving the trust responsibility so long as Congress has specifically imposed a conflicting duty on the government.[188] As a result, tribal interests will *always* lose out in conflicts situations involving the federal government's trust duties.[189]

United States v. Jicarilla Apache Nation,[190] decided in 2011, exemplifies the conflict of interest problem in the government's administration of its trust duties. There, the Supreme Court held that the government was not required under common law trust principles to produce litigation documents ostensibly protected by the attorney-client privilege.[191] There, the government was confronted with a very serious conflict problem raised by the fact that the trust beneficiary, an Indian tribe, was suing the government as trustee for breach of trust.[192]

Normally, a trustee must produce documents prepared in relation to a trust corpus to the beneficiary. Here, however, the Supreme Court noted that the government was not merely a trustee, but was acting in its capacity as the national sovereign.[193] Unless Congress specifically provided for the tribal beneficiary to have access to litigation documents produced in relation to the trust corpus, the government was not required to produce the documents.[194]

§ 5.3   Indian Treaties

The original legal relationships between Indian nations and the United States were established and governed by treaties. Indian treaties negotiated by the Executive branch and ratified by the

---

[186] Id.

[187] Nevada v. United States, 463 U.S. 110, 142 (1983).

[188] Ann Carey Juliano, A Step Backward in the Government's Representation of Tribes: The Story of Nevada v. United States, in Indian Law Stories 297, 323–24 (Carole E. Goldberg, Kevin K. Washburn, & Philip P. Frickey, eds. 2011).

[189] Id. at 324.

[190] 564 U.S. 162 (2011).

[191] Id. at 165.

[192] Id. at 166.

[193] Id. at 165.

[194] Id. at 178.

Senate are the supreme law of the law under the Constitution's Supremacy Clause.[195] From the point of view of Indian nations, Indian treaties are sacred, often familial arrangements that cannot be broken.[196] From the point of view of the United States, Indian treaties are nothing more than simple legislation that can be unilaterally abrogated by Congress. Under international law, a treaty relationship meant basically that the tribe had agreed to turn over its external sovereign rights to form military and other alliances with nations other than the United States—and nothing more.[197] Later treaties would provide for a greater intrusion in the internal sovereignty of Indian tribes, but not so much that they would lose their fundamental sovereign existence.[198] Hundreds of Indian treaties remain extant, and still form the foundational basis of federal Indian law.

Indian nations and the federal government executed over 400 ratified treaties with the United States between 1778 and 1868.[199] Over 200 of these treaties remain in force today. Each Indian treaty is unique, though there were many commonalities between treaties. In very loose terms, Indian treaties could be characterized as peace treaties, or treaties of military alliance; reservation establishment treaties; removal treaties; or land cession treaties. Some treaties could be characterized in more than one of these categories.

As demonstrated in Justice Thompson's dissenting opinion in *Cherokee Nation v. Georgia*,[200] these early treaties should be construed more like treaties of military or political alliance between foreign nations. The Treaty of Hopewell, for example, used the word "protection" as a term of art that memorializes this relation. Under international law precepts, according to Justice Thompson, a nation that entered into a treaty of "protection" with a more powerful nation did not give up all aspects of its sovereignty.[201] It remained a

---

[195] Const. Art. II, § 2, para. 2 (treaty clause); id., art. VI, cl. 2 (supremacy clause).

[196] See generally Robert A. Williams, Jr., Linking Arms Together: American Indian Treaty Visions of Law & Peace, 1600–1800 (1997); Nation to Nation: Treaties between the United States & American Indian Nations (Suzan Shown Harjo ed. 2014).

[197] Siegfried Wiessner, American Indian Treaties and Modern International Law, 7 St. Thomas L. Rev. 567, 574–77 (1995).

[198] Id. at 577–80.

[199] Treaty with the Delawares, Sept. 17, 1778, 7 Stat. 13; Treaty with the Nez Percés, Aug. 13, 1868, 15 Stat. 693; Treaty with the Navajo, June 1, 1868, 15 Stat. 667; Treaty with the Northern Cheyenne and Northern Arapaho, May 10, 1868, 15 Stat. 655; Treaty with the Crows, May 7, 1868, 15 Stat. 649; Treaty with the Cherokee, Apr. 27, 1868, 16 Stat. 727; Treaty with the Ute, Mar. 2, 1868, 15 Stat. 619.

[200] 30 U.S. 1 (1831).

[201] Id. at 53 (Thompson, J., dissenting).

separate nation, along of the lines of contemporary Luxembourg or the Vatican. The Cherokee Nation, and other tribes like it, entered into these treaties of protection wherein they gave up important aspects of external sovereignty, such as the right to ally with yet another nation, in exchange for protection from outsiders by the larger, more powerful nation; that is, the United States.

Consistent with these earlier treaties in important ways are the mid-1800s treaties with the Lakota and with the Navajo. In the 1868 Treaty of Fort Laramie, the Sioux Nation and the United States agreed to establish the Great Sioux Reservation, which included the Black Hills and much of the rest of South Dakota, for the permanent settlement of the tribe, with the United States in "solemnly agree[ment]" that no unauthorized persons "shall ever be permitted to pass over, settle upon, or reside in [this] territory."[202] The Supreme Court's commentary and interpretation of the Treaty of Fort Sumner with the Navajo[203] helped to reestablish the principle that federal law excluded state laws from interfering with tribal governance.[204] These treaties created vast reservations, larger than many eastern states, and separated Indians from Americans. Charles Wilkinson's theory of "measured separatism" included discussion of these treaties as evidence for the policy of keeping Indian tribes and individual Indians away from Americans and their state governments, not to mention the United States Army and other military units.[205] Measured separatism, in these treaties, again worked to establish both independent tribal sovereignty and exclusion from the American constitutional structure.

After the War of 1812, the American treaties with Indian tribes east of the Mississippi River changed character a great deal. Most post-1815 treaties involved massive land cessions by tribes and ever declining tribal fortunes and land bases. And with the advent of the 1830 Indian Removal Act,[206] all eastern Indian treaties involved discussion of removal to lands beyond the Mississippi River, with only a select few tribes avoiding that terrible fate. The land cession and removal treaties involved continued recognition of tribal sovereignty and the viability of Indian tribes, if for no other reason than the United States needed a functional sovereign with which to acquire lands.

---

202 Fort Laramie Treaty of April 29, 1868, art. 2, 15 Stat. 635.

203 Treaty of Fort Sumner, 15 Stat. 668.

204 Williams v. Lee, 358 U.S. 217 (1959).

205 Charles F. Wilkinson, American Indians, Time, and the Law 14 (1987).

206 Act of May 30, 1830, 4 Stat. 411–412.

The treaty era formally ended in 1871 when Congress barred the President from negotiating further treaties with Indian nations,[207] though tribes and the federal government continued entering into treaty-like arrangements later adopted as legislation by Congress.[208] The federal government continued to negotiate agreements with Indian tribes, recognizing their sovereignty in the process, with the only key change registering as the inclusion of the House of Representatives in the agreement approval process. Instead of a treaty that would require only the ratification of the Senate, post-1871 agreements involved ratification as legislation, and required both Houses to consent to the tribal agreement before it became valid. If the United States stopped recognizing tribal sovereignty and the viability of Indian tribes, it would have negotiated with individual Indians who purported to be members of those tribes.

United States v. Winans

United States v. Winans[209] is the first major Supreme Court decision interpreting treaty language to find tribal rights to fish. Winans also established the reserved rights doctrine, the principle that the rights contained in Indian treaties were not grants from the federal government, but a "reservation of those [rights] not granted."[210]

The Winans decision implicated the critically important Stevens treaties, several treaties between the United States and Pacific northwest tribes,[211] with primary credit for the negotiations given to Isaac Stevens, a military man and the Territory of Washington's first governor.[212] Governor Stevens' goals were to extinguish Indian title to the northwest, isolate Indian nations on a limited number of reservations with an eye toward eventually consolidating all reservations into one, and to establish the groundwork for statehood.[213] But the Stevens treaties also included

---

[207] Act of Mar. 3, 1871, 16 Stat. 544, 566 (1871), codified at 25 U.S.C. § 71.

[208] G. William Rice, 25 U.S.C. § 71: The End of Indian Sovereignty or a Self-limitation of Contractual Ability?, 5 Am. Indian L. Rev. 239 (1977).

[209] 198 U.S. 371 (1905).

[210] Id. at 381.

[211] See generally Symposium, The Isaac I. Stevens and Joel Palmer Treaties, 1855–2005, 106:3 Or. Hist. Q. 342 (2005).

[212] Michael C. Blumm & James Brunberg, "Not Much Less Necessary . . . Than the Atmosphere They Breathed": Salmon, Indian Treaties, and the Supreme Court—A Centennial Remembrance of United States v. Winans and Its Enduring Significance, 46 Nat. Res. J. 489, 501 (2006).

[213] Kent Richards, The Stevens Treaties of 1854–1855, 106:3 Or. Hist. Q. 342, 344–47 (2005).

important language reserving on- and off-reservation rights to fish that remain extant to this day.

The Supreme Court held for the government and tribal treaty rights.[214] The Court, in powerful language, concluded, that the treaty fishing rights "were not much less necessary to the existence of the Indians than the atmosphere they breathed."[215] The Court rejected the Winans brothers' argument that, despite the "in common" language of the treaty, private property owners could exclude Indians from the rivers.[216]

The Court noted that Indians and Indian tribes retained rights to fish off the reservation as well and, although limited to some extent, the Court described them as a "servitude" or "easement" upon lands off the reservation alienated by the federal government to non-Indians.[217] The Court noted that both on- and off-reservation rights had to be recognized in order to "give effect to the treaty."[218]

For details on the specific rights, including rights to water, **see Chapter 11**, and rights to hunt and fish, **see Chapter 12**.

§ 5.4   Canons of Construction of Indian Treaties

From the earliest years of the United States, the Supreme Court has liberally construed Indian treaties in favor of tribal interests. The Court recognized that treaties are agreements between sovereigns that are entitled to supremacy under the Constitution, but also that many treaties are the product of unequal bargaining power. The substance of the treaties themselves generally created a legal relationship between a superior sovereign agreeing to protect the people, lands, and sovereignty of Indian nations. The canons of construction are tools of judicial statutory construction that have been refined since their early incarnation in the Marshall Trilogy, and invoked hundreds of times by courts to interpret and construe Indian treaty language.

In general, the canons are:

(1)   A treaty must be liberally interpreted in favor of the Indians or tribes in question.

(2)   A treaty must be construed as the Indians understood it.

---

[214]   United States v. Winans, 198 U.S. 371, 384 (1905).

[215]   Id. at 381.

[216]   Id. at 382 See also Joseph C. Dupris, Kathleen S. Hill & William H. Rodgers, Jr., The Si'ailo Way: Indians, Salmon, and Law on the Columbia River 72 (2006).

[217]   United States v. Winans, 198 U.S. 371, 381 (1905) ("servitude"); id. at 384 ("easements").

[218]   Id. at 381.

(3) Doubtful or ambiguous expressions in a treaty must be resolved in favor of the given Indian tribe.

(4) Treaty provisions that are not clear on their face may be interpreted from the surrounding circumstances and history.

An important corollary to these canons is the clear statement rule, discussed in § 5.6.

The first canon is that courts must interpret Indian treaties liberally. In *Worcester v. Georgia*,[219] the Marshall Court held that Cherokee Nation willingly agreed to come under the "protection" of European nations in exchange for preservation of their internal governance, meaning that the Cherokee Nation's claim to sovereignty and independence from the encroachments of state law could be implied from the terms of the treaty.[220] While this language suggests that the *Worcester* majority was cognizant of the oft-unequal bargaining power during Indian treaty negotiations, an important basis for the canons of construction, Justice McLean's concurrence explicitly states that treaty language "should never be construed to the [Indians'] prejudice. If words be made use of which are susceptible of a more extended meaning than their plain import, as connected with the tenor of the treaty, they should be considered as used only in the latter sense."[221]

In the modern era, the Supreme Court acknowledged the origins of the canons and reaffirmed their viability: "The canon of construction applied over a century and a half by this Court is that the wording of treaties and statutes ratifying agreements with the Indians is not to be construed to their prejudice."[222]

The second canon requires courts to interpret Indian treaties as the Indians themselves would have understood the treaty language. The Supreme Court interprets ambiguous Indian treaties "to give effect to the terms as the Indians themselves would have understood them. . . ."[223]

In *Jones v. Meehan*,[224] the Supreme Court protected reservation lands set aside by a treaty from a private claim.[225] The

---

[219] 31 U.S. 515 (1832).

[220] Id. at 546–47 (emphasis added).

[221] Id. at 582 (M'Lean, J., concurring).

[222] Antoine v. Washington, 420 U.S. 194, 199 (1975) (citations omitted); see also Squire v. Capoeman, 351 U.S. 1, 6–7 (1956) (quoting Worcester v. Georgia, 31 U.S. 515, 582 (1832) (M'Lean, J., concurring)).

[223] Minnesota v. Mille Lacs Band of Chippewa Indians, 526 U.S. 172, 196 (1999).

[224] 175 U.S. 1 (1899).

[225] Id. at 32.

Court noted that Indian treaties were often negotiated under a regime of unequal bargaining power between the tribal and federal sides, and the fact that Indian treaties are written in English, a language foreign to Indian negotiators.[226] Similarly, in *Tulee v. Washington*,[227] the Supreme Court again interpreted the Treaty with the Yakima (as it had in *United States v. Winans*,[228] **see § 5.3**) and held,

> It is our responsibility to see that the terms of the treaty are carried out, so far as possible, in accordance with the meaning they were understood to have by the tribal representatives at the council and in a spirit which generously recognizes the full obligation of this nation to protect the interests of a dependent people.[229]

The third canon requires courts to interpret doubtful or ambiguous treaty language to the benefit of tribal interests. In *Winters v. United States*,[230] discussed in greater detail in **§ 11.1**, the Supreme Court concluded that a treaty had more than one meaning, and applied the canon to reach a conclusion favoring tribal interests.[231]

A fourth canon requires courts to take into consideration historical circumstances when interpreting Indian treaty language. For example, in *Williams v. Lee*,[232] discussed in greater detail in **§ 6.7**, the Supreme Court interpreted the Navajo Nation's primary treaty, the 1868 Treaty of Fort Sumner,[233] with the deep history of the treaty in mind.[234]

Choctaw Nation v. United States

In *Choctaw Nation v. United States*,[235] the Supreme Court applied the canons of treaty construction to hold that the Choctaw and Cherokee Nations retained mineral interests in the Arkansas River bed.

Several treaties established tribal ownership of the Arkansas River bed in the 19th century,[236] but the Curtis Act of 1898

---

[226] Id. at 10–11.

[227] 315 U.S. 681 (1942).

[228] 198 U.S. 371 (1905).

[229] Tulee v. Washington, 315 U.S. 681, 684–85 (1942) (citations omitted).

[230] 207 U.S. 564 (1908).

[231] Id. at 577.

[232] 358 U.S. 217 (1959).

[233] 15 Stat. 668.

[234] Williams v. Lee, 358 U.S. 217, 221–22 (1959) (footnotes omitted).

[235] 397 U.S. 620 (1970).

[236] Id. at 628–30.

terminated many tribal governments and set aside lands for the Choctaw, Chickasaw, and the Cherokee nations.[237] A 1906 statute provided for the disposition of remaining lands by transmuting the property to federal trust for the benefit of the Indian nations.[238] Oklahoma argued that there was no federal conveyance of the riverbed to the tribes.[239]

The Court began its analysis by invoking the canon of Indian treaty construction, noting that the government imposed the treaties on the tribes, and that they were poorly drafted.[240] The government's contemporaneous interpretation of the treaties further expressed the government's understanding that the treaty conveyed ownership of the riverbed to the tribes.[241]

§ 5.5 Canons of Statutory Construction

The Supreme Court also requires courts to construe federal legislation addressing Indian affairs liberally in favor of the Indians, again with ambiguous provisions interpreted to their benefit. Since Congress legislates in Indian affairs as protector and trustee to Indian tribes and individual Indians, courts presume the United States intends its enactments to benefit tribal interests. Standard rules of statutory interpretation do not apply, and courts interpret ambiguous provisions in federal statutes to the benefit of tribal interests.

In *Choate v. Trapp*,[242] the Supreme Court interpreted the Curtis Act of 1898[243] to reach the conclusion that the state did not taxation authority on the Indian land tax immunity established in that statute. The Act was an allotment act that allotted land to Indians but allowed for a period of years in which the land would not be taxable by the states.[244] Oklahoma attempted to impose a tax on the land before the expiration of the trust period on the theory that since Oklahoma was not a party to the statute, the tax immunity did not apply to state taxes.[245] The Court rejected the argument applying the canon of construing Indian statutes.[246]

---

[237] An Act for the Protection of the People of the Indian Territory, June 28, 1898, 30 Stat. 495.

[238] Act of April 26, 1906, 34 Stat. 148.

[239] Choate Nation v. United States, 397 U.S. 620, 630 (1970).

[240] Id. at 630–31.

[241] Id. at 631–32.

[242] 224 U.S. 665 (1912).

[243] An Act for the Protection of the People of the Indian Territory, June 28, 1898, 30 Stat. 495.

[244] Choate v. Trapp, 224 U.S. 665, 667 (1912).

[245] Id. at 670.

[246] Id. at 675.

More recent Supreme Court decisions hold that the foundational principle for the canon of statutory construction is the trust relationship and federal policies favoring tribal self-determination: "The canons of construction applicable in Indian law are rooted in the unique trust relationship between the United States and the Indians."[247]

Montana v. Blackfeet Tribe

In *Montana v. Blackfeet Tribe of Indians*,[248] the Supreme Court applied the canon of statutory construction applicable to federal legislation relating to Indian affairs.[249]

The Supreme Court upheld tribal immunity from state natural-resource-extraction royalty taxes. A 1921 federal statute regulating Indian oil and gas leasing expressly authorized state taxation of royalty interests in tribal lands.[250] However, the Court held that a later federal statute, the Indian Mineral Leasing Act,[251] silent as to taxation, but which Congress intended to use to "obtain uniformity so far as practicable of the law relating to the leasing of tribal lands for mining purposes," effectively overrode the 1921 Congressional authorization of the state taxes.[252]

§ 5.6   The Clear Statement Rule

The clear statement rule is that courts will not interpret a federal statute to abrogate an Indian treaty right (**§§ 5.7, 10.6, 12.4**), tribal sovereignty immunity (**§ 6.6**), an Indian or tribal tax immunity (**§ 8.6**), reservation boundary (**§ 7.2**), or any other tribal government power (**§§ 3.7, 3.11, 5.8**) absent a clear statement by Congress to that effect. In *Michigan v. Bay Mills Indian Community*,[253] discussed in greater detail in **§§ 6.6, 9.6**, the Supreme Court stated unequivocally that "courts will not lightly assume that Congress in fact intends to undermine Indian self-government," and that "such a congressional decision must be clear."[254]

The clear statement rule is a foundational and canonical principle of federal Indian law originating in the Marshall Trilogy, but being most aptly announced in the modern era in *Santa Clara*

---

[247] Oneida County, N.Y. v. Oneida Indian Nation of N.Y., 470 U.S. 226, 247 (1985) (citations omitted).

[248] 471 U.S. 759 (1985).

[249] Id. at 766.

[250] Act of May 29, 1924, 43 Stat. 244, codified at 25 U.S.C. § 398.

[251] Act of May 11, 1938, 52 Stat. 347, codified at 25 U.S.C. §§ 396a et seq.

[252] Montana v. Blackfeet Tribe, 471 U.S. 759, 766–67 (1985).

[253] 134 S.Ct. 2024 (2014).

[254] Id. at 2031–32.

Pueblo v. Martinez.[255] There, the Supreme Court stated that "a proper respect both for tribal sovereignty itself and for the plenary authority of Congress in this area cautions that we tread lightly in the absence of clear indications of legislative intent."[256] In the Indian Civil Rights Act (ICRA), Congress had imposed upon tribal governments the so-called "Indian Bill of Rights," which loosely tracked the federal constitution's individual rights protections.[257] However, Congress did nothing to abrogate tribal immunity from suits to enforce those rights in federal, state, or tribal courts, nor did Congress expressly provide a federal court cause of action to enforce the rights, except for habeas petitions.[258] The Court applied the clear statement rule to hold that ICRA did not abrogate tribal immunity,[259] nor allow for federal civil suits to enforce the Indian Bill of Rights.[260]

Similarly, in *Michigan v. Bay Mills Indian Community*,[261] the Supreme Court applied the clear statement rule to hold that Congress did not intend the Indian Gaming Regulatory Act (IGRA) to abrogate tribal sovereign immunity. IGRA does abrogate tribal immunity in one context: suits by states "to enjoin a class III gaming activity located *on Indian lands* and conducted in violation of any Tribal-State compact. . . ."[262] However, the Court held that since Michigan's suit was designed to stop a gaming facility *not* on Indian lands, the Congressional abrogation of immunity did not extend to that class of suit.[263] The Court rejected Michigan's ultimate argument that such a syllogism renders IGRA "senseless" by refusing to rewrite IGRA to conform with Michigan's views. The Court here strongly relied on the clear statement rule, arguing that Congress legislated extensively in relation to Indian gaming, and had abrogated tribal immunity for some purposes, but not to resolve disputes involving gaming on non-Indian lands.[264]

§ 5.7   Treaty Abrogation

The most prominent expression of the clear statement rule involves the abrogation of Indian treaties by Congress. While the

---

[255] 436 U.S. 49 (1978).

[256] Id. at 60.

[257] 25 U.S.C. § 1302(a).

[258] 25 U.S.C. § 1303.

[259] Santa Clara Pueblo v. Martinez, 436 U.S. 49, 58–59 (1978).

[260] Id. at 59–70.

[261] 134 S.Ct. 2024 (2014).

[262] 25 U.S.C. § 2710(d)(7)(A)(ii) (emphasis added); Michigan v. Bay Mills Indian Community, 134 S.Ct. 2024, 2032 (2014).

[263] Id.

[264] Id. at 2033–34.

United States has the power to abrogate Indian treaties, as it does with any treaty, the courts will not lightly infer the abrogation of Indian treaty rights.

The origin of the federal power to abrogate Indian treaty rights may ironically be *Lone Wolf v. Hitchcock*,[265] where the Court found clear Congressional intent to abrogate Indian treaty rights, and the constitutional authority to do so. *Lone Wolf* is an embarrassment to American rule of law, **see § 3.7**, but at least required a clear statement of intent to abrogate Indian treaty rights.

United States v. Dion

In *United States v. Dion*,[266] the Supreme Court held that the Endangered Species Act and the Bald Eagle Protection Act served to abrogate Indian treaty rights to harvest bald eagles.

The Court noted that the clear statement rule applied in force to treaty rights: "As a general rule, Indians enjoy exclusive treaty rights to hunt and fish on lands reserved to them, unless such rights were clearly relinquished by treaty or have been modified by Congress."[267] The Court noted that it would presume that Congress only intended to abrogate treaty rights to advance both national and tribal interests.[268] Moreover, the Court reaffirmed that it would not imply an abrogation of treaty rights in the absence of express statutory language.[269] Extraneous evidence of Congressional intent may suffice if the evidence is overwhelming.[270]

The Eagle Protection Act criminalized the harvest of golden and bald eagles by any person,[271] but allowed the Interior Secretary to authorize via regulation American Indians to take eagles.[272] The Court held that the provision allowing for a permitting process for American Indians constituted the requisite Congressional statement of intent to abrogate treaty rights.[273] The Court also found in the legislative history of the amendment to the Act protecting golden eagles evidence that Congress understood that the Act abrogated treaty rights.[274]

---

[265]   187 U.S. 553 (1903).

[266]   476 U.S. 734 (1986).

[267]   Id. at 738.

[268]   Id.

[269]   Id. at 738–39.

[270]   Id. at 739–40.

[271]   16 U.S.C. § 668(a).

[272]   16 U.S.C. § 668a.

[273]   United States v. Dion, 476 U.S. 734, 740 (1986).

[274]   Id. at 740–45.

§ 5.8   Federal Statutes of General Applicability

A much more difficult area is where a federal statute governs a particular field of law, but does not expressly state whether the statute applies to Indian nations. These statutes, often called federal statutes of general applicability, are silent as to their application to Indian nations, and therefore do not meet the exacting analysis of the clear statement rule. However, several lower courts have cobbled together a body of federal common law to hold that federal statutes of general applicability do apply to Indian nations.

The Supreme Court has not definitively addressed whether federal statutes of general applicability apply to Indian nations. In *Federal Power Commission v. Tuscarora Indian Nation*,[275] the Court held that the federal power of eminent domain allows the United States to take Indian lands,[276] but the Court did not address tribal governance authority in that case. Twice, the Supreme Court has placed the *Federal Power Commission* statement in jeopardy by reaching the opposite conclusion in regards to tribal governance authority—first, in *Merrion v. Jicarilla Apache Tribe*,[277] and then later in *Iowa Mutual Ins. Co. v. LaPlante*.[278] In *Merrion*, the Court declined to read into the tribe's constitution, approved by the Interior Secretary, an implied limitation on the tribe's power to tax nonmembers.[279] In *Iowa Mutual*, the Court squarely applied the clear statement rule in the context of a statute of general applicability; in that instance, the federal diversity jurisdiction statute.[280]

Numerous federal courts have applied federal employment laws silent as to their applicability to tribal or Indian country employers, relying in large part on the *Federal Power Commission* statement.[281] In the context of the National Labor Relations Act (NLRA),[282] which is silent as to its applicability to Indian nations, the D.C. Circuit concluded that the NLRA applies to Indian

---

[275]   362 U.S. 99 (1960).

[276]   Id. at 120–22.

[277]   455 U.S. 130 (1982).

[278]   480 U.S. 9 (1987).

[279]   455 U.S. 130, 149 n. 14 (1982).

[280]   Iowa Mutual Insurance Co. v. LaPlante, 480 U.S. 9, 18 (1987) (discussing 28 U.S.C. § 1332).

[281]   E.g., Smart v. State Farm Ins. Co., 868 F.2d 929, 932–36 (7th Cir. 1989) (applying Employee Retiremet Income Security Act of 1974); Reich v. Mashantucket Sand & Gravel, 95 F.3d 174, 177–81 (2d Cir. 1996) (applying Occupational Safety and Health Act).

[282]   29 U.S.C. §§ 151 et seq.

nations.[283] The court declined to employ the *Federal Power Commission*'s statement, finding instead that the tribal gaming operations in question were not sufficiently governmental in character to avoid the application of the statute.[284]

But in *NLRB v. Pueblo of San Juan*,[285] the Tenth Circuit sitting en banc held conclusively that the clear statement rule controls. The court drew from *Santa Clara Pueblo* rather than from *Federal Power Commission* as its starting point.[286]

Despite the D.C. Circuit's inclination not to choose between *Federal Power Commission* and *Santa Clara Pueblo*, the Supreme Court eventually is likely to choose between the two. *San Manuel* is not a rigorously principled decision, heavily relying upon incorrect assumptions about the relationship between tribal governance and gaming operations.[287] Conversely, the *San Juan Pueblo* analysis is rooted more in the clear statement rule articulated by the Supreme Court, despite perhaps suffering from the defect identified by the Second Circuit as "almost invariably compel[ling] the conclusion that every federal statute that failed expressly to mention Indians would not apply to them."[288]

---

[283] San Manuel Indian Bingo and Casino v. NLRB, 475 F.3d 1306 (D.C. Cir. 2007).

[284] Id. at 1315.

[285] 276 F.3d 1186 (10th Cir. 2002) (en banc).

[286] Id. at 1195 (citations omitted).

[287] Michigan v. Bay Mills Indian Community, 134 S.Ct. 2024, 2040–45 (2014) (Sotomayor, J., concurring).

[288] Mashantucket Sand & Gravel, 95 F.3d 174, 178 (2d Cir. 1996).

Chapter 6

TRIBAL SOVEREIGNTY AND NATIVE NATION-BUILDING

Analysis

§ 6.1   Introduction to Tribal Sovereignty

American Indian nations predate the European nations and the United States on the North American continent and, to a significant extent, retain many of the aspects of their traditional governance structures and methods. The diversity of tribal governance structures and philosophy is extensive. It is important to recognize that tribal governance often resembled nothing like the European powers that they confronted in the previous several centuries. Differences in law and governance between tribal groups and the American government form the basis for many conflicts in Indian country to this day.

Tribal sovereignty is a catch phrase in modern American Indian law. Since the American constitutional law treats the United States and the several states as "sovereigns," it is an easy and important fit for Indian nations to also be treated as sovereigns. In fact, after visiting three tribal courts in the 1990s, Supreme Court Justice Sandra Day O'Connor referred to Indian nations as the third sovereign, writing, "Today, in the United States, we have three types of sovereign entities—the Federal government, the States, and the Indian tribes. Each of the three sovereigns has its own judicial system, and each plays an important role in the administration of justice in this country."[1] Former Principal Chief of

---

[1]   Sandra Day O'Connor, Lessons from the Third Sovereign: Indian Tribal Courts, 33 Tulsa L.J. 1, 1 (1997).

the Cherokee Nation of Oklahoma Wilma Mankiller referred to American Indian sovereignty as a "sacred trust."[2]

For modern Indian nations engaged in the process of nation building, tribal sovereignty is the most critical legal instrument required to achieve self-determination.[3] Tribal sovereignty allows Indian nations to make their own decisions, free from the interference of federal, state, and local government entities. Absent tribal sovereignty, there would be no Indian nationhood, no ability of Indians to create and maintain their own governance structures, economies, and local laws.

§ 6.2 Tribal Governments as Sovereigns

Both the text of the United States Constitution and the earliest major Indian law decisions of the Supreme Court—the Marshall Trilogy, **see §§ 2.1, 2.2**—expressly recognized that tribal governments are sovereign entities. The Commerce Clause recognizes three types of sovereigns—states, foreign nations, and Indian tribes.[4] The United States entered into hundreds of treaties with Indian nations, continuing a practice started by French, Spanish, and British nations had started before, an additional recognition of Indian nations as sovereign entities.

The Supreme Court after the Marshall Trilogy struggled to articulate how Indian nations fit into the American constitutional polity. However, several important concepts are well settled. First, the United States Constitution has virtually no applicability to Indian nations. The Framers did not invite Indian nations to the Constitutional Convention, nor did they seek tribal ratification, nor is there a mechanism for tribal consent to the constitution.

Talton v. Mayes

In *Talton v. Mayes*,[5] the Supreme Court reviewed a petition for a writ of habeas corpus by a Cherokee Nation of Oklahoma member who had been convicted of murder by the Cherokee court and sentenced to be hanged.[6] Petitioner Mayes argued that the conviction violated both federal and tribal law; specifically, he argued that the grand jury that returned the indictment leading to his prosecution included only five members, a number insufficient

2   Wilma Mankiller, "Tribal Sovereignty is a Sacred Trust": An Open Letter to the Conference, 23 Am. Indian L. Rev. 479, 479 (1998–1999).

3   See generally David H. Getches, Charles F. Wilkinson, Robert A. Williams, Jr., Matthew L.M. Fletcher, and Kristen A. Carpenter, Cases and Materials on Federal Indian Law 415–16 (7th ed. 2017).

4   Const. Art. I, § 8, cl. 3.

5   163 U.S. 376 (1896).

6   Id. at 379.

under both federal and tribal law.[7] Cherokee law required 13 grand jury members, it appears, although one tribal statute merely required five grand jury members.[8] Both the defendant and the victims were Cherokee, and the defendant committed the crime on Cherokee lands.[9]

As an initial matter, Supreme Court, per Justice White, recognized the sovereignty of the Cherokee Nation and its authority to prosecute criminals, through various treaties between the tribe and the United States.[10] The existence of tribal sovereignty forced the recognized the authority of the Cherokee Nation to enact its own legislation to govern law and order, and the procedures by which the tribe would enforce its criminal code.[11] The Court further held that, because the Cherokee Nation retained its sovereignty, a crime on Cherokee territory was therefore a crime against the Cherokee Nation, and not the United States.[12] As such, federal law—including the Fifth Amendment of the Constitution—had no applicability to a crime against the tribe.[13]

The Court also considered whether the Fifth Amendment to the United States Constitution could apply to the Cherokee statute that allowed for a grand jury to be composed by as few as five persons on the theory the Cherokee prosecution was in actuality an exercise of federal rather than tribal power.[14] After all, it is Congress that enjoys plenary power over Indian affairs, and perhaps Indian nations, too. The Court firmly rejected that argument, holding that the Cherokees as a sovereign nation possessed inherent criminal prosecutorial power.[15] Moreover, the Court held that Cherokee sovereignty predates the Constitution, which by its terms does not limit or regulate Cherokee nationhood, foreclosing the notion that the Constitution applies to Indian nations.[16] In short, tribes are not arms of the federal government, and therefore beholden to federal constitutional law, merely because Congress possesses plenary power over Indian affairs. The *Talton* Court borrowed from its jurisprudence on whether provisions of the Bill of Rights applied to

---

[7]   Id.

[8]   Id. at 378.

[9]   Id. at 379.

[10]   Id. at 379–80.

[11]   Id. at 380.

[12]   Id. at 381.

[13]   Id. at 381–82.

[14]   Id. at 384.

[15]   Id.

[16]   Id. at 384 (citations omitted).

states, the so-called incorporation doctrine,[17] to conclude that the Fifth Amendment has no applicability to Indian nations.

Talton continues to stand for the key proposition that the United States Constitution by its own terms does not apply to limit or regulate tribal governments. Ironically, the Court relied upon cases such as *United States v. Kagama*,[18] which held that Indian nations and Indian people were so weak and dependent on the federal government for basic sustenance that Congress was authorized to extend federal criminal jurisdiction authority into Indian country.[19] It must seem strange that the Supreme Court could hold in the 1880s that Indian nations were so weak as to justify federal control over them, but in the 1890s to expressly recognize the authority an Indian nation to impose the death penalty. Context matters, in that the Hoopa, Yurok, Karuk, or Klamath tribes in the *Kagama* case likely did not establish a criminal justice system akin to that established by the Cherokee Nation throughout the 19th century.[20] **See § 3.7**.

That the United States Constitution was inapplicable to tribal governments became an issue in the mid-20th century, as civil rights began to dominate American political dialogue. In the original edition of the *Handbook of Federal Indian Law*, Felix S. Cohen condensed *Talton*'s theory of tribal sovereignty into the notion that Indian nations possessed "inherent" authority to govern, absent divestiture of that authority by Congress or the tribe through agreement.[21]

In *Native American Church of North America v. Navajo Tribal Council*,[22] the Tenth Circuit applied *Talton* in concluding that the First Amendment did not apply to tribal governments. There, the Navajo Nation Council criminalized the possession, sale, and use of peyote, a hallucinogenic bean used as a sacrament by the Native American Church, a pan-Indian religious group.[23] The court held, just as the *Talton* Court did, that the relevant constitutional provision did not, by its express terms, apply to Indian nations, any more than did the First Amendment by its own terms apply to

---

[17] Barron v. City of Baltimore, 32 U.S. 243 (1833).

[18] 118 U.S. 375 (1886).

[19] Id. at 383–84.

[20] Compare Byron Nelson, Jr., Our Home Forever: The Hupa Indians of Northern California 94 (1994) ("There was no legal channel through which an Indian could appeal the agent's judgment."), with John Howard Payne, Indian Justice: A Cherokee Murder Trial at Tahlequah in 1840 (1933) (Univ. of Oklahoma Press 2002) (detailing a Cherokee murder trial).

[21] Felix S. Cohen, Handbook of Federal Indian Law 122 (1941 ed.).

[22] 272 F.2d 131 (10th Cir. 1959).

[23] Id. at 132.

states.[24] Moreover, the federal incorporation doctrine that did expose states to many of the Bill of Rights, including the First Amendment, could not apply to tribes because tribes are not states.[25]

United States v. Wheeler

As the Supreme Court moved into the modern era of federal Indian law, the Court expressly adopted Cohen's inherent tribal authority theory. In *United States v. Wheeler*,[26] the Court addressed a challenge to a federal criminal prosecution of a Navajo Nation member for statutory rape.[27] The Navajo Nation had previously convicted him of tribal offenses related to the same facts and the defendant claimed the federal prosecution violated the Double Jeopardy Clause of the United States Constitution.[28]

Normally, prosecutions for the same criminal acts in state and federal courts do not violate the Double Jeopardy Clause.[29] American criminal law theory provides that when a person commits a criminal act, that act goes against the government, or the people, of the territory in which the act is committed. So a criminal act in South Dakota is a crime against the state or the people of South Dakota. If the criminal act is also a federal criminal act, then the criminal act implicates two sovereigns, federal and state. While the Double Jeopardy Clause bars the federal government, or a state government, from putting a criminal defendant in jeopardy more than once, both the federal government and a state government may each prosecute a defendant for the same crime—they are separate sovereigns.

Wheeler includes Indian nations in that equation, holding that a federal prosecution occurring after a tribal prosecution is not barred by the Double Jeopardy Clause under the Dual Sovereignty doctrine.[30] The Court concluded that Indian nations retain sovereign authority to prosecute tribal members.[31] Then the Court expressly adopted Cohen's inherent sovereignty theory, whereby tribal sovereignty over internal tribal relations remain extant unless that power is divested by Act of Congress or treaty—what Cohen and the Court referred to as "*inherent powers of a limited*

---

[24]   Id. at 134 (footnote omitted).

[25]   Id.

[26]   435 U.S. 313 (1978).

[27]   Id. at 315.

[28]   Id. at 314.

[29]   Bartkus v. Illinois, 359 U.S. 121 (1959); Abbate v. United States, 359 U.S. 187 (1959).

[30]   United States v. Wheeler, 435 U.S. 313, 318–21 (1978).

[31]   Id. at 322 (citations omitted).

sovereignty which has never been extinguished."[32] Indian nations are sovereign, and therefore retain "the inherent power to prescribe laws for their members and to punish infractions of those laws."[33]

The Court acknowledged that inherent tribal authority, however, may be limited, or divested, through the treaty process or through Act of Congress: "By specific treaty provision they yielded up other sovereign powers; by statute, in the exercise of its plenary control, Congress has removed still others."[34] Moreover, referencing the Court's own assertion of power to recognize the divestiture of inherent authority, as it had in cases like *Oliphant v. Suquamish Indian Tribe,*[35] **see § 7.6**, the Court noted that "[t]heir incorporation within the territory of the United States, and their acceptance of its protection, necessarily divested them of some aspects of the sovereignty which they had previously exercised."[36]

Even so, the *Wheeler* Court characterized inherent tribal sovereignty as extant, usually, until Congress expressly acts to limit tribal power. In compelling language, the Court wrote:

> But our cases recognize that the Indian tribes have not given up their full sovereignty. We have recently said that: "Indian tribes are unique aggregations possessing attributes of sovereignty over both their members and their territory. . . . [They] are a good deal more than 'private, voluntary organizations.'" . . . The sovereignty that the Indian tribes retain is of a unique and limited character. It exists only at the sufferance of Congress and is subject to complete defeasance. But until Congress acts, the tribes retain their existing sovereign powers. In sum, Indian tribes still possess those aspects of sovereignty not withdrawn by treaty or statute, or by implication as a necessary result of their dependent status.[37]

The Court then applied its inherent sovereignty framework and determined that neither the Navajo Nation nor Congress had acted to divest the tribe of prosecutorial authority.[38] The Navajo Nation had been party to 1850 and 1868 treaties that allowed for federal prosecution of tribal members for crimes against non-Indians, the Court concluded that the tribe had not relinquished its

---

[32] Id. (quoting F. Cohen, Handbook of Federal Indian Law 122 (1945) (emphasis in original)).

[33] Id. at 323.

[34] Id.

[35] 435 U.S. 191 (1978).

[36] United States v. Wheeler, 435 U.S. 313, 323 (1978).

[37] Id. at 323 (citations and footnote omitted).

[38] Id. at 323–25.

own authority to prosecute tribal members. Almost by definition, the treaty relationship between Indian nations and the United States constitutes the federal acknowledgment of inherent tribal authority, such as the power to prosecute: "[W]e have said that '[i]mplicit in these treaty terms . . . was the understanding that the internal affairs of the Indians remained exclusively within the jurisdiction of whatever tribal government existed.' "[39] The relevant Navajo treaty did include provisions for the punishment of Navajos who commit crimes against non-Indians by the United States, but was silent as to the tribal authority to prosecute Navajos.[40] As such, the inherent tribal sovereignty doctrine required the Supreme Court's acknowledgement of tribal authority to prosecute.

An additional critical aspect of the *Wheeler* decision was the rejection of the claim that when the Navajo Nation prosecutes a tribal member, it does so as an arm or instrumentality of the federal government.[41] The Court acknowledged that the Bureau of Indian Affairs had established the earliest incarnation of the Navajo justice system with a Court of Indian Offenses applying a tribal law and order code, and that the tribal code had been approved by the Interior Secretary.[42] While it was (and likely remains) true that the Navajo Nation relies heavily on federal appropriations and technical assistance to enforce criminal laws, even to this day, it does so as a nation largely independent of federal authority.[43]

Finally, the Supreme Court also opined that the power of Indian nations to prosecute tribal members for criminal offenses is a uniquely local governance activity that implicates core tribal values, and for even Congress to act to limit tribal authority would severely undermine tribal self-determination.[44] The Court noted that tribal justice systems serve as important regulators of tribal government conduct: "[T]ribal courts are important mechanisms for protecting significant tribal interests. Federal pre-emption of a tribe's jurisdiction to punish its members for infractions of tribal law would detract substantially from tribal self-government, just as federal pre-emption of state criminal jurisdiction would trench upon important state interests."[45]

---

[39]   Id. at 324 (quoting Williams v. Lee, 358 U.S. 217, 221–22 (1959)).

[40]   Id. at 324 & n. 20 (referencing the 1849 Treaty of Canyon de Chelly, 9 Stat. 974, and the 1868 Treaty of Fort Sumner, 15 Stat. 667).

[41]   Id. at 326–28.

[42]   Id. at 327.

[43]   Id. at 327–28.

[44]   Id. at 331–32.

[45]   Id. at 332 (footnote omitted).

§ 6.3   The Indian Civil Rights Act

After several years of taking testimony from Indian country witnesses about civil rights violations in Indian country by federal, state, and tribal governments, Congress enacted the Indian Civil Rights Act (ICRA).[46] Congress enacted ICRA as Title II of the 1968 Civil Rights Act. Portions of the ICRA that substantially mirror the Bill of Rights are popularly called the "Indian Bill of Rights." The Indian Bill of Rights extends most—but not all—of the constitutional protections of the Bill of Rights to individuals under the jurisdiction of Indian tribal governments. In order to preserve certain aspects of tribal government and sovereignty, some of the Bill of Rights were modified or left out.

The individual rights protections include: the rights to free exercise of religion, free speech, press, assembly, and to petition for a redress of grievances; the right to be free of unreasonable searches and seizures without a search warrant to be issued only upon a showing of probable cause; the right to be free from being placed in double jeopardy and from self-incrimination; the right to due process and equal protection; the right to be free from taking of property without just compensation; the rights to a speedy trial, confront witnesses, and the assistance of counsel; the freedom from excessive bail and cruel and unusual punishment; the freedom from bills of attainder and ex post facto laws; and the right to a jury of at least six persons in all criminal cases carrying the possibility of imprisonment.[47] The main differences include the absences of an establishment clause and a right to counsel for indigent criminal defendants at the government's expense. Also, ICRA prohibited Indian tribes from sentencing convicted criminals to more than six months in prison and $500 in fines, later amended to one year and $5000 in 1986.[48]

Specific provisions in the final version of the ICRA strongly imply that Congress intended to preserve as much of tribal culture as possible. Congress left out a provision equivalent to the Establishment Clause in order to preserve the rights of tribes to form and maintain theocratic government structures if they wished, as some tribes had.[49] Even in the area of criminal procedure, the

---

[46]   Pub. L. 90–284, Title II, § 201, Apr. 11, 1968, 82 Stat. 77, codified as amended at 25 U.S.C. §§ 1301 et seq.

[47]   25 U.S.C. § 1302(a).

[48]   25 U.S.C. § 1302(a)(7)(B), enacted by Pub. L. 99–570, Title IV, § 4217, Oct. 27, 1986, 100 Stat. 3207–146. In 2010, Congress authorized certified tribes to sentence convicted criminals to three years and a $5000 fine for any single offense. 25 U.S.C. § 1302(b), enacted by Pub. L. 111–211, Title II, § 234(a), July 29, 2010, 124 Stat. 2279.

[49]   Id. at 1358.

Senate explicitly questioned whether imposition of certain criminal procedures would injure tribal culture or significantly impact the tribal governmental capability, and limited federal intervention to a habeas right.[50]

On the question of whether Indian tribes should be obligated to provide attorneys to indigent defendants, the subcommittee appeared particularly concerned that tribal communities rarely enjoyed an adequate population of professional lawyers. The Interior Solicitor testified that Indian courts would no longer be able to function under that regime.[51] The Department of Justice also testified that there were few attorneys available on reservations and that, since most tribal prosecutions dealt with tribal customary and traditional law, attorneys were not necessary.[52]

Even so, ICRA plainly is "Congress's attempt to impose liberal democratic ideals on Indian nations."[53]

For the next several years, federal courts took jurisdiction over numerous internal tribal governance matters. Eventually, the Supreme Court closed federal courthouses to ICRA civil rights claims, leaving only the federal habeas cause of action in place.

Santa Clara Pueblo v. Martinez

In *Santa Clara Pueblo v. Martinez*,[54] Julia Martinez brought a claim under ICRA's equal protection clause against her tribe seeking membership for her children.[55] The Pueblo had enacted an enrollment ordinance that discriminated on the basis of sex against her and her children.[56] The Supreme Court initially held that the Santa Clara Pueblo could not be sued in federal court without its consent, and that waiver of tribal immunity must be "unequivocally expressed."[57] Congress had not expressly abrogated tribal sovereign immunity to allow enforcement of ICRA's provisions on the face of the Act,[58] or in its provision of federal court review of tribal court

---

[50] Hearing Before the Subcommittee on Constitutional Rights of the Senate Committee on the Judiciary, Amendments to the Indian Bill of Rights, 91st Cong., 1st Sess. 15 (1969) (Statement of Sen. Sam Ervin).

[51] Arthur Lazarus, Jr., Title II of the 1968 Civil Rights Act: An Indian Bill of Rights, 45 N.D. L. Rev. 337, 339 n. 12 (1969).

[52] Id. at 339–40.

[53] Wenona T. Singel, Cultural Sovereignty and Transplanted Law: Tensions in Indigenous Self-Rule, 15 Kan. J. L. & Pub. Pol'y, Winter 2006, at 357, 364.

[54] 436 U.S. 49 (1978).

[55] Id. at 52–53.

[56] Id. at 51.

[57] Id. at 58 (quoting United States v. Testan, 424 U.S. 392, 399 (1976)).

[58] Id. at 59.

convictions through the habeas writ.[59] However, as Martinez also named the chief executive officer of the pueblo as a defendant, the Court concluded that tribal officials violating federal law may be sued for injunctive, prospective relief, assuming a federal cause of action lies.[60]

The Court, per Justice Marshall, stated that complainants against tribal government actions must pursue a tribal forum, and that Congress created no federal cause of action to enforce ICRA's civil rights guarantees. First, the Court applied the clear statement rule and concluded that Congress did not state a clear intent to restrict tribal authority to regulate internal tribal affairs, such as membership, in enacting ICRA: "Although Congress clearly has power to authorize civil actions against tribal officers, and has done so with respect to habeas corpus relief in § 1303, a proper respect both for tribal sovereignty itself and for the plenary authority of Congress in this area cautions that we tread lightly in the absence of clear indications of legislative intent."[61]

After stating that principles of federal Indian law required the Court to "tread lightly," the Court noted that the only express avenue for federal court relief under ICRA was the habeas provision in 25 U.S.C. § 1303, which allows persons detained by a tribal government to file petitions for writs of habeas corpus in federal court: "ICRA was generally understood to authorize federal judicial review of tribal actions only through the habeas corpus provisions of § 1303."[62] Moreover, ICRA's overall purpose, to enhance tribal self-government, was exemplified by Congress's refusal to incorporate the Bill of Rights wholesale, instead "selectively incorporat[ing] and in some instances modif[ying] the safeguards of the Bill of Rights to fit the unique political, cultural, and economic needs of tribal governments."[63] Moreover, ICRA's structure, which provided for limitations on the reach of Public Law 280 and for strengthening tribal justice systems, supported limited federal court interference with tribal affairs.[64]

In critically important language, the Court hearkened back to *Williams v. Lee*'s approval of tribal court systems,[65] holding that

---

[59]   Id.

[60]   Id. at 59 (citing Ex parte Young, 209 U.S. 123 (1908)).

[61]   Id. at 59–60 (citations omitted).

[62]   Id. at 70.

[63]   Id. at 62.

[64]   Id. at 63–64.

[65]   359 U.S. 217 (1959).

tribal forums were available to allow ICRA claimants to enforce the Indian Bill of Rights.[66]

Finally, the Court noted that ICRA should be interpreted not to allow for a federal cause of action because many of the claims involving internal tribal affairs may involve analyses arising from tribal custom and tradition, beyond of the institutional competence of federal courts: "Congress may also have considered that resolution of statutory issues under § 1302, and particularly those issues likely to arise in a civil context, will frequently depend on questions of tribal tradition and custom which tribal forums may be in a better position to evaluate than federal courts."[67]

In 2012, the Santa Clara Pueblo voted to vacate its membership rules, replacing them in 2014 with modernized rules that eliminate the discriminatory aspects of the rules in place in 1978.

Habeas Corpus Review of Tribal Detention

The lone federal cause of action contained in ICRA is the provision allowing individuals convicted of a tribal offense to petition for a writ of habeas corpus in federal courts.[68] The meaning of this phrase has been extended by some federal courts to include banishment or exclusion from reservation lands. In *Poodry v. Tonawanda Band of Seneca Indians*,[69] the Second Circuit granted a petition for a writ of habeas corpus where the tribal council had banished several tribal members for treason.[70] The council also stripped them of their on-reservation property and citizenship within the tribe.[71] The banished individuals received no hearing prior to being deprived of their membership and property.[72] The Second Circuit panel expressed incredulity that it could not assert jurisdiction over the challenges to the tribal action: "The respondents invite us to hold that the petitioners—citizens of the United States residing within our borders—cannot challenge the threatened loss of their tribal membership, cultural and religious identity, and property under the laws of the United States."[73] With the tone of incredulity set, the court proceeded to apply American constitutional standards to the tribal decision: "We decline the

---

[66] Santa Clara Pueblo v. Martinez, 436 U.S. 49, 65–66 (1978) (citations and footnotes omitted).

[67] Id. at 71.

[68] 25 U.S.C. § 1303.

[69] 85 F.3d 874 (2d Cir.), cert. denied, 519 U.S. 1041 (1996).

[70] Id. at 876.

[71] Id.

[72] Id.

[73] Id. at 876.

respondents' invitation to hold that under current law basic American principles of due process are wholly irrelevant in these circumstances, or that the federal courts are completely divested of authority to consider whether the alleged actions of the members of the tribal Council of Chiefs conform to those principles."[74]

Other courts struggled to apply the *Poodry* analysis to tribal exclusion and banishment orders, which are increasingly being employed in both criminal and membership contexts. The Ninth Circuit in *Jeffredo v. Macarro*[75] followed the *Poodry* holding that actual detention is not required to invoke the § 1303 habeas right, but held under that mere "limitation on . . . access to certain tribal facilities does not amount to a 'detention.' "[76] Similarly, the court in *Alire v. Jackson* declined to extend federal habeas review to a Warm Springs Indian Reservation tribal council order excluding a nonmember Indian, who lost neither her tribal membership nor her federal government benefits available to tribal members.[77] The tribal council based its exclusion on the fact that the petitioner had been convicted of child abuse and had been employed as a caregiver to children on that reservation.[78] In *Tavares v. Whitehouse*,[79] the Ninth Circuit noted the Circuit's disagreement with much of the analysis of the Second Circuit's *Poodry* decision.[80] There, over a dissent, the court held that the temporary banishment of tribal members did not rise to the level of detention.[81]

Others have sought habeas review of tribal court decisions in matters resulting in civil fines. In *Moore v. Nelson*,[82] a Yurok Indian who had violated a tribal court order not to harvest timber on the Hoopa Valley Reservation sought review of that court's order to impound his logging equipment and fined him over $18,000.[83] The Ninth Circuit refused to grant the petition, emphasizing that the petitioner had never been criminally prosecuted or sentenced and never subjected to detention of any kind.[84] Similarly, in *Shenandoah v. Dept. of Interior*,[85] the Second Circuit refused to grant habeas review to petitioners who claimed to have been

---

[74] Id. at 876–77.

[75] 599 F.3d 913 (9th Cir. 2009), cert. denied, 560 U.S. 925 (2010).

[76] Id. at 919.

[77] 65 F. Supp. 2d 1124, 1129 (D. Or. 1999).

[78] Id. at 1125.

[79] 851 F.3d 863 (9th Cir., 2017).

[80] Id. at 875–76.

[81] Id. at 878.

[82] 270 F.3d 789 (9th Cir. 2001).

[83] Id. at 790.

[84] Id. at 791–92.

[85] 159 F.3d 708 (2d Cir. 1998).

terminated from tribal employment, denied government benefits, and ordered not to speak to other tribal members.[86] Later, the same court, in *Shenandoah v. Halbritter*,[87] rejected a habeas petition after the tribal government ordered the eviction of the petitioners from tribal housing as a means of enforcing the tribal housing ordinance.[88]

§ 6.4   The Special Problem of Disenrollment

The federal courts long have recognized the authority of Indian nations to determine their own membership or citizenship criteria.[89] Moreover, federal and state courts have no jurisdiction over tribal membership disputes. Individuals challenging tribal membership decisions often make herculean efforts to force federal court review, usually without success. In *Smith v. Babbitt*,[90] for example, the Eighth Circuit rejected a claim by members and nonmembers that the Mdewakanton Sioux Tribe, a highly successful gaming tribe, had violated the Indian Gaming Regulatory Act by illegally disbursing tribal gaming per capita payments.[91] The court held that the tribe's membership decisions were its own and could not be upended by a federal court, noting that "a membership dispute is an issue for a tribe and its courts."[92] The district court noted that the gaming act claims were merely pretexts for challenging tribal membership.[93]

Other claimants sue the United States as a means to get around the federal subject matter jurisdictional limitation, only to be confronted by tribal sovereign immunity. In *Lewis v. Norton*,[94] the court held that suing the federal government cannot avoid "the double jurisdictional whammy of sovereign immunity and lack of federal court jurisdiction to intervene in tribal membership disputes."[95] Even so, the court tapped into growing concern over the lack of accountability Indian tribes face when making membership

---

[86]   Id. at 714.

[87]   366 F.3d 89 (2d Cir. 2004).

[88]   Id. at 92.

[89]   E.g., Santa Clara Pueblo v. Martinez, 436 U.S. 49 (1978); Cherokee Intermarriage Cases, 203 U.S. 76 (1906); Roff v. Burney, 168 U.S. 218 (1897).

[90]   100 F.3d 556 (8th Cir. 1996), cert. denied sub nom., Feezor v. Babbitt, 522 U.S. 807 (1997).

[91]   Id. at 557.

[92]   Id. at 558 (citations omitted).

[93]   Id. at 559.

[94]   424 F.3d 959 (9th Cir. 2005).

[95]   Id. at 960.

decisions, arguing that its own decision was "deeply troubling on the level of fundamental substantive justice."[96]

The most controversial tribal membership decisions are disenrollments, where the tribal government has made a political decision to disenroll individuals who are enrolled.[97] Most federal court cases involving disenrollments are dismissed for lack of jurisdiction. Disenrollees may bring suits in tribal courts, however, to challenge the tribal decision, with some success.

In general, Indian nations that choose to engage in mass disenrollment are nations without a sitting judiciary, eliminating a forum for independent review of the decisions. Indian nations with judiciaries that engage in mass disenrollment often, but not always, raise tribal immunity or other jurisdictional defenses to judicial review.

§ 6.5   Tribal Sovereign Immunity

American Indian tribes are immune from suit by states, individuals, and businesses in federal, state, and tribal courts unless the tribe consents to suit or Congress abrogates tribal immunity for a particular statutory purpose. Indian tribes are not immune from suit by the federal government.

Foundational Cases

Tribal sovereign immunity is a long-standing doctrine, with Supreme Court and lower federal court cases recognizing tribal immunity from suit going back well in the 19th century. In *Parks v. Ross*,[98] the Supreme Court rejected a claim by Parks, the executor of a Cherokee citizen's estate, against John Ross, the Principal Chief of the Cherokee Nation, for debts allegedly owed under contract as part of the Cherokee removal in 1838 and 1839.[99] The Court noted to extraordinary status of the Cherokee Nation and held, in what appears to be the first instance of a court recognizing a nascent theory of tribal sovereign immunity, that the national status of the tribe foreclosed federal court authority.[100]

Eventually, the Supreme Court reaffirmed and cemented the doctrine of tribal sovereign immunity in *Puyallup Tribe, Inc. v. Department of Game of Washington*[101] and *Santa Clara Pueblo v.*

---

[96]   Id. at 963.

[97]   See generally Gabriel S. Galanda & Ryan D. Dreveskracht, Curing the Tribal Disenrollment Epidemic: In Search of a Remedy, 57 Ariz. L. Rev. 383 (2015).

[98]   52 U.S. 362 (1850).

[99]   Id. at 373.

[100]   Id. at 374.

[101]   433 U.S. 165 (1977).

Martinez.[102] In *Puyallup*, the Court tossed a state supreme court decision affirming a state court order asserting jurisdiction over the fishing activities of the Puyallup Tribe.[103] The Court held that tribal immunity foreclosed the state's jurisdiction absent waiver or consent by either the tribe or Congress.[104]

In *Martinez*, the Court held that the Indian Civil Rights Act also did not effect a waiver of tribal sovereign immunity.[105] The Court noted that the Act did not expressly abrogate tribal immunity, though Congress certainly had the authority to do so, and would not imply a Congressional waiver of tribal immunity in deference to tribal self-determination.[106]

The Supreme Court reaffirmed tribal sovereign immunity even in the face of a suit brought by a state government in *Oklahoma Tax Commission v. Citizen Band Potawatomi Tribe of Oklahoma*.[107] There, the tribe sued the state to enjoin state tobacco taxes for cigarettes sold on tribal trust lands, and the state countersued to force the tribe to collect and remit the state taxes.[108] The Court expressly noted that tribal sovereign immunity is subject to defeasance by Congress, but that the Legislature has repeatedly affirmed its approval of tribal immunity.[109]

Congress has frequently legislated in light of tribal sovereign immunity; perhaps most obviously in the context of the Indian Gaming Regulatory Act.[110] In the Act, Congress created a mechanism abrogating tribal immunity in limited situations; namely, for states and tribes to negotiate the question of casino-style gaming,[111] a mechanism that would be unnecessary if tribes possessed no immunity from state suit.

Oklahoma asked the Court to abrogate tribal immunity in instances where states had brought the claim, but the Court refused to do so even where the state lacked an effective judicial remedy to enforce its valid state taxes against the tribe.[112] Importantly, the

---

[102]   436 U.S. 49 (1978).

[103]   Puyallup Tribe, Inc. v. Department of Game of Washington, 433 U.S. 165, 167 (1977).

[104]   Id. at 173.

[105]   Santa Clara Pueblo v. Martinez, 436 U.S. 49, 58 (1978).

[106]   Id. at 58–59 (quoting United States v. Testan, 424 U.S. 392, 399 (1976), quoting in turn, United States v. King, 395 U.S. 1, 4 (1969)).

[107]   498 U.S. 505 (1991).

[108]   Id. at 507–08.

[109]   Id. at 510.

[110]   25 U.S.C. §§ 2701 et seq.

[111]   25 U.S.C. § 2710(d).

[112]   Id. at 514.

Court noted the state had other enforcement mechanisms, including perhaps a suit against tribal officials, who the Court noted are not immune from suits for injunctive, prospective relief.[113]

In *Kiowa Tribe of Oklahoma v. Manufacturing Technologies, Inc.*,[114] the Supreme Court affirmed tribal sovereign immunity from suits arising from off-reservation, commercial conduct.[115] The Court reaffirmed the general rule that Indian tribes are immune from suit absent consent or Congressional waiver.[116] The Court took a major turn at that point to conclude that tribal sovereign immunity, like foreign sovereign immunity, is "a matter of federal law."[117] The Court had not previously compared tribal immunity to the immunity of foreign nations, which Congress had expressly limited in the Foreign Sovereign Immunities Act of 1976.[118] Making that analogy allowed the Court to assert that "[a]s with tribal immunity, foreign sovereign immunity began as a judicial doctrine."[119] For the Court, if tribal immunity is judge-made law, then perhaps the Court can eliminate tribal immunity.

The Court in *Kiowa* instead roundly affirmed tribal immunity, even over the invitation by the tribe's opponent to confine tribal immunity to on-reservation, noncommercial activity.[120] The Court reviewed its precedents and confirmed, "To date, our cases have sustained tribal immunity from suit without drawing a distinction based on where the tribal activities occurred. . . . Nor have we yet drawn a distinction between governmental and commercial activities of a tribe."[121] Moreover, the Court relied on the fact that Congress has not acted either: "Tribes enjoy immunity from suits on contracts, whether those contracts involve governmental or commercial activities and whether they were made on or off a reservation. Congress has not abrogated this immunity, nor has petitioner waived it, so the immunity governs this case."[122]

At that point, the Supreme Court expressed its views as a policymaker, criticizing its own precedents recognizing and affirming tribal immunity and imploring Congress to abrogate

---

[113] Id.

[114] 523 U.S. 751 (1998).

[115] Id. at 753.

[116] Id. at 754.

[117] Id. at 759.

[118] 28 U.S.C. §§ 1604, 1605, 1607.

[119] Kiowa Tribe of Oklahoma v. Manufacturing Technologies, Inc., 523 U.S. 751, 759 (1998).

[120] Id. at 758.

[121] Id. at 754–55.

[122] Id. at 760.

tribal immunity. The Court first asserted that its prior recitations of tribal immunity rested on precedents "that assumed immunity without extensive reasoning. . . ."[123] Asserting that tribal immunity "developed almost by accident,"[124] the Court expressed a view that tribal immunity should not apply to commercial activities of Indian nations because commercial activities have no nexus to "traditional tribal customs and activities."[125] Asserting that modern tribal commercial activities that include ski resorts, gaming, and tobacco sales—"the Nation's commerce"—the Court argued that tribal immunity "extends beyond what is needed to safeguard tribal self-governance."[126]

Moreover, the Court argued that tort victims and contract partners unaware they are dealing with a tribe—neither of which were at issue in the *Kiowa* matter—could be severely affected by tribal immunity: "In this economic context, immunity can harm those who are unaware that they are dealing with a tribe, who do not know of tribal immunity, or who have no choice in the matter, as in the case of tort victims."[127] In the end, however, the Court declared that "we defer to the role Congress may wish to exercise in this important judgment."[128]

Michigan v. Bay Mills Indian Community

In *Michigan v. Bay Mills Indian Community*,[129] the Supreme Court re-affirmed the *Kiowa Tribe* decision, which had held that Indian tribes remain immune from suit in state courts, even in off-reservation disputes involving commercial activity absent Congressional abrogation or tribal waiver. **See §§ 5.6, 9.6**.

The Bay Mills Indian Community had purchased off-reservation fee land using proceeds from a trust fund account it acquired in the Michigan Indian Land Claims Settlement Act, quickly opening a casino on the lands.[130] The State and another Indian tribe, the Little Traverse Bay Bands of Odawa Indians, sued the tribe in federal claim to enjoin the operation of the casino, arguing that the operation violated the Indian Gaming Regulatory Act.[131] The *Bay Mills* Court's decision held first that the Indian

---

[123] Id. at 753.
[124] Id. at 756.
[125] Id. at 758.
[126] Id.
[127] Id.
[128] Id.
[129] 134 S.Ct. 2024 (2014).
[130] Id. at 2029 (citing Pub. L. 105–143, Dec. 15, 1997, 111 Stat. 2652).
[131] Id.

Gaming Regulatory Act did not authorize Michigan's suit.[132] The Court opened by reiterating that Congressional abrogation of tribal immunity "must be clear."[133] "The baseline position, we have often held, is tribal immunity; and [t]o abrogate [such] immunity, Congress must unequivocally express that purpose."[134] The Court concluded that the gaming act did not express abrogate tribal immunity in cases where a state sues a tribe in an off-reservation gaming case.[135] This portion of the opinion is discussed at greater detail in § 9.6.

The Court then re-affirmed tribal sovereign immunity by rejecting Michigan's plea to reverse or limit *Kiowa Tribe*.[136] The Court refused to disturb its precedents, noting first that *Kiowa* "reaffirmed a long line of precedents" recognizing tribal immunity for both commercial and governmental conduct, both on and off the reservation.[137] The Court noted next that it had also built its tribal immunity decisions around the doctrine, and that tribes, tribal business partners, and others had "negotiate[ed] their contracts and structur[ed] their transactions against a backdrop of tribal immunity."[138] The Court also recognized Congressional plenary power in the field of Indian affairs, and that Congress "remains free to alter what we have done."[139]

The final point is a critical one—the Court conclusively stated that it would not disturb the doctrine of tribal immunity "because it is fundamentally Congress's job, not ours, to determine whether or how to limit tribal immunity. The special brand of sovereignty the tribes retain—both its nature and its extent—rests in the hands of Congress."[140] Congress "has the greater capacity 'to weigh and accommodate the competing policy concerns and reliance interests' involved in the issue."[141] Importantly, the Court noted that since *Kiowa*, Congress had legislated in light of the Supreme Court's recent jurisprudence, and chosen not to broadly abrogate tribal immunity, but to legislate narrowly in the area.[142] The Court

---

[132] Id. at 2030–36.

[133] Id. at 2031.

[134] Id. (quoting C&L Enterprises, Inc. v. Citizen Band Potawatomi Tribe of Oklahoma, 532 U.S. 411, 418 (2001)) (quoting in turn Santa Clara Pueblo v. Martinez, 436 U.S. 49, 58 (1978) (quotation marks omitted)).

[135] Id. at 2032–35.

[136] Id. at 2036–39.

[137] Id. at 2036.

[138] Id.

[139] Id. (quotation and citation omitted).

[140] Id. at 2037.

[141] Id. at 2037–38 (quoting Kiowa Tribe of Oklahoma v. Manufacturing Technologies, Inc., 523 U.S. 751, 759 (1998)).

[142] Id. at 2038–39.

refused to upend Congress's policy choices, noting that to judicially vacate tribal immunity "would scale the heights of presumption: Beyond upending 'long-established principle[s] of tribal sovereign immunity,' that action would replace Congress's considered judgment with our contrary opinion."[143]

Waivers of Tribal Immunity—*C&L Enterprises*

In *C&L Enterprises Inc. v. Citizen Band Potawatomi Indian Tribe*,[144] the Supreme Court held that a tribe effectively waived its immunity to suit in state court by executing a boilerplate construction contract that included an arbitration clause that allowed for enforcement of an arbitration award in "any court of competent jurisdiction of this state."[145] The Court held that, while a tribe's waiver must be "clear," the arbitration clause and accompanying enforcement provision served as adequate clarity.[146]

Though the courts disfavor implied waivers of tribal immunity, following the doctrine that waivers of immunity must be clear, claims that a tribe has impliedly waived immunity have blossomed, especially in tribal courts.[147] For example, in *Bittle v. Bahe*,[148] the Oklahoma Supreme Court ruled that the tribe waived its immunity by signing onto a gaming compact that required the tribe to defend casino-related tort claims in "courts of competent jurisdiction," which the court held included state courts.[149] Some courts have ruled in favor claims that a tribal official executing contract documents waived tribal immunity even where the official had no authority to do so.[150]

Consistent with the purpose of protecting tribal governance, tribes use sovereign immunity to protect small tribal budgets, tribal lands, and tribal trusts for children, elders, and government programs. Nationwide, tribal governments have crafted limited

---

[143] Id. (quoting Oklahoma Tax Commission v. Citizen Band of Potawatomi Indians of Oklahoma, 498 U.S. 505, 510 (1991)).

[144] 532 U.S. 411 (2001).

[145] Id. at 416.

[146] Id. at 418.

[147] E.g., Johnson v. Navajo Nation, 5 Navajo Rep. 192 (Navajo Nation Supreme Court 1987); Kalantari Spirit Mountain Gaming, Inc., 5 Am. Tribal Law 94 (Confederated Tribes of Grand Ronde Community Tribal Court 2004), appeal dismissed, 6 Am. Tribal Law 94 (Confederated Tribes of Grand Ronde Community Court of Appeals 2005).

[148] 192 P.3d 810 (Okla. 2008).

[149] Id. at 828 n. 1 (Kauger, J., dissenting). Eventually, the court reversed itself and concluded that the language did not amount to a clear waiver. Sheffer v. Buffalo Run Casino, 315 P.3d 359 (Okla. 2013).

[150] E.g., Smith v. Hopland Band of Pomo Indians, 95 Cal. App. 4th 1 (2002); Rush Creek Solutions, Inc. v. Ute Mountain Ute Tribe, 107 P.3d 402 (Colo. App. 2004).

waivers of immunity both statutorily and contractually that work to preserve limited tribal assets and provide a forum to resolve disputes,[151] although it should be noted that many Indian tribes have not yet established a court system. Indian law scholars such as Frank Pommersheim have been warning tribal leaders and counsel for decades that if they do not solve the no-forum problem, someone else will—either Congress or the Supreme Court.[152] Progressive and forward-thinking Indian tribes by the dozens have already enacted ordinances governing tort and contract claims, as well as civil rights statutes that offer blanket but limited waivers of immunity.[153] Business-oriented tribes have also waived immunity contractually in many instances.[154] Tribes typically waive immunity to suits in tribal courts but often waive immunity in state or federal courts' jurisdiction as well. Cases in which a tribe successfully invokes immunity to preclude judicial review in any court still make news, but have become the exception rather than the rule.

Tribal Official Immunity

The Supreme Court has held that tribal officials engaged in ongoing violations of federal law may be sued in federal court for prospective, injunctive relief. Though the Court has made statements supportive of the proposition, the Court has not yet held that tribal officials violating state law may be sued, or whether they may be sued in federal and state court.

In at least four cases strongly affirming tribal sovereign immunity, the Supreme Court has suggested a rule analogous to *Ex parte Young*,[155] which authorizes suits against government officials, could apply to tribal officials acting outside of the scope of their official capacities, or in violation of federal law, as a means to avoid tribal immunity. In *Michigan v. Bay Mills Indian Community*,[156] the Court suggested that "tribal immunity does not bar . . . a suit for injunctive relief against individuals, including tribal officers,

---

[151] Kaighn Smith, Jr., Ethical "Obligations" and Affirmative Tribal Sovereignty: Some Considerations for Tribal Attorneys, Drummond Woodsum & MacMahon 3–5 (2006). E.g., 6 Grand Traverse Band Code §§ 201–11 (entitled "Waiver of Sovereign Immunity and Jurisdiction in Commercial Transactions"); Waganakising Odawa Tribal Code § 6.5005 (waiving immunity from suits against tribal officials for claims of discrimination).

[152] Frank R. Pommersheim, The Crucible of Sovereignty: Analyzing Issues of Tribal Jurisdiction, 31 Ariz. L. Rev. 329, 347–51 (1989).

[153] Patrice H. Kunesh, Tribal Self-Determination in the Age of Scarcity, 54 S.D. L. Rev. 398, 408–14 (2009).

[154] John F. Petoskey, Northern Michigan: Doing Business with Michigan Indian Tribes, 76 Mich. B.J. 440, 442–45 (1997).

[155] 209 U.S. 123 (1908).

[156] 134 S.Ct. 2034 (2014).

responsible for unlawful conduct."[157] In *Oklahoma Tax Commission v. Citizen Band Potawatomi Indian Nation*,[158] the Court stated: "We have never held that individual agents or officers of a tribe are not liable for damages in actions brought by the State."[159] In *Santa Clara Pueblo v. Martinez*,[160] the Supreme Court held that Lucario Padilla, a defendant in the civil rights complaint and an officer of the Pueblo, "is not protected by the tribe's immunity from suit."[161] Finally, the Court in *Puyallup Tribe, Inc. v. Washington Dept. of Game*,[162] held that "the doctrine of sovereign immunity . . . does not immunize the individual members of the Tribe."[163]

The so-called *Ex parte Young* exception allows for a suit against officers of a sovereign government where the plaintiffs allege continuing unlawful conduct, and where the plaintiffs seek declaratory and injunctive relief only.[164] In *Vann v. Kempthorne*,[165] the D.C. Circuit noted that the only two circumstances where a government official may be sued is where the official's actions go beyond the authority granted by statute, and were therefore ultra vires; or where the statute itself is alleged to be unconstitutional.[166]

As a general matter, tribal official immunity applies for activities undertaken off-reservation, suits brought for money damages, can include both members and nonmembers and unelected tribal officials, and derives from a tribal sovereignty that predates the Constitution.[167] Prior to *Martinez*, federal courts long had recognized that tribal officials may not be sued, largely because plaintiffs would sue tribal officials to avoid the general rule that Indian tribes may not be sued absent Congressional consent.[168] Cases in this vein hold that tribes and tribal officials are under the

---

[157] Id. at 2035.

[158] 498 U.S. 505 (1991).

[159] Id. at 514.

[160] 436 U.S. 49 (1978).

[161] Id. at 59 (citing Puyallup Tribe, Inc. v. Department of Game of Washington, 433 U.S. 165, 171 (1973); Young, 209 U.S. 123).

[162] 433 U.S. 165 (1973).

[163] Id. at 171–72.

[164] Seminole Tribe of Florida v. Florida, 516 U.S. 44, 73 (1996); Keweenaw Bay Indian Community v. Kleine, 546 F. Supp. 2d 509, 517 (W.D. Mich. 2008).

[165] Vann v. Kempthorne, 534 F.3d 741, 750–51 (D.C. Cir. 2008).

[166] Id. at 750–51.

[167] James Joseph Morrison Consultants, Inc. v. Sault Ste. Marie Tribe of Chippewa Indians, No. 2:97–CV–315, 1998 WL 1031492, at *3–4 (W.D. Mich., Aug. 6, 1998).

[168] E.g., Haile v. Saunooke, 246 F.2d 293, 297–98 (4th Cir. 1957); Adams v. Murphy, 165 F. 304, 309 (8th Cir. 1908); Seneca Constitutional Rights Organization v. George, 348 F. Supp. 48, 50 (W.D. N.Y. 1972); Barnes v. United States, 205 F. Supp. 97, 100 (D. Mont. 1962).

"tutelage" of the United States, and therefore immune absent a Congressional waiver.[169]

Immunity of Individual Tribal Employees—*Lewis v. Clarke*

In *Lewis v. Clarke*,[170] the Supreme Court held that a suit against a tribal employee in his individual capacity is not barred by tribal sovereign immunity. There, a married couple injured in an off-reservation automobile wreck sued a driver employed by the Mohegan Tribe's gaming operation who allegedly caused the accident. The tribe argued that it was the real party in interest, meaning that any judgment award against the driver would be paid by the employer, the tribe. The Court held that tribal employees sued in their individual capacities involve claims that do not implicate tribal sovereign immunity.[171] The *Lewis* Court left open several questions, notably how the official and qualified immunity doctrines that govern state and federal official actions will apply in the tribal government context, if at all.

---

[169] E.g., Twin Cities Chippewa Tribal Council v. Minnesota Chippewa Tribe, 340 F.2d 529, 532 (8th Cir. 1967); Leech Lake Citizens Community v. Leech Lake Band of Chippewa Indians, 355 F. Supp. 697, 700 (D. Minn. 1973).

[170] 137 S.Ct. 1285 (2017).

[171] Id. at 1292 (citing Larson v. Domestic and Foreign Commerce Corp., 337 U.S. 682, 687 (1949)).

Chapter 7

INDIAN COUNTRY AND CRIMINAL JURISDICTION

Analysis

§ 7.1   "Indian Country" Before the 1948 Codification

"Indian country" is a term of art that is most useful in the criminal jurisdiction context, but has a long and complicated history arising from its origins as a casual descriptor of where Indian people live. Indian country once meant everything west of the original 13 states, but that understanding was dynamic as the American republic crept westward. Indian country is now statutorily defined as three kinds of Indian lands—reservation lands, dependent Indian communities, and allotments.

In 1948, Congress codified the definition "Indian country" in the federal criminal code.[1] Section 1151 was an attempt by Congress in 1948 to consolidate conflicting and inconsistent provisions of the code, and to incorporate Supreme Court decisions establishing the federal common-law definition of "Indian country."[2]

---

[1]   The definition is:

> [T]he term "Indian country", as used in this chapter, means (a) all land within the limits of any Indian reservation under the jurisdiction of the United States Government, notwithstanding the issuance of any patent, and, including rights-of-way running through the reservation, (b) all dependent Indian communities within the borders of the United States whether within the original or subsequently acquired territory thereof, and whether within or without the limits of a state, and (c) all Indian allotments, the Indian titles to which have not been extinguished, including rights-of-way running through the same.

18 U.S.C. § 1151.

[2]   18 U.S.C. § 1151 note.

The definition is also used for civil jurisdiction purposes as well,[3] although it is perilous to do so as courts deciding tribal civil jurisdiction cases have been more restrictive in acknowledging Indian lands than the "Indian country" statute. **See § 8.1**.

The key factors the Supreme Court identified as relevant to whether a particular parcel of land was "Indian country" before 1948—whether the government set aside the lands for Indian purposes and whether the government continues to supervise the Indians on that land—are both random historical events and deeply paternalistic. The factors lead to results that can be under-inclusive.

Allotment lands are also Indian country so long as Indian ownership remains, subject to complex fact-based questions relating to the various ways lands have been allotted and the individual histories of Indian reservations. Even the Supreme Court has been uncertain about allotment lands. In *In re Heff*,[4] the Court held that once an Indian allotment's trust status expired, usually after 25 years, federal authority over the Indian and his property also expires.[5] Eleven years later, in *United States v. Nice*,[6] the Court reversed *Heff* and concluded that Indian-owned allotments remain lands over which Congress can legislate.[7]

On more than one occasion, the Supreme Court's determinations on whether lands constituted Indian country for purposes of criminal jurisdiction delved into its own ethnocentric views on whether the Indian people living on the lands were "civilized" or "dependent." In *United States v. Sandoval*,[8] the Supreme Court held that the federal courts could entertain jurisdiction over a federal criminal prosecution for bringing liquor in Indian country; namely, the Santa Clara Pueblo.[9] For more details on *Sandoval*, **see § 3.7**.

The 1948 Act "gave rise to an entirely new genre of litigation, today referred to as reservation boundary litigation."[10] Codification has not settled Indian country status, and reservation boundary litigation frequently arises.

---

[3]   Alaska v. Native Village of Venetie Tribal Government, 522 U.S. 520, 527 (1998); DeCoteau v. District Court, 420 U.S. 425, 427 & n.1 (1975) (per curiam).

[4]   197 U.S. 488 (1905).

[5]   Id. at 509.

[6]   241 U.S. 591 (1916).

[7]   Id. at 601.

[8]   231 U.S. 28 (1913).

[9]   Id. at 49.

[10]   Marc Slonim, Indian Country, Indian Reservations, and the Importance of History in Indian Law, 45 Gonz. L. Rev. 517, 526 (2009/2010).

§ 7.2   Reservation Boundaries Litigation

In the mid-20th century, the Supreme Court often attempted to resolve reservation boundaries litigation by limiting the checkerboarded patterns of Indian country jurisdiction created by allotment and other Congressional programs. Tribal interests often prevailed in these early cases. By the 1990s, however, the Supreme Court turned more to the demographic patterns of on-reservation residents, usually to the detriment of Indian nations.[11]

Seymour v. Superintendent of Washington State Penitentiary

In *Seymour v. Superintendent of Washington State Penitentiary*,[12] the Supreme Court considered a habeas petition by a Colville Indian Nation member convicted in state courts of burglary.[13] The lower court concluded that the land upon which the crime occurred was, at one time, Colville reservation land, but since that time the reservation had "dissolved."[14] President Grant established the Colville Indian Reservation in 1872 by Executive Order.[15] An 1892 Act of Congress did apparently alter the status of the so-called "North Half" of the reservation but Congress expressly stated that the "South Half" of the reservation, upon which the crime occurred, remained "reserved by the Government for their (the Colville Indians') use and occupancy."[16] Therefore, the 1892 Act did not change the character of the relevant reservation land.

Mattz v. Arnett

The next Supreme Court case to determine whether an Indian reservation remained Indian country was *Mattz v. Arnett*.[17] There, California state conservation officers confiscated the fishing equipment of a Yurok tribal member within an Indian reservation on the Klamath River.[18] President Pierce established the land as reservation lands in an 1855 Executive Order issued under the authority of an 1853 Act of Congress.[19] The reservation included a strip of land starting with the mouth of the Klamath River, going

---

[11]   David H. Getches, Charles F. Wilkinson, Robert A. Williams, Jr., Matthew L.M. Fletcher, and Kristen A. Carpenter, Cases and Materials on Federal Indian Law 522–23 (7th ed. 2017).

[12]   368 U.S. 351 (1962).

[13]   Id. at 352.

[14]   Id. at 353.

[15]   Id. at 354.

[16]   Id.

[17]   412 U.S. 481 (1973).

[18]   Id. at 484.

[19]   Id.

up the river 20 miles, and extending out one mile from the river in each direction.[20]

Mattz held that the 1892 Act allotting lands within the Hoopa Valley Reservation did not disestablish the Klamath River extension.[21] The Act provided that all lands within the former Klamath River Reservation were to be allotted to Yurok tribal members and the remainder to be sold under the federal homestead laws.[22] The Court held that the 1892 Act was merely a local implementation of the 1887 General Allotment Act, which authorized the President to allot Indian reservations to individual Indians, but left the sale of surplus lands to the President's discretion.[23] The 1887 Act, according to the Court, was not intended to disestablish Indian reservations, but instead was intended to "open the way for non-Indian settlers to own land on the reservation in a manner which the Federal Government, acting as guardian and trustee for the Indians, regarded as beneficial to the development of its wards."[24]

The *Mattz* Court required that a judicial determination that an Indian reservation has been diminished or disestablished be supported by a clear statement of Congress to that effect, noting that the 1892 Act did not include "clear termination language."[25] The Court concluded, "[W]e are not inclined to infer an intent to terminate the reservation."[26]

DeCoteau v. District County Court for the Tenth Judicial District

After *Mattz*, however, the Supreme Court would not confine its search for intent to diminish or disestablish an Indian reservation to statutory language. In *DeCoteau v. District County Court for the Tenth Judicial District*,[27] the Court held that the Lake Traverse Reservation of the Sisseton Wahpeton Oyate was disestablished by Congress in an 1891 Act.[28] As with *Seymour* and *Mattz*, *DeCoteau* involved the state's assertion of jurisdiction for acts occurring within reservation boundaries.[29]

---

[20] Id. at 483–84.
[21] Mattz v. Arnett, 412 U.S. 481, 494–95 (1973).
[22] Id. at 495.
[23] Id. at 496–97.
[24] Id. at 497 (quoting Seymour v. Superintendent, 368 U.S. 351, 356 (1962)).
[25] Id. at 504.
[26] Id.
[27] 420 U.S. 425 (1975).
[28] Id. at 427–28.
[29] Id. at 427.

The Court concluded that " 'the face of the Act,' and its 'surrounding circumstances' and 'legislative history,' all point unmistakably to the conclusion that the Lake Traverse Reservation was terminated in 1891."[30] The Court pointed to the language of the 1891 agreement, in which the tribe agreed to sell all of its unallotted lands.[31] The Court held that the United States and the Sisseton Wahpeton Oyate were both satisfied that tribal government could continue without any of the unallotted lands, and that "retention of allotments would provide an adequate fulcrum for tribal affairs."[32] The Court concluded, therefore, that "exclusive tribal and federal jurisdiction is limited to the retained allotments."[33]

Justice Douglas, joined by two others, dissented on the grounds that § 1151 defined "Indian country" to include lands " 'within the limits of' an Indian reservation 'notwithstanding the issuance of any patent.' "[34] The dissent criticized the majority for recognizing exclusive federal and tribal jurisdiction over only a small portion of the reservation, noting that even the local Indian office is located outside of that area.[35] The dissent noted that the tribe was the major employer and government entity on the reservation.[36]

Rosebud Sioux Tribe v. Kneip

Similarly, in *Rosebud Sioux Tribe v. Kneip*,[37] the Court held that Congress had diminished the Rosebud Sioux Reservation in a series of Congressional acts.[38] In 1889, the tribe and the United States treated for the creation of a 3.2 million acre reservation, covering most of what are now five counties in the state of South Dakota.[39] Three subsequent federal statues purported to dispose of unallotted lands in three of the counties.[40]

The three Acts of Congress were unilateral federal enactments done without tribal consent: "the Acts of 1904, 1907, and 1910 were unilateral Acts of Congress without the consent of three-quarters of the members of the tribe required by the original Treaty. . . ."[41]

---

[30]   Id. at 445.

[31]   Id.

[32]   Id. at 446.

[33]   Id.

[34]   Id. at 460 (Douglas, J., dissenting) (quoting 18 U.S.C. § 1151).

[35]   Id. at 464 (Douglas, J., dissenting).

[36]   Id. at 465 (Douglas, J., dissenting).

[37]   430 U.S. 584 (1977).

[38]   Id. at 585.

[39]   Id. at 585–86.

[40]   Id. at 586.

[41]   Id. at 587.

Relying on *Lone Wolf v. Hitchcock*,[42] the Court concluded that tribal consent "does not have any direct bearing" on the question at hand.[43]

The Court focused on a 1901 agreement between the tribe and the federal government, not ratified by Congress, would have diminished the reservation by an entire county.[44] In 1903, United States negotiators obtained consent from a majority of the "adult male Indians" to open up the same area as the 1901 area for settlement, which the federal negotiator claimed would diminish the reservation.[45] Members of Congress expressed their understanding that this outcome was also their understanding, that the Rosebud Sioux Reservation would diminish down to the shape of a square.[46] The agreement used language legally equivalent to the language used in the *DeCoteau* case, most notably, "cession."[47] But the agreement in *DeCoteau* was a "cession," in that the tribe consented to the sale. The agreement in *Kneip* could not be, in that the tribe's consent was not perfected, rendering the 1904 Act awkward at best. The Court was unconcerned: "The use of the word 'cession' in the 1904 Act, which was not consented to by the required extraordinary majority of the Tribe, does not make the meaning of the Act ambiguous as between diminution of the Reservation boundaries on the one hand, and merely opening up designated lands for settlement by non-Indians, on the other."[48]

As the Court did in *DeCoteau*, the *Kneip* Court addressed post-enactment "jurisdictional history."[49] Without responding to the federal government's particular arguments on its continued assertion of jurisdiction over the relevant land, the Court rejected the government's claims as "sporadic, and often contradictory, history of congressional and administrative actions. . . ."[50]

The Current Approach: *Solem v. Bartlett*

The leading case in the area of reservation boundaries litigation is *Solem v. Bartlett*,[51] a dispute over the reservation

---

[42]   187 U.S. 553 (1903).

[43]   Rosebud Sioux Tribe v. Kneip, 430 U.S. 584, 587 (1977).

[44]   Id. at 591–92.

[45]   Id. at 593–94.

[46]   Id. at 596.

[47]   Id. at 597 (citing DeCoteau v. District County Court, 420 U.S. 425, 445 (1975)).

[48]   Id.

[49]   Id. at 605.

[50]   Id. at 605 n. 27.

[51]   465 U.S. 463 (1984).

boundaries of the Cheyenne River Sioux Tribe.[52] The state of South Dakota convicted a tribal member with a felony, and he argued the state had no jurisdiction over him because the crime occurred within the reservation boundaries.[53]

The tribe and the federal government negotiated for the creation of the Cheyenne River Sioux Reservation in an agreement ratified by Congress in 1889.[54] In 1908, Congress passed an allotment statute relating to the reservation, providing for the sale of surplus lands.[55] The Court was careful to note that by 1908, "Congress was dealing with the surplus land question on a reservation-by-reservation basis, with each surplus land act employing its own statutory language, the product of a unique set of tribal negotiation and legislative compromise."[56] The Court further pointed out that Congress's codification of "Indian country" in 1948 "uncouple[d] reservation status from Indian ownership, and statutorily define Indian country to include lands held in fee by non-Indians within reservation boundaries."[57] Justice Douglas noted in dissent that the Court all but ignored the plain text of § 1151.

The *Solem* Court also made clear that the late 19th and early 20th century tribal and federal negotiators rarely considered questions of state jurisdiction in the manner of modern courts—either because Congress had not yet "uncouple[d]" Indian ownership with reservation status or because non-Indians believed Indian reservations would not last: "Congress naturally failed to be meticulous in clarifying whether a particular piece of legislation formally sliced a certain parcel of land off one reservation."[58]

Noting that the Court had reached different and frankly inconsistent outcomes in reservation boundaries prior to *Solem*, the Court articulated a legal test for analyzing the cases going forward. The first principle is that only Congress can divest a tribe of its reservation:

> Our precedents in the area have established a fairly clean analytical structure for distinguishing those surplus land acts that diminished reservations from those acts that simply offered non-Indians the opportunity to purchase land within established reservation boundaries. The first and governing principle is that only Congress can

---

[52]   Id. at 464.

[53]   Id.

[54]   Id. at 465.

[55]   Id. at 466.

[56]   Id. at 467.

[57]   Id. at 468.

[58]   Id. at 468.

divest a reservation of its land and diminish its boundaries. Once a block of land is set aside for an Indian Reservation and no matter what happens to the title of individual plots within the area, the entire block retains its reservation status until Congress explicitly indicates otherwise.[59]

The Court further held that reservation diminishment "will not be lightly inferred."[60] The Court would require Congress to "clearly evince an 'intent to change boundaries' before diminishment will be found."[61] If the Congressional act makes "[e]xplicit reference to cession or other language evidencing the present and total surrender of all tribal interests[,]" and when the "cession is buttressed by an unconditional commitment from Congress to compensate the Indian tribe for its opened land, there is an almost insurmountable presumption that Congress meant for the tribe's reservation to be diminished."[62]

However, the Court added that "explicit language of cession and unconditional compensation" are not absolute "prerequisites for a finding of diminishment"[63]—subsequent events approved of by Congress may also provide probative evidence of diminishment.[64]

The Court would also look to subsequent treatment of the lands in later enactments "[t]o a lesser extent": "Congress's own treatment of the affected areas, particularly in the years immediately following the opening, has some evidentiary value, as does the manner in which the Bureau of Indian Affairs and local judicial authorities dealt with unalloted open lands."[65]

Finally, the Court stated it would look at the "pragmatic" story of an Indian reservation as well, in particular the demographics of the reservation: "Where non-Indian settlers flooded into the opened portion of a reservation and the area has long since lost its Indian character, we have acknowledged that de facto, if not de jure, diminishment may have occurred."[66]

Turning to the relevant Act of Congress, the Court initially noted that the 1908 Cheyenne River Act did not reference the

---

[59]   Id. at 470 (citations and footnote omitted).

[60]   Id.

[61]   Id.

[62]   Id. at 470–71 (citations omitted).

[63]   Id. at 471.

[64]   Id.

[65]   Id.

[66]   Id.

"cession" of Indian lands by the tribe to the United States.[67] A mere sale, for the Court, appeared to me only that the Interior Secretary "was simply being authorized to act as the Tribe's sales agent."[68]

Moreover, the Court found that the Act's language and structure supported the continuation of the reservation. Section 1 authorized the Interior Secretary to set aside surplus lands "'for agency, school, and religious purposes, to remain reserved as long as needed, and as long as agency, school, or religious institutions are maintained thereon for the benefit of said Indians.'"[69] Section 2 authorized Indians to obtain allotments in the area otherwise set aside for surplus.[70] The Court noted that Congress did refer to the "diminished" portion of the reservation, and to "opened areas as being in the 'public domain,'"[71] but the language appeared as "isolated phrases" not sufficient to "carry the burden of establishing an express congressional purpose to diminish."[72]

The Court found that the circumstances of the agreement negotiations also did not support diminishment. A Senator introduced the bill, which pushed the Interior Secretary to send a negotiator to the reservation.[73] Few members of the tribe met with the federal negotiator, and after he returned to Washington, D.C. he was forced to acknowledge in his report that "he had never received formal approval from the Tribe."[74] The tenor of the legislative debates focused on the payment, not the "Act's effect on the reservation's boundaries or whether State or Federal officials would have jurisdiction over the opened areas."[75]

The jurisdictional history after the enactment of the Act was "so rife with contradictions and inconsistencies as to be of no help to either side."[76] Both the federal government and the state asserted jurisdiction over the opened areas, forcing the Court to conclude that "[n]either sovereign dominated the jurisdictional history of the opened lands in the decades immediately following 1908."[77]

Most importantly for the tribe, though, was the fact that most of the tribal members "obtained individual allotments on the lands

---

[67] Id. at 472–73.
[68] Id. at 473.
[69] Id. at 474.
[70] Id.
[71] Id. at 474.
[72] Id. at 475.
[73] Id. at 476.
[74] Id. at 477.
[75] Id. at 478.
[76] Id.
[77] Id. at 479.

opened by the Act," meaning that mostly Indians lived in the opened areas.[78] The tribe and the federal government maintained a strong presence on the opened area to the current era.[79]

Hagen v. Utah

In *Hagen v. Utah*,[80] the Supreme Court held that the Uintah Indian Reservation was diminished by Congress.[81] *Hagen* arose when the state prosecute a Uintah tribal member under state law.[82]

The *Hagen* Court held that the restoration of Indian reservation lands back into the "public domain" in a 1905 allotment act served to "extinguish[ ]" any previous public use.[83] The relevant Act in *Solem* also referenced the "public domain" in the context of the whether Indians could harvest timber on unalloted lands, but the *Hagen* Court distinguished that language, arguing that the 1902 Act used the phrase in its "*operative* language."[84] Following the *Solem* framework, the Court then found that the circumstances contemporary to the enactments supported diminishment.[85]

Justice Blackmun dissented.[86] He opened his dissent, one of his most powerful Indian law dissents, with a famous quote from Justice Black's dissent in *Federal Power Commission v. Tuscarora Indian Nation*:[87] "Great nations, like great men, should keep their word."[88] The dissent jumps on the ambiguity inherent in reservation boundaries litigation and would have applied a clear statement rule to the matter: "The Court relies on a single, ambiguous phrase in an Act that never became effective, and which was deleted from the controlling statute, to conclude that Congress must have intended to diminish the Uintah Valley Reservation."[89]

South Dakota v. Yankton Sioux Tribe

In *South Dakota v. Yankton Sioux Tribe*,[90] the Supreme Court again found that Congress intended an Indian reservation to be

---

[78]   Id. at 480.

[79]   Id.

[80]   510 U.S. 399 (1994).

[81]   Id. at 421–22.

[82]   Id. at 408.

[83]   Id. at 412.

[84]   Id. at 413 (emphasis in original).

[85]   Id. at 416.

[86]   Id. at 422 (Blackmun, J., dissenting).

[87]   362 U.S. 99 (1960).

[88]   Hagen v. Utah, 510 U.S. 399, 421 (1994) (Blackmun, J., dissenting) (quoting *Tuscarora*, 362 U.S. at 142) (Black, J., dissenting).

[89]   Id.

[90]   522 U.S. 329 (1998).

diminished, this time with additional reliance on the modern demographics of the reservation.[91] The question there involved a landfill owned by the state on non-Indian owned land within the reservation boundaries could be regulated by the tribe.[92]

The tribe and the federal government created a large reservation for the tribe in an 1858 treaty.[93] The federal government issued allotments on the reservation in accordance with the General Allotment Act of 1887.[94] The Interior Department began negotiations for the sale of the unallotted lands in 1892, and "[o]nce the Commissioners garnered a measure of support for the sale of the unallotted lands," proposed an agreement to the tribe.[95] Eventually, the Interior Department claimed they had received the consent of a majority of the adult male Indians and brought the agreement to Congress.[96] Despite claims of fraud in the acquisition of consent, a familiar story in the allotment-era negotiations, Congress ratified the agreement in 1894.[97]

In 1895, President Cleveland opened up the unallotted lands to settlement.[98] The Court found that "the total Indian holdings in the region consist of approximately 30,000 acres of allotted land and 6,000 acres of tribal land."[99]

The Court's analysis began, in accordance with *Solem*, with the 1892 agreement language. The agreement provided that the tribe will "cede, sell, relinquish, and convey to the United States all their claim, right, title, and interest in and to all the unallotted lands within the limits of the reservation. . . ."[100] The cession language was similar to language that appeared in the *DeCoteau* matter.[101]

Nebraska v. Parker

In *Nebraska v. Parker*,[102] the Supreme Court unanimously affirmed the continued viability of the Omaha Indian Reservation's reservation boundaries.[103] The Omaha Tribe enacted a liquor tax on all reservation businesses, including those in the village of Pender,

---

[91] Id. at 333.
[92] Id.
[93] Id. at 333–34.
[94] Id. at 337.
[95] Id.
[96] Id. at 339.
[97] Id.
[98] Id.
[99] Id. (citing Indian Reservations: A State and Federal Handbook 260 (1986)).
[100] Id. at 344.
[101] Id. (citing DeCoteau v. District County Court, 420 U.S. 425, 445 (1975)).
[102] 136 S.Ct. 1072 (2016).
[103] Id. at 1082.

which is populated mostly by nonmembers.[104] The federal government's authorized the tribe's tax under its Indian country liquor control powers.[105] The State of Nebraska eventually intervened, and claimed that the tribal tax was invalid because the village was located within a portion of the historic reservation that had been diminished by an 1882 Act of Congress.[106]

An 1854 treaty established the Omaha Indian Reservation, originally over 300,000 acres larger.[107] On behalf of the tribe, the United States sold off portions of the reservation in 1865 and 1872 not relevant to the Pender dispute.[108] In 1882, Congress authorized the Department of the Interior to aside 50,000 acres for sale on the public, after Omaha Indians had the opportunity to make selections of allotments.[109] Just a few tribal members made selections, and a nonmember named W.E. Peebles purchased the land that later became the base for the village of Pender.[110]

Unlike federal statutes held to diminish Indian reservations, the 1882 Act did not provide a large up-front payment to the tribe, but instead the government would pay the tribe money derived from sales to nonmembers.[111] Moreover, the two prior statutes involving the Omaha Tribe used language typically used in reservation diminishment cases, "cede" and "relininquish."[112] The 1882 Act used no such language.[113]

The Supreme Court did leave open the possibility that the Department of the Interior's approval of the tribe's liquor control regulation was barred by certain forms of equity previously announced in *City of Sherrill v. Oneida Indian Nation of New York*.[114] **See § 4.7.** The Court rejected Nebraska's argument on the record before it that "justifiable expectations" of the non-Indians in the area precluded tribal jurisdiction.[115] However, the Court noted that the tribe's history of not enforcing tribal laws on the village could be challenged under *Sherrill* in a future claim.[116]

---

[104] Id. at 1078.

[105] 18 U.S.C. § 1161.

[106] Act of Aug. 7, 1882, 22 Stat. 341.

[107] Treaty with the Omahas, Mar. 16, 1854, 10 Stat. 1043.

[108] Nebraska v. Parker, 136 S.Ct. 1072, 1077 (2016).

[109] Id.

[110] Id.

[111] Id. at 1079.

[112] Id. at 1080.

[113] Id.

[114] 544 U.S. 197 (2005).

[115] Nebraska v. Parker, 136 S.Ct. 1072, 1082 (2016).

[116] Id.

§ 7.3   Secretarial Trust Land Acquisitions

The most critical and occasionally controversial means by which Indian nations attempt to restore their lands is through the acquisition of land into trust by the Interior Secretary. Though the land is owned by the United States, Indian nations have the beneficial interest in the land and trust land, as this type of land is usually called, is the equivalent to reservation land and is "Indian country."

Section 5 of the Indian Reorganization Act, **see § 3.9**, authorizes the Interior Secretary to acquire land in trust for the benefit of Indians and tribes.[117] Section 7 authorized the Interior Secretary to declare new reservations on acquired trust lands.[118]

Congress intended Section 5 to respond to the massive dispossession of Indian lands resulting from the allotment policy.[119] Congress formally ended allotment in 1934 after Indians and tribes lost about 86 to 90 million acres.[120] In *Mescalero Apache Tribe v. Jones*,[121] the Supreme Court noted that Congress intended the IRA reflected "a new policy of the Federal Government and aimed to put a halt to the loss of tribal lands through allotment [and it] gave the Secretary of the Interior power to create new reservations. . . ."[122] Congress intended to IRA to "rehabilitate the Indian's economic life and to give him a chance to develop the initiative destroyed by a century of oppression and paternalism."[123]

Carcieri v. Salazar

In *Carcieri v. Salazar*,[124] the Supreme Court held that the Interior Secretary may not acquire land in trust for the benefit of the Narragansett Indian Tribe.[125] The state challenged the Secretary's decision to take land into trust on the ground that the tribe was not eligible to benefit from Section 5.

Section 5 authorizes the Interior Secretary to acquire land in trust for "Indians," a term of art defined a later section of the IRA as "all persons of Indian descent who are members of any

---

[117] 25 U.S.C. § 5108.

[118] 25 U.S.C. § 5110.

[119] Frank Pommersheim, Land into Trust: An Inquiry into Law, Policy, and History, 49 Idaho L. Rev. 519, 521–27 (2013).

[120] Id. at 522, 525.

[121] 411 U.S. 145 (1973).

[122] Id. at 151. The Court still found that tribal activities on off-reservation lands acquired under Section 5 are subject to state taxation.

[123] H.R. Rep. 73–1804 at 6 (1934).

[124] 555 U.S. 379 (2009).

[125] Id. at 382–83, 395–96.

recognized Indian tribe *now under Federal jurisdiction. . . .*"[126] The state argued that the Narragansett Indian Tribe, which the federal government recognized as an Indian tribe in 1983,[127] was not under federal jurisdiction in 1934, the date of the enactment of the IRA. The federal government and the tribe argued that "now" meant at the time of the Interior Secretary's decision to acquire land in trust. The Court agreed with the state.

The Court undertook a simple statutory construction under which it concluded that the definition of "Indian" was unambiguous.[128] The Court looked to the "ordinary meaning of the word 'now,'" and located contemporaneous dictionary definitions of the word that suggested the word "ordinarily" refers to a "present" time or moment.[129] Importantly, the Court pointed to a statement made by John Collier, architect of the IRA and the Commissioner of Indian Affairs, in 1936, two years after the IRA's enactment: "Section 19 of the Indian Reorganization Act . . . provides, in effect, that the term 'Indian' as used therein shall include—(1) all persons of Indian descent who are members of any recognized tribe *that was under Federal jurisdiction at the date of the Act. . . .*"[130]

The Court concluded by noting that no party ever claimed the Narragansett Indian Tribe was under federal jurisdiction in 1934, and shut the door to further proceedings by declaring that it would hear no evidence to the contrary.[131]

On March 12, 2014, the Interior Solicitor issued an opinion on the definition of "under federal jurisdiction" for IRA purposes.[132] The Solicitor opined that there is no plain meaning of "under federal jurisdiction."[133] The Solicitor then concluded that whether an Indian tribe was "under federal jurisdiction" in 1934 is a two-part inquiry, namely whether the tribe was ever under federal jurisdiction prior to 1934 and then whether the tribe was under federal jurisdiction in 1934.[134]

---

[126]   25 U.S.C. § 5129 (emphasis added).

[127]   Final Determination for Federal Acknowledgment of Narragansett Indian Tribe of Rhode Island, 48 Fed. Reg. 6177 (Feb. 10, 1983).

[128]   Carcieri v. Salazar, 555 U.S. 379, 388–89 (2009).

[129]   Id. at 388.

[130]   Id. at 390 (quoting Letter from John Collier, Commissioner, to Superintendents (Mar. 7, 1936)) (emphasis in original).

[131]   Id. at 395–96.

[132]   Dept. of Interior, Office of the Solicitor, The Meaning of "Under Federal Jurisdiction" for Purposes of the Indian Reorganization Act, M–37029 (March 12, 2014).

[133]   Id. at 18.

[134]   Id. at 19.

Match-E-Be-Nash-She-Wish Band of Pottawatomi Indians v. Patchak

In *Match-E-Be-Nash-She-Wish Band of Pottawatomi Indians v. Patchak*,[135] the Supreme Court held that Congress waived the federal government's immunity from suit to challenge Secretarial trust land acquisitions in the Administrative Procedure Act.[136] The suit involved the decision by the Interior Secretary to acquire land for the tribe, informally known as the Gun Lake Tribe, which Interior had acknowledged as a federally recognized tribe in 1999.[137]

The Interior Department's regulations on trust land acquisitions required the Secretary to wait 30 days to allow parties with standing to challenge a final decision to take land into trust.[138] The Interior Secretary's decision relating to the Gun Lake Tribe's trust application had already been the subject of suit in *Michigan Gambling Opposition v. Kempthorne*.[139] As that suit wound down, a local resident sued under the Administrative Procedure Act (APA) while that suit was still pending in order to bring a legal theory similar to the one advanced in *Carcieri*.[140] After the Supreme Court declined to review the D.C. Circuit's decision in *Michigan Gaming Opposition*, the Interior Secretary acquired the Gun Lake land in trust.[141]

The federal government and the tribe argued that the Quiet Title Act (QTA), a waiver of federal sovereign immunity allowing claimants to sue the United States to quiet title to federal lands.[142] However, the QTA does not apply to Indian lands, barring challenges to the federal government's title to Indian lands.[143]

The Supreme Court reasoned that the QTA's federal immunity bar applied only to claims to the tribe's land, not to final agency decisions about the tribe's land.[144] Patchak may not sue the

---

[135] 567 U.S. 209 (2012).

[136] Id. at 216–17.

[137] Id. at 212 (citing Final Determination to Acknowledge the Match-e-be-nash-she-wish Band of Pottawatomi Indians of Michigan, 63 Fed. Reg. 56936 (Oct. 23, 1999)).

[138] Id. at 213 (citing 25 C.F.R. § 151.12(b)).

[139] 477 F. Supp. 2d 1 (D.D.C. 2007), aff'd, 525 F.3d 23 (D.C. Cir. 2008), cert. denied, 555 U.S. 1137 (2009).

[140] Match-E-Be-Nash-She-Wish Band of Pottawatomi Indians v. Patchak, 567 U.S. 209, 213 (2012).

[141] Id.

[142] 28 U.S.C. § 2409a(d).

[143] 28 U.S.C. § 2409a(a).

[144] Match-E-Be-Nash-She-Wish Band of Pottawatomi Indians v. Patchak, 567 U.S. 209, 217 (2012).

government under the APA to claim he owned the property, and not the tribe or the government.[145] But Patchak may sue to challenge the Interior Secretary's decision on environmental or other grounds.[146]

§ 7.4   Federal Criminal Jurisdiction in Indian Country

Historical Background

Indian nations originally possessed inherent and exclusive sovereign authority to enforce criminal laws against lawbreakers, but tribal jurisdiction and authority receded through the treaty process and through the ravages of history. Federal authority replaced and occasionally removed tribal authority dating back to the colonial period.

Congress federalized Indian country criminal jurisdiction as early as the first Trade and Intercourse Act in 1790.[147] **See § 3.1**.

Indian Country Crimes Act, 18 U.S.C. § 1152

The Indian Country Crimes Act originated in section 5 of the initial Trade and Intercourse Act that extended federal criminal jurisdiction to Indian country crimes committed by American citizens against Indians.[148]

In 1817, Congress further extended federal criminal jurisdiction to crimes by Indians against non-Indians in Indian country.[149] Section 2 of the Act foreclosed federal jurisdiction over "any offense[s] committed by one Indian against another, within any Indian boundary."[150] Section 2 also preserved Indian treaty rights relating to criminal jurisdiction.[151]

The Supreme Court interpreted a precursor of the modern statute in *Ex parte Crow Dog*.[152] There, the Court determined that the statute did not authorize federal criminal jurisdiction over an Indian-on-Indian crime in Indian country.[153] Importantly, the Court also concluded that the 1868 Treaty of Fort Laramie,[154] which

---

[145]   Id. at 215.
[146]   Id.
[147]   1 Stat. 137 (1790).
[148]   1 Stat. 137, 138 (1790).
[149]   3 Stat. 383 (1817).
[150]   Id.
[151]   Id.
[152]   109 U.S. 556 (1883).
[153]   Id. at 571–72.
[154]   15 Stat. 635 (1868).

included the so-called "bad men" clause,[155] also did not authorize the federal prosecution of Crow Dog.[156] **See § 3.7**.

As finally amended in 1854, the Indian Country Crimes Act currently provides

> Except as otherwise expressly provided by law, the general laws of the United States as to the punishment of offenses committed in any place within the sole and exclusive jurisdiction of the United States, except the District of Columbia, shall extend to the Indian country.

> This section shall not extend to offenses committed by one Indian against the person or property of another Indian, nor to any Indian committing any offense in the Indian country who has been punished by the local law of the tribe, or to any case where, by treaty stipulations, the exclusive jurisdiction over such offenses is or may be secured to the Indian tribes respectively.[157]

In *United States v. McBratney*,[158] decided in 1891, the Supreme Court held that Colorado retained jurisdiction over a murder committed by a non-Indian against a non-Indian in Indian country, and not the federal courts.[159] Article 6 of the 1868 Indian treaty that formed the Ute Reservation in Colorado included a "bad men" clause requiring the tribe to turn over non-Indian lawbreakers to the federal government.[160] The Court held that the 1875 Act that admitted Colorado the Union placed the state on "equal footing" with previously admitted states, not an unusual provision.[161] And, for the Court, because the 1875 Act did not carve out Indian country as an exception to its general jurisdiction, the state could prosecute non-Indian-on-non-Indian murders on Indian reservations.[162]

In *Draper v. United States*,[163] the Supreme Court extended the *McBratney* ruling even to states that had disclaimed jurisdiction over Indian country in their admissions act.[164] There, a federal court convicted a non-Indian of murdering another non-Indian on the Crow Reservation.[165] In fact, the victim and perpetrator were

---

[155] Id. art. 1.

[156] Ex parte Crow Dog, 109 U.S. 556, 567–70 (1883).

[158] 104 U.S. 621 (1881).

[159] Id. at 624.

[160] 15 Stat. 619, 621 (1868).

[161] Id. at 623.

[162] Id. at 623–24.

[163] 164 U.S. 240 (1896).

[164] Id. at 247.

[165] Id. at 241.

both African-American.[166] Congress admitted Montana into the Union in 1889, and in the admission act, the state and its people disclaimed jurisdiction over Indian lands.[167] Surprisingly, the Court held that the equal footing doctrine trumped even the plain language of the admission act.[168]

Decades later, the Supreme Court extended the *McBratney-Draper* holdings to New York State, an original state, in *New York ex rel. Ray v. Martin*.[169] There, the Court held that crimes involving non-Indians generally do "not directly affect the Indians."[170]

Major Crimes Act

Congress enacted the original version of the Major Crimes Act in 1885 as a direct response to the Supreme Court's decision in *Ex parte Crow Dog*.[171] In *United States v. Kagama*,[172] the first Major Crimes Act prosecution, the Supreme Court affirmed the constitutionality of the Major Crimes Act. **See § 3.7**.

The Major Crimes Act originally extended federal criminal jurisdiction over seven felonies, but Congress amended the Act several times to include additional crimes. It currently provides:

(a) Any Indian who commits against the person or property of another Indian or other person any of the following offenses, namely, murder, manslaughter, kidnapping, maiming, a felony under chapter 109A, incest, a felony assault under section 113, an assault against an individual who has not attained the age of 16 years, felony child abuse or neglect, arson, burglary, robbery, and a felony under section 661 of this title within the Indian country, shall be subject to the same law and penalties as all other persons committing any of the above offenses, within the exclusive jurisdiction of the United States.

(b) Any offense referred to in subsection (a) of this section that is not defined and punished by Federal law in force within the exclusive jurisdiction of the United States shall be defined and punished in accordance with the laws of the

---

[166] Id.

[167] Id. at 244.

[168] Id. at 244–45.

[169] 326 U.S. 496, 500–01 (1946).

[170] Id. at 501.

[171] 109 U.S. 556 (1883). See also Keeble v. United States, 412 U.S. 205, 209 (1973).

[172] 118 U.S. 375 (1886).

State in which such offense was committed as are in force
at the time of such offense.[173]

United States v. Antelope

In *United States v. Antelope*,[174] the Supreme Court upheld the
Major Crimes Act from an equal protection claim under the Fifth
Amendment's Due Process Clause.[175] The government prosecuted
two tribal members for felony murder, which does not require
premeditation, under the Major Crimes Act.[176] The defendants
argued that had they been prosecuted for the same crime under
state law, in this instance Idaho, which had no felony murder
statute, they could not have convicted of murder.[177] Idaho requires
premeditation as an element of the crime of murder.[178] Only
because they were Indians could they be prosecuted for murder in
Idaho.[179]

Under the theory and holding of *Morton v. Mancari*,[180] **see
§ 3.12**, decided three years before *Antelope*, the Court concluded
that statutes relating to the federal government's Indian affairs
power are not based on racial classifications, but on political
classifications, thereby undermining the due process claim. [181]

In short, the race of the Indian defendants was irrelevant; the
Court concluded that they "were not subjected to federal criminal
jurisdiction because they are of the Indian race but because they are
enrolled members of the Coeur d'Alene Tribe."[182] Moreover, the
Major Crimes Act is a statute designed to implement an aspect of
the federal government's trust obligation to Indian nations to
preserve law and order in Indian country, or as the Court out it,
"federal regulation of criminal conduct within Indian country
implicating Indian interests. . . ."[183] Moreover, there was and could
be no claim that Congress treated the Indian defendants any
differently than others prosecuted under federal law for crimes
committed in other federal enclaves.[184]

---

[173]   18 U.S.C. § 1153.

[174]   430 U.S. 641 (1977).

[175]   Id. at 669–70.

[176]   Id. at 642–43.

[177]   Id. at 644.

[178]   Id.

[179]   Id.

[180]   417 U.S. 535 (1974).

[181]   United States v. Antelope, 430 U.S. 641, 645 (1977).

[182]   Id. at 646.

[183]   Id.

[184]   Id. at 647.

Normally, when Congress treats similarly situated persons differently on the basis of race, gender, sexual orientation, or other immutable characteristic, the Supreme Court will apply a strict scrutiny analysis under the Fifth Amendment in determining whether the treatment is constitutional.[185] But the Court in *Antelope* held that federal statutes implementing Congress's Indian affairs powers that treat Indians differently than non-Indians do so on the basis of the political relationship between Indian nations and their members and the United States. On occasion, federal treatment benefits Indians to the exclusion of others, such as the provision of federal housing or health care benefits. Those benefits originated with Indian treaty provisions included in dozens of treaties. Therein lay the political relationship. Other federal statutes implementing the trust responsibility have been to the detriment of Indian nations and Indian people, as in the case of *Antelope*, at least from the point of the view of the Indian defendants.

Indian Status

Indians are subject to prosecution under both the Indian Country Crimes Act and the Major Crimes Act. "Indian status" is an element of the offense under both statutes, and federal prosecutors must prove the "Indian status" of defendants beyond a reasonable doubt. As such, the Indian status of the perpetrator may also be subject to thorny litigation.[186]

Tribal membership is a factor, but it is not dispositive in either direction. For example, tribal members who are not Indians by ancestry cannot be prosecuted.[187] But many Indians, for whatever reason, are not either members or eligible for tribal membership may still be Indians under the Act. In *Ex parte Pero*,[188] the Seventh Circuit concluded that the son of tribal members, and who resided on a Lake Superior Ojibwe reservation in Wisconsin, but who was not a tribal member, may still be prosecuted in federal court.[189]

---

[185] E.g., Bolling v. Sharpe, 347 U.S. 497 (1954).

[186] See generally Brian L. Lewis, Do You Know What You Are? You Are What You Is; You Is What You Am: Indian Status for the Purpose of Federal Criminal Jurisdiction and the Current Split in the Courts of Appeals, 26 Harv. J. Racial & Ethnic Just. 241 (2010); Jacqueline F. Langland, Indian Status under the Major Crimes Act, 15 J. Gender Race & Just. 109 (2012).

[187] Cf. Alberty v. United States, 162 U.S. 499 (1896) (holding Cherokee Freedmen cannot be prosecuted under the Indian Country Crimes Act); United States v. Rogers, 45 U.S. 567 (1846) (holding federal court may prosecute non-Indian who was also member of Cherokee Nation under federal statue authorizing criminal jurisdiction over non-Indians).

[188] 99 F.2d 28 (7th Cir. 1938), cert. denied, 306 U.S. 643 (1939).

[189] Id. at 31.

The Indian in question was eligible for enrollment in what would later be known as the St. Croix Chippewa Indians of Wisconsin.[190]

The leading modern case on "Indian status" is the Ninth Circuit's recent en banc decision in *United States v. Zepeda*.[191] the Ninth Circuit adopted the following test: "We hold that proof of Indian status under the [Major Crimes Act] requires only two things: (1) proof of some quantum of Indian blood, whether or not that blood derives from a member of a federally recognized tribe, and (2) proof of membership in, or affiliation with, a federally recognized tribe."[192]

Judge Kozinski dissented, arguing that the test is "based solely on an unadorned racial characteristic" and therefore violates the Fifth Amendment's equal protection component.[193]

Assimilative Crimes Act

The Assimilative Crimes Act[194] is another critical general federal criminal jurisdictional statute with relevance to Indian country. The Act allows federal prosecutors to "assimilate" state criminal laws to govern state law crimes in federal enclaves by either Indians or non-Indians. Congress intended the statute to fill "voids in the criminal law applicable to federal enclaves created by the failure of Congress to pass specific criminal statutes."[195]

The Act is purely a gap-filler for federal prosecutors, and if the actions of the defendant have been criminalized in another federal statute, that statute controls. For example, in *Williams v. United States*,[196] the Supreme Court declined to apply an Arizona statute in accordance with the Act because "the precise acts upon which the conviction depends have been made penal by the laws of Congress. . . ."[197] The Court concluded that the Act cannot be used to "modify[ ] or repeal[ ] existing provisions of the Federal Code."[198]

The Act also does not apply to Indian-on-Indian crime because the Indian Country Crimes Act, from which the Assimilative Crimes Act is applied to Indian country, bars federal prosecutions for those crimes.[199] For example, in *United States v. Tsosie*,[200] the court

---

[190] Id. at 32.

[191] 792 F.3d 1103 (9th Cir. 2015) (en banc).

[192] United States v. Zepeda, 792 F.3d 1103, 1113 (9th Cir. 2015) (en banc).

[193] Id. at 1116 (Kozinski, C.J., dissenting).

[194] 18 U.S.C. § 13.

[195] United States v. Engelhorn, 122 F.3d 508, 510 (8th Cir. 1997).

[196] 327 U.S. 711 (1946).

[197] Id.

[198] Id. at 718.

[199] 18 U.S.C. § 1152.

dismissed an indictment assimilating Arizona's hit and run statute under the Act because both the victim and the defendant were Indians.[201] The Ninth Circuit relied upon legislative history from the 1966 revision of the Major Crimes Act, in which members of Congress expressed the view that several crimes not included in the Major Crimes Act could not be prosecuted under the Assimilative Crimes Act if neither the perpetrator nor the victim was an Indian.[202]

§ 7.5   State Criminal Jurisdiction in Indian Country

Historical Background

In the early decades of the Constitution, federal Indian policy excluded state governments from exercising jurisdiction in Indian country or interfering in Indian affairs. The First Congress enacted the Trade and Intercourse Acts, which included criminal jurisdiction provisions, to comprehensively regulate Indian affairs.[203] **See § 3.1.** The Marshall Trilogy roundly confirmed federal dominance in Indian affairs to the exclusion of states;[204] in *Worcester v. Georgia*, the Court held that state laws have "no force" in Indian country.[205] **See § 2.2.**

State-Specific Statutes

During the early years of the termination era, Congress dabbled with extending state laws and jurisdiction into Indian country in New York, Kansas, and parts of California (Agua Caliente Reservation), Iowa (Sac and Fox or Meskwaki), and North Dakota (Spirit Lake). In 1948, Congress granted the State of New York jurisdiction over crimes by or against Indians on Indian lands.[206] In 1950, Congress enacted a parallel statute relating to civil suits.[207] Congress also granted the State of Kansas criminal jurisdiction over Indian country concurrent with the federal government in 1940.[208] Congress did the same in relation to specific reservations, as it did with the Sac and Fox Indian Reservation in

---

[200] No. CR–12–08147–PHX–GMS, 2012 WL 6163075 (D. Ariz., Dec. 11, 2012).

[201] Id. at *3.

[202] Acunia v. United States, 404 F.2d 140, 143 (9th Cir. 1968).

[203] 1 Francis Paul Prucha, The Great Father 102–08 (1984).

[204] Johnson v. McIntosh, 21 U.S. 543 (1823); Cherokee Nation v. Georgia, 30 U.S. 1 (1831); Worcester v. Georgia, 31 U.S. 515 (1832).

[205] Id. at 561.

[206] 25 U.S.C. § 232.

[207] 25 U.S.C. § 233.

[208] 18 U.S.C. § 3243.

Iowa in 1948,[209] the Spirit Lake Sioux Reservation in 1946,[210] and the Agua Caliente Reservation in California in 1949.[211]

Public Law 280

In 1953, Congress enacted a statute extending state criminal and civil jurisdiction into Indian country in five additional states, and authorized other states to affirmatively assert jurisdiction by opting in.[212] Usually known as "Public Law 280" or "PL 280," the statute dramatically altered the structure of tribal-state-federal relations in dozens of states. It is now well established that the Public Law 280 experiment was a tremendous—and continuing—failure in most states.[213]

Section 2(a) of Public Law 280 transferred criminal jurisdiction from the federal government to the mandatory states—California, Minnesota (except Red Lake), Nebraska, Oregon (except Warm Springs), and Wisconsin (except Menominee).[214] Section 4(a) extended state civil jurisdiction to the mandatory states.[215] Sections 2(b) and 4(b) both preserved the federal government trust obligation's to the affected reservations, and protected tribal and Indian immunities from state regulation and taxation, as well as preserved treaty rights. Section 6 authorized states to amend their constitutions with disclaimer provisions to accept jurisdiction over Indian country, and Section 7 authorized all other states to assume jurisdiction. Congress added Alaska to the list of mandatory states in 1958.[216]

Several states asserted jurisdiction over the Indian reservations within their borders.[217] Florida, Idaho, Montana, Nevada, and Washington state all asserted either full or partial

---

[209] Act of June 30, 1948, 62 Stat. 1161.

[210] Act of May 31, 1946, 60 Stat. 229.

[211] Act of Oct. 5, 1949, 63 Stat. 705.

[212] Pub. L. 83–280, Aug. 15, 1953, 67 Stat. 588, codified in relevant part as amended at 18 U.S.C. § 1162 and 28 U.S.C. § 1360.

[213] See generally Duane Champagne & Carole Goldberg, Captured Justice: Native Nations and Public Law 280 (2012); Carole Goldberg & Duane Champagne, Searching for an Exit: The Indian Civil Rights Act and Public law 280, in The Indian Civil Rights Act at Forty (Kristen A. Carpenter, Matthew L.M. Fletcher, and Angela R. Riley, eds. 2011); Robert T. Anderson, Negotiating Jurisdiction: Retroceeding State Authority over Indian Country Granted by Public Law 280, 87 Wash. L. Rev. 915 (2012).

[214] Pub. L. 83–280, § 2, Aug. 15, 1953, 67 Stat. 588, codified in relevant part as amended at 18 U.S.C. § 1162.

[215] Pub. L. 83–280, § 4, Aug. 15, 1953, 67 Stat. 588, codified in relevant part as amended at 28 U.S.C. § 1360.

[216] Pub. L. 85–615, Aug. 8, 1958, 72 Stat. 545.

[217] Duane Champagne & Carole Goldberg, Captured Justice: Native Nations and Public Law 280, at 16–18 (2012).

jurisdiction over Indian country.[218] Montana and Utah conditioned their assumption of jurisdiction on tribal consent; only one tribe consented.[219]

In 1968, Congress repealed Section 7 of Public Law 280, requiring tribal consent before a state may assume jurisdiction over Indian country.[220] Congress also authorized states to retrocede jurisdiction back to the tribes and the federal government.[221] Nevada and Montana have retroceded jurisdiction back to the United States.[222] Some Washington tribes have as well.[223] Washington's legislature enacted retrocession legislation in 2012 that may expand the number of retroceded reservations.[224]

Kennerly v. District Court of the Ninth Judicial District of Montana

Public Law 280's contours have spawned hundreds of cases and affected thousands more. For example, in *Kennerly v. District Court of the Ninth Judicial District of Montana*,[225] the Supreme Court interpreted Section 7 of Public Law 280, which authorized states to assume jurisdiction over Indian country so long as "the people of the State . . . by affirmative legislative action" agree to do so,[226] and its successor, adopted in the 1968 amendments. The issue involved a suit to enforce a grocery store debt against Blackfeet tribal members.[227] Though Montana had invoked the pre-1968 amendment Section 7 to assume jurisdiction over the Flathead Reservation, it had not done so with regards to the Blackfeet Reservation.[228] However, the Blackfeet Tribal Council enacted a statute asserting that the tribal court and the state enjoyed "concurrent" jurisdiction over civil suits brought against Blackfeet

---

[218] Id.

[219] Id. at 16 n. 39 (Utah); id. at 17 (Confederated Salish & Kootenai Tribes in Montana).

[220] Pub. L. 90–284, Title IV, §§ 401(a), 402(a), April 11, 1968, 82 Stat. 77, codified at 25 U.S.C. §§ 1322(a), 1326.

[221] Pub. L. 90–284, Title IV, § 403(a), April 11, 1968, 82 Stat. 77, codified at 25 U.S.C. § 1323.

[222] Duane Champagne & Carole Goldberg, Captured Justice: Native Nations and Public Law 280, at 17 & n. 42 (2012).

[223] Id. at 17–18.

[224] Robert T. Anderson, Negotiating Jurisdiction: Retroceeding State Authority over Indian Country Granted by Public Law 280, 87 Wash. L. Rev. 915, 951–56 (2012).

[225] 400 U.S. 423 (1971) (per curiam).

[226] Pub. L. 83–280, § 7, Aug. 15, 1953, 67 Stat. 589.

[227] Kennerly v. District Court of the Ninth Judicial District of Montana, 400 U.S. 423, 424 (1971) (per curiam).

[228] Id. at 425.

tribal members.[229] The Supreme Court held that the original Section 7 expressly required state legislative action; since none had occurred, the state court had no jurisdiction.[230]

The Supreme Court then construed the amended Public Law 280, which required tribal consent before a state may assume jurisdiction.[231] That statute required "a majority vote of the adult Indians voting at a special election held for that purpose" before a state may assume jurisdiction.[232] A mere tribal council enactment, for the Court, was simply insufficient to confer jurisdiction with the state court.[233]

Washington v. Confederated Tribes and Bands of the Yakima Indian Nation

In *Washington v. Confederated Tribes and Bands of the Yakima Indian Nation*,[234] the Supreme Court rejected the tribe's arguments challenging Washington's assertion of partial jurisdiction over the tribe's reservation.[235] In 1963, Washington had assumed jurisdiction under Public Law 280 (prior to the 1968 amendment requiring tribal consent) over the reservation, except in eight subject areas in cases arising on tribal trust lands.[236] The Ninth Circuit had held that the resulting checkerboarding of the Yakima Indian Reservation was too "bizarre" to survive even a deferential Equal Protection Clause challenge to the state's partial assumption of jurisdiction.[237] The tribe argued further that the state's regime violated the Equal Protection Clause were suspect classifications based on race, and that partial assumption of jurisdiction could not be justified under the strict scrutiny test.[238]

The Court affirmed the constitutionality of Washington's assumption of partial jurisdiction by holding first that the state's legislation introduced "classifications based on tribal status and land tenure inhere[nt] in many of the decisions of this Court involving jurisdictional controversies between tribal Indians and

---

[229] Id.

[230] Id. at 429.

[231] 25 U.S.C. § 1326.

[232] Id.

[233] Kennerly v. District Court of the Ninth Judicial District of Montana, 400 U.S. 423, 429 (1971) (per curiam).

[234] 439 U.S. 463 (1979).

[235] Id. at 502.

[236] Id. at 465.

[237] Confederated Bands and Tribes Bands of Yakima Indian Nation v. State of Washington, 552 F.2d 1332, 1335 (9th Cir. 1977), rev'd, 439 U.S. 463 (1979).

[238] Washington v. Confederated Tribes and Bands of the Yakima Indian Nation, 439 U.S. 463, 500 (1979).

the States."[239] The Court further held that though the checkerboarding of the Yakima reservation might be "difficult to administer [, . . .] they are no more or less so than many of the classifications that pervade the law of Indian jurisdiction."[240] It seems Congress's allowance under Section 7 of Public Law 280 for states to assume jurisdiction that complicated and confused Indian country governance was an acceptable exercise of federal Indian affairs power.

Bryan v. Itasca County

In *Bryan v. Itasca County*,[241] the Supreme Court held that Public Law 280 states may not tax on-reservation personal property of reservation Indians.[242] Itasca County, Minnesota tax auditors levied a personal property tax on the mobile home of Minnesota Chippewa Tribe members Russell Bryan and Helen Bryan, assessing a $147.95 liability.[243] The Bryans lived on the trust land within the Leech Lake Reservation; she was a Leech Lake member and he was a White Earth Band of Ojibwe Indians member.[244]

The Supreme Court's analysis focused on Section 4 of Public Law 280.[245] Section 4(a) extended state "civil laws . . . of general application to private persons and property" into Indian country in Minnesota.[246] Section 4(b) stated that Public Law 280 did not operate to authorize Indian land sales or encumbrances, nor the "taxation of any real or personal property" held by an Indian under federal trust.[247] The Minnesota Supreme Court had held that Section 4(b) limitation on state taxation was an implicit recognition that Section 4(a) constituted "a general grant of the power to tax," or else Section 4(b) would constitute "limitations on a nonexistent power."[248]

The Supreme Court disagreed, applying the canons of construction of Indian statutes and the legislative history of Public Law 280.[249] The Court pointed out that states may not tax Indian

---

[239] Id. at 501.

[240] Id. at 502.

[241] 426 U.S. 373 (1976).

[242] Id. at 375.

[243] Bryan v. Itasca County, 426 U.S. 373, 375 (1976).

[244] Kevin K. Washburn, The Legacy of Bryan v. Itasca County: How a $147 County Tax Notice Helped Bring Tribes More Than $200 Billion in Indian Gaming Revenue, 92 Minn. L. Rev. 919, 923 (2008).

[245] 25 U.S.C. § 1360.

[246] 25 U.S.C. § 1360(a).

[247] 25 U.S.C. § 1360(c).

[248] Bryan v. Itasca County, 228 N.W.2d 249, 253 (Minn. 1975), rev'd 426 U.S. 373 (1976).

[249] Bryan v. Itasca County, 426 U.S. 373, 379 (1976).

lands or on-reservation Indian activity "absent congressional consent."[250] The *Bryan* Court strongly reestablished that the canons of construing legislation affecting American Indians is strongest in the context of Indian taxation.[251] At best, for the state, Section 4 of Public Law 280 was an ambiguous grant of authority from Congress to tax Indian lands, far from the clear expression required by the Court.

The legislative history of Public Law 280 was, for all the terminationist commentaries of the various Members of Congress, unhelpful to the state. The Court noted, in line with Professor Carole Goldberg's research, that Congress's primary purpose in enacting Public Law 280 was combatting lawlessness in Indian country.[252] The Court also noted "the virtual absence of expression of congressional policy or intent respecting § 4's grant of civil jurisdiction to the States."[253] Importantly, Congress barely noted Indian taxation issues in passing, and nothing approaching a clear statement that Congress intended to grant states the power to tax Indian country activities and resources.[254] To the extent Congress discussed the taxability of Indian lands in Public Law 280 states, it was in regard to the lack of funding available to states needed to effectively assume jurisdiction.[255]

Section 4(c) of Public Law 280 cemented the Court's conclusion that Congress did not intend to generally authorize state taxation of Indian lands and activities. That provision requires state courts to apply tribal law not inconsistent with applicable state law in lawsuits brought in state courts.[256] State civil procedure rules would govern the procedures used, but the substantive law would remain tribal. For example, in a dispute between Indian heirs brought in state court under Section 4, the tribal probate code effectively would trump state law. The *Bryan* Court read Section 4(c) to mean Congress did not mean to eradicate tribal law or to completely assimilate Indian people by enacting Public Law 280.[257]

Finally, the Court noted while that Congress was undoubtedly engaged in the business of termination in 1953, it could not have

---

[250] Id. at 376 (quoting Mescalero Apache Tribe v. Jones, 411 U.S. 145, 148 (1973)).

[251] Id. at 392 (citations omitted).

[252] Id. at 379 (citing Carole Goldberg, Public Law 280: The Limits of State Jurisdiction over Reservation Indians, 22 UCLA L. Rev. 535, 541–542 (1975)).

[253] Id. at 381.

[254] Id. at 381–85.

[255] Id. at 381–83.

[256] 28 U.S.C. § 1360(c).

[257] Bryan v. Itasca County, 426 U.S. 373, 388–89 (1976).

intended for Public Law 280 to operate as a termination act.[258] The same Congress that enacted Public Law 280, also terminated its relationship with the Klamath Tribe, the Alabama and Coushatta Tribes of Texas, the Paiute Indians of Utah, and the Menominee Tribe of Wisconsin.[259] Had Congress wanted to generally authorize state taxation of Indian lands and activities, it knew how to do so.

The Future of Public Law 280

History has not been kind to Public Law 280. Indian tribes opposed the extension of state jurisdiction on their lands without tribal consent from the beginning. Unilateral state action to assume jurisdiction, often in a piecemeal manner, created hostility from reservation communities as well as increasing territorial and subject matter checkerboarding of jurisdiction. When Congress first amended Public Law 280 to allow for state retrocession of jurisdiction and to require tribal consent for future state assumption of jurisdiction,[260] it did nothing to undo the damage done between 1953 and 1968. The 1968 amendments did halt further activity, and encouraged several states to retrocede or partially retrocede jurisdiction back to the federal and tribal governments.

In the 1990s and 2000s, research led by Carole Goldberg and others confirmed what Indian people in most Public Law 280 jurisdictions already knew—Public Law 280 is a dramatic failure on a wide variety of angles.[261] The law is an unfunded mandate, forcing states to spread out government resources.[262] The law does not reduce crime rates in Indian country, and most especially in states like Alaska, with vast open areas and nominal state resources.[263] States simply cannot and do not effectively patrol Indian country.[264] The law undermines tribal governance authority and legitimacy.[265] The law stands in the way of critical federal

---

[258] Id. at 389–90.

[259] Id. at 389 n. 15.

[260] Carole Goldberg & Duane Champagne, Is Public Law 280 Fit for the Twenty-First Century? Some Data at Last, 38 Conn. L. Rev. 697, 707 (2006).

[261] See generally Duane Champagne & Carole Goldberg, Captured Justice: Native Nations and Public Law 280 (2012).

[262] Angela R. Riley, Indians and Guns, 100 Geo. L.J. 1675, 1732 (2012).

[263] Indian Law and Order Commission, A Roadmap for Making Native America Safer: Report to the President & Congress of the United States (Nov. 2013).

[264] Carole Goldberg & Duane Champagne, Searching for an Exit: The Indian Civil Rights Act and Public Law 280, in The Indian Civil Rights Act at Forty 247, 249–54 (Kristen A. Carpenter, Matthew L.M. Fletcher & Angela R. Riley eds., 2012).

[265] Carole Goldberg, Public Law 280 and the Problem of Lawlessness in California Indian Country, 44 UCLA L. Rev. 1405, 1415–1437 (1997).

funding for Indian tribes,[266] despite the fact that the courts have roundly concluded that tribal governments retain concurrent jurisdiction over Indian lands in Public Law 280 states.[267]

In 2010, Congress amended Public Law 280 to allow Indian nations to request the United States to reassume federal criminal jurisdiction over Indian country concurrent with state and tribal governments.[268]

§ 7.6   Tribal Criminal Jurisdiction

Indian nations, in general, possess the full range of inherent sovereign powers that every sovereign possesses, subject to divestiture by the tribe through agreement or through the exercise of federal plenary power. Indian nations retain the authority to exercise criminal jurisdiction over tribal members in Indian country,[269] as well as nonmember Indians.[270] However, tribal authority to prosecute non-Indians is sharply restricted.[271] Only a small number of Indian nations have authority to prosecute non-Indians, and only for domestic violence and dating violence.[272] Moreover, the Indian Civil Rights Act restricts tribal sentencing authority for crimes to one year in jail and a $5000 fine.[273] Indian nations that guarantee certain criminal procedure rights may exercise enhanced sentencing authority, up to three years in jail and a $15,000 fine.[274]

Oliphant v. Suquamish Indian Tribe

The Suquamish Tribe's police department arrested Mark Oliphant, a Port Madison Reservation resident, for assaulting a police officer on August 19, 1973, during the tribe's unofficial national holiday, Chief Seattle Days.[275] He was drunk when he apparently assaulted another reveler, necessitating a call to tribal

---

[266] Carole Goldberg & Duane Champagne, A Second Century of Dishonor: Federal Inequities and California Tribes (March 27, 1996) (unpublished report), http://www.aisc.ucla.edu/ca/Tribes.htm.

[267] See generally Hoopa Valley Tribal Council v. Jones, 11 NICS App. 100, 104 (Hoopa Valley Tribal Court of Appeals 2013) (collecting cases).

[268] Tribal Law and Order Act, Pub. L. 111–211, § 221, 124 Stat. 2258, 2271–72, codified at 25 U.S.C. § 1321 and 18 U.S.C. § 1162.

[269] E.g., Talton v. Mayes, 163 U.S. 376 (1896). Cf. United States v. Wheeler, 435 U.S. 313 (1978) (acknowledging tribal criminal justice authority over tribal members).

[270] 25 U.S.C. § 1301(2); United States v. Lara, 541 U.S. 193 (2004).

[271] Oliphant v. Suquamish Indian Tribe, 425 U.S. 191 (1978).

[272] 25 U.S.C. § 1304.

[273] 25 U.S.C. § 1302(a)(7)(B)–(C).

[274] 25 U.S.C. § 1302(b).

[275] Oliphant v. Schlie, 544 F.2d 1007, 1009 (9th Cir. 1976), rev'd, 435 U.S. 191 (1978).

police, the only law enforcement authority on the reservation at that time, who arrested him at 4:30 a.m.[276] The tribe, which had established a provisional tribal court and adopted a law and order code, released Oliphant released him on his own recognizance.[277] A few months later, the tribe also arrested Daniel Belgarde after a high-speed chase through the Port Madison Reservation that ended "when Belgarde collided with a tribal police vehicle."[278] Mark Oliphant was in the car with Belgarde.[279] Upon their individual releases, Oliphant and Belgarde filed petitions for writs of habeas corpus in federal court. *Oliphant* was the first federal court case in a century involving the tribal prosecution of a non-Indian.[280]

The Supreme Court held with sweeping reasoning that the Suquamish Tribe may not prosecute non-Indians.[281]

The opinion opens with a brief description of the Suquamish Tribe, a tribe that was a signatory to the 1855 Treaty of Point Elliott.[282] The Court notes that few Suquamish tribal members lived on Port Madison Reservation, created out of the 1855 treaty, and describes the reservation as "a checkerboard of tribal community land, allotted Indian lands, property held in fee simple by non-Indians, and various roads and public highways maintained by Kitsap County."[283]

After setting that stage, the Court's proceeded to analyze the question on two fronts. The first area involved a complex historical discussion about whether the three branches of the federal government and Indian tribes acted with the presumption that Indian tribes enjoyed criminal jurisdiction over non-Indians.[284] Other than *Ex parte Kenyon*,[285] it appears that not a single federal

---

[276] Sarah Krakoff, Mark the Plumber v. Tribal Empire, or Non-Indian Anxiety v. Tribal Sovereignty?: The Story of Oliphant v. Suquamish Indian Tribe, in Indian Law Stories, 261, 270 (Carole Goldberg, Kevin K. Washburn & Philip P. Frickey, eds. 2011).

[277] Oliphant v. Schlie, 544 F.2d 1007, 1009 (9th Cir. 1976), rev'd, 435 U.S. 191 (1978).

[278] Oliphant v. Suquamish Indian Tribe, 435 U.S. 191, 194 (1978).

[279] Sarah Krakoff, Mark the Plumber v. Tribal Empire, or Non-Indian Anxiety v. Tribal Sovereignty?: The Story of Oliphant v. Suquamish Indian Tribe, in Indian Law Stories, 261, 271 (Carole Goldberg, Kevin K. Washburn & Philip P. Frickey, eds. 2011).

[280] The only previous federal case appears to be Ex parte Kenyon, 14 F. Cas. 353 (W.D. Ark. 1878) (No. 7720).

[281] Oliphant v. Suquamish Indian Tribe, 435 U.S. 191 (1978).

[282] 12 Stat. 927.

[283] Oliphant v. Suquamish Indian Tribe, 435 U.S. 191, 193 (1978). See also id. at 193 n. 1 (noting only 50 tribal members lived on the reservation).

[284] Id. at 196–206.

[285] 14 F. Cas. 353 (W.D. Ark. 1878) (No. 7720).

court ever addressed tribal criminal jurisdiction over non-Indians. The Court gathered a wide assortment of a legislative, Executive branch, and judicial authorities to reach the conclusion that there existed a "commonly shared presumption of Congress, the Executive Branch, and lower federal courts that tribal courts do not have the power to try non-Indians. . . ."[286]

The Court's historical analysis instead began with a discussion of the Choctaw Nation, which had executed an 1830 treaty with the United States and operated a formal court system in the 19th century.[287] As to the 1830 treaty, the Court points to Article 4 of the treaty, noting that the tribe "express[es] a wish that Congress may grant to the Choctaws the right of punishing by their own laws any white man who shall come into their nation, and infringe any of their national regulations."[288]

The Court also pointed to two Attorney General opinions relating to the Choctaw justice system after removal to the west.[289] The first was an 1834 opinion found that the Choctaw Nation did not have jurisdiction over a slave owned by a non-Indian who had murdered another slave.[290]

The second was an 1855 opinion finding that the Choctaw Nation operating under the terms of the 1830 treaty did not enjoy criminal jurisdiction over a non-Indian man who had married into the tribe, thereby acquiring tribal membership and property rights under tribal law.[291] But the opinion is limited to the Choctaw Nation, which had expressly asked for Congress to confer jurisdiction. The Attorney General pointed out that generally non-Indians who "connect" themselves to Indian tribes consent to that tribe's jurisdiction.[292] The Attorney General's conclusion was that Congress had chosen to expressly excise only the Choctaw Nation's criminal jurisdiction over non-Indians.[293]

In 1834, Congress seriously considered whether to start the Indian territory in what is now Oklahoma on the road to statehood, leading to bills and debates selectively relied upon by the *Oliphant* Court. First, the Court discussed a report published by the House Committee on Indian Affairs to accompany bills designed to

---

[286] Oliphant v. Suquamish Indian Tribe, 435 U.S. 191, 206 (1978).

[287] Id. at 197–98.

[288] Id. at 197 (quoting Treaty of Dancing Rabbit Creek art. IV, 7 Stat. 333, 334 (Sept. 27, 1830)).

[289] Oliphant v. Suquamish Indian Tribe, 435 U.S. 191, 198–99 (1978).

[290] 2 Op. Att'y Gen. 693 (1834).

[291] 7 Op. Att'y Gen. 174 (1855).

[292] Id. at 182–83.

[293] Id. at 185.

reorganize the Indian Department, to amend the trade and intercourse acts, and to establish a Western Territory.[294] The third bill, referred to by the Court as the "Western Territory" bills, which would have been the first step to statehood, never passed Congress.[295] The House Committee refers to the Western Territory proposal as a confederacy of Indian tribes, and parallels what would become the Indian Territory and, later, the State of Oklahoma. The Court first relied on the 1834 report by quoting a report by the Office of Commissioners of Indian Affairs for the proposition that only two or three tribes operated a justice system, and that all of Indian tribes "are without laws."[296]

At this point, the Court's opinion asserts that an "unspoken assumption" against tribal jurisdiction existed in 1834.[297] The Court first concluded that an 1854 statute denying federal prosecutors the authority to prosecute Indians who had already been prosecuted in tribal court meant that Congress must have assumed tribes could not prosecute non-Indians, or else Congress would have acted on that belief.[298]

The Court then turned to the Major Crimes Act, enacted in 1885, extending federal criminal jurisdiction over felonies occurring in Indian country.[299] The Court relied upon an uncertain interpretation of the statute that a few courts had adopted by the 1970s that the Major Crimes Act foreclosed tribal jurisdiction over the same crimes.[300]

The Court also addressed *Ex parte Kenyon*,[301] and a 1970 opinion of the Interior Solicitor that argued the *Kenyon* precedent foreclosed tribal criminal jurisdiction over non-Indians.[302] The Interior Solicitor opinion, withdrawn without comment in 1974,[303] limited itself to tribes that had not established tribal courts under

---

[294] H.R. Rep. 23–474 (1834).

[295] Oliphant v. Suquamish Indian Tribe, 435 U.S. 191, 202 n. 13 (1978). See generally Francis Paul Prucha, American Indian Policy in the Formative Years: The Indian Trade and Intercourse Acts, 1790–1834, at 250–73 (1962).

[296] Id. at 197.

[297] Oliphant v. Suquamish Indian Tribe, 435 U.S. 191, 203 (1978).

[298] Id. (citing Act of March 27, 1854, § 3, 10 Stat. 270).

[299] Act of March 3, 1855, 23 Stat. 385, codified as amended at 18 U.S.C. § 1153.

[300] Oliphant v. Suquamish Indian Tribe, 435 U.S. 191, 203 & n. 14 (1978).

[301] 14 F. Cas. 353 (W.D. Ark. 1878) (No. 7720).

[302] Interior Solicitor Opinion M–36810, 77 Int. Dec. 113 (Aug. 10, 1970).

[303] Oliphant v. Suquamish Indian Tribe, 435 U.S. 191, 201 n. 11 (1978).

written constitutions approved by the Interior Secretary under the Indian Reorganization Act.[304]

The Court then cited to its own precedent, *In re Mayfield*,[305] a 19th century case in which the Court stated in dicta its view that Congress did not intend Indian tribes to assert criminal jurisdiction over non-Indians.[306]

The Court's strongest historical evidence that Congress and others assumed tribes did not have criminal jurisdiction over non-Indians involves an Act of Congress designed to combat the destruction of reservation boundary and warning signs by non-Indians.[307] The Court's analysis focused on the 1960 Senate Report accompanying the bill.[308] There, for the first time in any of the materials proffered by the Court in the *Oliphant* opinion, a Congressional committee opined that Indian tribes flatly cannot prosecute non-Indians.[309] The Interior Department, mired in the Termination Era, concurred.[310]

The Court's historical analysis fails to address tribes that were similarly situated to the Suquamish Tribe and misrepresents the salience of Congress's views on tribal criminal jurisdiction. In the 19th century, if an "unspoken assumption" against tribal criminal jurisdiction existed, it was often rooted in racial bias. In the 20th century, if an "unspoken assumption" existed, it was rooted in Termination-era thinking.

The second portion of the opinion involved an analysis of the 1855 Treaty of Point Elliott, which did not expressly provide for or against tribal criminal jurisdiction over non-Indians.[311] The Court concluded that the silence in the treaty merely confirmed the unspoken assumption of the negotiating parties that the tribes did not possess that jurisdiction.[312]

The tribe argued also that the history of the Port Madison treaty also confirmed tribal criminal jurisdiction over non-Indians.[313] An early draft of the treaty borrowed from treaties

---

[304] Interior Solicitor Opinion M-36810, 77 Int. Dec. 113, 113 n. 1 (Aug. 10, 1970).

　[305] 141 U.S. 107 (1891).

　[306] Id. at 115–16.

　[307] 18 U.S.C. § 1164.

　[308] S. Rep. 1686, 86th Cong., 2d Sess. (June 24, 1960).

　[309] Id. at 2.

　[310] Id. at 4.

　[311] Oliphant v. Suquamish Indian Tribe, 435 U.S. 191, 206–8 (1978).

　[312] Id. at 206.

　[313] Brief for Respondents 41–45, Oliphant v. Suquamish Indian Tribe, 435 U.S. 191 (1978) (No. 76–5729), 1977 WL 189289.

concluded with other tribes, and provided that "Injuries committed by whites towards [Indians are] not to be revenged, but on complaint being made they shall be tried by the Laws of the United States and if convicted the offenders punished."[314] So, the early draft expressly stripped the tribe of jurisdiction. But the final draft deletes this language, and provides only for an extradition process if offenders try to conceal themselves on the reservation.[315] The Court concluded that this change had no meaning.[316]

Ultimately, the Court held that "Indians do not have criminal jurisdiction over non-Indians absent affirmative delegation of such power by Congress."[317] As the 1855 treaty did not expressly confer or recognize tribal jurisdiction, the Court would not do so either.

Drawing from 19th century cases, the Court stated that Indian tribes "ced[ed] their lands to the United States and announc[ed] their dependence on the Federal Government."[318] In critically important language, the Court noted, "Upon incorporation into the territory of the United States, the Indian tribes thereby come under the territorial sovereignty of the United States and their exercise of separate power is constrained so as not to conflict with the interests of this overriding sovereignty."[319]

Before *Oliphant*, it was understood that Congress through the exercise of its plenary power in Indian affairs could divest an Indian tribe of aspects of tribal sovereign authority, or Indian tribes could agree to divestiture of their authority by agreement. The Court in *Oliphant* adds an additional source of divestiture—the "overriding sovereignty" of the United States alone, without affirmative action. A few years later, the Court would extend this analysis to the civil side of tribal authority in *Montana v. United States*,[320] discussed in § 8.1.

Duro v. Reina

Duro v. Reina extended the *Oliphant* holding to include a class of individuals known as "nonmember Indians."[321] In 1984, Albert Duro shot and killed a 14-year-old boy on the Salt River Indian Reservation near Phoenix, Arizona.[322] Duro was a member of the

---

[314] Id. at 42.

[315] Treaty of Point Elliott art. IX, 12 Stat. 927 (1855).

[316] Oliphant v. Suquamish Indian Tribe, 435 U.S. 191, 206 n. 16 (1978).

[317] Id. at 208.

[318] Id.

[319] Id. at 209.

[320] 450 U.S. 544 (1981).

[321] 495 U.S. 676, 684–85 (1990).

[322] Id. at 679.

Torres-Martinez Band of Cahuilla Mission Indians, residing on the Salt River reservation while he worked a tribally-owned construction company, PiCopa Construction Company.[323] The victim was a member of yet another tribe, Gila River Indian Tribe of Arizona, also local to the Phoenix area.[324] The federal government declined to prosecute.[325] Tribal police arrested Duro, and the tribal prosecutor brought charges in the Pima-Maricopa Indian Community Court.[326] Since tribal code only allowed for the prosecution of misdemeanors, the prosecutor charged Duro with unlawful discharge of a firearm.[327]

Drawing from *Oliphant* and *Wheeler*, the Court concluded that a tribal prosecution that was a "manifestation of external relations between the Tribe and outsiders . . . " was unauthorized absent Congressional "delegation" of the requisite authority.[328] The Court clarified that the distinction between tribal members and nonmembers, even Indians, was important, especially in taxation and hunting and fishing rights.[329] Justice Kennedy began the majority opinion by noting that nonmembers could not vote in Pima-Maricopa elections, to hold tribal office, or to serve on tribal juries.[330] He repeated that statement in concluding that a nonmember Indian is no different than the non-Indians over whom the Suquamish Tribe could not assert criminal jurisdiction in *Oliphant*.[331]

Duro "Fix"

Fortunately for Indian nations, Congress quickly enacted the so-called "Duro fix." Tribal advocates argued that *Duro* established an arbitrary line by differentiating between members and nonmember Indians. Nonmember Indians play a significant role in the daily life of any American-Indian community—they participate in cultural ceremonies and powwows, they marry tribal members, they may be drawn to other American Indian communities through the operation of the foster care and adoption provisions of the Indian Child Welfare Act and federal health, housing, and

---

[323] Id.

[324] Id.

[325] Id. at 680.

[326] Id. at 681.

[327] Id. The current tribal code provision is titled, "Unlawful discharge of firearm." Salt River Pima-Maricopa Indian Community Code of Ordinances § 6–131.

[328] Duro v. Reina, 495 U.S. 676, 686 (1990).

[329] Id. at 686–87.

[330] Id. at 679 (citing Salt River Pima-Maricopa Indian Community Code of Ordinances §§ 3–1, 3–2, 5–40). By 2015, the tribe had amended its election code and these citations are no longer accurate.

[331] Id. at 688.

educational programs, and most importantly they are valued and essential members of the American Indian community.[332] For tribal advocates, the Court's reliance upon the membership of an American Indian was completely out of tune with the reality on the ground—nonmember Indians are far more integrated into an American Indian community than tourists in a foreign land. In response, Congress exercised its plenary authority and quickly enacted what became known as the "Duro fix," amending the Indian Civil Rights Act to restore and affirm the "inherent power of Indian tribes ... to exercise criminal jurisdiction over all Indians," expressly avoiding the language of a delegation of federal authority.[333]

United States v. Lara

The Supreme Court affirmed the validity of the Duro fix in *United States v. Lara*,[334] rejecting an argument by a nonmember Indian that his federal criminal prosecution for a crime previously prosecuted by an Indian nation was barred under the Double Jeopardy Clause.

How Congress crafted the Duro fix is critical to understanding the challenges to the statute. Congress in reversing the outcome in *Duro* had two options: it could delegate federal authority to prosecute nonmember Indians to Indian tribes, or it could reaffirm or recognize tribal inherent authority to prosecute nonmember Indians. Congress chose the latter.[335] Congress specifically noted that the Duro fix as enacted was not a Congressional delegation of federal power to Indian tribes.[336]

Billy Jo Lara was a member of the Turtle Mountain Band of Chippewa Indians, married to a member of the Spirit Lake Nation (Mne Wakan Oyate), and resided on that reservation.[337] According to the federal prosecutor, Assistant United States Attorney Janice Morley, and the Spirit Lake tribal prosecutor, Michelle Rivard, Lara began to repeatedly disturb the peace and perpetrate domestic violence, steadily increasing the violence of his crimes, until he was banished from the Spirit Lake Reservation.[338] As is the unfortunate signature of many domestic violence cases, Lara returned. He was

---

[332] Carole Goldberg-Ambrose, Of Native Americans and Tribal Members: The Impact of Law on Indian Group Life, 28 Law & Society Review 1123, 1128 (1994).

[333] 25 U.S.C. § 1301(2).

[334] 541 U.S. 193 (2004).

[335] H.R. Conf. Rep. 102–261, 102nd Cong., at 3 (1991).

[336] Id. at 3–4.

[337] United States v. Lara, 541 U.S. 193, 196 (2004).

[338] Matthew L.M. Fletcher, United States v. Lara: Affirmation of Tribal Criminal Jurisdiction over Nonmember Indians, 83 Mich. B.J., July 2004, at 24, 26.

arrested by a Bureau of Indian Affairs officer, who happened to be cross-deputized by the tribe.[339] When Lara knocked out one of the arresting officers, the tribe prosecuted Lara, followed shortly thereafter by the United States Attorney's Office prosecution for assaulting a federal officer.[340]

The Supreme Court in *Lara* expressly adopted Congress' view of the *Duro* decision.[341] The Court held as an initial matter that Congress in the Duro fix had merely chosen to relax statutory restrictions on tribal authority, establishing that the question was whether Congress had authority to relax restrictions on tribal authority.[342] The majority then firmly ratified Congress's long-standing practice of regulating the "metes and bounds of tribal sovereignty."[343] The Court deferred to Congress's policymaking in regards to the extent to which the United States would recognize tribal autonomy.[344] For example, Congress had, after all, terminated the federal government's relationship with the Menominee Tribe, only later to restore the tribe legislatively and reaffirm the tribe's governance authority.[345]

The Court identified the Indian Commerce Clause and the Treaty Power as the primary sources of Congressional plenary power, but also recognized that the Property Clause may also be a source of authority.[346] Justice Breyer added that, while it is silent as to Indian affairs, the Treaty Power adds to Congress's authority through "treaties ... [that] authorize Congress to deal with 'matters' with which otherwise 'Congress could not deal.' "[347] In his concurrence, Justice Thomas raised the specter of the 1871 Act of Congress that "purported to prohibit entering into treaties with the 'Indian nation[s] or tribe[s],' " and asserted that the Act "reflects the view of the political branches that the tribes had become a purely domestic matter."[348] The Court responded that the same 1871 Act also "saved existing treaties from being invalidated or impaired and

---

[339] Id.

[340] United States v. Lara, 541 U.S. 193, 196 (2004).

[341] Id. at 199–200.

[342] Id. at 200.

[343] Id. at 202.

[344] Id. at 205.

[345] Id. at 203 (citing Menominee Tribe v. United States, 391 U.S. 404 (1968); 25 U.S.C. §§ 903–903f).

[346] Id. at 200.

[347] Id. at 201 (quoting Missouri v. Holland, 252 U.S. 416, 433 (1920)).

[348] Id. at 218 (Thomas, J., concurring in judgment) (quoting 16 Stat. 566 (1871), codified at 25 U.S.C. § 71 (2000)).

this Court has explicitly stated that the statute in no way affected Congress' plenary powers to legislate on the problems of Indians."[349]

The Court also articulated for the first time a notion that congressional plenary and exclusive power over Indian affairs is authorized by "preconstitutional powers necessarily inherent in a Federal Government, namely, powers that this Court has described as 'necessary concomitants of nationality.' "[350] For this proposition, the Court cited *United States v. Curtiss-Wright Export Corp.*, a fairly radical and controversial decision about the origins of the federal national affairs power.[351]

---

[349] Id. at 201 (citation and internal quotation marks omitted).

[350] Id. at 201–02.

[351] 299 U.S. 304 (1938).

Chapter 8

TRIBAL AND STATE CONFLICTS OVER CIVIL JURISDICTION

Analysis

§ 8.1   Tribal Civil Regulatory Jurisdiction

Indian nations retain regulatory jurisdiction over tribal members within and without Indian country, and likely retain jurisdiction over nonmembers on Indian lands. **See § 8.3**. However, Indian nations generally do not possess inherent authority to regulate nonmember activity on nonmember-owned fee lands within reservation boundaries. This general rule has two exceptions; the first is that a tribe may regulate a nonmember that consents, and the second is that a tribe may regulate nonmember conduct that significantly imperils tribal self-government.

Montana v. United States

In *Montana v. United States*,[1] the Supreme Court addressed the authority of Indian tribes to regulate the activities of nonmembers on nonmember-owned fee lands within reservation boundaries.[2] The Court established a general rule that tribes do not possess inherent authority to regulate nonmember conduct on fee lands unless one of two exceptions are met.[3]

The *Montana* case arose out of a dispute between the Crow Tribe, the State of Montana, and several nonmember reservation

---

[1]   450 U.S. 544 (1981).
[2]   Id. at 547.
[3]   Id. at 565–66.

residents over the tribe's effort to prohibit nonmember hunting and fishing on all areas of the reservation.[4] The Crow Tribe had entered into treaties with the United States in 1851 and 1868.[5] The 1851 treaty expressly reserved "the privilege of hunting, fishing, or passing over any of the tracts of country. . . ."[6] The 1868 treaty established the tribe's reservation, and expressly "set apart [the reservation] for the absolute and undisturbed use and occupation" of the tribe.[7]

In 1920, Congress provided for the allotment of the Crow reservation, generating intense difficulties for the tribe.[8] About 30 percent of the reservation residents were nonmembers by the time the Ninth Circuit heard the case.[9]

The Court addressed treaty-based and inherent tribal sovereignty-based arguments by the tribe and the federal government purporting to authorize the tribe to ban hunting and fishing by nonmembers, rejecting them in turn. **See § 4.2**. First, the Court addressed whether the tribe had reserved ownership of the riverbed under the Big Horn River on the Crow Reservation through either the 1851 or 1868 treaties.[10] Normally, the presumption in interpreting Indian treaties is that the tribe retains all lands not expressly divested by the treaty; in the case of submerged lands under navigable waterways like the Big Horn River, the presumption is reversed.[11] The Court concluded that the 1851 treaty did not expressly reserve any lands to the tribe, and so it could not have reserved ownership of the lands to the tribe.[12] Similarly, the Court concluded that the 1868 treaty was of no help to the tribe even though it did expressly reserve lands to the tribe; it did not expressly reserve the riverbed.[13] Because title to the riverbed did not vest with the tribe (or the United States as trustee), the State of Montana acquired title to the riverbed upon its

---

[4]   Id. at 547.

[5]   John P. LaVelle, Beating a Path of Retreat from Treaty Rights and Tribal Sovereignty: The Story of Montana v. United States, in Indian Law Stories 535, 538 (Carole Goldberg, Kevin K. Washburn, and Philip P. Frickey, eds. 2011).

[6]   Id. (quoting First Treaty of Fort Laramie, art. II, 11 Stat. 749, Sept. 17, 1851).

[7]   Id. (quoting Second Treaty of Fort Laramie, art. V, 15 Stat. 649, 650, April 29, 1868).

[8]   Id. at 528–39.

[9]   Id. at 539 (citing United States v. Montana, 604 F.2d 1162, 1164 n. 3 (9th Cir. 1979), rev'd 450 U.S. 544 (1981)).

[10]   Montana v. United States, 450 U.S. 544, 550–57 (1981).

[11]   Id. at 552–53 (citing United States v. Holt State Bank, 270 U.S. 49, 58–59 (1926)).

[12]   Id. at 553.

[13]   Id. at 553–56.

admission to the Union.[14] As such, the Court held that the tribe could not rely upon the treaty for authority. Implied in the Court's decision is that if the tribe owned the land, the tribe *would* have jurisdiction, but that question remains open after later cases.

Second, the Court addressed the inherent sovereignty argument.[15] The Court noted that inherent sovereignty is limited: "[E]xercise of tribal power beyond what is necessary to protect tribal self-government or to control internal relations is inconsistent with the dependent status of the tribes, and so cannot survive without express congressional delegation."[16] In other words, inherent sovereignty is largely limited to power to regulate tribal members and internal reservation affairs only.

However, the general rule is not complete as the Court recognized that Indian nations possess considerable governance authority within reservation boundaries: "To be sure, Indian tribes retain inherent sovereign power to exercise some forms of civil jurisdiction over non-Indians on their reservations, even on non-Indian fee lands."[17] The Court articulated two exceptions the general rule that tribes do not possess inherent authority over nonmembers on non-Indian owned land. The first exception is that "[a] tribe may regulate, through taxation, licensing, or other means, the activities of nonmembers who enter consensual relationships with the tribe or its members, through commercial dealing, contracts, leases, or other arrangements."[18] The second exception is that "[a] tribe may also retain inherent power to exercise civil authority over the conduct of non-Indians on fee lands within its reservation when that conduct threatens or has some direct effect on the political integrity, the economic security, or the health or welfare of the tribe."[19]

The Court concluded that regulating nonmember hunting and fishing on nonmember-owned fee lands did not meet either exception. In the first instance, nonmembers had "not enter[ed into] any agreements or dealings with the Crow Tribe so as to subject

---

[14]   Id. at 556–57.

[15]   Id. at 563–67.

[16]   Id. at 564.

[17]   Id. at 565.

[18]   Id. (citing Williams v. Lee, 358 U.S. 217, 223 (1959); Morris v. Hitchcock, 194 U.S. 384 (1904); Buster v. Wright, 135 F. 947, 950 (8th Cir. 1905), appeal dismissed, 203 U.S. 599 (1906); Washington v. Confederated Tribes of Colville Indian Reservation, 447 U.S. 134, 152–154 (1980)).

[19]   Id. at 566 (citing Fisher v. District Court, 424 U.S. 382, 386 (1976); Williams v. Lee, 358 U.S. 217, 220 (1959); Montana Catholic Missions v. Missoula County, 200 U.S. 118, 128–129 (1906); Thomas v. Gay, 169 U.S. 264, 273 (1898)).

themselves to tribal civil jurisdiction."[20] As for the second, the tribe never alleged that the activities of the nonmembers would "imperil the subsistence or welfare of the Tribe."[21] The Court relied on the fact that the tribe had long allowed the State to regulate the river without imposing discriminatory regulations on tribal members.[22]

Brendale v. Confederated Tribes and Bands of the Yakima Indian Nation

In *Brendale v. Confederated Bands and Tribes of Yakima Indian Nation*,[23] the Court held that an Indian tribe may regulate nonmember land use through zoning ordinances in areas of an allotted reservation that have not been generally opened to public sale (loosely speaking, "closed" areas), but may not enforce zoning ordinances on nonmembers in areas that have been opened to public sale (loosely speaking, "opened" areas).[24] The sharply divided Court did not issue a majority opinion.

Brendale consisted of three consolidated appeals, with nonmember landowners and the State of Washington (and a county subdivision) arguing that the Yakima Indian Nation (now the Yakama Indian Nation) did not have authority to enforce its zoning ordinances against nonmember landowners on fee lands within the Yakama reservation.[25] The Yakama Reservation consists of "open" and "closed" areas.[26] The closed area consists mostly of forest land, more than 800,000 acres, with only 25,000 acres owned in fee.[27] By statute, the tribe closed that portion of the reservation to the general public in 1954, relying upon language from the 1855 treaty that assured "the Tribe 'exclusive use and benefit' of reservation lands. . . ."[28] In contrast, the "open" area consisted of more than 300,000 acres, nearly half of which was owned in fee as a result of the allotment of that portion of the reservation.[29]

---

[20] Id.

[21] Id.

[22] Id. at 566–67 & n. 16.

[23] 492 U.S. 408 (1989).

[24] Id. at 425 (opinion of White, J.) (opened areas); id. at 444 (opinion of Stevens, J.) (closed areas).

[25] Id. at 417 (opinion of White, J.) (suit by nonmember Indian); id. at 418 (opinion of White, J.) (suit by nonmember); id. at 419 (opinion of White, J.) (suit by tribe against Yakima County).

[26] Id. at 415–16 (opinion of White, J.).

[27] Id. at 438 (opinion of Stevens, J.).

[28] Id. (opinion of Stevens, J.) (quoting Treaty between the United States and the Yakima Nation of Indians, 12 Stat. 951).

[29] Id. at 445–46 (opinion of Stevens, J.).

A majority of the Court concluded that the tribe could regulate nonmember activity in the closed area, but not in the open area.[30] Justice Stevens' opinion on the question of the closed area focused on the tribe's authority to condition entry of nonmembers onto tribal lands, a broad power recognized in cases such as *New Mexico v. Mescalero Apache Tribe*.[31] **See § 12.3**. For Justice Stevens, because the closed area was overwhelmingly tribal in character, "it is enough to recognize that notwithstanding the transfer of a small percentage of allotted land the Tribe retains its legitimate interest in the preservation of the character of the reservation."[32]

On the question of the open area, Justice White's opinion relied far more on the *Montana* analysis, finding that the tribe's attempted regulation of nonmembers on nonmember-owned land was tantamount to regulating a "tribe's 'external relations.' "[33] Applying *Montana*'s second exception, Justice White argued that for a tribe to regulate nonmember impacts, "[t]he impact must be demonstrably serious and must imperil the political integrity, the economic security, or the health and welfare of the tribe. This standard will sufficiently protect Indian tribes while at the same time avoiding undue interference with state sovereignty and providing the certainty needed by property owners."[34] For Justice White, the presumption started with county jurisdiction, rebuttable by the tribal showing of imperilment of tribal self-government after the zoning regime decided upon by the county was in place.[35]

Justice Blackmun's opinion disputed both plurality opinions.[36] Justice Blackmun, like Justice White, would apply *Montana*, but he interpreted the general rule to be far more deferential to tribal interests: "[I]t is evident that *Montana* must be read to recognize the inherent authority of tribes to exercise civil jurisdiction over non-Indian activities on tribal reservations where those activities, as they do in the case of land use, implicate a significant tribal interest."[37]

---

[30]   See generally Joseph William Singer, Sovereignty and Property, 86 Nw. U. L. Rev. 1, 7 (1991) (counting votes).

[31]   Brendale v. Confederated Tribes and Bands of the Yakima Indian Nation, 492 U.S. 408, 435–36 (1989) (opinion of Stevens, J.) (citing and quoting New Mexico v. Mescalero Apache Tribe, 462 U.S. 324, 144–45 (1983)).

[32]   Id. at 442 (opinion of Stevens, J.).

[33]   Id. at 426 (opinion of White, J.) (quoting United States v. Wheeler, 435 U.S. 313, 326 (1978)).

[34]   Id. at 431 (opinion of White, J.).

[35]   Id. at 431–32 (opinion of White, J.).

[36]   Id. at 448–49 (Blackmun, J., concurring and dissenting).

[37]   Id. at 450 (Blackmun, J., concurring and dissenting).

The *Brendale* Court left tribal civil regulatory jurisdiction in disarray, with no agreement by the Court on whether *Montana* was the correct test, or what the import of *Montana* decision would be going forward.

South Dakota v. Bourland

In 1993, the Court decided *South Dakota v. Bourland*,[38] which did very little to clarify whether the *Montana* test was the correct standard, and whether Justice White's or Justice Stevens' views in *Brendale* would control how the Court would interpret that standard.

Bourland arose when the Cheyenne River Sioux Tribe attempted to exclude nonmember deer hunters from reservation lands and waters acquired by the United States for the Oahe Dam and Reservoir project.[39] The State of South Dakota sued to resolve the dispute with the tribe.[40] As in the *Montana v. United States* matter, the Court first analyzed whether the tribe's treaty rights or applicable federal statutes reserved or provided for tribal authority to regulate nonmembers on the federal lands.[41] Again like *Montana*, the *Bourland* Court did not find that authority in the treaty or the statute.[42] It then turned to inherent tribal authority.[43]

The Court appeared to reaffirm that the *Montana* standard applied to determine whether a tribe could regulate nonmember activities on nonmember-owned fee lands within the reservation, but remanded to the lower courts for a decision on whether either exception to *Montana*'s general rule applied to the activities on the federal lands.[44]

While the Supreme Court has not had occasion to reexamine tribal inherent authority to regulate nonmember conduct on nonmember-owned fee lands, the Court has held in cases involving tribal adjudicatory jurisdiction and tribal taxation authority that *Montana* is the governing rule. **See § 8.3.**

§ 8.2   Federal Authority Delegated to Indian Tribes

Congress may delegate federal authority to Indian tribes, usually in the context of implementing federal statutes. Indian

---

[38]   508 U.S. 679 (1993).

[39]   Id. at 681–82.

[40]   Id. at 685.

[41]   Id. at 688–95.

[42]   Id. at 693–94.

[43]   Id. at 694–97.

[44]   Id. at 695–96.

tribes retain inherent governmental authority sufficient to accept federal government delegation of authority to implement federal statutes and to administer federal government programs.

United States v. Mazurie

In *United States v. Mazurie*,[45] the Supreme Court affirmed that Congress may delegate federal authority to Indian tribes.[46] *Mazurie* involved a federal statute that gave tribes the option to regulate the introduction of liquor into Indian country.[47] The Wind River Reservation tribes enacted an ordinance in accordance with federal law that required liquor retailers to acquire both a state and a tribal license.[48] The nonmember owners of the Blue Bull bar attempted to obtain a license from the tribe, but after tribal residents complained, the tribe denied the license.[49] After a time, the Blue Bull reopened, and federal agents eventually shut down the bar and confiscated the liquor.[50] The bar owners challenged the statute, particularly the authority of the tribe to enforce the federal law.[51]

The Court held that Indian tribes "are unique aggregations possessing attributes of sovereignty over both their members and their territory . . . ; they are 'a separate people' possessing 'the power of regulating their internal and social relations. . . .' "[52] The Court added that when Congress delegates federal authority to Indian tribes, they are delegating authority to governmental entities that already "possess a certain degree of independent authority over matters that affect the internal and social relations of tribal life."[53]

Rice v. Rehner

In *Rice v. Rehner*,[54] the Court reaffirmed that Congress may delegate federal liquor regulatory authority to Indian tribes: "By enacting [18 U.S.C.] § 1161, Congress intended to delegate a portion of its authority to the tribes as well as to the States, so as to fill the void that would be created by the absence of the discriminatory

---

[45]   419 U.S. 544 (1975).

[46]   Id. at 557–59.

[47]   Id. at 547 (citing 18 U.S.C. § 1161).

[48]   Id. at 548.

[49]   Id.

[50]   Id.

[51]   Id.

[52]   Id. at 557 (citations omitted). See also id. ("Indian tribes within 'Indian country' are a good deal more than 'private, voluntary organizations. . . .' ").

[53]   Id.

[54]   463 U.S. 713 (1983).

federal prohibition."[55] Congress has also delegated authority to tribes to enforce federal and tribal laws in other contexts, such as environmental law.[56]

§ 8.3   Indian Country Civil Adjudicatory Jurisdiction

Suits Against Tribal Members

Indian tribal justice systems have exclusive jurisdiction over civil suits brought against tribal members arising on the reservation, whether or not those suits are brought by nonmembers. In *Williams v. Lee*,[57] **see § 6.7**, the Supreme Court held that state courts may not entertain civil suits against reservation Indians for claims arising in Indian country.[58]

The theory behind this bright-line rule is the so-called "infringement" test, whereby state action that infringes on tribal self-governance is invalid.[59] The infringement test derives from critical language in the *Williams* opinion: "Essentially, absent governing Acts of Congress, the question has always been whether the state action infringed on the right of reservation Indians to make their own laws and be ruled by them."[60] The Court noted that Congress long had acted in accordance with the view that states "have no power to regulate the affairs of Indians on a reservation." As a result, in the 19th and 20th centuries, Congress had both provided the foundation for federal control of Indian country and "encouraged tribal governments and courts to become stronger and more highly organized."[61] Though Congress had provided Arizona with the opportunity to assume jurisdiction over the Navajo Reservation under Public Law 280, it had not done so.[62]

The 1868 treaty between the Navajo Nation and the United States provided significant support for the infringement model.[63] Even though the tribe was an exiled people at the time of the treaty, foundational principles of federal Indian law recognize that

---

[55]   Id. at 733.

[56]   See generally Judith V. Royster & Rory SnowArrow, Control of the Reservation Environment: Tribal Primacy, Federal Delegation, and the Limits of State Intrusion, 64 Wash. L. Rev. 581 (1989).

[57]   358 U.S. 217 (1959).

[58]   Id. at 223.

[59]   Id. at 220.

[60]   Id. at 220 (citing Utah & Northern Railway Co. v. Fisher, 116 U.S. 28 (1885)).

[61]   Id. (citing 25 U.S.C. §§ 476, 477 [now § 25 U.S.C. §§ 5123, 5124]; other citations omitted).

[62]   Id. at 221.

[63]   Id. at 221–22.

"[i]mplicit in these treaty terms . . . was the understanding that the internal affairs of the Indians remained exclusively within the jurisdiction of whatever tribal government existed."[64] The United States also had assisted the tribe in developing its own tribal justice system in light of tribal self-government.[65] In conclusion, the Court stated, "There can be no doubt that to allow the exercise of state jurisdiction here would undermine the authority of the tribal courts over Reservation affairs and hence would infringe on the right of the Indians to govern themselves."[66]

In subsequent cases, the Supreme Court applied the infringement test to strike down state court suits against tribal members or Indian tribes not authorized by Congress as interfering with tribal self-government. In *Fisher v. District Court*,[67] the Court held that Montana courts did not enjoy jurisdiction over Indian child custody proceedings involving on-reservation children.[68] There, the Montana Supreme Court held that that state courts could assume jurisdiction over reservation child custody decisions because state courts had done so before the tribe established a court system in 1935.[69] The Court concluded in a summary reversal of the Montana Supreme Court that state court jurisdiction over a child custody dispute where all parties were reservation Indians would plainly infringe upon tribal self-government.[70]

State courts' subject matter jurisdiction is limited by the *Williams* infringement principle. For example, in *Sage v. Sicangu Oyate Ho, Inc.*,[71] the South Dakota Supreme Court held that state courts did not have jurisdiction over a contract claim by a school principal against an on-reservation school funded exclusively by federal, tribal, and private donors.[72] Additionally, in *State ex rel. Peterson v. District Court*,[73] the Wyoming Supreme Court examined *Williams* and *Fisher* in great detail to reach the conclusion that state courts did not have jurisdiction to adjudicate a claim between tribal members arising on a state highway on the Wind River Reservation.[74]

---

[64]   Id.

[65]   Id. at 222.

[66]   Id. at 223 (citations omitted).

[67]   424 U.S. 382 (1976) (per curiam).

[68]   Id. at 387–88.

[69]   Id. at 384 (citing State ex rel. Firecrow v. District Court, 536 P.2d 190 (Mont. 1975)).

[70]   Id. at 387–88.

[71]   473 N.W.2d 480 (S.D. 1991).

[72]   Id. at 482–83 (quoting Williams v. Lee, 358 U.S. 217, 221 (1959)).

[73]   617 P.2d 1056 (Wyo. 1980).

[74]   Id. at 1061–70.

The *Williams* holding also extends to all on-reservation lands, including state highways within reservation boundaries. For example, in *Winer v. Penny Enterprises, Inc.*,[75] the North Dakota Supreme Court held that state courts may not assume jurisdiction over a tort claim brought against a reservation Indian arising from a car accident on a state highway within reservation boundaries.[76]

Usually, the infringement test arises in the context of state taxation or regulation of on-reservation activity, and will be discussed in greater detail in §§ 8.6, 12.3.

State Court Personal and Subject Matter Jurisdiction in Indian Country

A state court must have both subject matter and personal jurisdiction over defendants in either a criminal or civil matter in order to adjudicate a defendant's rights. *Williams v. Lee*[77] and *Fisher v. District Court*[78] limit state courts' personal and subject matter jurisdiction over Indians that have allegedly engaged in off-reservation actions but have returned to the reservation. For example, in *Joe v. Marcum*,[79] the Tenth Circuit held that a state court may not order the garnishment of wages earned by a reservation Indian.[80] The Tenth Circuit's analysis there centered on the fact that the Navajo Nation's treaty established its right of self-government, and that Congress had enacted a statute (Public Law 280) establishing the procedure by which a state could assume civil jurisdiction over reservation Indians.[81] New Mexico had not assumed jurisdiction over Public Law 280, and to allow state courts to garnish the wages of on-reservation Indians would undermine tribal self-government.[82]

The case law on state court jurisdiction over cases arising in Indian country and involving Indian country parties is a bit in disarray, in large part because of the many permutations of facts that can occur. For example, in *Begay v. Roberts*,[83] the Arizona Court of Appeals held that the state court did not have jurisdiction to garnish the wages of a Navajo Nation member who lived and

---

[75]   674 N.W.2d 9 (N.D. 2004).

[76]   Id. at 11–17.

[77]   358 U.S. 217 (1959).

[78]   424 U.S. 382 (1976) (per curiam).

[79]   621 F.2d 358 (10th Cir. 1980).

[80]   Id. at 361.

[81]   Id.

[82]   Id.

[83]   807 P.2d 1111 (Ariz. App. 1990) , review denied, April 23, 1991.

worked on the reservation, even where the court retained personal jurisdiction over the employer (the Salt River Project).[84]

The complexity of the law of personal and subject matter jurisdiction creates excellent incentives for states and tribes to negotiate solutions to these issues. Tribal-state agreements on enforcing foreign judgments, extradition, law enforcement cooperation, and garnishments are routine.

Suits Against Nonmembers

As an initial matter, tribal civil adjudicatory jurisdiction is to be distinguished from tribal civil regulatory jurisdiction for purposes of clarity. Although the Supreme Court has held that the contours and extent of tribal adjudicatory and regulatory jurisdiction are equal, as a practical matter they are not. Thousands upon thousands of nonmembers consent to tribal jurisdiction as a matter of course; thousands, and perhaps hundreds of thousands, of nonmembers work for Indian tribes, live in tribal housing, receive direct tribal government services such as job training and health care, and engage in direct contractual relationships with Indian tribes. The only cases federal courts now review are the outlier cases, where nonmembers engage in almost herculean efforts to avoid often fairly noncontroversial assertions of tribal jurisdiction.

Tribal Court Exhaustion Doctrine

Nonmembers that wish to challenge the jurisdiction of the tribal courts over them must first exhaust their tribal remedies, usually in trial and appellate courts of Indian tribes. The Supreme Court acknowledged a federal common law right to be free of tribal jurisdiction and a federal common law cause of action to enforce that right. Nonmembers must exhaust tribal remedies unless a tribe does not have colorable or plausible jurisdiction.

National Farmers Union Ins. Cos. v. Crow Tribe of Indians

In *National Farmers Union Insurance Companies v. Crow Tribe of Indians*,[85] the Supreme Court established a federal common law right and cause of action. In *National Farmers Union*, a Crow tribal member sued an on-reservation public school district in tribal court after a motorcycle accident on the school's parking lot.[86] That case, captioned *Sage v. Lodge Grass School District*,[87] resulted in a default judgment in the amount of $153,000 against the school

---

[84] Id. at 1117.

[85] 471 U.S. 845 (1985).

[86] National Farmers Union Ins. Cos. v. Crow Tribe of Indians, 471 U.S. 845, 847 (1985).

[87] 10 Indian L. Rep. 6019, 6020 (Crow Tribal Court 1982).

district, which did not appear in the tribal court to defend the suit, apparently because the chairman of the school board failed to notify anyone the school had been sued.[88]

National Farmers Union dramatically expanded the reach of federal common law in the Indian law context, holding in a simple syllogism that whether tribal courts have jurisdiction over nonmember civil defendants in a given case is a question arising under federal law, and therefore Section 1331 of the Judicial Code authorizes federal courts to give an answer.[89] The Court had a long history of adopting federal common law causes of action in Indian law, but in each instance, Congress had created a right without any specified remedy.[90] For example, Congress had prohibited sales of Indian lands to anyone absent the consent of Congress but did not created a cause of action in federal court to void such sales, and so the Supreme Court created one.[91] Similarly, when the United States sued a county on behalf of an Indian tribe for interest in back taxes illegally collected by the county, the Court applied federal common law to determine whether such interest was recoverable.[92] In none of these prior circumstances had the Court created a federal common law cause of action from scratch, by articulating a common law right *and* a federal court remedy.[93]

The tribal court exhaustion doctrine is far from direct federal court review of tribal court judgments, however. The Court held that tribal courts must be the first to engage in "a careful examination of tribal sovereignty, the extent to which that sovereignty has been altered, divested, or diminished, as well as a detailed study of relevant statutes, Executive Branch policy as embodied in treaties and elsewhere, and administrative or judicial decisions."[94] Congressional support for tribal self-determination "favors a rule that will provide the forum whose jurisdiction is being challenged the first opportunity to evaluate the factual and legal

---

[88]   National Farmers Union Ins. Cos. v. Crow Tribe of Indians, 471 U.S. 845, 847–48 (1985).

[89]   Id. at 862.

[90]   E.g., Non-Intercourse Act, 25 U.S.C. § 177.

[91]   County of Oneida, N.Y. v. Oneida Indian Nation of N.Y., 470 U.S. 226, 237–39 (1985). The Court cited to numerous other instances where the Court assumed that a federal common law cause of action existed allowing suit to recover Indian lands. See id. at 235–36 (collecting cases).

[92]   Board of Commissioners of Jackson County v. United States, 308 U.S. 343, 349 (1939).

[93]   In the classic Supreme Court case creating a federal common law cause of action, Bivens v. Six Unknown Named Agents, 403 U.S. 388 (1971), the Court merely recognized the cause of action to enforce federal constitutional rights against federal officials, not the rights themselves.

[94]   National Farmers Union Ins. Cos. v. Crow Tribe of Indians, 471 U.S. 845, 855–56 (1985) (footnote omitted).

bases for the challenge."[95] Federal courts would also benefit from a "full record [being] developed in the Tribal Court before either the merits or any question concerning appropriate relief is addressed."[96] Tribal courts would also benefit from the opportunity to "explain to the parties the precise basis for accepting jurisdiction, and will also provide other courts with the benefit of their expertise in such matters in the event of further judicial review."[97]

The Court also addressed potential limitations on the tribal court exhaustion doctrine; specifically, exhaustion would not be required where tribal jurisdiction " 'is motivated by a desire to harass or is conducted in bad faith,' . . . or where the action is patently violative of express jurisdictional prohibitions, or where exhaustion would be futile because of the lack of an adequate opportunity to challenge the court's jurisdiction."[98]

Iowa Mutual Ins. Co. v. LaPlante

Two years later, in *Iowa Mutual Insurance Co. v. LaPlante*,[99] the Supreme Court clarified the tribal court exhaustion doctrine. The Court held that nonmembers must exhaust *all* of the tribal remedies available, and that includes any available tribal appellate review.[100]

Interestingly, given that later Supreme Court opinions backtracked from this view, the Court strongly suggested that tribes "presumptively" enjoy jurisdiction over nonmember activity on "reservation lands":

> Tribal authority over the activities of non-Indians on reservation lands is an important part of tribal sovereignty. . . . Civil jurisdiction over such activities presumptively lies in the tribal courts unless affirmatively limited by a specific treaty provision or federal statute. "Because the Tribe retains all inherent attributes of sovereignty that have not been divested by the Federal Government, the proper inference from silence . . . is that the sovereign power . . . remains intact."[101]

---

[95]   Id. at 856 (footnote omitted).

[96]   Id. (footnote omitted).

[97]   Id. at 857 (footnote omitted).

[98]   Id. at 856 n. 21 (citation omitted).

[99]   480 U.S. 9 (1987).

[100]   Id. at 16–17 (citations omitted).

[101]   Id. at 18 (quoting Merrion v. Jicarilla Apache Tribe, 455 U.S. 130, 149 (1982); other citations omitted).

This "presumption" has not yet been confirmed by Supreme Court decisions that have followed, and the Court in *Nevada v. Hicks* expressly left the question open.[102]

There are four exceptions to tribal court exhaustion:

(1) an assertion of tribal jurisdiction is motivated by a desire to harass or is conducted in bad faith; (2) the action is patently violative of express jurisdictional prohibitions; (3) exhaustion would be futile because of the lack of adequate opportunity to challenge the court's jurisdiction; or (4) it is plain that no federal grant provides for tribal governance of nonmembers' conduct on land covered by *Montana*'s main rule.[103]

Importantly, nonmembers are foreclosed from alleging bias or incompetence by the tribal court. Some nonmembers have sought to relieve their exhaustion burden by arguing that the assertion of tribal jurisdiction is conducted in bad faith.

The tribal court exhaustion doctrine has generated dozens of federal appellate decisions, and even a few state court decisions. In general, so long as it is "colorable" or "plausible" that a tribal court would have jurisdiction over the nonmember conduct, the federal appellate courts would require nonmembers to exhaust tribal remedies.[104] Nonmembers that fail to exhaust their tribal remedies through procedural default may be out of luck, with their failure to exhaust equivalent to a waiver of the right to challenge tribal jurisdiction.[105]

The *Montana* General Rule and Exceptions

Once tribal remedies have been exhausted or excused, federal courts then proceed to the merits of the tribe's assertion of jurisdiction over nonmembers. Tribal courts generally may not exercise jurisdiction over nonmember defendants in civil cases absent two exceptions rooted in nonmember consent or nonmember activities that significantly threaten tribal governance. How courts interpret the exceptions often depends on numerous factors such as whether the action arose on Indian lands, whether the action arose

---

[102] 533 U.S. 353, 358 n. 2 (2001).

[103] Burlington Northern R.R. Co. v. Red Wolf, 196 F.3d 1059, 1065 (9th Cir. 1999) (citations omitted).

[104] E.g., Elliott v. White Mountain Apache Tribal Court, 566 F.3d 842, 848 (9th Cir.) ("colorable or plausible"), cert. denied, 558 U.S. 1024 (2009); Ninigret Development Corp. v. Narragansett Indian Wetuomuck Housing Authority, 207 F.3d 21, 31 (1st Cir. 2000) ("colorable"); Stock West Corp. v. Taylor, 964 F.2d 912, 919–20 (9th Cir. 1992) ("plausible").

[105] E.g., Davis v. Mille Lacs Band of Chippewa Indians, 193 F.3d 990, 992 (8th Cir. 1999), cert. denied, 529 U.S. 1099 (2000).

in tort or in contract, and possibly other factors. It is important to know that federal court review of tribal jurisdiction is not direct review of the merits of the tribal court claim, only the tribal court's authority.

We now know that the "pathmarking" case—to borrow Justice Ginsburg's phrasing[106]—in tribal court jurisdiction is *Montana v. United States*,[107] although prior to *Strate v. A-1 Contracting*, the Supreme Court had not confirmed that the *Montana* general rule and its exceptions would apply to tribal courts.

The Supreme Court's application of the *Montana* general rule took a circuitous route. The first cases following *Montana* involving tribal authority over nonmembers barely mentioned *Montana*. In *New Mexico v. Mescalero Apache Tribe*,[108] the State sued the Tribe seeking a judgment that it had concurrent jurisdiction over hunting and fishing regulation involving nonmembers on tribal lands.[109] In *Mescalero*, the parties understood tribal governance interests on Indian lands to be so strong that the State conceded that the Tribe had authority to regulate nonmember hunting and fishing on tribal lands.[110] The Court agreed that *Montana* itself held that tribes may regulate nonmember hunting and fishing on tribal lands: "[A]s to 'lands belonging to the Tribe or held by the United States in trust for the Tribe,' we 'readily agree[d]' that a Tribe may 'prohibit nonmembers from hunting or fishing . . . [or] condition their entry by charging a fee or establish bag and creel limits.' "[111] Similarly in the previous year, in *Merrion v. Jicarilla Apache Tribe*,[112] the Court held that Indian tribes retain inherent authority to tax nonmember companies doing business on tribal lands without discussion of the *Montana* case.[113] Prior to *Montana*, the Court had also held that tribes may tax on-reservation sales to nonmembers.[114]

Strate v. A-1 Contractors

The next important tribal civil jurisdiction case[115] directly involved, for the first time, tribal civil adjudicatory jurisdiction over

---

[106] Strate v. A-1 Contracting, Inc., 520 U.S. 438, 445 (1997).

[107] 450 U.S. 544 (1981).

[108] 462 U.S. 324 (1983).

[109] Id. at 330.

[110] Id.

[111] Id. at 331 (quoting *Montana*, 450 U.S. at 557–67).

[112] 455 U.S. 130 (1982).

[113] Id. at 140.

[114] Washington v. Confederated Tribes of Colville Indian Reservation, 447 U.S. 134 (1980).

[115] South Dakota v. Bourland, 508 U.S. 679 (1993), discussed in **§ 8.1**, arose on non-Indian lands on the Cheyenne River Sioux Tribe set apart by a federal statute for a dam project, making it a relatively easy case for the Court. Id. at 690.

a nonmember defendant—*Strate v. A-1 Contractors*.[116] The case involved an automobile accident on a state-controlled highway located on tribal trust lands, and a tribal court suit filed by the non-Indian plaintiff against a non-Indian defendant.[117] The nonmember defendant was driving on the reservation only because the tribe had engaged it to perform landscaping work on tribal land.[118]

The Court first held that the state-controlled highway where the accident occurred was not tribal land,[119] which was consistent with the reasoning in earlier cases,[120] even though some commentators suggested that the Court had rewritten basic property law to reach that result.[121] The highway did cut through the Fort Berthold Reservation, but the state police patrolled the highway, the state maintained the highway, and the tribe and the United States had long ago consented to grant a right-of-way to the state for that purpose.[122] In many meaningful respects, the highway had lost much of its character as tribal lands, even though the land was technically owned by the Interior Secretary in trust for the tribe.

Once the Court concluded the case arose on non-Indian land, the Court applied *Montana*.[123] *Strate* is the first case in which the Court conclusively identified *Montana* as applying to all cases involving tribal civil jurisdiction over nonmembers,[124] but Justice Ginsburg was careful to note that *Montana* "governs" assertions of tribal jurisdiction on non-Indian lands.[125] As a result, *Strate* is a case about non-Indian land within reservation borders.

The Court first turned to the *Montana 1* exception—commercial consensual relations: "The first exception to the Montana rule covers activities of nonmembers who enter consensual relationships with the tribe or its members, through commercial dealing, contracts, leases, or other arrangements.' "[126] The Court refused to apply the exception on grounds that the accident had

---

[116]   520 U.S. 438 (1997).

[117]   Id. at 442.

[118]   Id. at 443.

[119]   Id. at 454.

[120]   Id. at 456.

[121]   E.g., Nancy Thorington, Civil and Criminal Jurisdiction over Matters Arising in Indian Country: A Roadmap for Improving Interaction among Tribal, State, and Federal Governments, 31 McGeorge L. Rev. 973, 1011 (2000).

[122]   Strate v. A-1 Contractors, Inc., 520 U.S. 438, 455–56 (1997).

[123]   Id. at 456–58.

[124]   Id. at 445 ("*Montana v. United States* . . . is the pathmarking case concerning tribal civil authority over nonmembers.").

[125]   Id. at 456.

[126]   Id. at 456 (quoting Montana v. United States, 450 U.S. 554, 565 (1981)).

nothing to do with the reason the non-Indian was on the reservation.[127] Justice Ginsburg asserted the underlying dispute was "distinctly non-tribal in nature" because it "arose between two non-Indians involved in [a] run-of-the-mill [highway] accident."[128]

The Court then addressed the second *Montana* exception— conduct that "threatens or has some direct effect on the political integrity, the economic security, or the health or welfare of the tribe."[129] The Court seemed unimpressed that the tribe was attempting to regulate nonmembers who had physically injured reservation residents with close ties to the tribal community: "Undoubtedly, those who drive carelessly on a public highway running through a reservation endanger all in the vicinity, and surely jeopardize the safety of tribal members. But if *Montana*'s second exception requires no more, the exception would severely shrink the rule."[130] The key analysis under *Montana 2* was whether the nonmember conduct "would trench unduly on tribal self-government."[131]

Nevada v. Hicks

The next major tribal civil jurisdiction case, *Nevada v. Hicks*,[132] is one of the most unusual opinions in the field. *Hicks* involved a Section 1983 claim brought against a state law enforcement official in tribal court for on-reservation conduct.[133] The filing of *federal* civil rights claims in *tribal* court against a *state* officer was likely unprecedented at the time of the suit. The state officer in question obtained a state court warrant to for a warrant to search the home of Floyd Hicks, a tribal member who resided on tribal lands.[134] The officer then had the state court warrant domesticated in the Fallon Paiute-Shoshone tribal court, state officials having no obvious authority to search residences on tribal lands.[135] The officer was looking for evidence that Hicks had poached a California bighorn sheep off the reservation.[136] Tribal police joined the state officer in the search found no incriminating evidence, but a year later a tribal police officer reported that he had seen two California bighorn

---

[127] Id. at 457.

[128] Id. (quoting A-1 Contractors, Inc. v. Strate, 76 F.3d 930, 940 (9th Cir. 1996) (en banc)).

[129] Strate v. A-1 Contractors, Inc., 520 U.S. 438, 457–59 (1997) (quoting Montana v. United States, 450 U.S. 544, 566 (1981)).

[130] Id. at 457–58.

[131] Id. at 458.

[132] 533 U.S. 353 (2001).

[133] Id. at 355–56.

[134] Id. at 355.

[135] Id.

[136] Id.

sheep heads in Hicks' home.[137] They searched again with a second state court warrant, again finding no evidence, but this time the state officer did not have his state court warrant domesticated in tribal court.[138] Hicks brought suit in tribal court, and ultimately the Ninth Circuit Court of Appeals held that the tribal court had jurisdiction to hear Section 1983 claims against state officers and that the officer was required to exhaust his tribal court remedies as to a qualified immunity defense before proceeding to federal court on that question.[139]

First, the majority began with a discussion of *Montana*.[140] The majority specifically held that *Montana* applies to actions arising on tribal lands, but also held that landownership remained an important, if not dispositive, factor.[141] However, the majority eventually held that state officers may enter Indian country to enforce state law,[142] rendering the *Montana* analysis unnecessary. Still, *Hicks* acknowledged that "*Montana* and *Strate* rejected tribal authority to regulate nonmembers' activities on land over which the tribe could not 'assert a landowner's right to occupy and exclude. . . .' "[143] Moreover, the majority also acknowledged that whether tribal authority over nonmembers on Indian lands exists remains an open question: "Our holding in this case is limited to the question of tribal-court jurisdiction over state officers enforcing state law. We leave open the question of tribal-court jurisdiction over nonmember defendants in general."[144]

Another important element of the *Hicks* case is Justice Souter's concurring opinion focusing on the possible (and again, hypothetical) consequences of tribal court jurisdiction over nonmembers. Justice Souter fleshed out the Court's concerns about the policy implications of tribal court jurisdiction over nonmembers first expressed in *Duro v. Reina*.[145] Justice Souter alleged that "outsiders" would not receive the benefit of adequate due process in tribal courts, citing respected scholarly works for the proposition

---

[137] Id.

[138] Id.

[139] State of Nevada v. Hicks, 196 F.3d 1020 (9th Cir. 1999).

[140] Id. at 358 ("The principle of Indian law central to this aspect of the case is our holding in *Strate v. A-1 Contractors*. . . .").

[141] Nevada v. Hicks, 533 U.S. 353, 360 (2001) ("[Land ownership] may sometimes be a dispositive factor.").

[142] Id. at 361–62 ("State sovereignty does not end at a reservation's border. . . . 'Ordinarily,' it is now clear, 'an Indian reservation is considered part of the territory of the State.' ") (citations omitted).

[143] Id. at 360 (quoting Strate v. A-1 Contractors, Inc., 520 U.S. 438, 546 (1997)); Montana v. United States, 540 U.S. 544, 557 (1981).

[144] Id. at 358 n. 2.

[145] 495 U.S. 676, 693 (1990).

that tribal courts had not interpreted the Indian Civil Rights Act's due process guarantees consistent with federal precedents.[146] Justice Souter mentioned first that tribal justice system structures differ from American court systems.[147]

In any event, the *Hicks* Court decided little, other than tribal courts may not entertain suits against state law enforcement officials, probably for federalism reasons.[148] The "open question" identified in *Hicks*, tribal civil jurisdiction over nonmembers on tribal lands, remains open more than a decade later.

Plains Commerce Bank v. Long Family Land and Cattle Co.

In 2008, the Supreme Court decided *Plains Commerce Bank v. Long Family Land and Cattle Co.*,[149] another case involving tribal court jurisdiction over tort and contract claims arising on nonmember owned land within reservation boundaries. *Plains Commerce* is notable not for its outcome but because the Court again declined an invitation by nonmembers to eliminate the possibility of tribal jurisdiction over nonmembers.

The facts are as convoluted as any law school essay exam. Kenneth Long, a non-Indian, and his spouse, Maxine Long, who was a Cheyenne River Sioux tribal member, together owned a farm and a house located within the Cheyenne River Sioux Tribe's reservation in South Dakota.[150] Maxine walked on, leaving Kenneth the sole owner.[151] In 1995, Kenneth walked on, he and the Long Company owed $750,000 to Bank of Hoven.[152] Kenneth's second wife, Pauline Long, conveyed the farm and the house to the Bank in lieu of foreclosure in exchange for a $478,000 credit on the outstanding debt.[153]

Ronnie Long, Kenneth's son and a Cheyenne River Sioux tribal member, inherited Kenneth's share in the farm and the Long Company, which amounted to 49 percent of the company.[154] Ronnie

---

[146] Id. at 384 (Souter, J., concurring) (citing Nell Jessup Newton, Tribal Court Praxis: One Year in the Life of Twenty Indian Tribal Courts, 22 Am. Indian L. Rev. 285, 344, n. 238 (1998)).

[147] Id.

[148] John P. LaVelle, Implicit Divestiture Reconsidered: Outtakes from the Cohen's Handbook Cutting-Room Floor, 38 Conn. L. Rev. 731, 775–76 & n. 266 (2006).

[149] 554 U.S. 316 (2008).

[150] Bank of Hoven (Plains Commerce Bank) v. Long Family Land and Cattle Co., 32 Indian L. Rep. 6001, 6001 (Cheyenne River Sioux Tribal Court of Appeals 2004).

[151] Id.

[152] Id.

[153] Id.

[154] Id.

and his wife, Lila Long, who is also a Cheyenne River Sioux tribal member, already owned the remaining 51 percent of the company.[155] Eventually, after negotiations on the reservation involving Ronnie and Lila Long, the Bureau of Indian Affairs, the Cheyenne River Sioux Tribe, and the Bank of Hoven (later, Plains Commerce Bank), the Bank agreed to a new deal by which the Bank would sell the farm back to the Longs through a 20 year contract for deed.[156] However, the Bank withdrew that offer in April 1996 on advice of counsel.[157] Instead, the Bank offered to lease the land to the Long Company for two years, with an option to purchase for the remaining $478,000 in debt.[158] The Bank also agreed to make an operating loan of $70,000 to allow the Long Company to operate during the coming winter.[159] The Bank and the Long Company completed the deal in December 1996.[160]

As the tribal appellate court found, the winter of 1996–97 was "horrific," but the Bank did not provide the promised $70,000 loan.[161] The Long Company lost much of its livestock and was not able to complete the purchase.[162] Though the Bank initially sued for foreclosure in state court, asking the tribal court to effectuate service on the Long Company, that suit never went anywhere.[163] Instead, the Bank sold the Long Company lands in two separate transactions in March and June 1999.[164] The Long Company remained in possession of 960 acres out of the original 2250 acres.[165] The Long Company sued the Bank in the Cheyenne River Sioux Tribal Court, and the Bank counterclaimed for possession.[166] After a two-day jury trial, the jury returned a general verdict in favor of the Long Company on three causes of action—breach of the loan agreement, race discrimination, and bad faith—and awarded damages in the amount of $750,000, plus $123,131 in prejudgment interest.[167]

The Bank appealed only the race discrimination claim, arguing that either the claim was a federal claim over which a tribal court

---

[155] Id.

[156] Id.

[157] Id.

[158] Id.

[159] Id.

[160] Id.

[161] Id.

[162] Id.

[163] Id.

[164] Id.

[165] Id.

[166] Id.

[167] Id.

could not have jurisdiction or that the claim was a tribal common law claim that did not exist as a matter of tribal law.[168] Importantly, the tribal appellate court noted that two other causes of action remained, and were foreclosed from further review because of the tribal court exhaustion doctrine.[169] And, because the jury verdict was a general verdict by which the monetary damages award could be supported by any of the three causes of action, the damages award would remain regardless of the appeal.[170]

Even so, the Supreme Court reversed, at least as to the tribal common law cause of action.[171] The Court first held that the land in question was nonmember land in principle, even if was under tribal member majority ownership, because once reservation land "is converted into fee simple, the tribe loses plenary jurisdiction over it."[172] Therefore, the *Montana* rubric applied.[173] Diverting the analysis from the tribal court and its jurisdiction, the Court instead held that since the tribe itself could not have had jurisdiction over the Bank's transaction, neither could the tribal court: "According to our precedents, 'a tribe's adjudicative jurisdiction does not exceed its legislative jurisdiction.' . . . We reaffirm that principle today and hold that the Tribal Court lacks jurisdiction to hear the Longs' discrimination claim because the Tribe lacks the civil authority to regulate the Bank's sale of its fee land."[174] The Court's opinion reads tribal interests narrowly, noting that, under *Montana*, Indian tribes' "sovereign interests are now confined to managing tribal land, . . . 'protect[ing] tribal self-government,' and 'control[ling] internal relations. . . .' "[175] Regulating the sale of nonmember lands to nonmembers, which the Court found was essentially what the tribal court was doing in applying tribal tort law against the Bank, was outside of that rubric: "It has already been alienated from the tribal trust. The tribe cannot justify regulation of such land's sale by reference to its power to superintend tribal land, then, because non-Indian fee parcels have ceased to *be* tribal land."[176]

The Supreme Court decided nothing in *Plains Commerce Bank*. The *Strate* holding that *Montana* applies in instances where tribal interests sue nonmembers in tribal courts under tort or contract on

---

[168] Id. at 6002.

[169] Id.

[170] Id.

[171] 554 U.S. 316 (2008).

[172] Id. at 329.

[173] Id.

[174] Id. at 330 (quoting Strate v. A-1 Contractors, 520 U.S. 438, 458 (1997)).

[175] Id. at 334 (quoting Worcester v. Georgia, 31 U.S. 515, 561 (1832), and Montana v. United States, 450 U.S. 544, 564 (1981)).

[176] Id. at 335–36 (quotation omitted) (emphasis in original).

nonmember-owned reservation land is still the law, despite the effort by the Bank to persuade the Court to eliminate tribal jurisdiction altogether. This is still a case about nonmember lands and nonmember parties, at least at the point of the transaction at issue—the one between the Bank and its nonmember purchasers. The Supreme Court still has not squarely addressed whether *Montana* applies to lands to Indians lands—that is, lands to which an Indian nation retains the exclusion power.

Moreover, the Long Company, still in possession of nearly 1000 acres, eventually restarted the tribal court suit to enforce the judgment, leading to a federal court decision ordering the Bank (now Plains Commerce Bank) to exhaust its tribal court remedies.[177] Eventually, the Bank and the Long Company reached a confidential settlement.

Post-*Plains Commerce Bank* Decisions

The Ninth Circuit held that *Montana* does not apply—or applies only in significantly watered-down form—in contract disputes involving nonmember defendants on tribal lands in *Water Wheel Camp Recreational Area, Inc. v. LaRance*.[178] The Colorado River Indian Tribes sued to evict the nonmember company from tribal trust lands and for back rent, damages, and attorney fees.[179] Water Wheel Camp was a holdover tenant as of July 7, 2007, and had for some before that failed to pay its rent.[180] The tribal court eventually awarded $1,486,146.42 plus interest for back rent and damages.[181]

The Ninth Circuit started its analysis by noting that Indian tribes retain the sovereign power to exclude undesirables from tribal lands.[182] The power to exclude then authorizes the tribe to regulate the activities of nonmembers on tribal lands, independent of the *Montana* analysis.[183] The court then gave teeth to the presumption of tribal jurisdiction over nonmembers on Indian lands first mentioned in *Iowa Mutual*: "We must therefore conclude that

---

[177] Plains Commerce Bank v. Long Family Land and Cattle Co., Inc., 910 F. Supp. 2d 1188 (D. S.D. 2012).

[178] 642 F.3d 802 (9th Cir. 2011).

[179] Colorado River Indian Tribes v. Water Wheel Camp Recreation Area, Inc., No. 08–0003, at 1–2 (Colorado River Indian Tribes Court of Appeals, Mar. 10, 2009), available at https://turtletalk.files.wordpress.com/2008/03/crit_ct_of_appeals_opinion.pdf.

[180] Id. at 2.

[181] Id.

[182] Water Wheel Camp Recreational Area, Inc. v. LaRance, 642 F.3d 802, 808 (9th Cir. 2011) (citing New Mexico v. Mescalero Apache Tribe, 462 U.S. 324, 333 (1983)).

[183] Id. at 810.

the CRIT's right to exclude non-Indians from tribal land includes the power to regulate them unless Congress has said otherwise, or unless the Supreme Court has recognized that such power conflicts with federal interests promoting tribal self-government."[184]

The Fifth Circuit used a different route in applying the first *Montana* exception to a tort claim arising on tribal trust lands against a nonmember company in *Dolgencorp, Inc. v. Mississippi Band of Choctaw Indians* (also known as *Dollar General Corp. v. Mississippi Band of Choctaw Indians*).[185] There, a tribal member child, who was a participating in a tribal employment program, sued the Dollar General Corporation and its employee Dale Townsend in tort, alleging that Townsend sexually assaulted the plaintiff at the store, located on tribal lands.[186] The Fifth Circuit rejected the nonmember's claim that *Plains Commerce* narrowed the *Montana* exceptions to nonmember activities that "intrude[ ]on the internal relations of the tribe or threaten[ ] self-rule."[187] Instead, the court held that "the ability to regulate the working conditions (particularly as pertains to health and safety) of tribe members employed on reservation land is plainly central to the tribe's power of self-government. Nothing in *Plains Commerce* requires a focus on the highly specific rather than the general."[188]

The question left open in *Nevada v. Hicks*,[189] whether and under what standard tribes can assert jurisdiction over nonmembers on Indian or tribal lands,[190] remains open after *Dollar General*.

Tribal Court Personal Jurisdiction over Nonmembers Beyond Indian Country

Courts once applied the classic due process analysis—notice and minimum contacts—in assessing tribal court personal jurisdiction outside of reservation boundaries.[191] However, Supreme

---

[184] Id. at 812 (citing Iowa Mutual Insurance Co. v. LaPlante, 480 U.S. 9, 18 (1987)).

[185] 746 F.3d 167 (5th Cir.), en banc petition denied, 748 F.3d 588 (5th Cir. 2014), aff'd by an equally divided court, 136 S.Ct. 2159 (2016).

[186] Doe v. Dollar General Corp., No. CV–02–05, at 2 (Mississippi Band of Choctaw Indians Supreme Court, Feb. 8, 2008), available at https://turtletalk.files. wordpress.com/2009/01/miss-band-choctaw-sct-opinion.pdf.

[187] Dolgencorp, Inc. v. Mississippi Band of Choctaw Indians, 746 F.3d 167, 175 (5th Cir.) (quoting Plains Commerce Bank v. Long Family Land and Cattle Co., Inc., 554 U.S. 316, 337 (2008)), aff'd by an equally divided court, 136 S.Ct. 2159 (2016).

[188] Id.

[189] 533 U.S. 353 (2001).

[190] Id. at 358 n. 2.

[191] E.g., Babbitt Ford, Inc. v. Navajo Indian Tribe, 519 F. Supp. 418, 431 (D. Ariz.), aff'd in part, rev'd in part on other grounds, 710 F.2d 587 (9th Cir. 1983), cert. denied, 466 U.S. 926 (1984).

Court jurisprudence on tribal court jurisdiction now focuses on jurisdiction under the *Montana* line of cases, incorporating elements of both subject matter and personal jurisdiction, but not entirely consistent with those lines of analyses.[192] The Ninth Circuit compared the first *Montana* exception favorably to a personal jurisdiction analysis. In *Smith v. Salish Kootenai College*,[193] the court suggested that the consensual relationships analysis was "perfectly consistent with principles of personal jurisdiction."[194]

In *Red Fox v. Hettich*,[195] a pre-*Strate* decision, the South Dakota Supreme Court analyzed whether a tribal member that had obtained a tort judgment against a nonmember in the Standing Rock Sioux Tribal Court could enforce that judgment in state court.[196] Like the accident in *Strate*, the tort claim here arose on a state highway within an Indian reservation.[197] The court concluded that the nonmember defendant did have sufficient minimum contacts with the reservation for the tribal court to assume personal jurisdiction over him because he was a reservation property and business owner.[198] The *Red Fox* court lamented that the Supreme Court's tribal jurisdiction analysis was unhelpful for lower courts in that the Court's analysis deviates from the typical personal and subject matter jurisdiction framework, and instead focuses on criminal, civil regulatory, and civil adjudicatory jurisdiction.[199]

Still, there are times when the courts must apply the minimum contacts analysis. For example, in *Water Wheel Camp Recreational Area, Inc. v. LaRance*,[200] the Ninth Circuit held that a nonmember defendant who resided on tribal lands and who was served on tribal lands had sufficient minimum contacts to confer personal jurisdiction.[201]

Tribal court jurisdiction is limited considerably by the *Montana* line of cases, and personal jurisdiction alone does not confer jurisdiction on tribal courts. Tribal courts must also have subject matter jurisdiction as well.

---

[192] Nevada v. Hicks, 533 U.S. 353, 367 n. 8 (2001).

[193] 434 F.3d 1127, 1138–39 (9th Cir.) (en banc), cert. denied, 547 U.S. 1209 (2006).

[194] Id. at 1138 (citing Stock West, Inc. v. Confederated Tribes of the Colville Reservation, 873 F.2d 1221, 1228–29 (9th Cir. 1989)).

[195] 494 N.W.2d 638 (S.D. 1993).

[196] Id. at 640.

[197] Id.

[198] Id. at 645.

[199] Id. at 642–43.

[200] 642 F.3d 802 (9th Cir. 2011).

[201] Id. at 819.

Membership-Based Jurisdiction

Indian nations may possess jurisdiction over tribal member activities outside of Indian country, as well. In *Settler v. Lameer*,[202] the court upheld the tribe's authority to enforce tribal fishing regulations against tribal members for fishing illegally on off-reservation fishing sites. The tribe's jurisdiction was tied to the retention of off-reservation fishing rights.[203] In *Littell v. Nakai*,[204] the court stated that off-reservation activities that involve tribal "internal affairs," such as the conduct of the tribe's chairman, should be addressed exclusively in tribal forums.[205]

In *Kelsey v. Pope*,[206] The Sixth Circuit held that a tribe in Michigan may exercise criminal jurisdiction over a tribal elected official's alleged off-reservation crime perpetrated on tribal fee lands.

§ 8.4   Enforcement of Tribal Court Judgments and Orders in State and Federal Courts

As there are only limited Constitutional or statutory mandates requiring federal and state courts to recognize and enforce tribal court judgments and orders, the ability of litigants to enforce tribal court judgments and orders differs from state to state. Most federal and state courts apply a comity analysis, while a few states apply a full faith and credit analysis. In more recent years, tribal courts or tribal governments have negotiated with state courts or state legislatures to enact a standard of review.

A few federal and state court decisions granted tribal court orders and judgments full faith and credit, including one 19th century Supreme Court case. The Constitution obligates states and state courts to grant full faith and credit to the "judicial Proceedings" of every other state.[207] Congress also enacted a statute that ensured federal courts would part of the full faith and credit regime.[208]

However, unless tribal lands are considered "Territories" under these provisions, then tribal courts are not included in the full faith

---

[202] 507 F.2d 231 (9th Cir. 1974).

[203] Id. at 237.

[204] 344 F.2d 486 (9th Cir. 1965).

[205] Id. at 490.

[206] Kelsey v. Pope, No. 1:09–CV–1015, 2014 WL 1338170 (W.D. Mich., March 31, 2014), aff'd, 809 F.3d 849 (6th Cir.), cert. denied sub nom., Kelsey v. Bailey, 137 S.Ct. 183 (2016).

[207] Const. Art. IV, § 1.

[208] 28 U.S.C. § 1738.

and credit regime. In *Mackey v. Coxe*,[209] the Supreme Court affirmed a lower court decision to grant full faith and credit to an order of the Cherokee tribal court.[210] The Court held that Cherokee territory did constitute a "Territory"—"a domestic territory—a territory which originated under our constitution and laws."[211] The Supreme Court cited that case with approval more than a century later,[212] but has not repeated that holding.

Other courts have agreed with this analysis. For example, in *Jim v. CIT Financial Services Corp.*,[213] the New Mexico Supreme Court held that the Navajo Nation was a "territory" under 28 U.S.C. § 1738.[214] *Jim* involved a tribal court judgment undoing the repossession of a truck, but courts were more likely to recognize tribal court judgments and orders relating to internal tribal affairs such as Indian child welfare.[215] Eventually, Congress statutorily granted full faith and credit to tribal court Indian child welfare judgments and orders in the Indian Child Welfare Act.[216] Congress later did the same in relation to tribal court protection orders,[217] child custody orders,[218] child support,[219] and some tribal property laws.[220]

Most state and federal courts confronted with a litigant seeking to enforce a tribal court judgment or order engage in a comity analysis. Comity is the term of art in which the court of one sovereign recognizes by courtesy, not obligation, the judgments and orders of another sovereign. Justice Sotomayor wrote recently that "[c]omity—that is, a proper respect for [a sovereign's] functions, . . .—fosters respectful, harmonious relations between governments. . . ."[221]

---

[209] 59 U.S. 100 (1856).

[210] Id. at 105.

[211] Id. at 103.

[212] Santa Clara Pueblo v. Martinez, 436 U.S. 49, 65 n. 21 (1978); United States v. Wheeler, 435 U.S. 313, 322 n. 18 (1978).

[213] 533 P.2d 751 (N.M. 1975).

[214] Id. at 752 (citing Mackey v. Coxe, 56 U.S. 100 (1856)).

[215] E.g., Matter of Adoption of Buehl, 555 P.2d 1334, 1342 (Wash. 1976); Sheppard v. Sheppard, 655 P.2d 895 (Idaho 1982).

[216] 25 U.S.C. § 1911(d).

[217] 18 U.S.C. § 2265.

[218] 28 U.S.C. § 1738A.

[219] 28 U.S.C. § 1738B.

[220] 25 U.S.C. § 2207 (Indian Land Consolidation Act); 25 U.S.C. § 3106 (National Indian Forest Resources Management).

[221] Michigan v. Bay Mills Indian Community, 134 S.Ct. 2024, 2041 (2014) (quoting Sprint Communications, Inc. v. Jacobs, 134 S.Ct. 584, 591 (2013), and Wood v. Milyard, 132 S.Ct. 1826, 1832–33 (2012)) (quotation marks omitted).

Concurrent Jurisdiction in Public Law 280 States

State and tribal courts in Public Law 280 states must confront the fact that they often exercise concurrent jurisdiction over the same matters. In *Teague v. Bad River Band of Lake Superior Tribe of Chippewa Indians*,[222] the Wisconsin Supreme Court was split on whether to apply comity or full faith and credit to a tribal court judgment where both a state and a tribal court had jurisdiction and had reached opposite conclusions.[223] The court annunciated numerous factors to consider in determining which court was best suited to hearing the matter in a concurrent jurisdiction scenario.[224] The *Teague* decision led to the so-called Teague protocol by which tribal and state court judges were to open lines of communication with each other when they learned that both courts had jurisdiction over the same case.

§ 8.5   Tribal Power to Tax

As a general matter, Indian nations retain the power to tax inherent to any sovereign government's menu of authorities, absent a clear statement from Congress abrogating the power to tax. **See §§ 5.6, 8.6**. Tribes may tax tribal members and others doing business or residing on Indian lands, but must comport with the *Montana* general rule and exceptions when seeking to tax nonmembers on nonmember-owned reservation lands.

The leading cases confirming the tribal power to tax are *Buster v. Wright*,[225] *Merrion v. Jicarilla Apache Tribe*,[226] and *Kerr-McGee Corp. v. Navajo Tribe*.[227] *Buster* involved a federally approved tribal permit tax issued on nonmembers for the privilege of doing business within reservation boundaries.[228] The court held that the tribe had "lawful authority" to enact the tax, tying the power to tax to the inherent authority of Indian nations as sovereigns.[229]

Merrion v. Jicarilla Apache Tribe

The Supreme Court did not return to the power to tax until the 1980s, and then engaged in a highly theoretical dissertation on the

---

[222] 665 N.W.2d 899 (Wis. 2003).

[223] Id. at 914 (Abrahamson, C.J., concurring).

[224] Chief Justice Shirley Abrahamson's opinion detailed 13 factors to consider. Id. at 917–18 (Abrahamson, C.J., concurring).

[225] 135 F. 947 (8th Cir. 1905), appeal dismissed, 203 U.S. 599 (1906).

[226] 455 U.S. 130 (1982).

[227] 471 U.S. 195 (1985).

[228] Buster v. Wright, 135 F. 947, 949 (8th Cir. 1905), appeal dismissed, 203 U.S. 599 (1906).

[229] Id. at 950.

origins of the power in *Merrion v. Jicarilla Apache Tribe.*[230] There, the tribe imposed a severance tax on oil and natural gas "removed from Tribal lands."[231] Nearly two dozen nonmember companies that leased land from the tribe for that exact purpose challenged the tribal tax.[232] The Court held that the tribal power to tax derives from the inherent sovereignty of Indian nations as nations: "The power to tax is an essential attribute of Indian sovereignty because it is a necessary instrument of self-government and territorial management."[233] Like all nations and governments, tribes require the power to tax to "to raise revenues for its essential services."[234] The Court noted that the nonmember companies "avail themselves of the 'substantial privilege of carrying on business' on the reservation."[235] And they "benefit from the provision of police protection and other governmental services. . . ."[236]

The Court also held that the tribal power to tax is inherent to tribal sovereignty. The dissent and the nonmember companies argued that the tribal power to tax arose only through the tribe's power to exclude persons from tribal lands akin to a landowner's power to exclude.[237] The basis of the argument stemmed from the fact that the tribe also required the nonmembers to pay royalties to the tribe in the lease arrangement with the nonmembers.[238] The argument held that since the tribe imposed the severance tax *after* the lease arrangements came into being and did not require the payment of the tax in the leases, the tribe more or less lost the ability to impose the tax.[239]

The majority concluded that inherent tribal sovereignty authorized the tax, and that tribes may tax nonmember activity "because the limited authority that a tribe may exercise over nonmembers does not arise until the nonmember enters the tribal jurisdiction."[240] This statement is consistent with the understanding that tribal sovereignty on tribal lands is robust.

The *Merrion* Court also focused on the status of the Jicarilla Apache Nation (as it is known now) was established as a tribal

---

[230] 455 U.S. 130 (1982).

[231] Id. at 133.

[232] Id.

[233] Id. at 137.

[234] Id.

[235] Id. (citations omitted).

[236] Id. (citations omitted).

[237] Id. at 141–44; see also id. at 172–72 (Stevens, J., dissenting).

[238] Id. at 136–37.

[239] Id. at 137.

[240] Id. at 142.

constitutional democracy under Section 16 of the Indian Reorganization Act.[241] The Nation's constitution in place at the time of the decision expressly authorized the tribal council to enact taxes "subject to approval by the Secretary of the Interior, to impose taxes and fees on non-members of the tribe doing business on the reservation."[242] The Interior Department approved the relevant taxes in 1976.[243] The internally imposed limitations on the tribe's power to tax—the requirement for Interior Department approval— led the Court to state at one point, "[T]he Tribe must obtain the approval of the Secretary before any tax on nonmembers can take effect."[244]

Kerr-McGee Corp. v. Navajo Tribe

That of course led to the next major tax case, *Kerr-McGee Corp. v. Navajo Tribe*.[245] The Navajo Nation, unlike the Jicarilla Apache Nation, does not operate under a constitution approved by the Interior Secretary, having famously rejected the opportunity to reorganize under the Indian Reorganization Act.[246] The Court held in a sparse, unanimous opinion that since no federal or tribal statute required the tribe to seek and receive approval to tax nonmembers, no federal approval was necessary.[247]

The Court wrote, "The power to tax members and non-Indians alike is surely an essential attribute of such self-government; the Navajos can gain independence from the Federal Government only by financing their own police force, schools, and social programs."[248]

Tribal Power to Tax Nonmembers

In general, absent an express Act of Congress to the contrary, Indian nations may tax the activities of nonmembers on tribal lands. However, the authority of Indian nations to tax nonmember activities on nonmember lands within Indian country is limited by the *Montana* general rule and its exceptions.

The Supreme Court's recognized the tribal power to tax nonmembers on tribal lands in *Washington v. Confederated Tribes*

---

[241] Id. at 134 (citing 25 U.S.C. § 476).

[242] Id. at 135 (quoting Revised Constitution of the Jicarilla Apache Tribe, art. XI, § 1(e)).

[243] Id. at 136.

[244] Id. at 141.

[245] 471 U.S. 195 (1985).

[246] Raymond D. Austin, Navajo Courts and Navajo Common Law: A Tradition of Tribal Self-Governance 14–15 (2009).

[247] Kerr McGee Corp. v. Navajo Tribe, 471 U.S. 195, 200 (1985).

[248] Kerr-McGee Corp. v. Navajo Tribe, 471 U.S. 195, 201 (1985) (citing Statement of President Ronald W. Reagan on American Indian Policy (Jan. 24, 1983)).

of the Colville Indian Reservation.[249] That case involved tribal taxes by three tribes on nonmember cigarette purchasers at Indian-owned smokeshops.[250] The Court held conclusively that the tribes do possess the power to tax the nonmembers on tribal lands: "The power to tax transactions occurring on trust lands and significantly involving a tribe or its members is a fundamental attribute of sovereignty which the tribes retain unless divested of it by federal law or necessary implication of their dependent status."[251] The Court relied on the Interior Solicitor's 1934 opinion and several federal cases in support of its holding.[252] Moreover, the Court found no Act of Congress abrogating the power to tax, nor an "overriding federal interest that would necessarily be frustrated by tribal taxation."[253]

On nonmember-owned lands, however, the Supreme Court limited the tribal power to tax in *Atkinson Trading Co., Inc. v. Shirley.*[254] A tribe must meet one of the two *Montana* exceptions to be authorized to impose a tax on nonmember activity on nonmember reservation lands.[255] The Cameron Trading Post, operated by Atkinson Trading, included "a business complex consisting of a hotel, restaurant, cafeteria, gallery, curio shop, retail store, and recreational vehicle facility."[256] But the parcel upon which the complex was located was nonmember owned land within the Navajo Reservation, which the Court hastened to note had expanded to engulf the parcel during one of several expansions of the reservation.[257]

For the first time, the Supreme Court applied the *Montana* analysis to tribal taxation power, equating tribal authority to tax with the tribal power to regulate and adjudicate nonmember rights.[258] The Court held that *Montana* "broadly addressed the concept of 'inherent sovereignty'" over nonmembers.[259] The Court distinguished *Merrion* on the grounds that *Merrion* involved

---

[249]   447 U.S. 134 (1980).

[250]   Id. at 144–45.

[251]   Id. at 152.

[252]   Id. at 153 (citing Powers of Indian Tribes, 55 Interior Dec. 14, 46 (1934); Buster v. Wright, 135 F. 947, 950 (8th Cir. 1905), appeal dismissed, 203 U.S. 599 (1906); other citations omitted).

[253]   Id. at 154 (citing Oliphant v. Suquamish Indian Tribe, 435 U.S. 191, 208–10 (1978)).

[254]   532 U.S. 645 (2001).

[255]   Id. at 647.

[256]   Id. at 648.

[257]   Id.

[258]   Id. at 649–54.

[259]   Id. at 651 (quoting Strate v. A-1 Contractors, Inc., 520 U.S. 438 (1997), quoting in turn Montana v. United States, 450 U.S. 544, 563 (1981)).

nonmember activity on tribal trust lands, not nonmember owned lands.[260]

The Court disposed of the Navajo Nation's *Montana 1* claim first. The tribe argued that the trading post and its hotel guests had a consensual relationship with the tribal government because of the "numerous services provided by the Navajo Nation"—including law enforcement and fire department services.[261] The Court held that "a nonmember's actual or potential receipt of tribal police, fire, and medical services does not create the requisite connection" described in *Montana*.[262] Reasoning that *Strate* rejected such a broad reading of the *Montana 1* exception, the Court added, "If [the first *Montana* exception] did [apply here], the exception would swallow the rule . . . ."[263] The Court noted that the trading post's hotel guests can reach the hotel "on United States Highway 89 and Arizona Highway 64, non-Indian public rights-of-way," never needing to enter tribal lands at all.[264]

§ 8.6   State Power to Tax in Indian Country

Clear Statement Rule

Absent a clear statement from Congress, states may not tax the activities, income, or property of Indian tribes and American Indians in Indian country. **See § 5.6**. As a general matter, Congress has not expressly authorized states to tax individuals and entities, except in limited circumstances.

Montana v. Blackfeet Tribe of Indians

In *Montana v. Blackfeet Tribe of Indians*,[265] the Supreme Court held that the Indian Mineral Leasing Act of 1938 did not authorize the state to tax tribal royalty interests under oil and gas leases to nonmember lessees. *Blackfeet* is one of the Court's most rigorous applications of the clear statement rule, as well as the canon of construing statutes relating to Indian affairs. **See §§ 5.5, 5.6**.

As the Court noted, Congress first authorized mineral leasing of Indian lands in 1891.[266] That Act was silent as to state taxation. In 1924, Congress expressly authorized the state taxation of

---

[260] Id. at 653 (citing Merrion v. Jicarilla Apache Tribe, 455 U.S. 130, 137 (1982)).

[261] Id. at 654.

[262] Id. at 655.

[263] Id. (quoting Merrion v. Jicarilla Apache Tribe, 455 U.S. 130, 137–38 (1982)) (footnote omitted).

[264] Id. at 656–57.

[265] 471 U.S. 759 (1985).

[266] Id. at 763 (citing Act of Feb. 28, 1891, 26 Stat. 795, codified at 25 U.S.C. § 397).

mineral production under leases authorized by the 1891 Act.[267] In 1938, Congress enacted the Indian Mineral Leasing Act "an effort to 'obtain uniformity so far as practicable of the law relating to the leasing of tribal lands for mining purposes.' "[268] The 1938 Act established uniform leasing procedures.[269] Though Section 7 of the Act provided that any federal statutes in conflict with the 1938 Act are repealed, the 1938 Act did not expressly repeal the 1924 authorization of state taxation.[270]

The Court applied the clear statement rule and the canons of construction of Indian statutes to reach the conclusion that the 1938 Act does not authorize state taxation of leases enacted under that statute.[271]

In *County of Yakima v. Confederated Tribes and Bands of the Yakima Indian Nation*,[272] the Supreme Court found a clear statement of Congressional intent to authorize state taxation of Indian allotments held in fee by Indians or the tribe. The Court held that the 1906 Burke Act, amending the 1887 General Allotment Act, authorized state taxation of Indian allotments after the Interior Secretary deemed an Indian competent and issued a patent in fee simple to that Indian.[273]

Lacking much guidance from Congress in other areas of taxation, the Supreme Court's views on state power to tax in Indian country has evolved (or devolved, depending on one's point of view) to favor state authority. In recent decades, the Supreme Court has repeatedly recognized the authority of states to tax nonmember individuals and entities inside of Indian country, even on lands owned and controlled by Indians and tribes.

Infringement of Indian Self-Government

In general, state taxes that infringe on Indian self-government are void. As Congress has left the contours of Indian self-government and infringement to the Supreme Court to resolve, federal common law governs this test. The cases support the notion that state taxes on Indian tribes, Indian- and tribally-owned and controlled lands, and the activities of Indians on Indian and tribal lands are void. Later, the Supreme Court would amend this rule to

---

[267] Id. (quoting Act of May 29, 1924, ch. 210, 43 Stat. 244, codified as 25 U.S.C. § 398).

[268] Id. (quoting S. Rep. 985, 75th Cong., 1st Sess. at 2 (1937)).

[269] 25 U.S.C. §§ 396b–396g.

[270] Montana v. Blackfeet Tribe of Indians, 471 U.S. 759, 764 (1985).

[271] Id. at 765–67.

[272] 502 U.S. 251 (1992).

[273] Id. at 262 (quoting Burke Act, 34 Stat. 182, 183).

focus on the legal incidence of a tax, effectively establishing a bright-line test akin to the infringement test articulated in *Williams v. Lee*.[274] **See § 6.7**.

The companion cases, *The Kansas Indians*,[275] and *The New York Indians*,[276] established that states may not tax tribally-owned land and Indian allotments established by treaties or Acts of Congress. *The Kansas Indians* involved three different tribal groups (Shawnee, Wea, and Miami) and treaty provisions, but similar facts. The portion of the opinion dealing with the Shawnee Indians involved provisions of an 1854 treaty that allowed tribal members to select lands within an area in Kansas, further allowing the Indians to own the land individually or in common.[277] In both types of land ownership, the treaty established restrictions on the alienation of the land by Indians.[278] Kansas argued that the 1854 treaty contained no express protections or recognition of the continuation of the tribal government, but the Court held instead that the United States continued to recognize the tribal government.[279] "As long as the United States recognizes their national character they are under the protection of treaties and the laws of Congress, and *their property is withdrawn from the operation of State laws.*"[280]

After the Supreme Court decided *Williams v. Lee*,[281] see § 6.7, the Court decided against state taxing authority in Indian country in several cases. In *Warren Trading Post v. Arizona State Tax Commission*,[282] the Court struck down state taxation of a nonmember retail business on the Navajo Reservation.[283] The Commissioner of Indian Affairs licensed the trading post under 19th century statutes empowering the Commissioner to employ "the sole power and authority to appoint traders to the Indian tribes," and to set prices on sales of goods to Indians.[284] The Court concluded that state taxation of the nonmember business would undermine federal policies in favor of tribal self-determination, as well as serve as a windfall of sorts for states who otherwise have

---

[274] 358 U.S. 217 (1959).

[275] 72 U.S. 737 (1867).

[276] 72 U.S. 761 (1867).

[277] The Kansas Indians, 72 U.S. 737, 753 (1967).

[278] Id.

[279] Id. at 757.

[280] Id. (emphasis added).

[281] 358 U.S. 217 (1959).

[282] 380 U.S. 685 (1965).

[283] Id. at 691–92.

[284] Id. at 689 (quoting 25 U.S.C. § 261).

little or no obligation to provide government services on the reservation.[285]

The *Warren Trading Post* Court's heavy reliance on the Indian trader licensing scheme to void state taxation would no longer be replicated after the late 1980s, and the Court's turn away from principles of tribal self-determination toward federal Indian affairs regulatory schemes initiated the dominance of federal Indian law preemption.

The next major case, *McClanahan v. Arizona State Tax Commission*,[286] continued the turn away from reliance on tribal sovereignty toward federal interests. There, the state imposed a tax on a Navajo tribal member who resided on the Navajo reservation and whose income derived solely from reservation sources.[287]

The *McClanahan* Court made express the Supreme Court's evolving understanding that Indian self-government was no longer a direct bar to state taxation of Indian country activities, and that the Court would analyze these conflicts under federal pre-emption principles: "[T]he trend has been away from the idea of inherent Indian sovereignty as a bar to state jurisdiction and toward reliance on federal pre-emption."[288] The Court relegated tribal sovereignty to a "backdrop."[289] But that backdrop served to establish that the principle that states do not have the power to tax absent "special authorization."[290]

In the companion case to *McClanahan*, *Mescalero Apache Tribe v. Jones*,[291] the Court held that the state could tax gross receipts of a tribally-owned ski resort located on federal lands outside of the tribe's reservation, but could not tax improvements made by the tribe to that property.[292] For the gross receipts tax, the Court relied on the general principle that "[a]bsent express federal law to the contrary, Indians going beyond reservation boundaries have generally been held subject to non-discriminatory state law otherwise applicable to all citizens of the State."[293] That the tribal lease of federal lands was consistent with the purposes of the Indian Reorganization Act's goal to "to rehabilitate the Indian's economic

---

[285] Id. at 691.

[286] 411 U.S. 164 (1973).

[287] Id. at 165.

[288] McClanahan v. Arizona State Tax Commission, 411 U.S. 164, 172 (1973).

[289] Id.

[290] Id. at 177. See also id. at 177 n. 16 (citing three statutes expressly authorizing state taxation).

[291] 411 U.S. 145 (1973).

[292] Id. at 157–58.

[293] Id. at 148–49.

life and to give him a chance to develop the initiative destroyed by a century of oppression and paternalism"[294] was insufficient to preserve the tribal immunity from state taxation: "But, in the context of the Reorganization Act, we think it unrealistic to conclude that Congress conceived of off-reservation tribal enterprises 'virtually as an arm of the Government.' "[295] Conversely, the Court held that the state's tax on the tribe's improvements to the ski resort were personal property attached to the federal lands entitled to immunity from taxation.[296]

Federal Indian Law Preemption

Federal Indian law pre-emption doctrine provides that where a state tax impermissibly interferes with federal law or federal policies, the state tax is invalid. A state tax might also be pre-empted by tribal law if the state law interferes with the marketing of on-reservation resources. Finally, a state tax that infringes on the right of reservation Indians to govern themselves is void. Whether a state tax is pre-empted is subject to a case-by-case analysis.

Conflicts between states and tribes over state taxation of Indian country activities came to a head in the 1970s as many tribal members and Indian tribes began operating and licensing smoke shops and gas stations that sold tobacco and motor fuel products free of state taxation. In *Moe v. Confederated Salish and Kootenai Tribes of the Flathead Reservation*,[297] the first major smokeshop case, Justice Rehnquist held that a state may impose its tobacco products tax on the sales by tribal members to nonmembers on Indian lands.[298]

Moe involved two questions: first, whether the state could tax on-reservation transactions between individual Indian retailers and nonmembers; and second, whether the state could tax transactions with tribal members. On the first question, the Court held not only that the state could tax the transactions between Indians and nonmembers, but could also force the Indian retailers to collect the tax for the state.[299] The Court distinguished *Warren Trading Post* by concluding that there was no impact or burden on trading between Indians and Indian traders.[300] The Court flatly rejected claims that the state's taxes impacted Indian trading, holding that nonmembers purchasing tobacco and motor fuel products without

---

[294] Id. at 152 (quoting H.R.Rep.No.1804, 73d Cong., 2d Sess., 6 (1934)).

[295] Id. at 152–53 (citing 25 U.S.C. § 465 [now 25 U.S.C. § 5108]).

[296] Id. at 158–59.

[297] 425 U.S. 463 (1976).

[298] Id. at 466.

[299] Id. at 481–83.

[300] Id. at 482.

paying state taxes were in violation of state law.[301] The Court further held that the imposition on Indian retailers to collect the state tax was no burden on "tribal self-government."[302] Here, the Court's holding seems to rely on the analytical play to distinguish Indians from their tribes as separate entities. In fact, the Court was simply wrong to not equate tribal self-government with the interests of individual tribal members. The interests of tribal members and Indian tribes are inextricably intertwined, and to find otherwise evidences real ignorance of federal Indian law and policy, as well as reservation realities. Law that allows for the enhancement of individual Indian income and business activities is law that supports tribal self-government; law that undercuts individual Indian economic activity undermines tribal self-government.

In *Moe*'s second holding, the Court rejected the state's argument that since the Flathead reservation Indians benefitted from the provision of various state services, could vote in state elections, and participated in non-Indian business and social activities, the state could tax reservation Indians like ordinary citizens.[303] However, the *Moe* Court relied on the *McClanahan* precedent, which pointed out that the Court in *The Kansas Indians* established that the status of Indian people could only be changed by Congress or by a "voluntary abandonment of their tribal organization."[304] In contrast to the first holding, this portion of the opinion demonstrates the understanding that Indians and tribes are closely aligned.

Colville Confederated Tribes

In *Washington v. Confederated Tribes of the Colville Indian Reservation*,[305] the Court addressed several issues, but primarily whether a state could tax smokeshop transactions where the home tribal government has imposed its own tax and whether states can collect taxes on nonmember Indians.[306]

On the first point, the tribes argued that the tribal tax on tobacco products was necessary to generate "revenues for the Tribes which they expend for essential governmental services, including programs to combat severe poverty and underdevelopment at the

---

[301] Id. at 481–82.

[302] Id. at 483 (citing Williams v. Lee, 358 U.S. 217, 219–20 (1959)).

[303] Id. at 476.

[304] Id. at 476 (citing McClanahan v. Arizona State Tax Commission, 411 U.S. 164, 173 & n. 12 (1973), quoting in turn The Kansas Indians, 72 U.S. 737, 757 (1867)).

[305] 447 U.S. 134 (1980).

[306] Id. at 151–52.

reservations. . . ."[307] Moreover, to allow the state to impose its tax on top of the tribal tax would put the tribes at "a competitive disadvantage as compared to businesses elsewhere."[308] The Court rejected the argument, holding that federal Indian law and policy simply does not "authorize Indian tribes thus to market an exemption from state taxation to persons who would normally do their business elsewhere."[309] The Court adopted a framework whereby on-reservation value added to a retail product may implicate tribal interests, but merely marketing an exemption from state taxation does not.[310]

The Court further held that Congress's interests in supporting tribal economic development through statutes such as the Indian Reorganization Act,[311] the Indian Financing Act of 1974,[312] and the Indian Self-Determination and Education Assistance Act of 1975,[313] did not evidence Congressional intent to "grant tribal enterprises selling goods to nonmembers an artificial competitive advantage over all other businesses in a State."[314]

On the second point, the Court held that a state could tax nonmember transactions, holding that no federal statute "demonstrate[d] a congressional intent to exempt such Indians from state taxation."[315] The Court's analysis betrayed its leanings—state authority to tax nonmembers in Indian country is presumed to be authorized even without Congressional authorization.

White Mountain Apache Tribe v. Bracker

Seventeen days after the Court decided *Colville*, the Court issued its classic federal Indian law preemption decision, *White Mountain Apache Tribe v. Bracker*,[316] and its companion case, *Central Machinery Co. v. Arizona Tax Commission*.[317] The *Bracker* opinion coalesced the Court's statements about the application of state law (in these cases, taxes) to Indian country into two parts: (1) federal Indian law preemption; and (2) infringement. Infringement was not at issue in *Bracker*. The Court's statements on preemption

---

[307] Id. at 154.

[308] Id.

[309] Id. at 155.

[310] Id. (citations omitted).

[311] 48 Stat. 984, 25 U.S.C. §§ 5101 et seq.

[312] 88 Stat. 77, 25 U.S.C. §§ 1451 et seq.

[313] 88 Stat. 2203, 25 U.S.C. §§ 5301 et seq.

[314] Washington v. Confederated Tribes of the Colville Indian Reservation, 447 U.S. 134, 155 (1979).

[315] Id. at 160–61.

[316] 448 U.S. 136 (1980).

[317] 448 U.S. 160 (1980).

were far from succinct and did not offer much guidance for future litigants, even noting that each instance of a state attempting to regulate or tax nonmembers in Indian country requires a case-by-case review, "a particularized inquiry into the nature of the state, federal, and tribal interests at stake, an inquiry designed to determine whether, in the specific context, the exercise of state authority would violate federal law."[318]

Still, the facts of the *Bracker* decision offer the prototypical example of how federal Indian law preemption works in its strong form—in short, federal control or significant direct support of a tribal initiative that would be undermined by the application of state is preempted. It is clear in *Bracker* that tribal interests are secondary to federal Indians in the preemption analysis. Yet, because *Bracker* established such a high bar for preemption, future tribal preemption claims suffered.

Bracker involved the application of state taxes to a non-Indian company, Pinetop Logging Co., doing business on the Fort Apache Reservation, and the White Mountain Apache Tribe's logging company, Fort Apache Timber Company, or FATCO.[319] The federal government through statute and regulation "comprehensive[ly]" regulated the tribal activity at issue—Indian country logging and timber production.[320] Federal statutes provided broad principles for the Interior Secretary to follow in terms of ensuring that Indian nations would receive the benefit of their on-reservation forest resources, and the Interior Secretary's regulations governed every aspect of timber production.[321] The Court concluded that "the federal regulatory scheme is so pervasive as to preclude the additional burdens sought to be imposed in this case."[322] The state taxes would directly affect the Bureau of Indian Affairs' activities on the reservation and undermine the federal goal of ensuring that only the tribe benefitted from timber production.[323]

If the state could tax the nonmember vendors and business partners, the Interior Secretary's calculations in allocating costs and fees relating to each contract would be affected.[324] The lone tribal interest at play in this analysis even had federal law at its heart: state taxes would affect the tribe's plans to "comply with the sustained-yield management policies imposed by federal law,"

---

[318] White Mountain Apache Tribe v. Bracker, 448 U.S. 134, 144 (1980).

[319] Id. at 137–39.

[320] Id. at 145–47 (citing 25 U.S.C. §§ 405–407 and 25 C.F.R. Part 141).

[321] Id.

[322] Id. at 148.

[323] Id. at 149.

[324] Id.

largely paid for by tribal timber revenues.[325] Finally, New Mexico offered no evidence that the state taxes would fund governmental services on the reservation.[326]

The paternalistic policies of the federal government inured to the benefit of tribal governance here by preempting state law. Federal goals, federal standards, federal assistance to the tribe, and federal administration of tribal contracting dominated this case.

Bracker's companion case, *Central Machinery Co. v. Arizona State Tax Commission*,[327] also involved federal Indian law preemption, but there through the Indian Trader statutes.[328] Arizona sought to impose a transactions tax on a company doing business with a tribally owned business entity.[329] The company was not licensed under the Indian trader statutes.[330] Still, the Court held, the transactions must comply with the statutes.[331] The goal of the statutes to prevent Indians and Indian nations from being defrauded would be undermined if a nonmember business simply chose not to be licensed: "One of the fundamental purposes of these statutes and regulations—to protect Indians from becoming victims of fraud in dealings with persons selling goods—would be easily circumvented if a seller could avoid federal regulation simply by failing . . . to obtain a federal license."[332] And therefore, the state tax on those transactions was preempted by federal law.[333]

The Supreme Court found other state taxes preempted under this analysis in the 1980s. For example, in *Ramah Navajo School Board v. Bureau of Revenue of New Mexico*,[334] the Court held that the state may not tax nonmember contractors that constructed a school for the reservation school board where federal money and regulations supported the school and the contractors passed the state taxes down to the school board.[335]

Cotton Petroleum v. New Mexico

The Supreme Court dramatically altered federal Indian law preemption analysis in *Cotton Petroleum v. New Mexico*.[336]

---

[325] Id. at 150.
[326] Id.
[327] 448 U.S. 160 (1980).
[328] Id. at 163–66.
[329] Id. at 163 (citing 25 U.S.C. §§ 261–264).
[330] Id. at 161.
[331] Id. at 164–65.
[332] Id. at 165.
[333] Id. at 166.
[334] 458 U.S. 832 (1982).
[335] Id. at 834.
[336] 490 U.S. 163 (1989).

Referring to this case as a "sequel" to *Merrion v. Jicarilla Apache Tribe*,[337] which upheld the tribe's power to tax, the Court in *Cotton Petroleum* held that the state's tax on the nonmember businesses engaged in mineral production on Indian trust lands was valid.[338]

A year prior, the Supreme Court eliminated the so-called intergovernmental tax immunity.[339] The intergovernmental tax immunity provided that a state tax that "burdened" the federal government's power to contract with, say, businesses or Indian nations by allowing for the passing of the tax burden onto the United States.[340] The new doctrine provided that "a State can impose a nondiscriminatory tax on private parties with whom the United States or an Indian tribe does business, even though the financial burden of the tax may fall on the United States or tribe."[341] The effect of the new understanding was to place the burden of identifying a Congressional tax immunity on the tribe or Indian country taxpayer[342]—in this case, Cotton Petroleum.

Cotton Petroleum pointed to the 1938 Indian Mineral Leasing Act, which recognized tribal authority to enter into mineral leases with the Interior Secretary's approval.[343] The Court concluded that Congress did not intend to allow mineral production under tribal leases to be free of state taxation, noting that the Act is silent as to state taxation.[344] The Court also noted that by 1938 it was clear that states could tax tribal mineral leases on federal public lands, so Congress must have been legislating with that notion in mind.[345] The Court also imputed Congressional intent, or at least acquiescence to state taxation of tribal mineral leases, from the Indian Oil Leasing Act of 1924, which expressly allowed for state taxation of mineral production on treaty-established reservations.[346] Despite the fact that the Jicarilla Apache Tribe's reservation was established by Executive Order and not subject to the 1924 Act, the Court held that state taxation of tribal mineral leases was the norm by the time Congress authorized leasing of Executive Order reservations in 1927.[347]

---

[337] Id. at 166 (citing Merrion v. Jicarilla Apache Tribe, 455 U.S. 130 (1982)).

[338] Id. at 173.

[339] South Carolina v. Baker, 485 U.S. 505, 520 (1988).

[340] Cotton Petroleum Corp. v. New Mexico, 490 U.S. 163, 174 (1989) (citing Gillispie v. Oklahoma, 257 U.S. 501 (1922)).

[341] Id. at 175 (citing Montana v. Blackfeet Tribe, 471 U.S. 759, 765 (1985)).

[342] Id.

[343] Id. at 177 (citing 25 U.S.C. §§ 396 et seq.).

[344] Id. at 177–78.

[345] Id. at 179.

[346] Id. at 181 (43 Stat. 244, codified as 25 U.S.C. § 398).

[347] Id. at 181.

Legal Incidence

The Supreme Court has moved toward a more objective and still simpler analysis of whether state taxes are preempted under federal Indian law—the legal incidence of the tax now governs whether the state tax is valid. For example, if the legal incidence of the tax is on an Indian nation or tribal entity, or on a reservation Indian, then the tax is invalid. State legislatures may simply identify in their taxing scheme where the legal incidence of the tax lies, and that identification will govern.

The legal incidence is simply what actor in the chain of commerce the legislature intends the tax to tax. In a tobacco products or motor fuels case, the actors typically could include the manufacturer, the distributor or wholesaler, the retailer, and the consumer. Oft-times in smokeshop cases, the Indian nation or a tribal member is the retailer, selling tobacco products. In more recent years, tribes or Indian businesses have entered the manufacture and distribution business.

The leading case is *Oklahoma Tax Commission v. Chickasaw Nation*.[348] There, the state sought to tax motor fuel sales by the tribe on tribal lands to tribal members, and also to tax the income of tribal members employed by the tribe but who live outside of Indian country.[349] The Court held that "[i]f the legal incidence of an excise tax rests on a tribe or on tribal members for sales made inside Indian country, the tax cannot be enforced absent clear congressional authorization."[350] Conversely, "if the legal incidence of the tax rests on non-Indians, no categorical bar prevents enforcement of the tax; if the balance of federal, state, and tribal interests favors the State, and federal law is not to the contrary, the State may impose its levy. . . ."[351]

Tribal Immunity from State Efforts to Collect

Complicating the state's rights to tax nonmember transactions on Indian lands, Indian nations are immune from state suits to force collection of state taxes. The Supreme Court held conclusively in *Oklahoma Tax Commission v. Citizen Band of Potawatomi Indian Tribe of Oklahoma*,[352] see **§ 6.6**, that Indian nations retain their immunity from state suit even where the state has a right to tax nonmember transactions.

---

[348] 515 U.S. 450 (1995).

[349] Id. at 453.

[350] Id. at 459 (citations omitted).

[351] Id. (citations omitted).

[352] 498 U.S. 505 (1991).

In *Potawatomi*, the Supreme Court held that the State of Oklahoma was free to tax the tribal member retail sales to nonmembers.[353] However, the Court left the State of Oklahoma with what the State called "a right without any remedy" by also holding that the tribe's immunity precluded the State from enforcing its laws in court.[354] The Court expressly stated that the State had several options for collecting its tax; it could "collect the sales tax from cigarette wholesalers[,] . . . enter into agreements with the Tribes to adopt a mutually satisfactory regime . . . [,or] seek appropriate legislation from Congress."[355]

§ 8.7   Tribal-State Tax Agreements

Drawing from the Supreme Court's prescription in *Oklahoma Tax Commission v. Citizen Band of Potawatomi Indian Tribe of Oklahoma*,[356] many Indian tribes and states have been negotiating in earnest over Indian country tax issues. Negotiation offers numerous benefits over litigation. Tribes and states can literally redraw maps of Indian country borders, and can determine how to share tax revenues from Indian country activities. Litigation over Indian taxation often leaves both tribes and states unhappy with the results. Tribes worry about how courts will apply the Indian preemption doctrine, and states are often confronted with the inability to collect taxes even if they win in court.

§ 8.8   Jurisdiction over Indian Child Welfare

Perhaps the most difficult and tragic area of federal Indian law is Indian child welfare, with its centuries of conflict between Indian people, the federal government, and more recently state governments—with Indian children paying an incredible price as a result.[357]

Indian Child Welfare Act

Congress enacted the Indian Child Welfare Act (ICWA) in 1978,[358] after more than four years of hearings, deliberation, and debate, in order to alleviate a terrible crisis of national proportions—the "wholesale separation of Indian children from

---

[353] Id. at 512.

[354] Id. at 514.

[355] Id.

[356] 498 U.S. 505, 512 (1991).

[357] See generally Margaret D. Jacobs, A Generation Removed: The Fostering & Adoption of Indigenous Children in the Postwar World 1–162 (2014) (detailing the Indian child welfare crisis and the efforts to enact the Indian Child Welfare Act).

[358] Public Law 95–608; 25 U.S.C. §§ 1901–1963.

their families. . . ."³⁵⁹ Hundreds of pages of legislative testimony taken from Indian Country over the course of four years confirmed for Congress that many state and county social service agencies and workers, with the approval and backing of many state courts and some federal Bureau of Indian Affairs officials, had engaged in the systematic, automatic, and across-the-board removal of Indian children from Indian families and into non-Indian families and communities.³⁶⁰ State governmental actors following this pattern and practice removed between 25 and 35 percent of all Indian children nationwide from their families, placing about 90 percent of those removed children in non-Indian homes.³⁶¹

To remedy the problem, Congress enacted the Indian Child Welfare Act, a statute designed to guarantee minimum procedural safeguards for Indian tribes and Indian families in non-tribal adjudicative forums and to clarify jurisdictional gray areas between state and tribal courts. In June 2016, the Bureau of Indian Affairs promulgated regulations to interpret ICWA.³⁶² They became binding on December 12, 2016. Also in December 2016, the Bureau issued new guidelines.³⁶³

In cases where a state court has jurisdiction in an Indian child custody case, ICWA provides for minimum procedural guarantees with which each state court must comply. A state court must provide notice to both the Indian parents and the Indian tribe if a state agency is petitioning for foster care placement or termination of parent rights.³⁶⁴ Additionally, in these state court actions, Indian parents have the right to court-appointed counsel.³⁶⁵ If the state court does order a placement, it must give preference to the Indian

---

³⁵⁹ Establishing Standards for the Placement of Indian Children in Foster or Adoptive Homes, to Prevent the Breakup of Indian Families, and for Other Purposes, H. R. Rep. 95–1386, at 9 (July 24, 1978).

³⁶⁰ 25 U.S.C. § 1901(4)–(5); see also Mississippi Band of Choctaw Indians v. Holyfield, 490 U.S. 30, 32–33 (1989).

³⁶¹ Indian Child Welfare Program, Hearings before the Subcommittee on Indian Affairs of the Senate Committee on Interior and Insular Affairs, 93rd Cong., 2d Sess., at 3 (April 8–9, 1974) (statement of William Byler); see also American Indian Policy Review Commission Task Force Four, Report on Federal, State, and Tribal Jurisdiction 79 (July 1976).

³⁶² 25 C.F.R. Part 23.

³⁶³ U.S. Department of the Interior Office of the Assistant Secretary—Indian Affairs Bureau of Indian Affairs Guidelines for Implementing the Indian Child Welfare Act (Dec. 2016), available at https://turtletalk.files.wordpress.com/2016/12/december2016guidelines.pdf.

³⁶⁴ 25 U.S.C. § 1912(a).

³⁶⁵ 25 U.S.C. § 1912(b).

child's extended family or, failing that, another tribal community placement.[366]

Before the state court can order foster care placement or termination of Indian parental rights, the state agency must prove that it has provided "active efforts" to prevent the breakup of the Indian family.[367] Of additional importance, the state agency seeking termination of Indian parental rights must prove beyond a reasonable doubt the case for termination.[368]

Congress's intent in requiring that state agencies provide "active efforts" before the termination of the rights of Indian parents to their children arose out of substantial testimony that state agencies rarely, if ever, provided competent services to Indian parents before state officials took away Indian children. The phrase "active efforts" in the context of preventive and rehabilitative governmental services to families and children in need is "unique in American law."[369] As a result of its origins and its function in ICWA, "active efforts" has a "distinctly Indian character."[370]

Mississippi Band of Choctaw Indians v. Holyfield

In *Mississippi Band of Choctaw Indians v. Holyfield*,[371] the Supreme Court held that the tribal court had exclusive jurisdiction over twin tribal member babies born off the reservation to Indian parents who were domiciled on the reservation. The case turned on the technical understanding of "domicile," a term not defined by the Indian Child Welfare Act.

The case involved unmarried parents who were members of the Mississippi Band of Choctaw Indians.[372] The mother already was a single parent, and the father was married to another woman with children of his own.[373] They were to have twins, eventually born in December 1985.[374] Through contacts at a Methodist Church, the

---

[366] 25 U.S.C. § 1915(a), (b); cf. Wisconsin Potawatomis v. Houston, 393 F. Supp. 719, 726 (W.D. Mich. 1973). (noting testimony of tribal expert about tribal family law).

[367] 25 U.S.C. § 1912(d).

[368] 25 U.S.C. § 1912(f).

[369] C. Eric Davis, In Defense of the Indian Child Welfare Act in Aggravated Circumstances, 13 Mich. J. Race & L. 433, 442 (2008).

[370] Mark Andrews, "Active" Versus "Reasonable" Efforts: The Duties to Reunify the Family Under the Indian Child Welfare Act and the Alaska Child in Need of Aid Statutes, 19 Alaska L. Rev. 85, 87 (2002).

[371] 490 U.S. 30 (1989).

[372] Id. at 37.

[373] Solangel Maldonado, Race, Culture, and Adoption: Lessons from Mississippi Band of Choctaw Indians v. Holyfield, 17 Colum. J. Gender & L. 1, 1 (2008).

[374] Mississippi Band of Choctaw Indians v. Holyfield, 490 U.S. 30, 37 (1989).

Holyfields, who were non-Indian and much older than most prospective adoptive couples, agreed to adopt the twins independent of an adoption agency.[375] The pregnant mother moved 200 miles away from the reservation to stay with the Holyfields partly upon the advice of counsel, who pointed out that state courts had no jurisdiction to confirm the private adoption unless the birth and adoption occurred off the reservation.[376] The parents and the Holyfields concluded the private adoption in state court in January 1986.[377] In March 1986, the tribe challenged the adoption.[378]

The Mississippi Supreme Court held that the twins never resided on or were domiciled on the reservation.[379] Under Mississippi precedents, children's domicile follows that of the parents, and "the parents went to some efforts to prevent the children from being placed on the reservation as the mother arranged for their birth and adoption in Gulfport Memorial Hospital, Harrison County, Mississippi."[380] The court concluded that since the twins were born off the reservation, the state court had jurisdiction to complete the adoption.[381]

The Supreme Court reversed, holding that Congress expressed no intent to rely upon state law definitions of "domicile" to interpret ICWA.[382] The Court noted first that Congressional intent in enacting ICWA was to protect "the rights of Indian families and Indian communities vis-à-vis state authorities."[383] The Court pointed out that Congress expressly stated that state courts and state agencies were "partly responsible for the problem it intended to correct."[384] The Court added that to rely upon one state's definition of "domicile" would create disarray in the application of ICWA nationwide, observing that New Mexico had reached the opposite outcome in a similar case relying on state law.[385]

---

[375] Solangel Maldonado, Race, Culture, and Adoption: Lessons from Mississippi Band of Choctaw Indians v. Holyfield, 17 Colum. J. Gender & L. 1, 1–2 (2008).

[376] Id. at 3.

[377] Id. at 6–7.

[378] Id. at 7.

[379] Matter of B.B., 511 So.2d 918, 921 (Miss. 1987), rev'd sub nom., Mississippi Band of Choctaw Indians v. Holyfield, 490 U.S. 30 (1989).

[380] Id.

[381] Id.

[382] Mississippi Band of Choctaw Indians v. Holyfield, 490 U.S. 30, 43–47 (1989).

[383] Id. at 45.

[384] Id. (citing 25 U.S.C. § 1901(5)).

[385] Id. at 45–46 (citing In re Adoption of Baby Child, 700 P.2d 198, 200–201 (N.M. App. 1985)).

The Court then determined what definition of "domicile" would apply, concluding that the twins and the birth mother were both domiciled on the reservation.[386] The Court surveyed state laws to find the generally accepted definition, which suggested that the Mississippi Supreme Court's understanding was an outlier; in fact, most states' laws would hold that since both birth parents lived on the reservation (and the mother returned there immediately after the adoption), the twins were also domiciled there.[387] Babies who have never been to a particular location may be domiciled there.[388]

Congressional intent further supported this understanding. The Court recognized that ICWA recognizes tribal rights to participate in decisions about Indian children, such as the right to intervene in all relevant cases involving Indian children in state courts, meaning that "[t]ribal jurisdiction . . . was not meant to be defeated by the actions of individual members of the tribe. . . ."[389] Moreover, Congress was also concerned with the adoption of Indian children by non-Indian homes, given the "evidence of the detrimental impact on the children themselves of such placements outside their culture."[390]

As the twins domicile was the reservation, the Court held that the state court had no jurisdiction to complete the adoption.[391]

Adoptive Couple v. Baby Girl

In 2013, the Supreme Court decided perhaps the most dramatic and wrenching federal Indian law case in modern history, *Adoptive Couple v. Baby Girl*.[392] The Court determined that certain of ICWA's protections favoring Indian parents in involuntary termination proceedings do not apply to parents who did not have custody of the child.[393] The Court further held that state courts are not required to ensure that the state engaged in active efforts to prevent the break-up of an Indian family are not required when an Indian parent abandons a child before birth.[394] The Court also held that ICWA's adoptive placement preferences favoring Indian

---

[386] Id. at 48–54.

[387] Id. at 48–49.

[388] Id. at 48 ("[I]t is entirely logical that '[o]n occasion, a child's domicile of origin will be in a place where the child has never been.' ") (quoting Restatement (Second) Conflict of Laws § 14, Comment b (1971)).

[389] Id. at 49.

[390] Id. at 49–50.

[391] Mississippi Band of Choctaw Indians v. Holyfield, 490 U.S. 30, 53 (1989).

[392] 133 S.Ct. 2552 (2013).

[393] Id. at 2557 (citing 25 U.S.C. § 1912(f)).

[394] Id. (citing 25 U.S.C. § 1912(d)).

families in adoption cases are inapplicable when no Indian family comes forth in an attempt to adopt the child.[395]

The case arose out of the adoption of an Indian child by a non-Indian parent in South Carolina in 2009.[396] The birth mother was Hispanic, but non-Indian, and the birth father was a member of the Cherokee Nation of Oklahoma.[397] They were unmarried but engaged.[398] The father was in the United States Army, called to active duty at the time many of the salient facts occurred. While the mother was pregnant, the father suggested they marry before the birth, in part because his tribal membership status entitled both the mother and unborn child federal health and other benefits.[399] The birth mother rejected the proposal, and then broke off their relationship.[400] The parties disputed whether the father (and his mother) attempted to contact the birth mother after that break up.[401] However, the birth mother contacted the birth father by text, asking him whether he would rather pay child support or terminate his parental rights.[402] He responded via text that he would rather relinquish his rights.[403] Later, he would testify that he believed he was relinquishing his rights to the child to the birth mother, not for adoption.[404] The birth mother did not inform the birth father that she was considering adoption at that time.[405]

A month before the baby girl was born, counsel for the birth mother sent notice to the Cherokee Nation of Oklahoma. Counsel misspelled birth father's name, causing the Cherokee Nation to state that they could not verify the birth father's membership based on that information.[406] The Cherokee Nation's response stated that its determination could change if counsel provided additional or updated information on the birth father.[407]

After the break up, the birth mother contacted an adoption agency. Through the adoption agency, the adoptive couple came into play. They were domiciled in South Carolina, while the birth

---

[395] Id. (citing 25 U.S.C. § 1915(a)).

[396] Adoptive Couple v. Baby Girl, 731 S.E.2d 550, 552 (S.C. 2012), rev'd, 133 S.Ct. 2552 (2013).

[397] Id. at 552, 554.

[398] Id. at 552–53.

[399] Id. at 553 & n.3.

[400] Id. at 553.

[401] Id.

[402] Id.

[403] Id.

[404] Id.

[405] Id.

[406] Id. at 554.

[407] Id.

parents were both domiciled in Oklahoma. After the baby girl was born on September 15, 2009, the birth mother voluntarily terminated parental rights the next day,[408] likely violating ICWA's requirement that parents may not voluntarily terminate rights to an Indian child for ten days.[409] On that same day, the birth mother and the adoptive couple executed a form required by the Interstate Compact on the Placement of Children, which notifies the State of Oklahoma that the families were intending to move the baby girl from Oklahoma to South Carolina. They identified the baby girl as Hispanic only, not Cherokee.

The South Carolina Supreme Court noted from these facts that "it appears that there were some efforts to conceal [the birth father's] Indian status." Though the birth mother knew that the birth father was a Cherokee Nation member, the adoptive couple believed otherwise.[410]

Three days later, the adoptive couple began the adoption process in South Carolina.[411] A few days later, Oklahoma granted its consent to the adoption of an Oklahoma child.[412] They did not notify the birth father of the adoption action until January 2010, four months after baby girl was born, days before the birth father was to be deployed to Iraq.[413] On that day, a process server approached the birth father with papers while the birth father was at a local mall near his base.[414] According to the birth father, the process server required the birth father to sign a document in order to see the papers—that document was a legal document voluntarily consenting to the termination of his parental rights.[415] Birth father later alleged he did know what he was signing.[416] The birth father claimed that in the same interaction with the process server, he realized that instead of relinquishing his parental rights to the birth mother, he had relinquished his parental rights to the adoptive couple.[417]

The birth father then sought legal counsel through the military, and filed a stay on the action under the Servicemembers'

---

[408] Id. at 554–55.

[409] 25 U.S.C. § 1913(a).

[410] Adoptive Couple v. Baby Girl, 731 S.E.2d 550, 554 (S.C. 2012), rev'd, 133 S.Ct. 2552 (2013).

[411] Id. at 555.

[412] Id.

[413] Id.

[414] Id.

[415] Id.

[416] Id.

[417] Id.

Civil Relief Act.[418] He departed for Iraq a few days later.[419] The Cherokee Nation then confirmed the birth father was a member.[420] The Cherokee Nation intervened in the South Carolina adoption action in April 2010.[421] The birth father returned from Iraq in December 2010. The South Carolina family court determined in July 2011 that ICWA applied.[422] During this entire period, the baby girl resided with the adoptive couple.

The family court decided the matter in November 2011 in favor of the birth father.[423] The court made a finding of fact that the birth father did not voluntarily consent to the adoption, and that appellants failed to prove in accordance with ICWA that his rights should be terminated or that granting custody to the birth father would result in serious emotional or physical to the child.[424] The court ordered the transfer of custody to the birth father.[425] The South Carolina Supreme Court ultimately affirmed the family court order in July 2012.[426]

The Supreme Court reversed, 5–4. The Court's first holding related to 25 U.S.C. § 1912(f), which provides that no termination of parental rights under ICWA may be ordered if "continued custody" of the Indian child will not harm the child.[427] The Court reasoned that since the birth father could not be protected by § 1912(f) because he never had "legal or physical custody" of the baby girl.[428] Justice Sotomayor's dissent argued that the majority's reasoning stripped all noncustodial parents of rights under ICWA, even those who "have embraced the financial and emotional responsibilities of parenting."[429]

The Court's second holding was that 25 U.S.C. § 1912(d) also did not apply to the birth father.[430] Section 1912(d) requires the lower courts to find that "active efforts" be made, usually by the state agency, to "prevent the breakup of an Indian family."[431] Private adoption agencies normally do not make "active efforts" to

---

[418]   Id. (citing 50 U.S.C. App. §§ 501–597b).

[419]   Id.

[420]   Id.

[421]   Id.

[422]   Id. at 556.

[423]   Id.

[424]   Id.

[425]   Id.

[426]   Id. at 657–58.

[427]   Adoptive Couple v. Baby Girl, 133 S.Ct. 2552, 2560–62 (2013).

[428]   Id. at 2562.

[429]   Id. at 2573 (Sotomayor, J., dissenting).

[430]   Id. at 2562–64.

[431]   Id. at 2562.

prevent the adoption of an Indian child where the adoption is voluntary. The birth father here, relying on the family court's findings of fact, argued that since he never consented to the adoption, active efforts were required to prevent the breakup of his family. The Court determined instead that the birth father's consent was irrelevant because it found he abandoned the "child prior to birth and . . . never had custody of the child."[432]

The Court's final holding was that 25 U.S.C. § 1915(a), which established placement preferences for adoptions favoring an Indian child's extended family, other tribal members, and other Indian families, did not apply.[433] The Court noted that no Indian family had offered to adopt the baby girl, and therefore the provision was inapplicable.[434] Of course, the birth father and his family could not have guessed that the Court would put them in the position of being required to adopt his own biological child.

---

[432] Id. at 2563.

[433] Id. at 2564–65.

[434] Id.

Chapter 9

INDIAN GAMING

Analysis

Gaming has completely changed the face of vast swaths of Indian country in the past few decades on economic, political, legal, and socioeconomic levels. Many Indian nations at the beginning of the self-determination era in the 1970s had virtually no sources of government revenue save for federal appropriations. Now most Indian nations outside of Alaska operate at least one gaming operation. It is fair to say that most gaming tribes have not become fabulously wealthy, but they have moved their citizenry from abject poverty to the lower middle class.

As early as the 1940s, one or two Indian nations enacted ordinances to allow and regulate private gaming operations on reservation lands.[1] In the 1970s, a few Indian tribes in California, Florida, Maine, New York, and Wisconsin desperate for tribal government revenue opened high stakes bingo parlors.[2] Indian gaming has developed from these humble origins to become a massive source of tribal government revenue, and is now a market greater than $28 billion a year nationally.[3]

---

[1]   E.g., United States v. Sosseur, 181 F.2d 873 (7th Cir. 1950) (Lac du Flambeau Indian Reservation). The Keweenaw Bay Indian Community enacted the first tribal gaming ordinance in 1974, but no casino appeared there until 1983. Bradley T. Dakota, The Father of Indian Casino Gaming, 20:1 Indian Gaming, Jan. 2010, at 44.

[2]   Kathryn R.L. Rand & Steven Andrew Light, Indian Gaming Law and Policy 23 (2d ed. 2014) (California and Florida).

[3]   The National Indian Gaming Commission announced the 2014 Indian gaming revenues as $28.5 billion. National Indian Gaming Commission, 2014 Indian Gaming Revenues Increased 1.5%, Press Release, July 1, 2015.

§ 9.1 *California v. Cabazon Band of Mission Indians*

California v. Cabazon Band of Mission Indians,[4] the first Supreme Court decision involving Indian gaming may be the most momentous decision in federal Indian law in the last 50 years. The decision provided a federal law basis for Indian tribes to engage in high stakes bingo and other gaming activities without state regulation, even in so-called Public Law 280 states like California that have criminal jurisdiction inside of Indian country. *Cabazon Band* provoked Congress to finally codify a regulatory scheme for Indian gaming, including an enactment that authorized under specific conditions Vegas-style casino gaming, in the Indian Gaming Regulatory Act of 1988.[5]

The State of California allowed the playing of bingo games within the state for charity purposes, so long as the prizes did not exceed $250 a game. Riverside County, the home of the Cabazon Band of Mission Indians and the Morongo Band of Mission Indians, regulated these bingo games, and further banned so-called card rooms. The Cabazon and Morongo Bands opened up high-stakes bingo halls (Cabazon also operated a card room) and purported to operate them without regard to the state law and the county ordinances. California and the county sued, and the lower courts held that the state and county laws did not apply to the tribe.[6] The Supreme Court granted certiorari.

The Supreme Court affirmed the Ninth Circuit in a 6–3 decision. The *Cabazon* majority opinion reaffirmed and clarified two important aspects of federal Indian law, the civil-regulatory/criminal-prohibitory analysis under Public Law 280 and the federal Indian law preemption analysis. Perhaps because the Court has retreated somewhat from those doctrines, the most important aspect of the opinion is the public policy analysis employed by the Court. California argued that state restrictions on gaming should apply in Indian Country because of the possibility of organized criminal infiltration of tribal gaming operations, and the possible zones of unethical behavior that the state alleged would develop if gaming continued without state intervention. The tribes responded, and California had no choice but to concede, that the state had authorized multiple forms of gaming, such as the lottery, card rooms, horse and dog racing, charity bingo, and other forms of

---

[4]   480 U.S. 202 (1987).

[5]   25 U.S.C. §§ 2701 et seq.

[6]   See generally Ralph A. Rossum, The Supreme Court and Tribal Gaming: California v. Cabazon Band of Mission Indians 9–24, 84–133 (2011).

gambling. The state really couldn't argue with any force that gaming-related criminal activity was unique to Indian country when so much gaming occurred in accordance with state law, though it certainly tried.

The tribes also argued forcefully, and persuasively it turned out, that the gaming operations constituted to sole source of economic activity on the reservations.[7] In the most critical component of *Cabazon*'s majority opinion, the Court noted how much federal interests paralleled the tribal interests, with several federal agency decisions permeating tribal gaming development.[8]

Tying tribal and federal interests together in this manner significantly undercut the State's public policy assertions. Federal interests are far more important to the Supreme Court than tribal interests, as the Court has held repeatedly over the decades.

§ 9.2   The Indian Gaming Regulatory Act

On October 17, 1988, Congress enacted the Indian Gaming Regulatory Act (IGRA). The Act was a compromise between the interests of Indian tribes that had been recognized and validated by the Supreme Court and the interests of the states and local governments. Congress, authorized to take action in this arena by the Indian Commerce Clause, created a novel scheme for the codification, authorization, and regulation of Indian gaming. Congress intended to codify the *Cabazon Band* decision as applied to high stakes bingo, authorize tribes to conduct casino-style gaming in certain states (which also operated as a limitation on inherent tribal sovereignty to open up casinos), and create an overall regulatory scheme.

Congress made clear that the purpose of the Act was to benefit Indian tribes, not states, and to expand tribal opportunities for self-determination, self-government, economic development, and political stability.

IGRA defined Class II gaming to mean high stakes bingo,[9] the types of games tribes first began in California, Florida, Michigan, and New York and the type at issue in the *Cabazon Band* litigation. Congress intended to leave the regulation of Class II games to Indian tribes, intending to codify the *Cabazon Band* decision, except to the extent the National Indian Gaming Commission is required

---

[7]   California v. Cabazon Band of Mission Indians, 480 U.S. 202, 218–19 (1987).

[8]   California v. Cabazon Band of Mission Indians, 480 U.S. 202, 218–19 (1987).

[9]   25 U.S.C. § 2703(7)(B).

to approve Class II tribal gaming ordinances and to issue gaming licenses.[10]

IGRA defined Class III games to include all other gaming.[11] This broad definition includes casino-style gaming, such as slot machines, poker, blackjack, craps, keno, and so on. Class III gaming is the kind of gaming that can be very lucrative for Indian tribes,[12] although some forms of Class II gaming can also generate enormous revenues.[13] It is here where Congress's regulatory and authorization scheme became the most creative—and complicated. Congress created a structure whereby Indian tribes could not conduct Class III gaming without entering into a Class III gaming compact with the governor of the state where the tribe wished to begin gaming.[14] In the compact, the tribe and the state would decide basic issues about the tribal gaming operations such as which sovereign would handle the regulation of the facility, what types of games could be played at the facility, and other logistical questions.[15] Congress also prohibited Class III gaming in states that prohibited all forms of these games,[16] importing the *Cabazon Band* analysis into the Class III schema. In states such as Nebraska or Texas, where no one was authorized to operate slot machines at any time, Congress did not authorize Indian tribes to engage in Class III gaming.[17]

IGRA also created the National Indian Gaming Commission (NIGC) to serve as the federal component of the regulatory scheme.[18] Congress intended for federal and state regulation of Indian gaming to be light, unless the tribe consented to such regulation, and did not intend the NIGC to act as a massive bureaucratic regulatory body.[19] In fact, for several years, the

---

[10]   25 U.S.C. § 2710(b)(2), (c)(1); S. Rep. No. 100–446, at 1 (1988).

[11]   25 U.S.C. § 2703(8). The National Indian Gaming Commission later promulgated a more specific definition of Class III gaming. 25 C.F.R. § 502.4.

[12]   Raymond Cross, Tribes as Rich Nations, 79 Or. L. Rev. 893, 949 (2000).

[13]   Kevin K. Washburn, Federal Law, State Policy, and Indian Gaming, 4 Nev. L.J. 285, 290 (2004) (referencing "so-called 'Class II' slot machines"). E.g., Seneca-Cayuga Tribe of Oklahoma v. National Indian Gaming Commission, 327 F.3d 1019 (10th Cir. 2003), cert. denied, 540 U.S. 1218 (2004); United States v. Santee Sioux Tribe of Neb., 324 F.3d 607 (8th Cir. 2003), cert. denied, 540 U.S. 1229 (2004); Diamond Game Enters. v. Reno, 230 F.3d 265 (D.C. Cir. 2000).

[14]   25 U.S.C. § 2710(d)(1)(C).

[15]   25 U.S.C. § 2710(d)(3)(C).

[16]   25 U.S.C. § 2710(d)(1)(B).

[17]   Neb. Op. Atty. Gen. No. 02001 (2002); Tex. Atty. Gen. Op. No. GA–0278 (2004).

[18]   25 U.S.C. §§ 2702(3), 2704.

[19]   See generally Franklin Ducheneaux, The Indian Gaming Regulatory Act: Background and Legislative History, 42 Ariz. St. L.J. 99 (2010).

NIGC's annual budget was limited to a mere $8 million[20] and did not authorize the NIGC to promulgate substantive regulations. The tribes would be the exclusive regulator of Class II.[21] IGRA left Class III gaming to the tribes and the states.[22] As a final and important touch, IGRA prohibited states from collecting taxes on Indian gaming operations and revenues.[23]

§ 9.3　Class III Gaming Compacts

In the arena of Class III gaming, Congress anticipated the problem that could arise when states would refuse to negotiate a gaming compact with the tribes.[24] First, IGRA placed the burden on the states to negotiate in good faith with the tribes.[25] Then, if the state refused to negotiate in good faith, IGRA created an enforcement mechanism against the states by extending jurisdiction to the federal courts to hear claims from a tribe that a state had refused to negotiate in good faith.[26] Congress intended a scheme where, if a state stonewalled the tribe, the tribe could still commence Class III gaming operations.[27] Absent this enforcement mechanism against the states, Congress might not have included a compact requirement.[28]

The earliest series of lawsuits arising out of IGRA were the so-called "good faith" lawsuits. In 1996, the Supreme Court struck down the portion of the gaming act that authorized federal courts to hear claims against states brought by tribes alleging that the state had failed to negotiate in good faith.

---

[20]　Sandra J. Ashton, The Role of the National Indian Gaming Association in the Regulation of Tribal Gaming, 37 New Eng. L. Rev. 545, 546 (2003).

[21]　25 U.S.C. § 2710(b).

[22]　25 U.S.C. § 2710(d)(1).

[23]　25 U.S.C. § 2710(d)(4).

[24]　Franklin Ducheneaux, The Indian Gaming Regulatory Act: Background and Legislative History, 42 Ariz. St. L.J. 99, 176 (2010).

[25]　25 U.S.C. § 2710(d)(3)(A).

[26]　25 U.S.C. § 2710(d)(7)(A).

[27]　S. Rep. No. 100–446, at 5–6, 18–19 (1988).

[28]　United States v. Spokane Tribe of Indians, 139 F.3d 1297, 1300 (9th Cir. 1998) (quoting Implementation of Indian Gaming Regulatory Act: Oversight Hearings Before the House Subcommittee on Native American Affairs of the Committee on Natural Resources, 103rd Cong., 1st Sess., Serial No. 103–17, Part 1, at 63 (April 2, 1993) (Statement of Sen. Inouye, Chair, Senate Indian Affairs Committee)); see also Hearing on Review of Court Decision on Indian Gambling Before the Senate Indian Affairs Committee, S. Hrg. No. 104–513 (May 9, 1996) (Prepared statement of Alex Tallchief Skibine) ("Had we known that Congress could not waive the state's sovereign immunity, there is no doubt in my mind that we would have selected the Secretary of Interior as the recourse in cases where states failed to negotiate in good faith.") (hereinafter Alex Skibine Testimony).

Seminole Tribe of Florida v. Florida

States believed that Congress did not have authority under the Commerce Clause to abrogate state sovereign immunity and force state negotiations, and the Supreme Court agreed in *Seminole Tribe of Florida v. Florida.*[29]

The critical legal question identified by the Court was "whether Congress has acted 'pursuant to a valid exercise of power,'" in its attempt to waive state sovereign immunity under the Eleventh Amendment.[30] IGRA was an attempt by Congress to exercise its authority under the Indian Commerce Clause.[31] Rather than delve into the Court's precedents about the scope of Congressional authority under the Indian Commerce Clause or even the Framers' views about the Clause, Chief Justice Rehnquist's majority opinion concluded that the Indian Commerce Clause and the Interstate Commerce Clause were jurisprudentially the same.

The Court first noted that the Court had recognized Congressional authority to abrogate Eleventh Amendment immunity in only two circumstances—in accordance with Section 5 of the Fourteenth Amendment and in accordance with the Interstate Commerce Clause.[32] The opinion glossed over Congressional authority under the Indian Commerce Clause,[33] choosing instead to focus on the lone Interstate Commerce Clause case that had recognized Congressional authority to abrogate Eleventh Amendment immunity—*Pennsylvania v. Union Gas Co.*[34] The Court, per Chief Justice Rehnquist, overruled that case.[35]

Though the Court did conclude that, "[i]f anything, the Indian Commerce Clause accomplishes a greater transfer of power from the States to the Federal Government than does the Interstate Commerce Clause,"[36] it did not decide how much or what kind of authority Congress had under the Indian Commerce Clause in

---

[29]   517 U.S. 44 (1996).

[30]   Id. at 55 (quoting Green v. Mansour, 474 U.S. 64, 68 (1985)).

[31]   Id. at 60 (citing Brief for Petitioner 17, Seminole Tribe of Florida v. Florida, 517 U.S. 44 (1996) (No. 94–12)).

[32]   Id. at 59 (citing Fitzpatrick v. Bitzer, 427 U.S. 445, 453 (1976) (Section 5 of the Fourteenth Amendment), and Pennsylvania v. Union Gas Co., 491 U.S. 1, 19 (1989) (plurality opinion) (Interstate Commerce Clause)).

[33]   Id. at 60–61 (citing Cotton Petroleum Corp. v. New Mexico, 490 U.S. 163, 192 (1989); County of Oneida of N.Y. v. Oneida Indian Nation of N.Y., 470 U.S. 226, 234 (1985); United States v. Kagama, 118 U.S. 375, 383–84 (1886)).

[34]   491 U.S. 1 (1989).

[35]   Seminole Tribe of Florida v. Florida, 517 U.S. 44, 63–73 (1996).

[36]   Id. at 62; see also id. ("This is clear enough from the fact that the States still exercise some authority over interstate trade but have been divested of virtually all authority over Indian commerce and Indian tribes.").

relation to the Eleventh Amendment. The Court held that "the plurality opinion in *Union Gas* allows no principled distinction between the Indian Commerce Clause and the Interstate Commerce Clause."[37]

Seminole Tribe returned to the states much of the bargaining power they had lost in *Cabazon Band*. For about two years after the decision, no tribe was successful in negotiating a Class III compact, but that changed quickly after the Department of Interior began to acquiesce in a series of nifty legal maneuvers that have benefitted both tribes and states over the last two decades.

Prior to *Seminole Tribe*, two important states, Connecticut and Michigan, negotiated revenue sharing provisions with the eight tribes located within their borders. "Revenue sharing" is not much different than a tax on Indian gaming, a tax prohibited by IGRA. But the tribes in those states, faced with reticent state governors, agreed to share revenue (10 percent in Michigan and 25 percent in Connecticut) in exchange for what would later become known as a "meaningful concession."[38] In those states, the tribes negotiated for a monopoly on Vegas-style gaming within the entire state. After *Seminole Tribe*, other tribes in other states began to follow suit, and Class III gaming began to mushroom.

For more than ten years after *Seminole Tribe*, Indian gaming expanded almost exponentially. The state leadership of California and Oklahoma, states with enormous gaming markets, finally entered into Class III gaming compacts with significant revenue sharing provisions. Each state could be said to have a percentage of Indian gaming revenue at which the state leadership could demand in exchange for a gaming compact.

However, the promise of market exclusivity also began to erode as more and more tribes entered the gaming market, and some states began to authorize various forms of gaming under state law. States seemed to be demanding higher and higher percentages in exchange for a smaller economic benefit to tribes. In 2010, the Ninth Circuit held that California had negotiated in bad faith with the Rincon Band of Luiseño Mission Indians when it sought 10–15 percent of tribal gaming revenue in exchange for what the court found was virtually nothing of value in *Rincon Band of Luiseño Mission Indians of the Rincon Reservation v. Schwarzenegger*.[39] Revenue sharing between tribes and states is in a state of confusion

---

[37]   Id. at 63.

[38]   Ezekiel J.N. Fletcher, Negotiating Meaningful Concessions from Statutes in Gaming Compacts to Further Tribal Economic Development: Satisfying the Economic Benefits Test, 54 S.D. L. Rev. 419 (2009).

[39]   602 F.3d 1019 (9th Cir. 2010), cert. denied, 131 S.Ct. 3055 (2011).

and uncertainty, and this question will affect the future of tribal gaming.[40]

Revenue Sharing

The Interior Secretary is charged with reviewing Class III gaming compacts.[41] The regulations state that the Secretary must approve or disapprove a compact submitted for approval within 45 days.[42] After *Seminole Tribe* (and in a few occasions before), states and tribes pressured the Interior Secretary to approve revenue sharing provisions because, without Secretarial approval, the tribes would not be able to engage in casino-style gaming.

Both states and tribes had reasons to seek agreement. Indian gaming had too much potential to generate government revenue for states to ignore. While the states, enjoying multiple and massive revenue options given the relative strength of the 1990s American economy could afford to reject gaming in some instances, Indian tribes could not because they often do not have a sufficient tax base.[43]

The financial advantage for the states to enter into Class III gaming compacts with Indian tribes was obvious—states could generate revenue without doing much to earn it. And after *Seminole Tribe*, states could dictate terms to the tribes. As a result, the states began to—in the eyes of tribal interests—extort Indian tribes.[44]

Tribal and state negotiations and compacts in the post-*Seminole Tribe* atmosphere have one major commonality—revenue sharing with states and state subdivisions. Under the creative legal structures created by states and tribes, and authorized by the Interior Department, revenue sharing is justified through an arm's length transaction where the state receives revenue sharing and the tribes receive exclusive gaming markets. One problem, as the

---

[40] See generally Zeke Fletcher, Indian Gaming and Tribal Self-Determination: Reconsidering the 1993 Tribal-State Gaming Compacts, 89 Mich. B. J., Feb. 2010, at 38.

[41] 25 U.S.C. § 2710(d)(7)(3)(B).

[42] 25 C.F.R. § 283.10(a).

[43] Cf. Michigan v. Bay Mills Indian Community, 134 S.Ct. 2024, 2043–44 (2014) (Sotomayor, J., concurring) (quoting Matthew L.M. Fletcher, In Pursuit of Tribal Economic Development as a Substitute for Reservation Tax Revenue, 80 N. D. L. Rev. 759, 774 (2004), and citing Robert A. Williams, Jr., Small Steps on the Long Road to Self-Sufficiency for Indian Nations: The Indian Tribal Governmental Tax Status Act of 1982, 22 Harv. J. Legis. 335, 385 (1985)).

[44] Kathryn R.L. Rand & Steven A. Light, Do "Fish and Chips" Mix? The Politics of Gaming in Wisconsin, 2 Gaming L. Rev. 129, 140 (1998); Jerry Useem, The Big Gamble: Have American Indians found their new buffalo?, Fortune, Oct. 2, 2001, at 222, available at 2000 WLNR 7913728.

following examples show, is that revenue sharing percentages have increased while exclusive gaming markets have begun to disappear.

Rincon Band

The saturation of the gaming market in many areas of the United States has begun to affect how courts and the Interior Department review revenue sharing agreements.

In 2010, the Ninth Circuit held that California's demand for 10–15 percent of the gaming revenues of the Rincon Band of Luiseño Mission Indians violated IGRA.[45] While most states have not waived immunity from good faith negotiation suits, California has.[46]

California's gaming market is saturated, and the state simply could not offer market exclusivity in any meaningful way to the tribe in exchange for revenue sharing. The court first noted that IGRA requires the courts to treat a "demand" by a state in Class III gaming compact negotiations to be considered evidence of bad faith.[47] The court did reaffirm its own precedent when it stated that while a state may not "impose" a tax on Indian gaming, it may negotiate for revenue sharing payments in exchange for "meaningful concessions."[48] The court noted that it had approved the state's promise of market exclusivity in 1999 gaming compacts in California, but a decade later the saturation of the market had all but eliminated market exclusivity as a viable economic benefit: "[T]he calculations presented by the State's own expert reveal that the financial benefit to Rincon from the amendments proposed would be negligible: Rincon stood to gain only about $2 million in additional revenues compared to the State's expected $38 million."[49]

After the Ninth Circuit held that California did not meet its obligation to negotiate in good faith, the Interior Secretary disapproved two gaming compacts for failure to show that tribes would gain a substantial economic benefit from revenue sharing.[50]

---

[45]   Rincon Band of Luiseño Mission Indians of the Rincon Reservation v. Schwarzenegger, 602 F.3d 1019 (9th Cir. 2010), cert. denied, 131 S.Ct. 3055 (2011).

[46]   Cal. Gov't Code § 98005.

[47]   Rincon Band of Luiseño Mission Indians of the Rincon Reservation v. Schwarzenegger, 602 F.3d 1019, 1029–32 (9th Cir. 2010), cert. denied, 131 S.Ct. 3055 (2011).

[48]   Id. at 1036.

[49]   Id. at 1038.

[50]   Letter from Larry Echo Hawk, Assistant Secretary of the Interior for Indian Affairs, to Chairperson Sherry Treppa, Habematolel Pomo of Upper Lake (Aug. 17, 2010); Letter from Larry Echo Hawk, Assistant Secretary of the Interior for Indian Affairs, to Chairwoman Leona Williams, Pinolevill Pomo Nation (Feb. 25, 2011).

The Secretarial Procedure, 25 CFR Part 291

In reaction to the *Seminole Tribe* ruling, the Interior Department promulgated regulations intended to patch the structure Congress established to ensure that states would not be able to block Class III gaming compacts by refusing to negotiate.

Before *Seminole*, Congress intended the Interior Department to serve as a mediator of state interests in crafting a Class III gaming compact where a state refused to negotiate in good faith and after a tribe successfully proved in federal court that the state failed to comply.[51] Congress gave the Secretary a mandate to enforce and implement gaming compacts selected by a mediator.[52]

After *Seminole*, the Interior Secretary promulgated a procedure that would allow a tribe to invoke this provision where a state refused to negotiate a Class III gaming compact in good faith, invoking its Eleventh Amendment immunity from suit.[53]

If Part 291 is a valid exercise of the Secretary's authority, this procedure would be a very effective tool for tribes to avoid the intransigence of a state refusing to engage in good faith compact negotiations. A split panel of the Fifth Circuit, however, struck down the regulation.[54] IGRA still retains a requirement that a federal court must make a determination that the state "has failed to negotiate in good faith with the Indian tribe to conclude a Tribal-State compact governing the conduct of gaming activities. . . ."[55] The Secretary argued in promulgating the final rule, Part 291 restores a critical portion of IGRA and fulfills Congressional intent.[56] The Ninth Circuit suggested, without making a ruling, that this procedure would not have been valid in the pre-*Seminole Tribe* legal world,[57] but, in a post-*Seminole Tribe* world, the procedure might be a valid exercise of Secretarial discretion that would satisfy Congressional intent in passing IGRA.[58]

---

[51]   25 U.S.C. § 2710(d)(7)(B)(vii) .

[52]   25 U.S.C. § 2710(d)(7)(B)(iv) .

[53]   Class III Gaming Procedures, 64 Fed. Reg. 17535, 17536–37 (April 12, 1999). The rules are codified at 25 C.F.R. Part 291.

[54]   Texas v. United States, 497 F.3d 491 (5th Cir. 2007), cert. denied sub nom., Kickapoo Traditional Tribe of Texas v. Texas, 555 U.S. 811 (2008).

[55]   25 U.S.C. § 2710(d)(7)(B)(iii).

[56]   Class III Gaming Procedures, 64 Fed. Reg. 17535, 17536 (April 12, 1999).

[57]   Spokane Tribe of Indians v. Washington, 28 F.3d 991, 997 (9th Cir. 1994), vacated on other grounds, 517 U.S. 1129 (1996).

[58]   United States v. Spokane Tribe of Indians, 139 F.3d 1297, 1301–02 (9th Cir. 1997) (citing Seminole Tribe of Florida v. Florida, 11 F.3d 1016, 1029 (11th Cir. 1994)).

§ 9.4   Class II Bingo

IGRA does not provide a role for states to play in the regulation of Class II gaming.[59] Class II gaming is classified as bingo and pull tabs, including "electronic, computer, or other technologic aids."[60] However, Congress provided that "electronic or electromechanical facsimiles of any game of chance or slot machines of any kind" are not Class II.[61] Congress intended to codify *California v. Cabazon Band of Missions Indians*,[62] see § 9.2, at least in relation to bingo.[63]

Those tribes unable to execute a Class III gaming compact with a state could commence Class II gaming without a compact. As "technologic aids"—namely, computer graphics—improved, Class II bingo machines began to look more and more like Class III slot machines.[64] States, the National Indian Gaming Commission, and the Department of Justice all challenged the new games, arguing that the technology advances were "electronic or electromechanical facsimiles" barred by IGRA and not "technologic aids" authorized by IGRA. What constitutes a Class II bingo or pull tabs device and what constitutes a Class III machine must be determined on a case-by-case basis.[65]

In *Seneca-Cayuga Tribe of Oklahoma v. National Indian Gaming Commission*,[66] *United States v. Santee Sioux Tribe of Nebraska*,[67] and *Diamond Gaming Enterprises, Inc. v. Reno*,[68] the Tenth, Eighth, and D.C. Circuits respectively held that the Johnson Act, a federal law prohibiting the possession of slot machines in Indian country not authorized by a Class III gaming compact, did not apply to Class II technologic aids.[69] Typically, these games offer

---

[59]   25 U.S.C. § 2710(b)(1).

[60]   25 U.S.C. § 2703(7)(A)(i).

[61]   25 U.S.C. § 2703(7)(B)(ii).

[62]   480 U.S. 202 (1987).

[63]   25 U.S.C. §§ 2701(5), 2702(1); S. Rep. No. 100–446, at 22–23 (1988).

[64]   Seneca-Cayuga Tribe of Oklahoma v. National Indian Gaming Commission, 327 F.3d 1019, 1025 (10th Cir. 2003), cert. denied sub nom., Ashcroft v. Seneca-Cayuga Tribe of Oklahoma, 540 U.S. 1218 (2004); United States v. Santee Sioux Tribe of Nebraska, 324 F.3d 607, 610 (8th Cir. 2003), cert. denied, 540 U.S. 1229 (2004).

[65]   Heidi McNeil Staudenmaier and Andrew D. Lynch, The Class II Gaming Debate: The Johnson Act vs. The Indian Gaming Regulatory Act, 8 Gaming L. Rev. 227, 288 (2004).

[66]   327 F.3d 1019 (10th Cir. 2003), cert. denied sub nom., Ashcroft v. Seneca-Cayuga Tribe of Oklahoma, 540 U.S. 1218 (2004).

[67]   324 F.3d 607 (8th Cir. 2003), cert. denied, 540 U.S. 1229 (2004).

[68]   230 F.3d 365 (D.C. Cir. 2000).

[69]   Seneca-Cayuga Tribe of Oklahoma v. National Indian Gaming Commission, 327 F.3d 1019, 1036–44 (10th Cir. 2003), cert. denied sub nom., Ashcroft v. Seneca-Cayuga Tribe of Oklahoma, 540 U.S. 1218 (2004); United States v. Santee Sioux Tribe of Nebraska, 324 F.3d 607, 610–16 (8th Cir. 2003), cert. denied,

technological advances that allow players to play bingo or pull tabs games quickly, so much so that the experience is similar to playing electronic slot machines and other casino style games normally classified as Class III.

The National Indian Gaming Commission now defines "electronic, computer, or other technologic aid" broadly to incorporate "pull tab dispensers and/or readers, telephones, cables, televisions, screens, satellites, bingo blowers, electronic player stations, or electronic cards for participants in bingo games."[70]

Tribes in states with massive gaming markets such as California, Florida, and Oklahoma played Class II games for many years before finally concluding Class III gaming compacts with their respective states.

§ 9.5   Gaming on After-Acquired Lands

IGRA generally bars gaming on "after-acquired lands"—that is, lands acquired by an Indian tribe for gaming purposes after the enactment of IGRA in 1988. However, there are several exceptions to the ban on gaming on after-acquired lands (in other words, lands not already in trust or located in a reservation or "off-reservation").[71] Former Interior Department official George Skibine provided the following rubric in testimony before the Senate Committee on Indian Affairs:

(1)   The lands are located within or contiguous to the boundaries of the tribe's reservation as it existed on October 17, 1988 [25 U.S.C. § 2719(a)(1)];

(2)   The tribe has no reservation on October 17, 1988, and "the lands are located in a State other than Oklahoma and are within the Indian tribe's last recognized reservation within the state or states where the tribe is presently located" [25 U.S.C. § 2719(a)(2)(B)];

(3)   The "lands are taken into trust as part of: (i) the settlement of a land claim; (ii) the initial reservation of an Indian tribe acknowledged by the Secretary under the Federal acknowledgement process; or (iii) the restoration of lands for an Indian tribe that is restored to Federal recognition." [25 U.S.C. § 2719(b)(1)(B)];

* * *

---

540 U.S. 1229 (2004); Diamond Gaming Enterprises, Inc. v. Reno, 230 F.3d 365, 368–71 (D.C. Cir. 2000).

[70]   25 C.F.R. § 502.7(c).

[71]   See generally 25 U.S.C. § 2719(a) & (b).

[4] [G]aming can occur on the land if the Secretary, after consultation with appropriate state and local officials, and officials of nearby tribes, determines that a gaming establishment on newly-acquired land will be in the best interest of the tribe and its members, and would not be detrimental to the surrounding community, but . . . only if the Governor of the state in which the gaming activities are to occur concurs in the Secretary's determination[, the so-called "two-part determination" exception at 25 U.S.C. § 2710(b)(1)(A)].[72]

In short, there are numerous exceptions incorporated into these four areas.

Normally, these exceptions may be invoked only after the Interior Secretary agrees to acquire land for the Indian tribe in trust under Section 5 of the Indian Reorganization Act.[73] Interior Department regulations governing these kinds of trust land acquisitions for gaming purposes are codified at 25 C.F.R. Part 292.

There are no Supreme Court decisions reviewing challenges to federal decisions on Indian gaming on after-acquired lands, but numerous lower court and agency decisions. The following sections focus on the exceptions subject to more numerous legal challenges.

Restored Lands/Restored Tribes Exceptions

Congress provided that Indian lands acquired by an Indian nation after the passage of IGRA may be used for gaming purposes so long as the land qualifies as land "restored" to the tribe, or if the land is owned by a tribe "restored" to status as a federally recognized Indian tribe.[74] The Interior Secretary promulgated regulations that provide guidance on these questions.[75]

An Indian tribe may qualify as a "restored tribe" if the tribe's federal recognition had been terminated by an Act of Congress or through the actions of the Executive branch, and then later Congress took action "recognizing, acknowledging, affirming, reaffirming, or restoring" the tribe to federal recognition.[76] A tribe

---

[72] Oversight Hearing on Lands Eligible for Gaming Pursuant to the Indian Gaming Regulatory Act Before the Senate Indian Affairs Committee, 109th Cong., 1st Sess. 225–26 (July 27, 2005) (Prepared Statement of George T. Skibine).

[73] 25 U.S.C. § 5108.

[74] 25 U.S.C. § 2719(b)(1)(B)(iii).

[75] 25 C.F.R. §§ 292.7–292.12.

[76] 25 C.F.R. § 292.10(a).

may also be recognized through the Federal Acknowledgment Process,[77] or by federal court order.[78]

What constitutes restored lands is highly controversial. The Interior Secretary's regulations derive from numerous federal court decisions and National Indian Gaming Commission "Indian lands opinions."[79]

The leading restored lands case is *City of Roseville v. Norton*.[80] The city argued that the Auburn Indian Band could not commence gaming on after-acquired lands in Place County, California not originally located on the tribe's former reservation.[81] Congress had legislatively terminated the tribe during the termination era, but then had restored the tribe under the Auburn Indian Restoration Act.[82] The restoration act included provision designating Placer County as an area in which the Interior Secretary could take land into trust.[83] The question was whether IGRA's restored lands exception required the tribe to own lands in Placer County prior to restoration in order to qualify as restored lands. The court noted that Congress could have not intended for that to be the case, given that the original Auburn Indian reservation area was no longer available for use by the tribe.[84] The court further noted that the public policy behind the various exceptions to the bar on gaming on after-acquired lands supported a reading deferential to tribal interests.[85]

The leading case on the "restored tribes" exception is *Grand Traverse Band of Ottawa and Chippewa Indians v. Office of the U.S. Attorney for the Western District of Michigan*.[86] In the case, the Grand Traverse Band had been administratively "terminated" by

---

[77]   25 C.F.R. § 292.10(b). See also 25 C.F.R. Part 83 (detailing the Federal Acknowledgment Process); § 5.1.

[78]   25 C.F.R. § 292.10(c).

[79]   E.g., Kevin K. Washburn, General Counsel, National Indian Gaming Commission to Hon. Douglas W. Hillman, Senior United States District Judge, United States District Court (W.D. Michigan) (Aug. 31, 2001) (Indian lands opinion regarding Grand Traverse Band of Ottawa and Chippewa Indians); Derril B. Jordan, Associate Solicitor, Division of Indian Affairs to George Skibine, Director, Indian Gaming Management Staff (Aug, 5, 1999) (Indian lands opinion regarding Little Traverse Bay Bands of Odawa Indians). Other Indian lands opinions are available at the National Indian Gaming Commission website, http://www.nigc.gov/.

[80]   348 F.3d 1020 (D.C. Cir. 2003), cert. denied sub nom., Citizens for Safer Communities v. Norton, 541 U.S. 974 (2004).

[81]   Id. at 1021–22.

[82]   Pub. L. 103–434, Title II, Oct. 31, 1994, 108 Stat. 4533.

[83]   Id. § 2(c).

[84]   City of Roseville v. Norton, 348 F.3d 1020, 1027–29 (D.C. Cir. 2003), cert. denied sub nom., Citizens for Safer Communities v. Norton, 541 U.S. 974 (2004).

[85]   Id. at 1030.

[86]   369 F.3d 960 (6th Cir. 2004).

improper federal agency action in the 19th century.[87] The tribe became the first tribe administratively recognized under what is now termed the Federal Acknowledgment Process in 1980.[88] The court's analysis relied upon the plain language of IGRA, focusing on the phrase "the restoration of lands for an Indian tribe that is restored to Federal recognition."[89]

The courts have concluded that several Michigan tribes administratively terminated by the Interior Department in the 19th century, then later restored to federally recognized status administratively or through an Act of Congress are eligible for the restored tribe and restored lands exceptions.[90]

Settlement of a Land Claim

A less often utilized exception involves Indian lands acquired through the settlement of a land claim.[91] Some Congressionally-ratified land claims settlement statutes forbid Indian nations from gaming on lands acquired through the settlement,[92] but others do not.

The Seneca Nation compact arose out of a Congressionally-approved land claims settlement between the State and the Nation, the Seneca Nation Settlement Act.[93] This land settlement statute required the Secretary to acquire parcels in Buffalo and Niagara Falls to be held in trust for the benefit of the Seneca Nation, which would allow the Nation to engage in what Interior Secretary Norton called "off-reservation gaming."[94]

Two-Part Determination

For Indian nations who have not been restored or are not eligible for the other specific exceptions to the bar on after-acquired gaming, they may apply to game on after-acquired lands after

---

[87]   Id. at 961–62 & n. 2.

[88]   Id. at 962.

[89]   25 U.S.C. § 2719(b)(1)(B)(iii) .

[90]   E.g., Michigan Gambling Opposition v. Kempthorne, 525 F.3d 23 (D.C. Cir. 2008) (Match-E-Be-Nash-She-Wish Band of Pottawatomi Indians), cert. denied, 555 U.S. 1137 (2009); Citizens Exposing Truth about Casinos v. Kempthorne, 492 F.3d 460 (D.C. Cir. 2007) (Nottawseppi Huron Band of Potawatomi Indians); TOMAC v. Norton, 433 F.3d 852 (D.C. Cir. 2006) (Pokagon Band of Potawatomi Indians); Sault Ste. Marie Tribe of Chippewa Indians v. United States, 78 F. Supp. 2d 699 (W.D. Mich. 1999) (Little Traverse Bay Bands of Odawa Indians).

[91]   25 U.S.C. § 2719(b)(1)(B)(i).

[92]   E.g., Narragansett Indian Tribe v. National Indian Gaming Commission, 158 F.3d 1335 (D.C. Cir. 1998) (discussing Rhode Island Indian Claims Settlement Act, Pub. L. 95–395, Sept. 30, 1978, 92 Stat. 813).

[93]   Pub. L. 101–503, Nov. 3, 1990, 104 Stat. 1292.

[94]   Letter from Gale A. Norton, Secretary of Interior, to Hon. Cyrus Schindler, Nation President, Seneca Nation of Indians at 5 (Nov. 12, 2002) (citation omitted).

completing the so-called two-step determination.[95] This is a highly political process that requires the Interior Secretary to conduct a comprehensive study of whether the off-reservation gaming activity would be in the best interest of the tribe that must be concurred in by the Governor of the State in which the tribe's proposed gaming operation is located. Few tribes have successfully navigated this exception.

Michigan v. Bay Mills Indian Community

The Supreme Court in *Michigan v. Bay Mills Indian Community* held that IGRA does not allow a state to bring suit against an Indian tribe engaged in gaming operations on fee lands outside of the tribe's reservation; in other words, lands not considered "Indian lands" under IGRA.[96]

Bay Mills involves the tribe's efforts to open a casino on lands normally ineligible for Indian gaming—tribally owned fee lands under state jurisdiction off the reservation. The tribe is the beneficiary of the Michigan Indian Land Claims Settlement Act of 1997 (MILCSA), an act designed to conclude an Anishinaabe land claim brought before the Indian Claims Commission.[97] Section 107(a)(3) of MILCSA authorizes the tribe to purchase land with the settlement funds through a tribal land trust, providing that "[a]ny land acquired with funds from the Land Trust shall be held as Indian lands are held."[98] The tribe argued that the lands it purchased using the land settlement trust in Vanderbilt, Michigan were eligible for gaming under IGRA and its gaming compact with the State of Michigan. The Department of the Interior disagreed, and determined that the casino was illegal as it was not located on "Indian lands."[99] The National Indian Gaming Commission, interestingly, concluded that it could exercise its enforcement authority on the tribe because IGRA only authorized the Commission to shut down illegal Indian casinos on Indian lands.[100]

After the State of Michigan sued the tribe to enjoin the casino, the tribe successfully argued in the Sixth Circuit that since its casino was not located on Indian lands, IGRA was effectively

---

[95]   25 U.S.C. § 2719(b)(1)(A).

[96]   134 S.Ct. 2024 (2014).

[97]   Michigan Indian Land Claims Settlement Act of 1997, Pub. L. 105–143, 111 Stat. 2652.

[98]   Id. § 107(a)(3).

[99]   Letter from Hilary C. Tompkins, Solicitor, Dep't of the Interior, to Michael Gross, Assoc. Gen. Counsel, Nat'l Indian Gaming Comm'n (Dec. 21, 2010).

[100] Memorandum from Michael Gross, Assoc. Gen. Counsel, Nat'l Indian Gaming Comm'n, for the Chairwoman (Dec. 21, 2010).

inapplicable.[101] IGRA does abrogate tribal sovereign immunity to allow states or tribes to "to enjoin a class III gaming activity located on Indian lands and conducted in violation of any Tribal-State compact . . . that is in effect."[102] The court held that the State's allegation that the Vanderbilt parcel was not "Indian lands" eliminated federal court jurisdiction over the suit.[103]

§ 9.6   Tribal Self-Determination

In IGRA, Congress mandated that tribal gaming profits must be used for tribal governance purposes.[104] For the 230 or so Indian tribes that operate gaming facilities profitably, the revenues have helped bring the members of those tribes up from economic destitution to the lower middle class, an important development.[105] Most successful gaming tribes can afford to supplement the federal housing, health, public safety, and other federal appropriations with gaming revenues, but only a small number—likely under 20—of tribes have enough gaming revenue to be truly self-determinative.

That said, there are two additional positive consequences to Indian gaming. The first is the development of tribal institutions arising out of the need to strictly regulate gaming enterprises. The National Indian Gaming Commission, state regulators, tribal regulators, and even tribal creditors have placed layer over layer of regulation and strict compliance mechanisms on Indian gaming to ensure that Indian gaming is clean and protected from bad elements like organized crime. The beneficiaries of this incredible amount of regulation are tribal governance institutions. Tribal members employed by the gaming entity either as gaming managers or regulators learn quickly multiple and pervasive aspects of governance, from surveillance, regulatory paperwork, and financials. Tribal gaming employees often move back and forth from the tribal government side, and they bring with them their expertise in business management and regulation.

A second important contribution of Indian gaming is improvement in tribal-state-local relationships. IGRA requires that tribes and state governors negotiate gaming compacts before casino-style gaming can take place.[106] State officials and tribes that

---

[101] State of Michigan v. Bay Mills Indian Community, 695 F.3d 406 (6th Cir. 2012), aff'd, 134 S.Ct. 2024 (2014).

[102] 25 U.S.C. § 2710(d)(7)(A)(ii).

[103] State of Michigan v. Bay Mills Indian Community, 695 F.3d 406, 412 (6th Cir. 2012), aff'd, 134 S.Ct. 2024 (2014).

[104] 25 U.S.C. § 2710(b)(2)(B).

[105] See generally Steven Andrew Light & Kathryn R.L. Rand, Indian Gaming and Tribal Sovereignty: The Casino Compromise 77–118 (2005).

[106] 25 U.S.C. § 2710(d).

otherwise might not talk to each other in a civil manner find it expedient to talk, and once that barrier is down, negotiations on any number of previously impassable tribal-state-local conflicts can develop. Tribal gaming revenue sharing encourages cooperation between all these levels of government, and even better, where revenue sharing is not an option, tribes are being smart and progressive about their ability to use gaming revenues in creative ways to open doors at the state and local level. All of this comes out of the Supreme Court's *Cabazon Band* decision and related cases where state and local officials who once used shotguns and threats of incarceration to influence Indian tribes are now dealing with Indian tribes as peers.

Finally, one dark side to Indian gaming is the inequity amongst tribes that gaming has fostered. The large majority of Indian tribes have no gaming enterprise at all, and only a very small minority of tribes could be said to be overly successful. To some extent, there is a "one percent" problem in Indian gaming as there is in the rest of the American economy.

Chapter 10

INDIAN RELIGION AND CULTURE

Analysis

§ 10.1   Indian Cultural Property

Along with land and other natural resources, Indian nations and Indian people have been fighting for centuries to protect and preserve tribal cultures, languages, and cultural property. The federal government's assimilation program worked dramatic and sometimes irreparable harm on Indian cultures. In the 1970s, the United States finally began to recognize the importance of preserving and protecting tribal cultures. The federal government's progress in this area is slow, and often hampered by Supreme Court decisions and non-Indian resistance.

§ 10.2   American Indian Religious Freedom Act

In 1978, Congress enacted the American Indian Religious Freedom Act,[1] a statement of policy supporting Indian religious freedom in light of concerted efforts by federal agencies and officials to thwart them. The Act defined the practice of "traditional religions" to include, without limitation, "access to sites, use and possession of sacred objects, the freedom to worship through ceremonials and traditional rites."[2]

The impetus for the Act was a study conducted by the House of Representatives that concluded the federal government was

---

[1]   42 U.S.C. § 1996.
[2]   Id.

restricting Indian religious freedom in at least three ways.[3] First, federal agencies such as the United States Forest Service, National Park Service, and the Bureau of Land Management frequently prevented Indians from entering federal land where sacred sites were located.[4] Moreover, the agencies refused to allow the burial of tribal leaders in tribal cemeteries located on federal land.[5] Second, federal law enforcement officials regularly confiscated substances, such as peyote, used by Indians for religious purposes, even though federal cases had protected the use of these substances as a bona fide religious sacrament.[6] Federal officials also confiscated the use of animal parts, such as turkey and eagle feathers, from endangered species that Indians used in religious ceremonies.[7]

Third, Congress found that federal agents directly and indirectly interfered with tribal ceremonies and religious practices. For example, federal officers had a long history of opposing and restricting the practice of tribal religions through the enforcement of Bureau of Indian Affairs-authored reservation law and order codes that prohibited or severely restricted Indian religious ceremonies.[8] These law and order codes were enforced in of Courts of Indian Offenses, with judges hand-picked by federal officers. Federal courts in cases such as *United States v. Clapox* upheld federal regulations often used to prosecute Indians engaging in traditional religious practices.[9] **See § 3.7.** On-reservation federal Indian agents, as a matter of administrative practice, obstinately remained on the grounds at Rio Grande pueblos during religious ceremonies requiring that no non-Indian be present.[10] And federal law enforcement officers would also do little or nothing to stop unwelcome on-lookers from interfering in tribal religious ceremonies. Congress also found that federal officials had either directly interfered or allowed interference in tribal religious practices because they personally opposed Indian religions.[11]

---

[3]   H. Rep. No. 95–1308 (1978).

[4]   Id. at 2.

[5]   Id.

[6]   Id.

[7]   Id. at 3.

[8]   Vine Deloria, Jr. & Clifford M. Lytle, American Indians, American Justice 230–39 (1983).

[9]   35 F. 575, 577 (D. Or. 1888).

[10]   Felix S. Cohen, The Erosion of Indian Rights, 1950–1953: A Case Study in Bureaucracy, 62 Yale L. J. 348, 359 (1953).

[11]   H. Rep. No. 95–1308, at 3 (1978).

In 1996, President Clinton issued an Executive order that required all federal agencies to accommodate access to sacred sites for Indian religious practitioners and avoid negatively impacting those sites.[12] Like AIRFA, the executive order does not contain an enforcement provision. Executive Order No. 13007 imposes a duty on federal agencies to take into consideration tribal interests, to consult with tribal leaders on the subject of Indian religion, and to not interfere with tribal religious practices.

§ 10.3 *Lyng v. Northwest Indian Cemetery Protective Association*

The Supreme Court has held that the federal government does not have an obligation under federal law to preserve and protect American Indian sacred sites on federal lands, even where federal action would destroy the site and severely compromise the religion.

In *Lyng v. Northwest Indian Cemetery Protective Association*,[13] tribal interests attempted to prevent the United States Forest Service from constructing a road through an area in northern California sacred to the Yurok, Karuk, and Tolowa Indians, who called the Klamath River home.[14] The proposed road, which would have run from Gasquet to Orleans, became known as the "G-O Road."[15] The government planned to run the road through what the tribes called the High Country.[16] The High Country was sacred to the Indian people of the region, so sacred that only a few people were allowed to go there: "[O]nly highly trained Indian doctors or those undergoing doctor training were permitted to visit the High Country—and these individuals went after cleansing themselves through days of fasting."[17] The preservation of the High Country was essential to the entire world of the Indian people there, and the exploitation of its resources would destroy the tribal cultures there.[18]

---

[12]   Executive Order No. 13007 (May 26, 1996).

[13]   485 U.S. 439 (1988).

[14]   Amy Bowers & Kristen A. Carpenter, Challenging the Narrative of Conquest: The Story of Lyng v. Northwest Indian Cemetery Protective Association, in Indian Law Stories 489, 489 (Carole Goldberg, Kevin K. Washburn & Philip P. Frickey eds. 2011).

[15]   Id. at 505.

[16]   Id.

[17]   Id. at 497.

[18]   Id. See generally Abby Abinanti, A Letter to Justice O'Connor, 1 Indigenous Peoples' J. L. Culture & Resistance 1 (2004).

The federal government claimed ownership of the High Country. In 1848, the United States acquired California through the Treaty of Guadalupe Hidalgo, in which the government agreed to respect land titles of Indian nations and others.[19] In 1851, the United States set up a land claims process through which any land not claimed by the beneficiaries to the 1848 treaty (including Indian nations) would be effectively forfeited to the federal government.[20] Klamath River tribes did not make a claim, perhaps because they were unaware of the land claims process.[21] Even so, these Indian nations likely would not have disclosed the critical character of the High Country to the federal government.[22] Though the tribes and the government engaged in decades worth of negotiation and conflict over the establishment of protected Indian lands in the region, the High Country was not included in those discussions.[23] Federal officers interfered with the ability of the Klamath River Indians to visit the High Country thereafter.[24] Like so many other Indian religions and cultures, the Klamath River Indians' beliefs about the High Country were forced underground until the 1970s.

In 1973, the Forest Service proposed clear-cutting much of northern California, and in 1974 proposed the G-O Road.[25] Tribal interests protested, and so the government commissioned a study of Yurok, Karuk, and Tolowa cultural interests.[26] The study concluded that the G-O Road would significantly and negatively affect Indian religion and culture, and recommended canceling the project.[27] The government chose to proceed anyway, leading to the Supreme Court decision in *Lyng*.

The Supreme Court ruled in favor of the government. Conceding that the construction of the road would be "devastating" to the religion[28] (but doubting that it would "doom" the religion[29]),

---

[19] Treaty of Peace, Friendship, Limits and Settlement between the United States of America and the Mexican Republic, Feb. 2, 1848, 9 Stat. 822 (1848).

[20] Amy Bowers & Kristen A. Carpenter, Challenging the Narrative of Conquest: The Story of Lyng v. Northwest Indian Cemetery Protective Association, in Indian Law Stories 489, 498 (Carole Goldberg, Kevin K. Washburn & Philip P. Frickey eds. 2011).

[21] Id.

[22] Id.

[23] Id. at 498–500.

[24] Id. at 503 & n. 51.

[25] Id. at 505.

[26] Id. at 506.

[27] Id.

[28] Lyng v. Northwest Indian Cemetery Protective Association, 485 U.S. 439, 451 (1988).

[29] Id. at 451.

the majority opinion focused on two points. First, the land at issue was owned by the federal government and the Court disfavored outsider attempts to control federal land projects.[30] Second, the Court was concerned that it would be forced to choose one religion over another,[31] second-guess the salience of religious belief,[32] or interpret the religious tenets of unfamiliar religions.[33] The Court noted that its validation of the tribal claim would result in a situation where "government . . . were required to satisfy every citizen's religious needs and desires."[34] The Court's concern about limiting principles in limiting principles in *Lyng* effectively dominates analysis of American Indian religious freedom to this day.[35]

Bear Lodge

In *Bear Lodge Multiple Use Association v. Babbitt*,[36] the Tenth Circuit dismissed on standing grounds constitutional challenges to the federal government's imposition of voluntary restrictions on the use of the place known to the Lakota as Mato Tipila, or Bear Lodge, more popularly known as Devil's Tower.[37] The location is a site sacred to many Plains Indian nations.[38] Mato Tipila is a popular tourist and adventurer destination, and the number of people visiting the location began to significantly interfere with Indian religious experiences and practices, as well as the environment.[39] There were 200 named climbing routes and 600 metal bolts implanted in the mountain.[40]

After *Lyng*, the United States amended the National Historic Preservation Act[41] to make Indian sacred sites eligible for treatment as historic sites entitled to some federal protections, and requiring consultation with Indian nations before the government

---

[30]   Id. at 453.

[31]   Id. at 457.

[32]   Id. at 449.

[33]   Id. at 457–58.

[34]   Id. at 452.

[35]   See generally Kristen A. Carpenter, Limiting Principles and Empowering Practices in American Indian Religious Freedoms, 45 Conn. L. Rev. 387 (2012).

[36]   175 F.3d 814 (10th Cir. 1999), cert. denied, 529 U.S. 1037 (2000).

[37]   Id. at 815–16.

[38]   Kristen A. Carpenter, Limiting Principles and Empowering Practices in American Indian Religious Freedoms, 45 Conn. L. Rev. 387, 450 (2012).

[39]   Id. at 450–51.

[40]   Id.

[41]   Pub. L. 89–665, Oct. 15, 1966, 80 Stat. 915, codified as amended at 16 U.S.C. §§ 470 et seq.

may disrupt the sites.[42] The government issued a management plan that barred additional metal bolts, limited climbing times to protect birds, and asked climbers to voluntarily refrain from climbing in June to allow Indian religious practitioners to practice their religions without interference.[43] Earlier drafts of the management plan called for a total ban of climbing in June, save for religious practitioners.[44] The Tenth Circuit upheld the voluntary ban, holding that the petitioners did not suffer an injury due to a voluntary ban.[45] A mandatory ban, the court appeared to presume, would amount to an establishment of Indian religions as the primary governing factors in the administration of the location in violation of the First Amendment.[46]

The Bear Lodge dispute raised critically important questions yet to be fully resolved by the Supreme Court, including to what extent federal government respect for Indian culture and religions implications the First Amendment's Establishment Clause and also to what extent the Indian culture and religions are protected at all from federal government burdens under the First Amendment.

§ 10.4 *Employment Division v. Smith*

In *Employment Division v. Smith*,[47] the Supreme Court articulated a new First Amendment test to determine whether governmental burdens on the exercise of religion that was far more deferential to government decisions, that "the Free Exercise Clause provided no protection at all the religious believers facing regulations—even, potentially, imprisonment—under 'neutral, generally applicable' laws."[48]

Peyote is a small cactus that grows in the desert southwest used by many Indian people as a religious sacrament.[49] Indian

---

[42] 16 U.S.C. §§ 470a(d)(6)(A)–(B), 470f; Amy Bowers & Kristen A. Carpenter, Challenging the Narrative of Conquest: The Story of Lyng v. Northwest Indian Cemetery Protective Association, in Indian Law Stories 489, 529 (Carole Goldberg, Kevin K. Washburn & Philip P. Frickey eds. 2011).

[43] Bear Lodge Multiple Use Association v. Babbitt, 175 F.3d 814, 818 (10th Cir. 1999), cert. denied, 529 U.S. 1037 (2000).

[44] Id. at 820.

[45] Id. at 822.

[46] Cf. Bear Lodge Multiple Use Association v. Babbitt, 2 F. Supp. 2d 1448, 1455 (D. Wyo. 1998), aff'd, 175 F.3d 814, 818 (10th Cir. 1999), cert. denied, 529 U.S. 1037 (2000).

[47] 494 U.S. 872 (1990).

[48] Garrett Epps, The Story of Al Smith: The First Amendment Meets Grandfather Peyote, in Constitutional Law Stories 477, 477 (Michael C. Dorf ed. 2004).

[49] Id. at 478.

people have used the cactus for over 10,000 years, according to anthropologists.[50] Some Indian people successfully use peyote, which is not habit-forming, as a means of controlling alcoholism.[51] In *People v. Woody*,[52] decided by the California Supreme Court in 1964, the court vacated the convictions of several Navajo Indians who had ingested peyote as members of the Native American Church. Since that time, peyote use by religious practitioners usually had been protected by the laws of many states, and from federal laws by the judiciary.[53]

The dispute arose when two Native American Church practitioners—one of whom, Al Smith, was a member of the Klamath Tribe[54]—who were employees of a private drug rehabilitation organization were fired for ingesting peyote as a sacrament.[55] After their termination, they sought unemployment benefits but were denied because state law categorized the use and possession of peyote as a crime.[56] The Oregon Supreme Court rejected the state's argument, applying the First Amendment's strict scrutiny test to conclude that the state had infringed on the free exercise of religion, and the state's interests did not meet the compelling governmental interest test.[57]

For religious exercise interests, *Smith* was a disaster. The Supreme Court held that "the right of free exercise does not relieve an individual of the obligation to comply with a 'valid and neutral law of general applicability on the ground that the law proscribes (or prescribes) conduct that his religion prescribes (or proscribes).'"[58] *Smith* upset decades of precedents imposing a strict scrutiny analysis of any governmental action that burdened the free

[50]   H.R. Rep. 103–675, at 3 (Aug. 5, 1994).

[51]   Id. See also Bernard J. Albaugh & Phillip O. Anderson, Peyote in the Treatment of Alcoholism among American Indians, 131 Am. J. Psychiatry 1247 (1974).

[52]   394 P.2d 813 (Cal. 1964).

[53]   E.g., Peyote Way Church of God, Inc. v. Smith, 742 F.2d 193 (5th Cir. 1984); Native American Church v. United States, 468 F. Supp. 1247 (S.D.N.Y.1979), aff'd, 633 F.2d 205 (2d Cir. 1980).

[54]   Garrett Epps, The Story of Al Smith: The First Amendment Meets Grandfather Peyote, in Constitutional Law Stories 477, 479 (Michael C. Dorf ed. 2004).

[55]   Employment Division v. Smith, 494 U.S. 872, 874 (1990).

[56]   Id. at 876 (citing Employment Division v. Smith, 763 P.2d 146, 148 (Or. 1988)).

[57]   Black v. Employment Division, 721 P.2d 451 (Or. 1986); Smith v. Employment Division, 721 P.2d 445 (Or. 1986).

[58]   Employment Division v. Smith, 494 U.S. 872, 879 (1990) (citation omitted).

exercise of religion by excluding a large class of statutes from strict scrutiny.[59]

Congress reacted to the *Smith* decision by enacting the Religious Freedom Restoration Act.[60] The statute was intended to restore the previous Supreme Court test of strict scrutiny of government action that "substantially burden[s]" the free exercise of religion.[61] The Supreme Court in *City of Boerne v. Flores*[62] struck down that statute as applied to states, but the statute remains viable as applied to the federal government.[63] Congress attempted to reverse *Boerne* in the Religious Land Use and Institutionalized Persons Act of 2000.[64] Congress also formally extended protection to peyote users in 1994.[65]

San Francisco Peaks

What constitutes a substantial burden on free exercise by federal government action is a heavily litigated question, but in the case of American Indian religious freedoms, has been a difficult test for Indian claimants to meet. The leading case is *Navajo Nation v. United States Forest Service*,[66] where the Ninth Circuit held that federal government action that does not completely bar a tribal religion does not impose a substantial burden on free exercise.

Indian religious communities and Indian nations have been unsuccessfully challenging the federal government's approval and subsidization of the so-called Arizona Snowbowl ski lodge on the San Francisco Peaks for decades.[67] In *Wilson v. Block*,[68] several

---

[59]   Id. at 892 (O'Connor, J., concurring in the judgment). See also Douglas Laycock, The Supreme Court's Assault on Free Exercise, and the Amicus Brief that was Never Filed, 8 J. L. & Religion 99, 99 (1990) ("The opinion removes many of the issues discussed in this journal from the scope of positive constitutional law.").

[60]   Pub. L. 103–141, Nov. 16, 1993, 107 Stat. 1488, codified at 42 U.S.C. §§ 2000bb et seq.; City of Boerne v. Flores, 521 U.S. 507, 512 (1997).

[61]   52 U.S.C. § 2000bb(b) ("The purposes of this chapter are . . . to restore the compelling interest test as set forth in Sherbert v. Verner, 374 U.S. 398 (1963) and Wisconsin v. Yoder, 406 U.S. 205 (1972) and to guarantee its application in all cases where free exercise of religion is substantially burdened; and . . . to provide a claim or defense to persons whose religious exercise is substantially burdened by government.").

[62]   521 U.S. 507 (1997).

[63]   Gonzales v. O Centro Espirita Beneficente Uniao Do Vegetal, 546 U.S. 418 (2006).

[64]   42 U.S.C. §§ 2000cc et seq.

[65]   American Indian Religious Freedom Act Amendments of 1994, Pub. L. 103–344, Oct. 6, 1994, 108 Stat. 3125, codified at 42 U.S.C. § 1996a.

[66]   535 F.3d 1058 (9th Cir. 2008) (en banc), cert. denied, 556 U.S. 1281 (2009).

[67]   Save the Peaks Coalition v. United States Forest Service, 669 F.3d 1025 (9th Cir. 2012); Navajo Nation v. United States Forest Service, 535 F.3d 1058 (9th Cir. 2008) (en banc), cert. denied, 556 U.S. 1281 (2009); Wilson v. Block, 708 F.2d 735

Indian tribes demonstrated that the Peaks held critical religious significance, most notably the Navajo[69] and Hopi[70] tribes. The Snowbowl was a ski lodge first established by the Forest Service in 1937.[71] In 1977, the Forest Service agreed to transfer operations to a private company, and to allow the company to expand the footprint of the Snowbowl.[72] The tribes objected, claiming that the expansion of the ski lodge would burden the free exercise of Indian religions.[73] The court rejected the claim, noting that Indian people could still access the area, and that expansion of the Snowbowl would not "prevent [Indians] from engaging in any religious practices."[74]

In *Navajo Nation v. United States Forest Service*,[75] the most recent incarnation of the San Francisco Peaks controversy, arising after the United States enacted the Religious Freedom Restoration Act,[76] the Forest Service approved the use of sewage effluent to make artificial snow on the Peaks for the benefit of the ski resort,[77] which as a result of changing climate conditions could no longer generate a sufficient snow pack on its own.[78] The tribes most vociferously objected to the use of treated sewage on the sacred peaks.[79]

(D.C. Cir.), cert. denied, 464 U.S. 956 (1983); Hopi Tribe v. City of Flagstaff, No. 1 CA–CV 12–0370, 2013 WL 1789859 (Ariz. App., April 25, 2013). See also John Petoskey, Indians and the First Amendment, in American Indian Policy in the Twentieth Century 221 (Vine Deloria, Jr. ed. 1985). See also John Petoskey, Indians and the First Amendment, in American Indian Policy in the Twentieth Century 221, 227–31 (Vine Deloria, Jr. ed. 1985) (summarizing issues in *Wilson v. Block*).

[68] 708 F.2d 735 (D.C. Cir.), cert. denied, 464 U.S. 956 (1983).

[69] Id. at 738.

[70] Id.

[71] Id.

[72] Id.

[73] Id. at 744.

[74] Id.

[75] Navajo Nation v. United States Forest Service, 535 F.3d 1058, 1080 (9th Cir. 2008) (en banc), cert. denied, 556 U.S. 1281 (2009).

[76] 42 U.S.C. §§ 2000bb et seq.

[77] Navajo Nation v. United States Forest Service, 535 F.3d 1058, 1080 (9th Cir. 2008) (en banc) (W. Fletcher, C.J., dissenting), cert. denied, 556 U.S. 1281 (2009). It is telling the majority opinion does not mention the word "sewage" at all.

[78] Navajo Nation v. United States Forest Service, 479 F.3d 1024, 1030 (9th Cir. 2007), rev'd 535 F.3d 1058 (9th Cir. 2008) (en banc), cert. denied, 556 U.S. 1281 (2009).

[79] Kristen A. Carpenter, Limiting Principles and Empowering Practices in American Indian Religious Freedoms, 45 Conn. L. Rev. 387, 455 (2012).

A Ninth Circuit panel initially agreed with the tribal petitioners. The panel held that there were two kinds of burdens imposed on the various tribal religions:

> (1) the inability to perform a particular religious ceremony, because the ceremony requires collecting natural resources from the Peaks that would be too contaminated—physically, spiritually, or both—for sacramental use; and (2) the inability to maintain daily and annual religious practices comprising an entire way of life, because the practices require belief in the mountain's purity or a spiritual connection to the mountain that would be undermined by the contamination.[80]

The panel pointed to Navajo[81] and Hualapai[82] testimony that contamination of the Peaks and the resources there would prevent their religious practitioners from performing particular religious practices. The panel pointed to Hopi[83] and Havasupai[84] testimony that desecration of the Peaks and resources there would undermine their religious practices.

On rehearing, the Ninth Circuit sitting en banc held that these facts were insufficient to demonstrate a "substantial burden" on Indian free exercise under the Religious Freedom Restoration Act.[85] The court held that a "substantial burden" was where "the government has coerced the Plaintiffs to act contrary to their religious beliefs under the threat of sanctions, or conditioned a governmental benefit upon conduct that would violate the Plaintiffs' religious beliefs. . . ."[86] The en banc court recalled the *Lyng* Court's concern about limiting principles when it stated that millions of citizens could object to any federal action.[87] The en banc court reasoned that this effort to stop government action on federal land, no matter the impact of the action on tribal religious practices, was

---

[80]　Navajo Nation v. United States Forest Service, 479 F.3d 10124, 1039 (9th Cir. 2007), rev'd 535 F.3d 1058 (9th Cir. 2008) (en banc), cert. denied, 556 U.S. 1281 (2009).

[81]　Id. at 1039–40.

[82]　Id. at 1040–41.

[83]　Id. at 1041.

[84]　Id. at 1042.

[85]　Navajo Nation v. United States Forest Service, 535 F.3d 1058 (9th Cir. 2008) (en banc), cert. denied, 556 U.S. 1281 (2009).

[86]　Id. at 1063.

[87]　Id. at 1063–64.

no different than the federal action held by the *Lyng* Court to be acceptable.[88]

§ 10.5 Native American Graves Protection and Repatriation Act

In 1990, Congress passed the Native American Graves Protection and Repatriation Act.[89] The Act required museums to catalog all human remains and funerary objects,[90] and then repatriate Indian remains to lineal descendants or relevant tribes at their request.[91] The Act also created a review committee to monitor the implementation of the statute.[92] Finally, the Act recognized that Indian nations should have ownership and control over Indian remains discovered going forward.[93]

Congress recognized that the removal of American Indian human remains had occurred en masse during the 19th and early 20th centuries.[94] Hundreds of thousands of Indian remains were housed in museums around the nation.[95] Many members of the scientific community were reluctant to return remains and funerary objects, concerned their access to important scientific study would be compromised or eliminated.[96] Private art dealers objected to the new rules, though admitting that the private market for Indian remains involved staggering sums.[97] Ongoing controversies include the problem of unidentifiable human remains and cultural objects.[98]

The Ancient One ("Kennewick Man")

The most controversial NAGPRA case is *Bonnichsen v. United States*.[99] There, the court vacated a federal agency's decision to turn over culturally unidentifiable remains to the Indian nations that resided on the lands where the remains were found.

---

[88] Id. at 1072.

[89] Pub. L. 101–601, Nov. 16, 1990, 104 Stat. 3048, codified at 25 U.S.C. §§ 3001 et seq.

[90] 25 U.S.C. § 3003.

[91] 25 U.S.C. § 3005.

[92] 25 U.S.C. § 3006.

[93] 25 U.S.C. § 3002.

[94] H.R. Rep. 101–877, at 10 (Oct. 15, 1990).

[95] Id.

[96] Id. at 13.

[97] Id.

[98] Id. at 16.

[99] 367 F.3d 864 (9th Cir. 2004).

The case involved the discovery of a skull, and later most of an entire skeleton, in shallow water in the Columbia River near Kennewick, Washington.[100] Radiocarbon dating allowed scientists to estimate the age of the remains at 8340 to 9200 years.[101] The area upon which the remains were found is the traditional territory of numerous modern Indian nations, "including the Confederated Tribes of the Umatilla Indian Reservation, the Confederated Tribes and Bands of the Yakama Indian Nation, the Confederated Tribes of the Colville Reservation, the Nez Perce Tribe of Idaho, and the Wanapum Band."[102]

The Yakama Nation took the lead, claimed the remains as an ancestor, and demanded that the Ancient One be reburied at once: "When a body goes into the ground, it is meant to stay there until the end of time. When remains are disturbed and remain above the ground, their spirits are at unrest. . . . To put these spirits at ease, the remains must be returned to the ground as soon as possible."[103] Scientists objected, arguing that study of the Ancient One might "shed light on the origins of humanity in the Americas" and that the shape of the face and skull were, in their opinion, unlike that of modern Indians.[104]

The Ninth Circuit sided with the scientists. The court first pointed to the statute, which defined "Native American" as "of, or relating to, a tribe, people, or culture that is indigenous to the United States."[105] The court held that "the statute unambiguously requires that human remains bear some relationship to a presently existing tribe, people, or culture to be considered Native American."[106] Concomitantly, the court held that "Congress was referring to presently existing Indian tribes when it referred to 'a tribe, people, or culture *that is* indigenous to the United States.' "[107]

Indian nations often argue that they are the caretakers of the lands upon which they currently reside, even if they have not always resided upon those lands since time immemorial. Many Indian nations have been displaced by historical events before and after contact with European nations. Indian nations routinely

---

[100] S. Alan Ray, Native American Identity and the Challenge of Kennewick Man, 79 Temp. L. Rev. 89, 95 (2006).

[101] Id. at 96.

[102] Id. (footnote omitted).

[103] Id. (footnote omitted).

[104] Bonnichsen v. United States, 367 F.3d 864, 870 (9th Cir. 2004).

[105] 25 U.S.C. § 3001(9).

[106] Bonnichsen v. United States, 367 F.3d 864, 875 (9th Cir. 2004).

[107] Id. (emphasis in original).

assert a relationship to the relatives that are buried in the ground even if those relatives would have been considered members of other Indian nations. The NAGPRA regulations, not promulgated until after the *Bonnichsen case* was decided, reflect this view:

> A museum or Federal agency that is unable to prove that it has right of possession ... to culturally unidentifiable human remains must offer to transfer control of the human remains to Indian tribes and Native Hawaiian organizations in the following priority order:
>
> (i) The Indian tribe or Native Hawaiian organization from whose tribal land, at the time of the excavation or removal, the human remains were removed.; or
>
> (ii) The Indian tribe or tribes that are recognized as aboriginal to the area from which the human remains were removed. Aboriginal occupation may be recognized by a final judgment of the Indian Claims Commission or the United States Court of Claims, or a treaty, Act of Congress, or Executive Order.[108]

In 2015, scientists concluded that the Ancient One was actually of American Indian descent.[109]

Another controversial case involves the remains of famed American Indian athlete Jim Thorpe. Decades ago, a Pennsylvania town acquired his remains from members of his family, buried him there, and renamed their community Borough of Jim Thorpe. Thorpe's other descendants who are Sac and Fox Nation members brought a suit under NAGPRA seeking the repatriation of remains to Oklahoma. The Third Circuit rejected the claim in *Thorpe v. Borough of Jim Thorpe*,[110] on the grounds that the Borough was not a museum or other institution subject to NAGPRA.

§ 10.6   The Eagle Acts

The Eagle Protection Act[111] criminally prohibits the taking of bald and golden eagles, and the possession of eagle parts.[112] The Act allows the Interior Secretary to issue permits allowing individuals

---

[108] 43 C.F.R. § 10.11(c)(1).

[109] Morten Rasmussen et al., The ancestry and affiliations of Kennewick Man, 523 Nature 455 (July 23, 2015).

[110] 770 F.3d 255 (3d Cir. 2014), cert. denied, 136 S.Ct. 84 (2015).

[111] Act of June 8, 1940, 54 Stat. 250 (Bald Eagle Protection Act), codified as amended at 16 U.S.C. § 668 et seq.

[112] 16 U.S.C. § 668.

to take and possess eagles for religious and cultural purposes.[113] The Supreme Court held that the Act generally abrogated Indian treaty rights to take eagles.[114] The implementation of the permits through the National Eagle Repository has generated several Indian free exercise challenges to federal agency action, and the exemption for Indian religious purposes has generated establishment of religion challenges.

United States v. Dion

In *United States v. Dion*,[115] the Supreme Court held that the Eagle Protection Act abrogated the treaty rights of Indian people to take and possess eagles. **See § 5.6**.

The Supreme Court held against Dion.[116] The government conceded that Dion and other reservation Indians retained the right to hunt and fish in general,[117] but focused its argument on the treaty abrogation claim.

The Court reviewed its precedents on the clear statement rule, and reaffirmed that the United States will not abrogate an Indian treaty absent a clear statement of intent by Congress to do so:

> We have required that Congress' intention to abrogate Indian treaty rights be clear and plain. . . . "Absent explicit statutory language, we have been extremely reluctant to find congressional abrogation of treaty rights. . . ." . . . We do not construe statutes as abrogating treaty rights in "a backhanded way" . . .; in the absence of explicit statement, " 'the intention to abrogate or modify a treaty is not to be lightly imputed to the Congress.' " . . . Indian treaty rights are too fundamental to be easily cast aside.[118]

However, the Court noted that even in the absence of express language of abrogation, the judiciary might also rely on "clear and

---

[113] 16 U.S.C. § 668a.

[114] United States v. Dion, 476 U.S. 734 (1986).

[115] 476 U.S. 734 (1986).

[116] United States v. Dion, 476 U.S. 734 (1986).

[117] Id. at 737–38.

[118] Id. at 738–39 (citing Charles F. Wilkinson & John M. Volkman, Judicial Review of Indian Treaty Abrogation: "As Long as Water Flows, or Grass Grows Upon the Earth"—How Long a Time Is That?, 63 Calif. L. Rev. 601 (1975); other citations omitted).

reliable" evidence from the legislative history of a statute to find abrogation.[119]

The Court then analyzed the Eagle Protection Act in light of the clear statement rule. The statute references Indian religious rights,[120] but nothing about treaties. One way to interpret the statute, as the Eighth Circuit did,[121] was to hold that the statute applied to off-reservation hunting, or to non-treaty right hunting. The clear statement rule would seem to support such an interpretation.

Instead, the Court held that the legislative history of the 1962 amendments to the Eagle Protection Act, which included the language now in 18 U.S.C. § 668a, was proof of intent to abrogate treaty rights.[122] The Interior Secretary recommended that express protections for American Indian religious practices be incorporated into the Eagle Act.[123] Congress did so, and reported in its legislative history that eagle feathers were important to Indians, and that eagles are threatened by tourists in Indian country and bounty hunters in Texas.[124] Decades later, the Supreme Court would view this legislative history as evidence that Congress was concerned that Indian harvesting of eagles for religious purposes was "one of the threats to the continued survival of the golden eagle that necessitated passage of the bill."[125]

The Court also ignored the import of the contemporaneous opinion of the Interior Solicitor, who had argued that the original version of the Eagle Protection Act did not apply within Indian reservations.[126] The court stated, without evidence, that Congress was unaware of the opinion letter.[127] Then, in direct contradiction to the clear statement rule, the Court simply asserted that the original version of the Eagle Act, which was completely silent as to Indians, did apply to Indians.[128] The Court may have been persuaded by the

---

[119] Id. at 739 (quoting Cohen's Handbook of Federal Indian Law 223 (1982 ed.); other citations omitted).

[120] 16 U.S.C. § 668a.

[121] United States v. White, 508 F.2d 453 (8th Cir. 1974).

[122] United States v. Dion, 476 U.S. 734, 740–45 (1986).

[123] Id. at 741–42.

[124] H.R. Rep. 87–1450, at 2 (1962).

[125] Id. at 743.

[126] Id. at 744 (citing Memorandum from Assistant Solicitor Vaughn, Branch of Fish and Wildlife, Office of the Solicitor to the Director, Bureau of Sport Fisheries and Wildlife, Apr. 26, 1962.).

[127] Id.

[128] Id.

reality that in the decades leading up to 1986, eagles were in serious danger of extinction more than the federal government's trust obligations to Indian people.[129]

§ 10.7   Indian Cultural Property

Indian nations and Indian people have long laid claim to property rights in cultural artifacts, symbols, and knowledge, with mixed results.

Indian cultural property for our purposes includes items considered critical, if not sacred, to Indian people and Indian nations.[130] These items may include items of religious or historical significance, or both. In the early 20th century, for example, the Onondaga Nation unsuccessfully sued in New York courts to recover wampum belts improperly sold by the official wampum keeper of the Onondaga Indian to a collector.[131] While the Onondaga Nation failed to recover those particular wampum belts, the story of the recovery of other wampum belts by the Grand River Six Nations Haudenosaunee nation in Canada, which pursued repatriation of several wampum belts for decades until final recovery,[132] exemplifies the lengths to which Indian nations will go to recover their cultural property.

Chilkat Indian Village v. Johnson

The efforts of the Chilkat Indian Village in Alaska to preserve possession and to repatriate its cultural property made new law both in federal Indian law and in American Indian tribal law. Tribal members, descendants of keepers of tribal cultural property, made efforts over several years to remove cultural items from the tribal community and allegedly sell them to non-Indian collectors. The tribal village was able to successfully block those efforts through a combination of federal and tribal law.

In *Johnson v. Chilkat Indian Village (Chilkat I)*,[133] the tribal member plaintiff brought suit in federal court to adjudicate whether she held property rights over cultural artifacts, arguing that her ancestor had owned them and therefore she owned them through

---

[129] Roberto Iraola, The Bald and Golden Eagle Protection Act, 68 Alb. L. Rev. 973, 974 n. 9 (2005).

[130] See generally Kristen A. Carpenter, Sonia K. Katyal & Angela R. Riley, In Defense of Property, 118 Yale L.J. 1022, 1024–25 (2009).

[131] Onondaga Nation v. Thacher, 62 N.E. 1098 (N.Y. 1901), aff'd, 189 U.S. 306 (1903).

[132] William N. Fenton, Return of Eleven Wampum Belts to the Six Nations Iroquois Confederacy on Grand River, Canada, 36:4 Ethnohistory 392 (1989).

[133] 457 F. Supp. 384 (D. Alaska 1978).

the simple rights of an heir under tribal law.[134] The village objected to her understanding of tribal law, and instead argued that the village owned the items communally.[135] She had twice previously attempted to remove the objects to her home in Arizona, and after those efforts, the tribal council enacted laws to bar the removal of tribal cultural property, including a judicial process to review council decisions.[136] The court dismissed the property rights arguments, reasoning that the tribal judicial process was the only court competent to review the complex tribal legal issues at play.[137]

In 1984, tribal members succeeded in removing the cultural artifacts to an art dealer in Arizona.[138] The village notified law enforcement officials of the State of Alaska of the theft, and the state confiscated the items, holding them in a warehouse.[139] The village brought suit to recover the items under a federal criminal statute that prohibited theft from a tribal organization.[140] In *Chilkat Indian Village v. Johnson* (*Chilkat II*),[141] the Ninth Circuit held that the statute did not authorize or imply a private cause of action to enforce it, and dismissed the tribe's claims.[142]

Having been unsuccessful in utilizing federal law to adjudicate the ownership of the items, the village turned to its own positive law regulating tribal cultural property and sued in tribal court. In *Chilkat Indian Village v. Johnson* (*Chilkat III*),[143] the tribal court enforced the tribe's ordinance, which provided:

> No person shall enter onto the property of the Chilkat Indian Village for the purpose of buying, trading for, soliciting the purchase of, or otherwise seeking to arrange a removal of artifacts, clan crests, or other traditional Indian art work owned or held by members of the Chilkat Indian Village or kept within the boundaries of the real property owned by the Chilkat Indian Village, without

---

[134] Id. at 385–86.

[135] Id. at 386.

[136] Id.

[137] Id. at 388.

[138] Chilkat Indian Village v. Johnson, 870 F.2d 1469, 1471 (9th Cir. 1989).

[139] Id.

[140] Chilkat Indian Village v. Johnson, 643 F. Supp. 535, 535–36 (D. Alaska 1986) (citing 18 U.S.C. § 1163), aff'd 870 F.2d 1469 (9th Cir. 1989).

[141] 870 F.2d 1469 (9th Cir. 1989).

[142] Id. at 1472.

[143] Chilkat Indian Village v. Johnson, 20 Indian L. Rep. 6127 (Chilkat Tribal Court 1993).

first requesting and obtaining permission to do so from the Chilkat Indian Village Council.[144]

It is far easier to define tangible cultural property such as wampum belts and other artifacts than to define and understand intangible cultural property.[145] Intangible cultural property may include "tribal names, symbols, stories, and ecological, ethnopharmacological, religious, or other traditional knowledge."[146]

---

[144] Angela R. Riley, "Straight Stealing": Toward an Indigenous System of Cultural Property Protection, 80 Wash. L. Rev. 69, 124 (2005) (quoting tribal law).

[145] Gerald C. Carr, Protecting Intangible Cultural Resources: Alternatives To Intellectual Property Law, 18 Mich. J. Race & L. 363, 363–64 (2013).

[146] Id. at 364.

Chapter 11

INDIAN WATER RIGHTS

Analysis

American Indian rights to water in the arid west are tied to the doctrine of federal reserved water rights, a controversial area of law, and often Indian treaties. As a result, Indian water rights claims are often superior to those of states, localities, and private property owners, despite periods of neglect of Indian rights by the federal government.[1] Resistance to Indian water rights is robust.[2] Western water rights disputes typically involve hundreds or thousands of parties with competing claims to a limited amount of water, and more recent disputes can only be concluded through settlement.

§ 11.1 *Winters v. United States*

In *Winters v. United States*,[3] the Supreme Court held that a federal law setting aside lands for Indian exclusive use and occupancy may also create Indian rights to water even in the absence of express language in the statute reserving those rights.

In 1888, Congress established a permanent reservation now called the Fort Belknap Indian Reservation.[4] The legislation was the product of a negotiated agreement involving the Assiniboine, Gros Ventre, Blackfeet, and Crow Indians to create three permanent reservations for the tribes.[5] The Ninth Circuit referred

---

[1]   Robert T. Anderson, Water Rights, Water Quality, and Regulatory Jurisdiction in Indian Country, 34 Stan. Envtl. L. J. 195, 204 (2015).

[2]   Id.

[3]   207 U.S. 564 (1908).

[4]   Act of May 1, 1888, 25 Stat. 113.

[5]   Id.

to the agreement as a treaty,[6] and the federal district court judge, Judge Hunt, described the 1888 agreement exclusively as a treaty.[7]

The agreement provided that each Indian nation would receive a federal guarantee to a separate reservation, with exclusive rights to use and occupancy.[8]

The creation of the reservation came at a time when the United States was formally encouraging the development of agriculture throughout the country. By 1895, non-Indian farmers began to divert water from the Milk River upstream from the Fort Belknap Indian Reservation.[9] In 1898, the Fort Belknap Indian Agency also began taking water from the river for agricultural purposes on behalf of the tribes.[10] In 1904 and 1905, a severe drought hit the area, and preventing any water from reaching the Indian users.[11] For the Indian people, the loss of water meant possible starvation.[12] The federal government sued on behalf of the tribes, seeking and receiving an injunction on upstream non-Indian water users.[13]

The Supreme Court affirmed.[14] The Court, per Justice McKenna, who also wrote the opinion in *United States v. Winans*,[15] discussed in § 5.3, noted that while the Fort Belknap Indian Reservation was formally established in its present form by simple legislation in 1888,[16] was originally part of a treaty-established reservation, "a very much larger tract which the Indians had the right to occupy and use. . . ."[17] The non-Indian farmers argued that the Indian negotiators had not reserved water rights for themselves, implying that they were really bison hunters and that it was only the federal government that was interested in the

---

[6]   Winters v. United States, 148 F. 684, 685 (9th Cir. 1906) (referencing "the treaty which is involved in the present case"), aff'd, 207 U.S. 564 (1908); Winters v. United States, 143 F. 740, 741 (9th Cir. 1906) ("This Indian reservation was established by the treaty or convention between the government of the United States and the Indians May 1, 1888. . . .").

[7]   Norris Hundley, Jr., The "Winters" Decision and Indian Water Rights: A Mystery Reexamined, 13:1 W. Hist. Q. 17, 26 n. 27 (1982).

[8]   Act of May 1, 1888, art. I, 25 Stat. 113.

[9]   Barbara Cosens, The Legacy of Winters v. United States and the Winters Doctrine, One Hundred Years Later, in The Future of Indian and Federal Reserved Water Rights 5, 7 (Barbara Cosens & Judith V. Royster, eds. 2012).

[10]   Id.

[11]   Id.

[12]   Norris Hundley, Jr., The "Winters" Decision and Indian Water Rights: A Mystery Reexamined, 13:1 W. Hist. Q. 17, 20 (1982).

[13]   Winters v. United States, 143 F. 740, 741 (9th Cir. 1906); Winters v. United States, 148 F. 684, 685 (9th Cir. 1906), aff'd, 207 U.S. 564 (1908).

[14]   Winters v. United States, 207 U.S. 564, 574–77 (1908).

[15]   198 U.S. 371 (1905).

[16]   Winters v. United States, 207 U.S. 564, 574–75 (1908).

[17]   Id. at 575.

water.[18] The Court rejected that claim, applying the law of Indian treaty and agreement interpretation.[19] For the Supreme Court, to establish a reservation upon arid land—which the Court at one point noted was "valueless" without irrigation[20]—only to deny the right to irrigate that land was not the government's intent.[21]

The *Winters* decision established that when the United States set aside land for a particular purpose, water rights are inherent to that set-aside where the land is arid and the purpose is agricultural. In this instance, it mattered that the government did so on behalf of Indians, but the federal water rights could be considered independent of the tribal interests.[22]

§ 11.2 Indian Reserved Water Rights

After *Winters v. United States*,[23] **see § 11.1**, federal courts tended to recognize Indian reserved water rights in an "open-ended" manner, with some tribes winning court orders preserving contemporaneous uses of water and allowing for tribes to petition for additional water if uses change.[24] "Thus, by the middle of the twentieth century it was clear that Indian reservations with an agricultural purpose included water rights sufficient for irrigation and that the amount of water with a date of reservation priority would increase as tribal needs increased."[25]

Prior Appropriation and Reserved Rights

Winters established that the creation of Indian reservations by federal action automatically reserve Indian water rights necessary to effectuate the purposes of the reservation—Indian treaty rights are reserved, after all.[26] *Winters* cannot be understood properly except in the context of understanding western water law's primary thrust, prior appropriation and beneficial uses.[27] In the arid west,

---

[18]   Id. at 576.

[19]   Id. at 576–77.

[20]   Id. at 570.

[21]   Id. at 577.

[22]   Barbara Cosens, The Legacy of Winters v. United States and the Winters Doctrine, One Hundred Years Later, in The Future of Indian and Federal Reserved Water Rights 5, 8–9 (Barbara Cosens & Judith V. Royster, eds. 2012).

[23]   207 U.S. 564 (1908).

[24]   Robert T. Anderson, Indian Water Rights and the Federal Trust Responsibility, 46 Nat. Res. J. 399, 414 (2006).

[25]   Id. at 416.

[26]   Norris Hundley, Jr., The "Winters" Decision and Indian Water Rights: A Mystery Reexamined, 13:1 W. Hist. Q. 17, 35 (1982).

[27]   Thomas H. Pacheco, How Big Is Big? The Scope of Water Rights Suits Under the McCarran Amendment, 15 Ecology L.Q. 627, 629 (1988).

the notion of "first in time, first in right" is a maxim.[28] In other words, the first beneficial use of water creates a priority date to the water going forward, with all subsequent users acceding to the prior users.[29] The prior users, however, can lose priority through the abandonment or forfeiture of their use.[30] Most eastern states utilize the riparian rights method of water utilization, with water users closest to the source of the water receiving the strongest claim.[31]

Winters recognized that a competing doctrine of law that would trump state appropriation law—federal and Indian reserved water rights based on the Constitution.[32] Yes, *Winters* placed Indian reservation users (Indian nations or individual Indians) at the first priority. But Indian and federal reserved water rights, it appears, cannot be forfeited by abandonment or through other creature of state law.

Only decades later did the Supreme Court affirm the outer contours of those rights through the adoption of the practically irrigable acreage standard.

Arizona v. California I

In *Arizona v. California*,[33] the Supreme Court reaffirmed the *Winters* ruling, and rejected state attacks on Indian water rights. The Court also adopted a test to determine the quantity of water to which an Indian reservation was entitled—practicably irrigable acreage. The Court suggested that the critical question in determining whether Indian reserved rights existed was to look for federal enactments.[34]

Numerous western states and Indian nations, as well as the federal government, had made "extravagant" claims on the Colorado

---

[28] Id. at 630.

[29] Robert A. Anderson, Indian Water Rights, Practical Reasoning, and Negotiated Settlements, 98 Calif. L. Rev. 1133, 1137 (2010).

[30] Id.

[31] David H. Getches, Water Scarcity in the Americas: Common Challenges—A Northern Perspective, in Water for the Americas: Challenges and Opportunities 15, 16 (Alberto Garrido & Mordechai Shecher, eds. 2014).

[32] Robert A. Anderson, Indian Water Rights, Practical Reasoning, and Negotiated Settlements, 98 Calif. L. Rev. 1133, 1139 (2010). See also Thomas H. Pacheco, How Big Is Big? The Scope of Water Rights Suits Under the McCarran Amendment, 15 Ecology L.Q. 627, 630–31 (1988).

[33] 373 U.S. 546 (1963).

[34] Robert A. Anderson, Indian Water Rights, Practical Reasoning, and Negotiated Settlements, 98 Calif. L. Rev. 1133, 1141 (2010) ("In most modem cases, however, and as the Supreme Court found in both Winters and Arizona I, the question is whether a reservation of water should be implied from congressional action to fulfill the purposes of the reservation.").

River water flows.[35] The states began to negotiate water apportionment in the early 20th century, reaching a draft accord in 1922, the Colorado River Compact.[36] The compact divided the states' shares of the Colorado River into the upper and lower river, with each portion of the river accounting for 7.5 million acre feet.[37] However, Arizona, Nevada, and California were all growing and developing, with Arizona and California competing for the 7.5 million.[38]

In 1952, the State of Arizona sued the State of California under the Supreme Court's original jurisdiction.[39] Several States, and the United States on behalf of its own interests and the interests of 20 Indian nations on five reservations, intervened.[40] At the time of the suit, Arizona claimed 2.8 million acre feet, and California was already using 4.6 million acre feet.[41]

In *Arizona v. California*, the Supreme Court adjudicated the States' claims, but also adjudicated the federal government's Indian water rights claims.[42] In short, the Court reaffirmed the principles of the *Winters v. United States* decision. The federal government claimed about 1 million acre feet on behalf of the Indian nations collectively.[43] The Court substantially affirmed, under *Winters*, the government's water claims on behalf of tribal interests. Justice Black's key reasoning sounded heavily influenced by Justice McKenna's opinion in *Winters*:

> It is impossible to believe that when Congress created the great Colorado River Indian Reservation and when the Executive Department of this Nation created the other reservations they were unaware that most of the lands were of the desert kind—hot, scorching sands—and that water from the river would be essential to the life of the Indian people and to the animals they hunted and the crops they raised.[44]

---

[35] Frank J. Trelease, Arizona v. California: Allocation of Water Resources to People, States, and Nation, 1963 S.Ct. Rev. 158, 160.

[36] Id. at 160–61.

[37] Id. at 163.

[38] Id. at 165.

[39] Arizona v. California, 373 U.S. 546, 550 (1963).

[40] Frank J. Trelease, Arizona v. California: Allocation of Water Resources to People, States, and Nation, 1963 S.Ct. Rev. 158, 162–63.

[41] Id. at 165.

[42] Arizona v. California, 373 U.S. 546, 595–601 (1963).

[43] Id. at 596.

[44] Id. at 598–99.

Justice Black further quoted a delegate for the Territory of Arizona in 1865 who strongly supported Indian water rights lest the Indian nations in the area perish.[45]

The Court expressly held that the government had reserved Indian water rights long before Congress first legislated water rights on the Colorado River, and held that the Indian rights predated all other claims and therefore were entitled to priority.[46] The Court also concluded that the reserved water rights included water needed for contemporaneous and future uses on the reservation. In 1979, the Court issued a supplemental decree that, in the event of a shortage, Indian water rights retained priority over other users.[47]

The Court also adopted the so-called "practically irrigable acreage" (PIA) standard as a means for lower courts to address tribal water quantification claims.[48]

The amorphous PIA standard all but guaranteed more litigation in relation to Indian water rights. Even which courts would adjudicate those questions remained unsettled in 1963.

Agua Caliente Band v. Coachella Water District

In *Agua Caliente Band of Cahuilla Indians v. Coachella Water District*,[49] the Ninth Circuit confirmed that *Winters* rights include the right to groundwater.[50] On the Agua Caliente Reservation, like many locations in the west, there is no adequate supply of surface water.[51] The court held that "survival" depends on access to groundwater.[52] The court specifically tied the reasoning behind *Winters* rights—survival of tribal communities—to access to groundwater as a reserved right.[53]

§ 11.3   Jurisdiction

In 1952, Congress enacted a statute usually referred to as the McCarren Amendment, in which the United States consented to suit in state courts to adjudicate water rights.[54] Whether that

---

[45]   Id. at 599.

[46]   Id. at 600.

[47]   Arizona v. California, 439 U.S. 419 (1979) (per curiam).

[48]   Arizona v. California, 373 U.S. 546, 600 (1963).

[49]   849 F.3d 1262 (9th Cir. 2017).

[50]   Id. at 1270.

[51]   Id. at 1271 (citing In re Gen. Adjudication of All Rights to Use Water in Gila River Sys. & Source, 989 P.2d 739, 746 (Ariz. 1999)).

[52]   Id.

[53]   Id. at 1271–72.

[54]   Act of July 10, 1952, 66 Stat. 560, codified at 43 U.S.C. § 666.

waiver of federal sovereign immunity would require Indian nations to adjudicate their water rights in state court was decided in 1976.

Colorado River Water Conservation District v. United States

In *Colorado River Water Conservation District v. United States*,[55] the Supreme Court held that the federal policy behind the McCarren Amendment compelled dismissal of a federal suit brought by the United States to adjudicate Indian water rights where a parallel state court action was pending.[56]

The government brought suit to adjudicate water rights of the United States and two Indian nations to the San Juan River, which runs through Colorado, New Mexico, and Utah, before meeting up with the Colorado River.[57] The government used under the general federal statute that allows the United States bring any civil actions in federal courts "[e]xcept as provided by any other Act of Congress."[58] The Court through Justice Brennan first held that the McCarren Amendment did not repeal the general federal statute.[59] In other words, federal courts could still entertain federal and Indian water rights claims.

However, the Court then held that the McCarren Amendment should be interpreted to require federal courts to abstain from adjudicating federal and Indian water rights claims where a concurrent state court action is pending, creating a new federal court abstention doctrine in the process.[60] The Court noted that the primary focus of the McCarren Amendment was reduce complex, intertwined stream adjudications into one court—state court.[61] To allow a concurrent federal court matter to adjudicate only special federal interests such as Indian water rights ran counter, for the Court, the Congressional intent.[62] However, the Court did not adopt the brightest of bright-line rules, providing in dicta that if extensive federal court proceedings had already occurred, or if the state court proceedings were somehow not adequate to resolve federal claims, perhaps abstention would not be required.[63]

---

[55]　424 U.S. 800 (1976).

[56]　Id. at 806.

[57]　Brief of the United States 5, Colorado River Water Conservation District v. United States, 424 U.S. 800 (1976) (Nos. 74–940 and 74–949), 1975 WL 173750.

[58]　28 U.S.C. § 1345.

[59]　Colorado River Water Conservation District v. United States, 424 U.S. 800, 807–09 (1976).

[60]　Id. at 817–20.

[61]　Id. at 819.

[62]　Id. at 819–20.

[63]　Id. at 820.

Arizona v. San Carlos Apache Tribe

In *Arizona v. San Carlos Apache Tribe*,[64] the Supreme Court held that federal courts were required to abstain from adjudicating Indian water rights under the McCarren Amendment even in states that disclaimed all "right and title" to Indian property rights, and arguably have no interest in adjudicating Indian water rights.[65]

Justice Brennan, again writing for the Court, began by noting that it is a matter of mere historical accident whether a western state has disclaimed interest in Indian property rights.[66] The Court noted that these disclaimers contained in state enabling acts had barely merited "anything more than a passing mention" in the Court's state jurisdiction cases.[67] The fact that most of Indian country in the western states was located in states with a disclaimer contained in their enabling acts, curiously counseled in favor of applying the McCarren Amendment and the *Colorado River Conservation District* reasoning to all western states.[68]

The Court further rejected claims that states normally have no business in Indian affairs.[69] The fact that the McCarren Amendment waived federal sovereign immunity in state courts, along with the fact that the United States is usually a party to Indian water rights cases, meant that state courts could have jurisdiction over Indian water rights cases.[70] If state courts have jurisdiction, then federal court jurisdiction could create the same inefficient, duplicative proceedings the Court found improper in *Colorado River Conservation District*.[71]

§ 11.4 Quantification

The Supreme Court in *Arizona v. California* adopted the practically irrigable acreage standard for quantifying Indian reserved water rights. **See § 11.2.** The Court would return to the question of quantifying Indian reserved water rights in that same case in *Arizona v. California II*.[72] Indian nations argued that circumstances had changed and that they required additional

---

[64]   463 U.S. 545 (1983).

[65]   Id. at 559.

[66]   Id. at 561–62.

[67]   Id. at 563.

[68]   Id. at 564.

[69]   Id. at 565–70.

[70]   Id. at 567.

[71]   Id.

[72]   460 U.S. 605 (1983).

water.[73] Tribal interests also claimed that the United States had not alleged sufficient water requirements for the five affected reservations.[74] The Special Master agreed with the tribes, and raised the tribes' allocation by 35 percent.[75] The Supreme Court largely rejected the Special Master's recommendations, holding that a "strong interest in finality" counseled against reopening water rights adjudications after they have been decided.[76]

Federal adjudications of Indian reserved water rights have occurred. In *United States v. Adair*,[77] the Ninth Circuit held that the water rights of the Klamath Indians survived its Congressional termination.[78] But because of the McCarren Amendment, **see § 11.3**, state courts have decided many (if not most) suits to determine the quantity of Indian water rights.[79] These suits, usually called "general stream adjudications," can involve the United States, Indian nations, states, local governments, and hundreds or thousands of individual private interests.[80]

Big Horn River Adjudication (Wyoming v. United States)

In *In re General Adjudication of All Rights to Use Water in the Big Horn River System*,[81] the Wyoming Supreme Court held that Indian nations retained reserved rights amounting to over 400,000 acre-feet of water, "the majority of the river's annual flow."[82]

The matter involved the Wind River Indian Reservation, which is home to two federally recognized Indian nations, the Eastern Shoshone Tribe and the Northern Arapaho Tribe. The history of the Wind River Reservation is recounted in more detail in **§ 4.2**, in relation to two Supreme Court decisions, *Shoshone Tribe of Indians of Wind River Reservation in Wyoming v. United States I and II*.[83]

---

[73]   David H. Getches, Charles F. Wilkinson, Robert A. Williams, Jr., Matthew L.M. Fletcher, and Kristen A. Carpenter, Cases and Materials on Federal Indian Law 860 (7th ed. 2017).

[74]   Id.

[75]   Id.

[76]   Arizona v. California, 460 U.S. 506, 620 (1983).

[77]   723 F.2d 1394 (9th Cir. 1983), cert. denied sub nom., Oregon v. United States, 467 U.S. 1252 (1984).

[78]   Id. at 1397.

[79]   Robert A. Anderson, Indian Water Rights, Practical Reasoning, and Negotiated Settlements, 98 Calif. L. Rev. 1133, 1136 (2010).

[80]   Id. at 1133; Thomas H. Pacheco, How Big Is Big? The Scope of Water Rights Suits Under the McCarran Amendment, 15 Ecology L.Q. 627, 635–43 (1988).

[81]   753 P.2d 76 (Wyo. 1988), aff'd sub nom., Wyoming v. United States, 494 U.S. 406 (1989) (per curiam).

[82]   David H. Getches, Charles F. Wilkinson, Robert A. Williams, Jr., Matthew L.M. Fletcher, and Kristen A. Carpenter, Cases and Materials on Federal Indian Law 858 (7th ed. 2017).

[83]   299 U.S. 476 (1937); 304 U.S. 111 (1938).

The Wyoming Supreme Court first addressed whether the 1868 treaty establishing the present outer boundaries of the Wind River reservation reserved water rights for Indian purposes, holding that it did.[84] The court noted that the 1868 treaty was silent as to water rights, but appeared to apply the reserved rights doctrine and presumed that the United States and the tribe intended to reserve water rights for the reservation.[85]

The history of the reservation and the state in which it is located was both instructive and inconclusive, but since the court was applying a presumption that water rights were reserved, the court required the opponents to tribal interests to prove that water rights were *not* reserved. In one example noted by the court, in 1890, Congress admitted Wyoming into the United States, but forced Wyoming to disclaim all jurisdiction over Indian lands.[86] The court concluded that the admission act and the disclaimer offered no evidence that the United States did not intend to reserve water rights for the reservation.[87] Similarly, the fact that the United States did not always assert Indian water rights did not evidence an intent not to reserve them.[88]

The court then addressed the quantity of water reserved for Indian purposes, and reached the conclusion that the federal and tribal governments reserved the Wind River Indian Reservation for agricultural purposes: "Considering the well-established principles of treaty interpretation, the treaty itself, the ample evidence and testimony addressed, and the findings of the district court, we have no difficulty affirming the finding that it was the intent at the time to create a reservation with a sole agricultural purpose."[89] The court noted that in four separate articles of the 1868 treaty, the parties referenced agricultural and farming purposes.[90] The court did reject the claim that the reservation was also created for the purpose of providing a fishery or mineral estate to the tribes.[91]

The Supreme Court affirmed the decision without opinion on an equally divided vote, with Justice O'Connor recused.[92]

---

[84] In re General Adjudication of All Rights to Use Water in the Big Horn River System, 753 P.2d 76, 91–94 (Wyo. 1988), aff'd sub nom., Wyoming v. United States, 494 U.S. 406 (1989) (per curiam).

[85] Id. at 91.

[86] Id. (citing Wyoming Constitution, Art. 21, § 26).

[87] Id. at 92.

[88] Id. at 93.

[89] Id. at 96.

[90] Id.

[91] Id. at 97–98.

[92] Wyoming v. United States, 492 U.S. 406 (1990). Dean David Getches uncovered a draft opinion written by Justice O'Connor made available in Justice

Purposes of the Reservation

The *Winters* Court reasoned that an Indian nation and the United States would not create a reservation in an arid area without providing sufficient water to fulfill the tribal and federal parties' interests. Subsequent courts have engaged in efforts to determine the purposes of creating a reservation. Courts have acknowledged that, for the most part, a reservation is created to provide a homeland for an Indian nation, but that question is not helpful for quantifying water rights. So courts have delved into whether a reservation was created for specific purposes, such as agriculture, hunting, fishing, mining, and so on. There is no set standard on determining the purpose or purposes of a reservation, and small even arbitrary bits of historical data may rise to monumental importance in a court's analysis.

The Ninth Circuit has held that the purposes for which an Indian reservation was formed is critical to determining the quantity of Indian water rights. In *Colville Confederated Tribes v. Walton*,[93] the court held that the Colville reservation was formed for two purposes—agriculture and fisheries.[94] The court allowed a supplement quantity of water to provide an adequate fishery for the reservation's tribes in addition to the water needed for agriculture.[95]

The Arizona Supreme Court has applied a "minimal need" analysis to determining the purposes of the creation of a reservation, and therefore the water needed for the reservation.[96] The court held that the PIA standard might guarantee too much water to an Indian nation to the detriment of non-Indian water users. The court critiqued the PIA analysis on multiple levels: the standard discriminates against tribes arbitrarily on the basis of location;[97] the standard requires tribes to "pretend" to be farmers in

---

Marshall's papers that was apparently intended to be a majority opinion that would have altered the practicably irrigable acreage standard to include an assessment "of the reasonable likelihood that future [Indian] irrigation projects will actually be built." David H. Getches, Conquering the Cultural Frontier: The New Subjectivism of the Supreme Court in Indian Law, 84 Calif. L. Rev. 1573, 1640–41 (1996). Such a decision would have dramatically altered, and perhaps effectively abrogated, *Winters* rights.

[93]   647 F.2d 42 (9th Cir. 1981), cert. denied, 454 U.S. 1092 (1981).

[94]   Id. at 47–49. See also Robert A. Anderson, Indian Water Rights, Practical Reasoning, and Negotiated Settlements, 98 Calif. L. Rev. 1133, 1150 (2010).

[95]   Id.

[96]   In re Gen. Adjudication of All Rights to Use Water in the Gila River Sys. & Source, 35 P.3d 68, 79 (Ariz. 2001).

[97]   Id. at 98.

order to receive water;[98] and the standard requires or strongly encourages tribes to engage in "inflated, unrealistic irrigation projects" to qualify for water.[99] The Arizona court would force the fact finder to engage in a fact- and reservation-specific inquiry that reviews

> a history of the water uses of cultural significance, the tribal land's geography, topography, and natural resources, "groundwater availability," the optimal manner of "creating jobs and income for the tribes and the most efficient use of water," the tribe's economic infrastructure, historic uses of water, present and projected population, and other relevant information.[100]

Of course, such an inquiry could require an Indian nation with few resources to plan out its entire political, economic, and social plan for decades in advance, again prejudicing those tribes to the advantage of other parties (including wealthier tribes) with resources and capacity to make those claims. Quantification is a highly technical, complicated analysis requiring extensive expert witness study and testimony.[101] "At least four disciplines are involved: soil science, hydrology, engineering, and economics."[102] According to commentators, economics is the most controversial aspect of the analysis, for "[i]f economics were no constraint, almost any land could be made irrigable."[103]

§ 11.5 Indian Water Rights Settlements

The modern trend in reserved water rights adjudications is to negotiate a settlement.[104] One commentator noted that the Supreme Court's decision in *Arizona v. San Carlos Apache Tribe*,[105] discussed

---

[98] Id.

[99] Id.

[100] David H. Getches, Charles F. Wilkinson, Robert A. Williams, Jr., Matthew L.M. Fletcher, and Kristen A. Carpenter, Cases and Materials on Federal Indian Law 863 (7th ed. 2017).

[101] Id. at 860.

[102] Id.

[103] Id.

[104] See generally David H. Getches, Charles F. Wilkinson, Robert A. Williams, Jr., Matthew L.M. Fletcher, and Kristen A. Carpenter, Cases and Materials on Federal Indian Law 872–882 (7th ed. 2017); Robert A. Anderson, Indian Water Rights, Practical Reasoning, and Negotiated Settlements, 98 Calif. L. Rev. 1133, 1153–59 (2010); Robert A. Anderson, Indian Water Rights: Litigation and Settlements, 42 Tulsa L. Rev. 23 (2006).

[105] 463 U.S. 545 (1983).

in § 11.3, "represents the clear beginning of the era of Indian water rights settlements."[106]

The multiple petitions for certiorari in the Big Horn River adjudication—every major party petitioned—perhaps exemplify the limitations of judicial quantification. Judges must cut bright line divisions based on law that is universally applicable, and not context specific. Negotiated settlements can cut across settled law and reach conclusions that are closer to the on the ground realities.[107] Settlements can allow the parties to anticipate changes in advance, unlike courts, and address other issues not squarely before the court.[108] However, negotiated settlements are hard to reach, with thousands of parties potentially having a stake in the settlement. Most importantly, the federal government will be present in the negotiations but usually will not take a position on the settlement until it is finalized.[109] Federal politics may also play a role in the final approval of a settlement.[110] Moreover, negotiated settlements still require significant judicial participation, especially if the parties cannot reach a consensus on specific, discreet legal questions.

When the United States, the state government and its subdivisions, tribal interests, business and other private interests, and other interests wade through their competing interests and reach agreement, the result is a complicated and often expensive exercise in ongoing, cooperative federalism.[111] Usually, though not

---

[106] Jeanne S. Whiteing, Indian Water Rights: The Era of Settlement, in The Future of Indian and Federal Reserved Water Rights 136, 137 (Barbara Cosens & Judith V. Royster, eds. 2012).

[107] Id. at 138–39.

[108] Id. at 138.

[109] Id. at 140.

[110] Id. at 141.

[111] Commonalities in water rights settlements include:

(1) a federal investment in water development facilities or acquisition of water to enable tribes to put their water to use without infringement on established non-Indian uses; (2) non-federal cost sharing—state and local contributions toward the costs of construction and other elements of the settlement; (3) creation of substantial Indian trust funds from federal and non-federal [money] that may be used by the tribes to develop their water and for other purposes; (4) limited off-reservation water marketing, allowing tribes to gain economic benefits from their water resources and non-Indians to use water that would otherwise be unavailable if tribes put it all to use on the reservations; (5) deference to states and to interstate water compacts (such as the "Law of the River" when the Colorado River system is involved; (6) emphasis on efficient management, conservation, and environmental concerns and; (7) a strategy of tying Indian water delivery projects to proposed projects that are beneficial to non-Indian interests.

always, Indian water rights settlements do not create a precedent for or against other Indian nations that are not a party to the settlement.[112]

§ 11.6 Marketing and Regulating Indian Water

Selling water rights may be a beneficial action for Indian nations to take in some instances, especially where a tribe's capacity to utilize the available water may be limited by a tribe's lack of resources or development. But Indian nations likely may not market their water rights without federal authorization.[113] Water rights settlements may authorize an Indian nation to market some of its water, especially to non-Indian water users who might use the water more efficiently. Water rights settlements involving Arizona tribes allowed major cities there to purchase Indian water.[114]

Whether Indian nations may market water without federal authorization technically is unsettled, but the safe bet is that federal authorization should be acquired. However, the requirement of federal authorization may put Indian nations in a disadvantage when negotiating settlements. Most water rights settlements include limited marketing authority, but very few authorize tribes to possess full authority to market their water.[115]

In the Colorado Ute Indian Water Rights Settlement Act of 1988[116] and amendments to that agreement in 2000,[117] Congress authorized the Animas-La Plata Project, a massive water reclamation project that created Lake Nighthorse in Colorado.[118] About half of the water reclaimed in the project is Indian reserved water, most of which will be marketed by the affected tribes for non-

---

David H. Getches, Charles F. Wilkinson, Robert A. Williams, Jr., Matthew L.M. Fletcher, and Kristen A. Carpenter, Cases and Materials on Federal Indian Law 876 (7th ed. 2017) (citations omitted).

[112] Robert T. Anderson, Indian Water Rights, Practical Reasoning, and Negotiated Settlements, 98 Calif. L. Rev. 1133, 1154–55 (2010).

[113] David H. Getches, Management and Marketing of Indian Water: From Conflict to Pragmatism, 58 U. Colo. L. Rev. 515, 542 (1988) (citing 25 U.S.C. § 177 and collecting cases).

[114] David H. Getches, Charles F. Wilkinson, Robert A. Williams, Jr., Matthew L.M. Fletcher, and Kristen A. Carpenter, Cases and Materials on Federal Indian Law 878 (7th ed. 2017).

[115] Denise D. Fort, Policy Questions Concerning Tribal Water Marketing, American Bar Association, 30th Annual Water Law Conference (Feb. 2012), available at https://papers.ssrn.com/sol3/papers.cfm?abstract_id=2153873.

[116] Pub. L. 100–585, Nov. 3, 1988, 102 Stat. 2973.

[117] Pub. L. 106–554, Dec. 21, 2000, 114 Stat. 2763.

[118] David H. Getches, Charles F. Wilkinson, Robert A. Williams, Jr., Matthew L.M. Fletcher, and Kristen A. Carpenter, Cases and Materials on Federal Indian Law 877–78 (7th ed. 2017).

Indian municipal purposes.[119] One commentator critical of the project argue the tribal water marketing here is mere "water laundering" wrapped in an "Indian blanket" that does not help tribal interests.[120] Still, the potential for tribal water use is there.

Conflicts over the regulation of Indian water also arise. State water rules may be preempted under a federal Indian law preemption analysis, as in *Colville Confederated Tribes v. Walton*.[121] However, in *United States v. Anderson*,[122] the court applied the *Montana* analysis to conclude that the state, not the Indian nation, had authority to regulate non-Indian water use on non-Indian-owned reservation lands.[123]

---

[119] Jesse Harlan Alderman, Winters and Water Conservation: A Proposal to Halt "Water Laundering" in Tribal Negotiated Settlements in Favor of Monetary Compensation, 31 Va. Envtl. L.J. 1, 2–3 (2013).

[120] Id. at 3.

[121] 647 F.2d 42, 51–53 (9th Cir. 1981).

[122] 736 F.2d 1358 (9th Cir. 1984).

[123] Id. at 1363–66.

Chapter 12

FISHING AND HUNTING RIGHTS

Analysis

§ 12.1   *United States v. Washington* (Boldt Decision)

The first major Indian treaty rights case seeking judicial confirmation of off-reservation fishing rights *and* quantifying them is *United States v. Washington*,[1] filed in 1970 and which remains the longest running active federal district court matter in American history. The initial trial court decision recognized extant and continuing Indian fishing rights guaranteed under the so-called Stevens treaties, and further provided that Indians were entitled to half of the total annual fishery harvest each year.

The decision is colloquially referred to as the "Boldt decision," after the federal judge who decided the case, Judge George H. Boldt.

The Boldt decision involved the interpretation of the so-called Stevens Treaties, a series of treaties with Pacific Northwest Indian tribes and Isaac Stevens, who later became the first territorial governor of Washington.[2] **See § 5.3.** One provision that appears in common with all the Stevens treaties involves the tribal reservation of rights to fish in all the usual and accustomed places in lands ceded to the United States. Article five of the Treaty of Point Elliott is an example:

---

[1]   No. C70–9213 (W.D. Wash.). In the late 1960s, a federal court recognized extant Indian treaty rights to fish in Sohappy v. Smith, 302 F. Supp. 899 (D. Or. 1969). But quantification required additional litigation. Charles Wilkinson, Messages from Frank's Landing: A Story of Salmon, Treaties, and the Indian Way 50 (2000).

[2]   The treaties included six treaties entered into by the United States and Indian nations living in the State of Washington in 1854 and 1855: Treaty of Medicine Creek, 10 Stat. 1132; Treaty of Point Elliott, 12 Stat. 927; Treaty of Point No Point, 12 Star. 933; Treaty with the Makahs (Treaty of Neah Bay), 12 Stat. 939; Treaty with the Quinaielts (Treaty of Olympia), 12 Stat. 971; and Treaty with the Yakimas, 12 Stat. 951.

The right of taking fish at usual and accustomed grounds and stations is further secured to said Indians in common with all citizens of the Territory, and of erecting temporary houses for the purpose of curing, together with the privilege of hunting and gathering roots and berries on open and unclaimed lands. Provided, however, That they shall not take shell-fish from any beds staked or cultivated by citizens.[3]

The Stevens treaties all included some form of this language, though "[v]ariations were made in the treaties to suit local needs. The Makah Indians and nearby groups on the Olympic Peninsula, for example, insisted on the right to take seals and whales."[4]

Dozens of Indian nations agreed to massive land cessions in the Pacific northwest in exchange for the continued right to fish in the rivers and in the ocean guaranteed in this provision. Pacific northwest Indian nations relied heavily on anadromous fish that swim upstream from the ocean to spawn, nonanadromous fish, and seals and whales.[5] Every regional Indian nation celebrates some form of the first salmon ceremony, a hugely important ceremony conducted at the beginning of the annual salmon run.[6] Tribal ceremonies have been the subject of numerous curious anthropological studies.[7] In short, fish was critical to the survival of the Pacific northwest Indians, and for the entire period between the treaty era and the modern day fish-ins of the 1960s and 1970s, Indians continued to fish.[8] Even so, the rapid development of commercial fishing operations and agricultural enterprises systematically destroyed many of the best fishing places in the region.

In the 1960s, Indian treaty fishers from the Pacific Northwest region exercising their fishing rights both on and off the reservation faced increasing hostility from non-Indians sports and commercial fishers. The State of Washington became more aggressive in its investigation and prosecution of treaty fishers in violation of the treaties.

---

[3]   Treaty of Point Elliott, Jan. 22, 1855, 12 Stat. 927 (ratified in 1859).

[4]   Donald L. Parman, Inconstant Advocacy: The Erosion of Indian Fishing Rights in the Pacific Northwest, 1933–1956, 53:2 Pac. Hist. Rev. 163, 166 n. 5 (1984).

[5]   Id. at 164.

[6]   Pamela T. Amoss, The Fish God Gave Us: The First Salmon Ceremony Revived, 24:1 Arctic Anthro. 56, 56 (1987).

[7]   E.g., Erna Gunther, An Analysis of the First Salmon Ceremony, 28:4 Am. Anthro. 605 (1926); Helen H. Roberts, The First Salmon Ceremony of the Karuk Indians, 34:3 Am. Anthro. 426 (1932).

[8]   Donald L. Parman, Inconstant Advocacy: The Erosion of Indian Fishing Rights in the Pacific Northwest, 1933–1956, 53:2 Pac. Hist. Rev. 163, 165 (1984).

Eventually, the United States sued in federal court to enjoin the State from interfering with the treaty fishing rights of the western Washington tribes. At trial, the court heard extensive and exhaustive testimony from Dr. Barbara Lane, who established that the lead federal treaty negotiator, Isaac Stevens, repeatedly promised that the treaties would preserve fishing rights: "As one example, at the Point No Point treaty negotiations, Stevens told the tribes that 'This paper secures your fish.' "[9]

The Boldt decision recognized that western Washington treaty tribes have a right to take fish in common with non-Indians in off-reservation waters.[10] Judge Boldt's even more controversial ruling was that Indian nations have a right to take as much as 50 percent of the harvestable fish off the reservation.[11] Non-Indians labeled the split a "travesty," given that Indians made up less than one percent of the population and were only taking about five percent of the fish at trial.[12]

As Charles Wilkinson noted, the Boldt decision "was extraordinarily difficult to enforce."[13] State officials and non-Indians ignored the court's rulings and enforcement orders for years.[14] When the Supreme Court took up the Boldt decision on collateral review from a state court decision, the Court noted that the case had become one of "unusual significance" due to the widespread defiance of federal court orders and federal law.[15]

The complexity of subject area, coupled with state and private defiance of his orders forced Judge Boldt to oversee the entire fishery under the court's continuing jurisdiction over the case. One Ninth Circuit judge lamented the district court's status as "perpetual fishmaster" as a result of the continuing jurisdiction of the court over disputes arising under the Boldt decision between the tribes and the state and also between tribes.[16]

---

[9]   Charles Wilkinson, Messages from Frank's Landing: A Story of Salmon, Treaties, and the Indian Way 52 (2000).

[10]   United States v. Washington, 384 F. Supp. 312, 333 (W.D. Wash. 1974) ("There is no indication that the Indians intended or understood the language 'in common with all citizens of the Territory' to limit their right to fish in any way."), aff'd, 520 F.2d 676 (9th Cir. 1975), cert. denied, 423 U.S. 1086 (1976).

[11]   Id. at 402, 416–17.

[12]   Charles Wilkinson, Messages from Frank's Landing: A Story of Salmon, Treaties, and the Indian Way 56 (2000).

[13]   Id.

[14]   Id. at 58–59.

[15]   Washington v. Washington State Commercial Passenger Fishing Vessel Assn., 443 U.S. 658, 674–75 (1979).

[16]   United States v. Washington, 520 F.2d 676, 693 (9th Cir. 1975) (Burns, D.J., concurring), cert. denied, 423 U.S. 1086 (1976).

Over time, *United States v. Washington* has spawned increasing cooperation between the treaty tribes and the State. Under the Boldt decision, the tribes and the State share responsibility for regulating the resource.[17]

The Supreme Court's foray into the Boldt decision is discussed in § 12.4.

U&A Subproceedings

The Boldt decision and the continuing jurisdiction of the federal court have generated an entire series of subproceedings within the *United States v. Washington* docket. Most of these subproceedings involve intertribal conflicts over fishing territories, usually referred to as "U&A" adjudications, after the "usual and accustomed" fishing places referenced the Stevens treaties.[18] The Boldt decision and several decisions in the same case that followed drew up fishing territories for the affected tribes based on Dr. Lane's historical testimony. Newly recognized tribes and original tribes challenge each other's fishing territories intermittently. Recently, a Ninth Circuit judge addressing yet another intertribal conflict wondered why these purely intertribal conflicts require the continued expenditure of federal judicial resources, and strongly recommended that the continuing jurisdiction of the federal court be brought to a conclusion.[19]

Shellfish Subproceeding

In the shellfish subproceeding, 16 Stevens treaty tribes brought a claim that the treaty right entitled them to take one half of the shellfish in their usual and accustomed places.[20] However, and the tribes conceded this, the right to take shellfish (if any) was limited by the so-called shellfish proviso, which provided, "[Indians] shall not take shellfish from any beds staked or cultivated by citizens."[21]

The trial pitted the tribal interests and the federal government against the State of Washington, which had sold tidelands to

---

[17] See generally Zoltán Grossman, Unlikely Alliances: Treaty Conflicts and Environmental Cooperation between Native American and Rural White Communities, 29:4 Am. Indian Culture & Res. J. 21, 26–28 (2005).

[18] E.g., United States v. Washington, 593 F.3d 790 (9th Cir. 2009) (en banc) (rejecting effort by Samish Tribe to re-open Boldt decision); United States v. Muckleshoot Tribe, 235 F.3d 429 (9th Cir. 2000) (rejecting claims of Muckleshoot Tribe); United States v. Lummi Tribe, 841 F.2d 317 (9th Cir. 1988) (adjudicating dispute between Tulalip and Lummi tribes).

[19] Upper Skagit Indian Tribe v. State of Washington, 590 F.3d 1020, 1026 (9th Cir. 2010).

[20] United States v. Washington, 157 F.3d 630, 638–39 (9th Cir. 1998), cert. denied, 526 U.S. 1060 (1999).

[21] Id. at 639.

private individuals in the 1950s.[22] The Ninth Circuit, affirming the district court, held that the word "fish" in the treaty includes shellfish, and that the State could demonstrate a limitation on species.[23] The court also held that the treaty right extends to privately-owned tidelands.[24] Further, the court held that the shellfish proviso applied only to artificially planted shellfish beds, not natural beds.[25] Finally, the court reaffirmed the fifty-fifty split in the shellfish take, subject to limitations based on non-Indian growers' enhancement of natural shellfish beds.[26]

Culverts Subproceeding

The Stevens treaty tribes banded together once more in an effort to challenge the State of Washington's ongoing destruction of the anadromous fish habitat in the culverts subproceeding.[27] In short, the tribes argue that the rivers and streams inherently critical to the fish habitat are cut off by roads constructed and permitted by the State, and that the culverts that artificially allow river and stream water to pass under the roads are unfit for preserving the habitat. The culverts subproceeding, which is pending appeal, may be the largest and most expensive decision in the history of *United States v. Washington*.[28]

In 2017, the Ninth Circuit held in favor of the treaty tribes, affirming Judge Ricardo Martinez's decision below.[29] Judge William Fletcher held that the fishing rights contained in the Stevens treaties guaranteed access to fish, as Issac Stevens promised, "forever."[30] Even absent this promise, the court held, the *Winters* decision mandated that promise.[31]

---

[22]   Jay Miller, The Shell(Fish) Game: Rhetoric, Images, and (Dis)Illusions in Federal Court, 23:4 Am. Indian Culture & Res. J. 159, 161 (1999).

[23]   United States v. Washington, 157 F.3d 630, 643 (9th Cir. 1998).

[24]   United States v. Washington, 157 F.3d 630, 646–47 (9th Cir. 1998), cert. denied, 526 U.S. 1060 (1999).

[25]   Id. at 648.

[26]   Id. at 653.

[27]   United States v. Washington, 20 F. Supp. 3d 986, 1023–26 (W.D. Wash. 2013), aff'd, 827 F.3d 836 (9th Cir. 2016), amended, 853 F.3d 946 (9th Cir. 2017).

[28]   See generally Michael C. Blumm & Jane G. Steadman, Indian Treaty Fishing Rights and Habitat Protection: The Martinez Decision Supplies a Resounding Judicial Reaffirmation, 49 Nat. Resources J. 653 (2009).

[29]   United States v. Washington, 827 F.3d 836 (9th Cir. 2016), amended, 853 F.3d 946 (9th Cir. 2017).

[30]   853 F.3d at 961.

[31]   Id. (citing Winters v. United States, 207 U.S. 564, 576, 577 (1908)).

§ 12.2 *United States v. Michigan* (Fox Decision)

In *United States v. Michigan*,[32] Judge Fox held that the Indian nations that were signatories to the 1836 Treaty of Washington retained off-reservation rights to fish the Great Lakes with gillnets. Unlike the Boldt decision, where Judge Boldt and his successors remain "perpetual fishmasters," the five Indian nations, the State of Michigan, and the federal government have entered into consent decrees that resolved the large majority of disputes over the treaty rights.

The Fox decision involved the interpretation of Article 13 of the 1836 Treaty of Washington.[33] That provision reads, "The Indians stipulate for the right of hunting on the lands ceded, with the other usual privileges of occupancy, until the land is required for settlement."[34]

Judge Fox's decision focused on the "settlement" language of Article 13, reasoning that the waters of the Great Lakes simply cannot be "settled," and therefore the right to take fish from those waters was reserved in the treaty:

> The language contained in Article Thirteenth of the Treaty of 1836, by its own terms could not have limited the Indians' right to fish in the waters of the Great Lakes because these large bodies of water could not possibly be settled by homes, barns and tilled fields. While the Indians might have been willing to give up their right to hunt on various parcels of land as that land became occupied with settlers, the vital right to fish in the Great Lakes was something that the Indians understood would not be taken from them and, indeed, there was no need to do so. The western movement of non-Indian settlers could be accommodated without requiring the Indians to relinquish their aboriginal and treaty rights to fish. While the United States has the power to abrogate treaties by subsequent treaty or statute, it must do so expressly and emphatically. No such abrogation of the reserved treaty right to fish can be found.[35]

The Anishinaabe treaty negotiators "fully appreciated the treaty's provision for usufructuary rights of the natural resources in

---

[32] United States v. Michigan, 471 F. Supp. 192 (W.D. Mich. 1979), aff'd as modified, 653 F.2d 277 (6th Cir.), cert. denied, 454 U.S. 1124 (1981).

[33] 7 Stat. 491.

[34] Id.

[35] United States v. Michigan, 471 F. Supp. 192, 253 (W.D. Mich. 1979).

their territory."[36] Subsequent federal courts have recognized that the rights of the Michigan Anishinaabeg are "unabridged, aboriginal, tribal right[s] to fish derived from thousands of years of occupancy and use of the fishery of the waters of Michigan."[37] The Sixth Circuit even held that treaty fishers must be given access to municipal mooring points along Lake Michigan.[38]

Great Lakes Consent Decrees

The consent decree reached on March 28, 1985, by the United States, the State of Michigan, the Bay Mills Indian Community, the Grand Traverse Band of Ottawa and Chippewa Indians, and the Sault Ste. Marie Tribe of Chippewa Indians settled—for fifteen years—many of the major disputes over treaty fishing in the Great Lakes under the 1836 Treaty, while leaving many issues inland rights for another day.[39]

The agreement created an executive council, with representatives of each of the parties, to decide all major disputes between the parties. The agreement also allocated the fishery between Indians and non-Indians, and between tribes. The parties created zones in Lakes Michigan, Huron, and Superior that created territories in which tribes would share the resources with others, and some territories in which a tribe had exclusive fishing rights. The agreement created a cooperative regulatory scheme over the fishery. But the decree also contained structural incentives to overharvest the fishery.

The cooperative character of the agreement is evidenced by Judge Enslen's 1992 comments during a federal court proceeding to decide a dispute involving the tribes. He stated:

> But through your acceptance of the 1985 Consent Decree, you committed to working together until the conflict was resolved, at least until the year 2000. That means I do not view these proceedings . . . as adversarial proceedings. We have a common goal, and that goal is the just implementation of the consent agreement.[40]

---

[36]   James M. McClurken, Ottawa Adaptive Strategies to Indian Removal, Mich. Hist. Rev., Spring 1986, at 29, 35.

[37]   United States v. Michigan, 505 F. Supp. 467, 472 (W.D. Mich. 1980).

[38]   Grand Traverse Band of Ottawa & Chippewa Indians v. Dir., Mich. Dep't of Natural Res., 141 F.3d 635, 638–39 (6th Cir.), cert. denied sub nom., Township of Leland v. Grand Traverse Band of Ottawa and Chippewa Indians, 525 U.S. 1040 (1998).

[39]   United States v. Michigan, 12 Indian L. Rep. 3079 (W.D. Mich. 1985).

[40]   Transcript of Opening Remarks and Concluding Findings, Rulings, Statements of the Court at 7, United States v. Michigan, M26–73 (W.D. Mich. Oct. 9, 1992).

Inland Consent Decree

In 2007, the five 1836 Treaty tribes concluded four years of negotiations with the State of Michigan over inland treaty rights by preserving for all time the right to hunt, fish, and gather on federal and state public lands within the territory ceded in the treaty.[41] The agreement had no termination date, and so it preserves the treaty rights indefinitely. The five federally recognized 1836 Treaty tribes agreed to limits on walleye and steelhead fishing and a ban on gillnetting on inland waters, but also agreed to expansive deer hunting on state and federal lands and extensive gathering rights. Tribes also preserved the right to use trap nets on inland waters, in certain circumstances. Another key victory for the tribes was to preserve the tribal authority to regulate their own tribal member hunting and fishing, even on public lands, and to issue licenses.

§ 12.3 On-Reservation Hunting and Fishing Regulation

Indian nations and the federal government as trustee serve as the primary governmental entities regulation on-reservation hunting and fishing, subject only to a state's right to regulate Indian hunting and fishing for conservation purposes.

The *Puyallup* Cases

The Puyallup trilogy involved the State of Washington's effort to regulate (and in many instances) bar Indian fishing on the Puyallup and Tulalip Rivers, and Commencement Bay, on areas both within the exterior boundaries of the tribes' reservations but also at the usual and accustomed places off-reservation.[42] Initially, the *Puyallup* decisions were about off-reservation fishing, because the State argued—and the Supreme Court assumed for sake of argument—that the Puyallup reservation had been disestablished.[43]

Puyallup I held that the state could not limit the manner of fishing, namely the method by which the treaty fishers harvested fish.[44] The State further claimed that it could regulate the amount

---

[41] Consent Decree, United States v. Michigan, No. 2: 73 CV 26 (W.D. Mich., Nov. 2007), available at https://turtletalk.files.wordpress.com/2007/11/consent-decree.pdf.

[42] Puyallup Tribe v. Dept. of Game, 391 U.S. 392 (1968) (Puyallup I); Dept. of Game v. Puyallup Tribe, 414 U.S. 44 (1973) (Puyallup II); Puyallup Tribe, Inc. v. Department of Game of Washington, 433 U.S. 165 (1977) (Puyallup III).

[43] David H. Getches, Charles F. Wilkinson, Robert A. Williams, Jr., Matthew L.M. Fletcher, and Kristen A. Carpenter, Cases and Materials on Federal Indian Law 909–10 (7th ed. 2017).

[44] Puyallup Tribe v. Dept. of Game, 391 U.S. 392, 398 (1968).

of the treaty fish harvest for conservation purposes, and apparently counsel for the tribes conceded that the then-current treaty fishing practices would "virtually exterminate" some fishing runs.[45] The Court rejected the tribes' claims that the state court could not regulate treaty fishing in a manner " 'necessary for the conservation of fish.' "[46] The Court quoted *United States v. Winans*,[47] discussed in § 5.3, the first major Indian treaty fishing case, for the proposition that a state could regulate treaty fishing.[48] The Court remanded the matter to the state courts for determinations of the state conservation standard to be applied to the treaty fishers.[49] The power of a state to regulate Indian treaty rights was harshly criticized at the time the Supreme Court decided *Puyallup I* as in conflict with the Supremacy Clause.[50]

In *Puyallup II*,[51] the Supreme Court struck down the state's regulation banning all tribal treaty steelhead fishing on the Puyallup River. On remand from *Puyallup I*, the Washington Department of Game did not its regulation barring steelhead fishing with nets on the Puyallup River.[52] The Court noted, and the state confirmed, that "[t]he ban on all net fishing in the Puyallup River for steelhead grants, in effect, the entire run to the sports fishermen."[53] Justice Douglas' opinion for the majority held that the state's regulation discriminated against tribal treaty fishers: "There is discrimination here because all Indian net fishing is barred and only hook-and-line fishing, entirely pre-empted by non-Indians, is allowed."[54] The Court instructed the state to try again, and offered relatively little guidance, suggesting only that experts were needed.[55] On the conservation standard, the Court held firm on suggesting that treaty fishers did not have the right to exterminate a species, but offered little assistance there as well.[56]

Shortly after the Supreme Court decided *Puyallup II*, the Ninth Circuit held in a parallel case that the Puyallup Indian reservation, where the Puyallup River ran, had not been

---

[45] Id. at 402 n. 15.

[46] Id. at 399 (quoting Tulee v. Washington, 315 U.S. 681, 684 (1942)).

[47] 198 U.S. 371 (1905).

[48] Puyallup Tribe v. Dept. of Game, 391 U.S. 392, 394 (1968).

[49] Id. at 401–03.

[50] Ralph W. Johnson, The State Versus Indian Off-Reservation Fishing: A United States Supreme Court Error, 47 Wash. L. Rev. 207 (1972).

[51] Dept. of Game v. Puyallup Tribe, 414 U.S. 44 (1973).

[52] Id. at 46.

[53] Id. at 46–47.

[54] Id. at 48.

[55] Id. at 48–49.

[56] Id. at 49.

disestablished.[57] Though the state had previously conceded that it could not regulate on-reservation treaty fishing, the state courts on remand from *Puyallup II* nonetheless held that the state could regulate on-reservation fishing.[58]

In *Puyallup III*,[59] the Supreme Court addressed the state's assertion of jurisdiction over on-reservation Indian treaty fishing, and held that tribal sovereign immunity precluded certain aspects of the state's regulatory scheme relating to the tribe, but also held that individual Indians were subject to regulation.[60] The Puyallup River's lowest seven miles ran exclusively through the Puyallup reservation, and the Court noted that recognizing the exclusive tribal right to take all fish in the lower seven miles would abrogate *Puyallup I* and *II*.[61] The state court had concluded that tribal treaty fishers were entitled to 45 percent of the steelhead take, a conclusion the Supreme Court affirmed.[62] The Court restated that lower courts must apply a "standard of conservation necessity" when determining state authority to regulate treaty fishing,[63] but again offered no additional clarification.

The federal court in *United States v. Washington*, **see § 12.1**, eventually took control over all aspects of the anadromous fishery in the area, and today the State and the Indian nations collectively govern the fishery.

New Mexico v. Mescalero Apache Tribe

In *New Mexico v. Mescalero Apache Tribe*,[64] the Supreme Court held that Indian tribes, and their federal trustee, has exclusive authority to govern on-reservation hunting and fishing activities by nonmembers. The Mescalero Apache reservation is reservation created by a series of Executive orders comprising more than 460,000 acres.[65] The tribe and the federal government cooperated to develop on-reservation fish and wildlife resources that largely did

---

[57]   United States v. Washington, 496 F.2d 620 (9th Cir.), cert. denied, 419 U.S. 1032 (1974).

[58]   David H. Getches, Charles F. Wilkinson, Robert A. Williams, Jr., Matthew L.M. Fletcher, and Kristen A. Carpenter, Cases and Materials on Federal Indian Law 910 (7th ed. 2017).

[59]   Puyallup Tribe v. Dept. of Game, 433 U.S. 165 (1977).

[60]   Id. at 173.

[61]   Id. at 176–77.

[62]   Id. at 177.

[63]   Id.

[64]   462 U.S. 324 (1983).

[65]   Id. at 326.

not exist prior to their efforts.[66] Tribal law governed the regulation of those resources.[67]

The Court held that the principles of federal Indian law preemption, **see § 8.6**, applied to on-reservation hunting and fishing regulation.[68] Several federal criminal statutes preserved and recognized tribal authority to regulate on-reservation hunting and fishing.[69] The Court further concluded that the inconsistent state regulations would undermine effective and efficient on-reservation regulation under tribal law.[70]

§ 12.4   Off-Reservation Hunting and Fishing Rights

The most controversial treaty rights reserved by Indian nations involve off-reservation hunting, fishing, and gathering rights, as evidenced by the highly contested cases, *United States v. Washington*, **see § 12.1**, *United States v. Michigan*, **see § 12.2**, and numerous other treaty cases. In short, the courts have overwhelmingly concluded that off-reservation treaty rights are extant under the reserved rights doctrine of Indian treaty rights, but have also concluded that states have an interest in regulating hunting, fishing, and gathering rights in accordance with the states' interests in conserving those resources. As noted before, in general, regulatory conflicts between tribes, states, and the federal government are often resolved by agreement and continuing cooperation.[71]

As early as *United States v. Winans*,[72] **see § 5.3**, and *Tulee v. Washington*,[73] the Supreme Court had suggested that states had an interest in regulating treaty fishing for conservation purposes.[74] In the *Puyallup* trilogy, **see § 12.3**, the Court expressly recognized states' rights to regulate off-reservation fishing for conservation purposes.

---

[66]   Id. at 327–28.

[67]   Id. at 328–29.

[68]   Id. at 333–36.

[69]   Id. at 337–38.

[70]   Id. at 338.

[71]   See generally David H. Getches, Charles F. Wilkinson, Robert A. Williams, Jr., Matthew L.M. Fletcher, and Kristen A. Carpenter, Cases and Materials on Federal Indian Law 903–05 (7th ed. 2017) (surveying cooperative agreements).

[72]   198 U.S. 371 (1905).

[73]   315 U.S. 681 (1942).

[74]   David H. Getches, Charles F. Wilkinson, Robert A. Williams, Jr., Matthew L.M. Fletcher, and Kristen A. Carpenter, Cases and Materials on Federal Indian Law 908–10 (7th ed. 2017).

Washington v. Washington State Commercial Passenger Fishing Vessel Association

In *Washington v. Washington State Commercial Passenger Fishing Vessel Association (Fishing Vessel)*,[75] the Supreme Court both affirmed the major thrust of the Boldt decision, **see § 12.1**, but also largely affirmed Judge Boldt's orders dividing the off-reservation fishery take between Indian and non-Indian fishers.

Fishing Vessel was the culmination of a series of cases pending in state and federal courts over the meaning and implementation of the off-reservation fishing rights guaranteed to numerous Washington Indian nations in the so-called Stevens treaties. **See §§ 5.3, 12.1**. The Supreme Court would review Judge Boldt's original determination that treaty fishers were entitled to one-half the fish harvest, and the federal court's ongoing jurisdiction to manage the fishery where the state courts' and agencies' failed to protect tribal treaty fishers and to implement tribal treaty fishing rights.[76]

The Court first recognized the complexity and importance of the fishery: anadromous fish travel through international, nation, and tribal jurisdictions, and governments have made competing political decisions on how to allocate the harvest.[77] The Court also recognized that the fishery is of great economic value to fishers, while also noting that tribal fishers are wholly outnumbered by non-Indian commercial and sports fishers.[78]

The Court's opinion also reaffirmed Judge Boldt's findings as to the importance of fish to the Indian people of the area during pre-contact and treaty times, most notably how tribal culture and life revolved around the fishery.[79] The Court also reaffirmed Judge Boldt's findings that the Stevens treaties were intended by both American and Indian negotiators to protect and preserve the right to take fish at "usual and accustomed places."[80] The Court pointed out that the treaty negotiators did not anticipate that non-Indian fishing would grow in size and efficiency to eventually dominate the

---

[75]   443 U.S. 658 (1979).

[76]   Brief of the United States 4, Washington v. Washington State Commercial Passenger Fishing Vessel Assn., 443 U.S. 658 (1979) (Nos. 77–983, 78–119 and 78–139), 1979 WL 199416.

[77]   Washington v. Washington State Commercial Passenger Fishing Vessel Assn., 443 U.S. 658, 663–64 (1979).

[78]   Id. at 664.

[79]   Id. at 665–66.

[80]   Id. at 666–67.

entire fishery and undermine Indian fishing, often with the benefit of "discriminatory" state regulatory practices.[81]

The Court described Judge Boldt's decision and orders as adopting the position advanced by the federal government that the treaty fishers were entitled to 45–50 percent of the harvestable fish run, as determined river-by-river and stream-by-stream, on-reservation and tribal cultural fish take excluded.[82] The state fisheries agency eventually promulgated regulations in accordance with Judge Boldt's order, but the state supreme court enjoined enforcement of the state rules as violative of the Fourteenth Amendment's Equal Protection Clause.[83] The Court's first ruling in *Fishing Vessel* was to reverse the state supreme court's decisions on federal constitutional law, holding that federal and state laws creating special classifications in relation to Indians and tribes are not unconstitutional if rationally related to the special relationship between Indian nations and the United States.[84]

The Court also addressed the serious and ongoing problem relating to the granting of full faith and credit of federal court orders in state courts, a question about the supremacy of federal law. In short, the Supreme Court affirmed and reinvested federal authority in the federal district court to complete the journey started in the Boldt decision.[85]

On the merits of the treaty interpretation, whether the tribal treaty right included a mere right to "access," as the state contended, or whether the treaty right included "a greater right—a right to harvest a share of the runs of anadromous fish that at the time the treaties were signed were so plentiful that no one could question the Indians' capacity to take whatever quantity they needed," the Court sided with tribal interests and the United States.[86]

The Court's reasoning detailed how the federal treaty negotiator, Isaac Stevens, understood that an off-reservation fishing right would have to be robust in order to persuade the Indian negotiators to part with their claims to hundreds of thousands of

---

[81]   Id. at 668–69.

[82]   Id. at 671.

[83]   Washington State Commercial Passenger Fishing Vessel Assn. v. Tollefson, 571 P.2d 1373 (Wash. 1977); Puget Sound Gillnetters Assn. v. Moos, 565 P.2d 1151 (Wash. 1977).

[84]   Washington v. Washington State Commercial Passenger Fishing Vessel Assn., 443 U.S. 658, 673 n. 20 (1979).

[85]   Id. at 695–96.

[86]   Id. at 675.

acres of land.[87] The Court noted that other provisions in the treaties appeared to presume that the right was more than "merely the chance, shared with millions of other citizens, occasionally to dip their nets into the territorial waters."[88] The Court concluded that the tribal treaty right was "unambiguous."[89] Despite a holding that the treaty purpose and intent was unambiguous, the Court noted that the canons of construing treaty language were to be applied.[90] Moreover, six times the Court had previously interpreted the same treaty language in favor of tribal interests, and against the same interpretation proposed by the state.[91]

The Court did not, however, that both tribal and non-tribal parties have secured a treaty right in the Stevens treaties; non-Indian interests may not use state power or property law to defeat the tribal right, and Indian interests may use totally exclude non-Indian fishing.[92] The "fair share" reached by Judge Boldt—essentially a 50–50 split—had previously been ratified in similar form by several state and federal courts previously, and so the Supreme Court here affirmed Judge Boldt's general division and the federal judicial supervision of the details of that division.[93] The Court was careful to note that the federal court could adjust a given tribe's share downward from the 50–50 split if certain conditions changed, such as the dwindling of tribal population numbers down to "just a few members."[94]

Fishing Vessel is a figurative watershed in American Indian treaty law, and serves as an important foundation for both the recognition and implementation of Indian fishing rights in the modern era.

Lac Courte Oreilles Band of Lake Superior Chippewa Indians v. Voigt

In *Lac Courte Oreilles Band of Lake Superior Chippewa Indians v. Voigt*,[95] and related cases, federal courts affirmed the off-reservation treaty hunting and fishing rights of six Wisconsin Indian nations: the Lac Courte Oreilles Band of Lake Superior Chippewa Indians, the Red Cliff Band of Lake Superior Chippewa

---

[87]   Id. at 676–77.

[88]   Id. at 678–79.

[89]   Id. at 679.

[90]   Id. at 675–76.

[91]   Id. at 679.

[92]   Id. at 684–85.

[93]   Id. at 685.

[94]   Id. at 686–87.

[95]   700 F.2d 341 (7th Cir.), cert. denied sub nom., Besadny v. Lac Courte Oreilles Band of Lake Superior Chippewa Indians, 464 U.S. 805 (1983).

Indians, the Sokaogon Chippewa Indian Community/Mole Lake Band of Wisconsin, the St. Croix Chippewa Indians of Wisconsin, the Bad River Band of Lake Superior Chippewa Indians, and the Lac du Flambeau Band of Lake Superior Chippewa Indians.[96] Non-Indian hostility toward Indian treaty rights during and after the *Lac Courte Oreilles* decision was vicious and dramatic.[97]

The nations are signatories to treaties dating back to 1837, 1842, and 1854.[98] The 1837 treaty was a massive land cession treaty by which the Lake Superior Ojibwe nations sold their interest in lands "east of the Mississippi as far as the Wisconsin River. . . ."[99] The Ojibwe negotiators agreed to cede the land but retained usufructuary rights. Article 5 provided:

> The privilege of hunting, fishing, and gathering the wild rice, upon the lands, the rivers and the lakes included in the territory ceded, is guarantied to the Indians, during the pleasure of the President of the United States.[100]

In 1842, after Douglas Houghton had described mineral interests in the region the federal government,[101] the Lake Superior Ojibwe again agreed to a land cession treaty. Article 2 of that treaty again reserved off-reservation usufructuary rights:

> The Indians stipulate for the right of hunting on the ceded territory, with the other usual privileges of occupancy, until required to remove by the President of the United States, and that the laws of the United States shall be continued in force, in respect to their trade and inter course with the whites, until otherwise ordered by Congress.[102]

The "pleasure of the President" proviso in the 1837 treaty, and similar language in the 1842 treaty, should make any lawyer believe that the promise of off-reservation rights was a kind of illusory promise. However, in 1837, the federal treaty negotiators

---

[96]   Charles F. Wilkinson, To Feel the Summer in the Spring: The Treaty Fishing Rights of the Wisconsin Chippewa, 1991 Wis. L. Rev. 375, 375 n. 1.

[97]   Id. at 376.

[98]   Treaty of St. Peter's, July 29, 1837, 7 Stat. 536; Treaty of La Pointe, Oct. 4, 1842, 7 Stat. 591; Treaty of La Pointe, Sept. 30, 1854, 10 Stat. 1109. See also Charles F. Wilkinson, To Feel the Summer in the Spring: The Treaty Fishing Rights of the Wisconsin Chippewa, 1991 Wis. L. Rev. 375, 383 n. 38.

[99]   Benjamin Ramirez-Shkwegnaabi, The Dynamics of American Indian Diplomacy in the Great Lakes Region, 27:4 Am. Indian Culture & Res. J. 53, 67 (2003).

[100]   Treaty of St. Peter's, July 29, 1837, 7 Stat. 536.

[101]   Robert H. Keller, Jr., On Teaching Indian History: Legal Jurisdiction in Chippewa Treaties, 19:3 Ethnohistory 209, 215 (1972).

[102]   Treaty of La Pointe, Oct. 4, 1842, 7 Stat. 591.

represented to the *ogimaag* that the President would not need the land for any purpose other than pine timber extraction for "many years."[103] In 1837, the federal negotiators represented to the *ogimaag* that the lands were valuable to the United States only for timber, and would never be needed for agriculture.[104] Moreover, federal treaty negotiators in both negotiations apparently never made clear to the *ogimaag* that the land cessions were equivalent to a sale of land to the United States that was permanent.[105] Two tribes even ceded away *all* of their lands, leaving no reservation at all.[106] The fact that the federal government recognized ongoing usufructuary rights on ceded lands perhaps confused the situation. The Ojibwe believed, based on representations from the federal negotiators, that their continued rights to the ceded territory and their reservations would exist so long as the Indian "behaved themselves."[107]

In 1850, federal Indian affairs officials persuaded the President to issue an Executive order purporting to revoke the off-reservation usufructuary rights.[108] The Executive order attempted to revoke tribal usufructuary rights to off-reservation lands and also imposed what appears to be a removal order. Though the 1837 and 1842 treaties were negotiated at a time when national federal Indian policy was geared toward removing Indian nations to lands west of the Mississippi River, the federal government did not inform the Wisconsin Ojibwe nations that removal to western lands was a possibility, except in the far future, if at all.[109] The 1842 treaty mentioned the possibility of removal, but the Ojibwe nations understood that removal there meant to stand aside while the federal government or others extracted minerals from the lands, or if they misbehaved.[110] Moreover, the United States had no plans to force the Ojibwe nations to remove from their lands to the west.[111]

---

[103] Benjamin Ramirez-Shkwegnaabi, The Dynamics of American Indian Diplomacy in the Great Lakes Region, 27:4 Am. Indian Culture & Res. J. 53, 66 (2003).

[104] Charles E. Cleland, Faith in Paper: The Ethnohistory and Litigation of Upper Great Lakes Indian Treaties 108 (2011).

[105] B.G. Armstrong, Early Life Among the Indians 12 (1892).

[106] Charles F. Wilkinson, To Feel the Summer in the Spring: The Treaty Fishing Rights of the Wisconsin Chippewa, 1991 Wis. L. Rev. 375, 388.

[107] B.G. Armstrong, Early Life Among the Indians 12 (1892).

[108] Lac Courte Oreilles Band of Lake Superior Chippewa Indians v. Voigt, 700 F.2d 341, 346 (7th Cir.), cert. denied sub nom., Besadny v. Lac Courte Oreilles Band of Lake Superior Chippewa Indians, 464 U.S. 805 (1983).

[109] Charles E. Cleland, Faith in Paper: The Ethnohistory and Litigation of Upper Great Lakes Indian Treaties 109 (2011).

[110] Id. at 121.

[111] Id. at 115.

Ojibwe resistance and non-Indian opposition to removal forced the government to suspend the removal order in 1851,[112] though officials made some attempt to implement it.[113] Largely, removal failed.

In 1854, the United States entered into a treaty with the Minnesota Ojibwe, and those Indian nations ceded much of their territory to the United States, while retaining off-reservation usufructuary rights.[114] Article 11 of the treaty provided in relevant part:

> [T]he Indians shall not be required to remove from the homes hereby set apart for them. And such of them as reside in the territory hereby ceded, shall have the right to hunt and fish therein, until otherwise ordered by the President.[115]

In construing the language of the 1837 and 1842 treaties, the Seventh Circuit applied the canon of construing Indian treaties that the treaty language must be interpreted as the Indians understood the terms at the time of the negotiation.[116] The court held that the Ojibwe nations understood that the President's discretion to revoke the off-reservation rights was dependent on whether the Indians misbehaved toward non-Indian settlers.[117] The court further held that the 1850 Executive order was invalid. Presidential orders cannot contravene an Act of Congress or a treaty. Since the Ojibwe nations understood that they would remain entitled to usufructuary rights unless they misbehaved, then the President was authorized to revoke those rights only if he found that the Indians had misbehaved. He made no such finding.[118]

Wisconsin Indians in the 1970s and 1980s resisted state efforts to undo their treaty rights,[119] and the federal courts ultimately affirmed their rights. However, the State of Minnesota would keep up the fight against Ojibwe treaty rights in parallel treaties well in the 1990s.

---

[112] Lac Courte Oreilles Band of Lake Superior Chippewa Indians v. Voigt, 700 F.2d 341, 347 (7th Cir.).

[113] Charles E. Cleland, Faith in Paper: The Ethnohistory and Litigation of Upper Great Lakes Indian Treaties 122 (2011).

[114] Treaty of La Pointe, Sept. 30, 1854, 10 Stat. 1109.

[115] Id.

[116] Lac Courte Oreilles Band of Lake Superior Chippewa Indians v. Voigt, 700 F.2d 341, 356 (7th Cir.), cert. denied sub nom., Besadny v. Lac Courte Oreilles Band of Lake Superior Chippewa Indians, 464 U.S. 805 (1983).

[117] Id.

[118] Id. at 362.

[119] Larry Nesper, Twenty-five Years of Ojibwe Treaty Rights in Wisconsin, Michigan, and Minnesota, 36:1 Am. Indian Culture & Res. J. 47, 50 (2012).

Minnesota v. Mille Lacs Band of Chippewa Indians

In *Minnesota v. Mille Lacs Band of Chippewa Indians*,[120] the Supreme Court held that the same 1837 treaty and 1850 removal order interpreted by the Seventh Circuit in *Lac Courte Oreilles Band of Lake Superior Chippewa Indians v. Voigt* reserved and retained usufructuary rights on ceded lands. The Court also interpreted the 1855 Treaty of Washington[121] favorably toward the retention of tribal usufructuary rights.

The 1837 treaty at issue in *Lac Courte Oreilles* involved both Wisconsin and Minnesota Ojibwe nations.[122] Therefore, to the extent that the 1850 Executive order applied to the Wisconsin Ojibwe nations, it could also apply to the Minnesota Ojibwe signatories to the 1837 treaty.

The State of Minnesota did not participate in the *Lac Courte Oreilles* matter, and since Minnesota is located in the Eighth Circuit, asserted that the Seventh Circuit's interpretation was inapplicable to Minnesota.[123] Notably, the *Lac Courte Oreilles* matter never reached a trial, with the courts adjudicating motions for summary judgment based on factual stipulations made by the parties. *Mille Lacs* would proceed to a trial on the merits.[124]

After trial, the federal judge made numerous and detailed findings of fact that supported the tribe's positions and strategies. The tribe hoped to prove that the off-reservation rights were "of profound spiritual, cultural, and economic importance to the Chippewa at the time of the treaty" and thereafter;[125] that the President's discretion to revoke the rights was restricted by the good faith of the President;[126] that the 1837 treaty council involved no discussion of removal;[127] that the 1850 removal order was in response to non-Indian pressure to exploit economic activities, not Indian depredations;[128] that the 1837 treaty never authorized removal, rendering the 1850 removal order invalid; and that the

---

[120]   526 U.S. 172 (1999).

[121]   10 Stat. 1165 (March 3, 1855).

[122]   Treaty of St. Peter's, July 29, 1837, 7 Stat. 536.

[123]   Marc Slonim, Milles Lacs Band of Chippewa Indians et al. v. State of Minnesota et al., District of Minnesota, Case No. 4–90–605, in Faith in Paper: The Ethnohistory and Litigation of Upper Great Lakes Indian Treaties 132, 133 (2011).

[124]   Id. at 135.

[125]   Id.

[126]   Id.

[127]   Id. at 135–36;

[128]   Id. at 136.

tribe never agreed to relinquish its off-reservation rights in the 1855 treaty.[129]

A split Supreme Court affirmed, holding 5–4 in favor the Mille Lacs Band.[130] The Court first reaffirmed the Seventh Circuit's original holding in the *Lac Courte Oreilles* matter that the 1850 removal order was invalid.[131] The State of Minnesota conceded that the 1850 Executive order did not authorize the removal of the Minnesota Ojibwe nations, but argued that the order could still be interpreted to revoke the off-reservation rights of the Ojibwe through the doctrine of severability.[132] The state argued that if the President had known that a removal order was invalid, he could still have merely revoked the usufructuary rights in the ceded territories, perhaps as an "incentive" to encourage the Ojibwe to leave.[133] The Court rejected that claim as unsupported by the historical facts, and also nonsensical.[134]

The State of Minnesota next argued that the Minnesota Ojibwe nations divested themselves of their off-reservation rights in the 1855 treaty, a treaty of cession that included the following provision:

> And the said Indians do further fully and entirely relinquish and convey to the United States, any and all right, title, and interest, of whatsoever nature the same may be, which they may now have in, and to any other lands in the Territory of Minnesota or elsewhere.[135]

The Court disagreed, first noting that there is no reference to the rights reserved by the 1837 treaty, let alone language of abrogation.[136] Moreover, the treaty negotiations make no reference at all to the off-reservation rights, strongly suggesting there was no intent by the parties—and certainly not the Minnesota Ojibwe—that the 1855 treaty would abrogate usufructuary rights.[137]

Minnesota next argued that the Equal Footing doctrine as applied in the state's entry into the Union abrogated the treaty rights,[138] relying on *Ward v. Race Horse*.[139] There, the Supreme

---

[129] Id. at 137.

[130] Minnesota v. Mille Lacs Band of Chippewa Indians, 526 U.S. 172 (1999).

[131] Id. at 188–95.

[132] Id. at 190–91.

[133] Id. at 192.

[134] Id. at 192–93.

[135] Id. at 195 (quoting Treaty of Washington, March 3, 1855, 10 Stat. 1165).

[136] Id.

[137] Id. at 198.

[138] Id. at 203.

[139] 163 U.S. 504 (1896).

Court held that off-reservation rights to hunt elk "on the unoccupied lands of the United States, so long as game may be found thereon, and so long as peace subsists among the whites and Indians on the borders of the hunting districts" did not survive Wyoming's admission to the Union.[140] In particular, the Court noted that off-reservation treaty rights could not coexist with a state's sovereignty over its public lands.[141]

Race Horse stands in stark contrast to the Court's decision less than a decade later in *United States v. Winans*.[142] **See § 5.3.** There, the Court announced the reserved rights doctrine, where Indian treaty rights are retained absent a clear statement of intent by Congress to abrogate them. The reserved-rights doctrine is now understood to be the primary understanding of Indian treaty rights that overrides *Race Horse*'s reasoning.[143] Several Supreme Court cases decided in the early 20th century confirm that *Race Horse*'s holding on the Equal Footing doctrine was not controlling.[144]

In *Mille Lacs*, the Supreme Court noted that *Race Horse*'s bare holding "has been qualified by later decisions of this Court."[145] The Court explained that states' rights can coexist with Indian treaty rights, so treaty abrogation is far from automatic when a state enters the Union,[146] and rejected Minnesota's final argument.

---

[140] Id. at 514–16.

[141] Id. at 509.

[142] 198 U.S. 371 (1905).

[143] State v. Buchanan, 978 P.2d 1070, 1083 (Wash. 1999), cert. denied, 528 U.S. 11 1154 (2000); see also id. (recognizing that *Mille Lacs* "effectively overruled *Race Horse*").

[144] E.g., Dick v. United States, 208 U.S. 14 340, 405–406 (1908); Winters v. United States, 207 U.S. 564, 577 (1908).

[145] Minnesota v. Mille Lacs Band of Chippewa Indians, 526 U.S. 172, 203 (1999).

[146] Id. at 204.

Chapter 13

ALASKA NATIVES

Analysis

The United States' disparate treatment of Alaska Natives and Alaska Native tribal governments forced them to walk a substantially different path than Indian nations in the lower 48 states. The federal government did not enter into treaties with Alaska Natives, and imposed modified forms of allotment, assimilation, state jurisdiction, and tribal government reorganization on Alaska Natives. Still, in recent decades, the federal government has slowly begun narrowing the differences between Alaska Native tribal governments and other federally recognized Indian nations.

§ 13.1 Alaska Native Claims Settlement Act

In 1971, Congress enacted the Alaska Native Claims Settlement Act (ANCSA),[1] a statute that forms the primary governing document in Alaska Native affairs. The Act rewrote much of the law that governed Alaska Native affairs from the purchase of the territory from Russia to 1971.

The United States purchased national interests in Alaska from Russia in the 1867 Treaty of Cession.[2] Article 3 of that treaty provided, "The uncivilized tribes will be subject to such laws and regulations as the United States may, from time to time, adopt in regard to aboriginal tribes of that country."[3] Congress made no such law until the Alaska Organic Act,[4] and even there, the government did not impose any regulation on Alaska Natives. Instead, the

---

[1]   Pub. L. 92–203, Dec. 18, 1971, 85 Stat. 688, codified at 43 U.S.C. §§ 1601 et seq.

[2]   15 Stat. 539.

[3]   Id.

[4]   23 Stat. 24.

United States preserved Alaska Native occupancy rights and reserved for another day the question of how Alaska Native lands might be acquired.[5]

In the early part of the 20th century, Congress passed the Alaska Native Allotment Act of 1906[6] and the Alaska Native Townsite Act of 1926.[7] Both of these statutes arose from the ashes of decades of early federal policy that tended to treat Alaska Natives differently than other American Indian nations.[8] It was understood that the General Allotment Act of 1887,[9] **see § 3.6**, was inapplicable to Alaska Natives.[10] There was little American settler pressure on the federal government to open up reservation lands for public sale and exploitation, but there were few legal rights and opportunities available for Alaska Natives to protect their property interests in land.[11] Even so, the federal government asserted ownership interests in lands claimed by Alaska Native communities, families, and bands, ultimately resulting in *Tee-Hit-Ton Indians v. United States*.[12] **See § 4.1**.

The United States vested Alaska with statehood in 1958. The statute admitting Alaska contained a disclaimer typical for western states that precluded the state from asserting jurisdiction over Alaska Native lands.[13]

Shortly after statehood, Alaska banned all fish traps in the state and began prosecuting Alaska Natives for the continued use of the traps.[14] Two suits brought by Alaska Native tribal governments challenged the law on the grounds that Alaska had disclaimed jurisdiction over them. The first suit, *Metlakatla Indian Community v. Egan*,[15] was brought by a tribal community recognized as an Indian reservation by an Act of Congress.[16] The tribe and the federal government argued that the Interior Secretary's regulations

---

[5]   23 Stat. at 26.

[6]   Act of May 17, 1906, 34 Stat. 197.

[7]   Act of May 25, 1926, 44 Stat. 629.

[8]   David S. Case & David A. Voluck, Alaska Natives and American Law 24 (3rd ed. 2012).

[9]   24 Stat. 388 (1887), codified as amended at 25 U.S.C. §§ 331 et seq.

[10]   David S. Case & David A. Voluck, Alaska Natives and American Law 115–17 (3rd ed. 2012).

[11]   Id. at 117–20.

[12]   348 U.S. 272 (1955) (citations omitted).

[13]   Pub. L. 85–508, July 7, 1958, 72 Stat. 339.

[14]   David S. Case & David A. Voluck, Alaska Natives and American Law 108 (3rd ed. 2012).

[15]   369 U.S. 45 (1962).

[16]   Act of March 3, 1891, § 15, 26 Stat. 1195, 1101.

allowing fish traps controlled over the state's ban.[17] However, the Court struck down the regulations as not authorized by the proper federal statute, and remanded to the Interior Secretary.[18] In a companion case, *Organized Village of Kake v. Egan*,[19] brought by two Alaska Native tribal governments for which Congress had not established reservations, the Court held that Alaska could impose the fish trap ban on their lands, which the Court held were not Indian lands.[20]

The statehood act also authorized the State of Alaska to select more than 100 million acres of land for its own use, and naturally the State selected the most valuable lands, much of which had already been claimed and occupied by Alaska Natives.[21] The discovery of vast oil reserves generated conflicts between the federal government, the state, and the Alaska Native communities that only Congress could conclude.

The Alaska Native Claims Settlement Act of 1971 "amounted to one of the greatest land transactions in history."[22] The Alaska Natives received $962.5 million, and selection rights to 44 million acres.[23] A surface estate of 22 million acres would be transferred to around 200 village corporations identified in the Act.[24] A subsurface, mineral estate of 22 million acres would be transferred to 12 regional corporations, with a surface estate of 16 million acres transferred to six of the regional corporations.[25] These corporations were chartered under state law.[26] Alaska Natives alive at the time of the Act were to become shareholders in regional and perhaps village corporations.[27] Previously established Alaska Native reservations would be revoked for the most part, excepting the Metlakatla Indian Community.[28] Lands selected and acquired by Alaska Native corporations would be held in fee simple, but with limitations on state taxation set to expire in 1991.[29] In 1987,

[17] Metlakatla Indian Community v. Egan, 369 U.S. 45, 58–59 (1962).

[18] Id. at 59.

[19] 369 U.S. 60 (1962).

[20] Id. at 62.

[21] David H. Getches, Charles F. Wilkinson, Robert A. Williams, Jr., Matthew L.M. Fletcher, and Kristen A. Carpenter, Cases and Materials on Federal Indian Law 960 (7th ed. 2017).

[22] Id.

[23] Id. at 961.

[24] Id.

[25] Id.

[26] Id.

[27] Id.

[28] Id. at 962.

[29] Id.

Congress amended the Act to allow corporations greater control over the alienability of shares and to extend the state property tax immunity indefinitely, or until the lands are developed.[30]

Alaska Native villages that had organized under the Indian Reorganization Act,[31] or that had governed under traditional tribal law, were unaffected by the ANCSA. Land is owned by the corporations but the tribal village governments remain.

§ 13.2 *Alaska v. Native Village of Venetie Tribal Government*

The first major Supreme Court case interpreting the Alaska Native Claims Settlement Act, *Alaska v. Native Village of Venetie Tribal Government*,[32] held that lands owned by village corporations are not Indian country, and therefore the village did not have the power to tax activities on that land.

The Venetie Tribe of Neets'aii Gwich'in Indians is organized under the Indian Reorganization Act as the Native Village of Venetie.[33] After the passage of the Alaska Native Claims Settlement Act (ANCSA),[34] **see § 13.1**, Venetie tribal lands were owned communally by two Alaska Native village corporations, Venetie and Arctic Village.[35] Taking advantage of provisions in ANCSA that allowed "village corporations the option of taking fee title to their former reservation lands in lieu of sharing in the monetary, land, regional corporation, and other provisions and obligations of the Act," the tribe conveyed their lands to the village tribal government and dissolved the village corporations.[36] And so by the time the dispute arose leading to the Supreme Court's decision, the tribal government owned Venetie lands in fee.[37]

The dispute arose when the tribe attempted to impose—and enforce in tribal tax court—a tribal tax on a non-Indian

---

[30] Id.

[31] 25 U.S.C. § 5123.

[32] 522 U.S. 520 (1998).

[33] Kristen A. Carpenter, Interpreting Indian Country in State of Alaska v. Native Village of Venetie, 35 Tulsa L.J. 73, 76 (1999).

[34] Pub. L. 92–203, Dec. 18, 1971, 85 Stat. 688, codified at 43 U.S.C. §§ 1601 et seq.

[35] Kristen A. Carpenter, Interpreting Indian Country in State of Alaska v. Native Village of Venetie, 35 Tulsa L.J. 73, 77 (1999).

[36] Id. (citing 43 U.S.C. § 1618(b)).

[37] Brief for the Respondents 1, Alaska v. Native Village of Venetie Tribal Government, 522 U.S. 520 (1998) (No. 96–1577), 1997 WL 631801.

construction contractor building a state-funded school on tribally owned lands.[38]

The Supreme Court's analysis focused exclusively on whether Alaska Native-owned lands are Indian country, presuming that if the land upon which the activities that Alaska Native tribal governments were trying to tax were not in Indian country, then the power to tax would be lacking. ANSCA revoked Alaska Native reservations, and there were not allotments at issue, so the Court determined that the only way the Alaska Native governmental lands could be Indian country under 18 U.S.C. § 1151 was whether the lands were "dependent Indian communities" under § 1151(c) . See § 7.1.

Dependent Indian communities are lands that are not reservation lands, trust lands, or allotments, and otherwise might be consider outside of Indian country. However, dependent Indian communities include areas in which the federal government has set aside lands for Indian or tribal purposes and that are under federal superintendence. For example, some tribal housing projects located outside reservation lands or allotments may be considered dependent Indian communities. New Mexico pueblos, whose lands are owned in fee simple under grants from Spain and who have retained sovereignty over their territory through confirmation of their land ownership by Congress, are the source of the term.

The Supreme Court concluded that lands must be set aside by the federal government for Indian purposes over which the federal government maintains jurisdiction.[39] The lands alleged to be "Indian country" in Venetie had not been reservation lands after the enactment of ANCSA. Moreover, the Act stated that the lands acquired by the Alaska Native village corporations would not "creat[e] a reservation system or lengthy wardship or trusteeship."[40] Relying on the language, the Court noted that "ANCSA transferred reservation lands to private, state-chartered Native corporations, without any restraints on alienation or significant use restrictions, and with the goal of avoiding 'any permanent racially defined institutions, rights, privileges, or obligations.' "[41] Without ongoing federal guardianship as evidenced, for example, by restraints on alienation, the lands could not be Indian country.

---

[38]   Alaska v. Native Village of Venetie Tribal Government, 522 U.S. 520, 525 (1998).

[39]   Id. at 530–31.

[40]   43 U.S.C. § 1601(b).

[41]   Alaska v. Native Village of Venetie Tribal Government, 522 U.S. 520, 532–33 (1997).

Venetie's legacy was to allow the State of Alaska to continue to challenge the inherent tribal authority of the Alaska Native tribal governments by asserting that there could be no sovereignty without lands classified as Indian country, a largely failed claim. Moreover, Alaska Native communities often had little contact with state officials and agencies.[42]

§ 13.3 *John v. United States* (Katie John)

Alaska Native subsistence rights are as critical to Alaska Native communities as treaty rights to hunt and fish are to Indian nations in the lower 48 states. In fact, it is likely subsistence hunting and fishing is more important, and critical to Alaska Native tribal cultures.[43] The federal government's regulations providing legal protection for subsistence hunting and fishing have survived legal challenges in the so-called Katie John cases.

Katie John was one of a group of tribal elders dependent on subsistence fishing that brought suit to challenge the federal government's interpretation of the Alaska National Interest Lands Conservation Act (ANILCA).[44] Congress passed ANILCA, in part, to impose federal conservation laws on the federal public lands in Alaska.[45] ANILCA was also intended to protect Alaska subsistence hunters and fishers, and authorized the Interior Secretary to promulgate regulations to that effect.[46] ANILCA also provided that state regulation that adequately implemented federal subsistence priorities would preclude the need for federal regulation.[47]

In 1982, the Interior Secretary certified state regulations established in 1978 linking subsistence fishing rights to particular communities.[48] The Alaska Supreme Court held that statute invalid because many Alaskans living in towns and villages remained dependent on subsistence hunting and fishing.[49] In 1989, the

---

[42] Kristen A. Carpenter, Interpreting Indian Country in State of Alaska v. Native Village of Venetie, 35 Tulsa L.J. 73, 156 (1999).

[43] Id. at 160–61.

[44] Pub. L. 96–487, Dec. 2, 1980, 94 Stat. 2374, codified at 16 U.S.C. §§ 3101 et seq.

[45] David H. Getches, Charles F. Wilkinson, Robert A. Williams, Jr., Matthew L.M. Fletcher, and Kristen A. Carpenter, Cases and Materials on Federal Indian Law 960 (7th ed. 2017).

[46] 16 U.S.C. § 3114.

[47] 16 U.S.C. § 3115(d).

[48] John v. United States, 720 F.3d 1214, 1219 (9th Cir. 2013), cert. denied sub nom., Alaska v. Jewell, 134 S.Ct. 1759 (2014).

[49] Madison v. Alaska Dept. of Fish & Game, 696 P.2d 168 (Alaska 1985).

Alaska Supreme Court struck down an amended statute on state constitutional grounds.[50]

The Interior Secretary decertified Alaska and promulgated its own regulations on subsistence rights on federal public lands in 1992.[51] Those regulations excluded all navigable waterways from federal public lands on which subsistence rights could be exercised, prompting several federal suits. In *Alaska v. Babbitt*,[52] the Ninth Circuit struck down the regulations on the ground that at least some navigable waterways should be eligible for the exercise of subsistence rights, and remanded back to the Interior Secretary.[53]

The new regulations, promulgated in 1999, described navigable waterways on which there were federal reserved water rights and extended federal subsistence rights on those waters.[54] The Katie John plaintiffs complained that the 1999 rules did not extend the federal subsistence priority to enough waters, and the State argued that the rules went too far. The Ninth Circuit rejected both challenges, and upheld the 1999 rules.[55]

§ 13.4　Alaska Native Sovereignty

Alaska Native sovereignty is exercised in large part by tribal governments formed under the authority of the Indian Reorganization Act,[56] **see § 3.8**, and to a lesser extent by the state village and regional corporations formed under the Alaska Native Claims Settlement Act,[57] **see § 13.1**. Through the historical, legal, and political complexities, Alaska Native tribal governments still retain inherent authority to govern. Alaska Native tribal justice systems may be more or less formal that state or federal courts, but generally are effective in governing.[58]

---

[50]　McDowell v. State, 785 P.2d 1, 9 (Alaska 1989).

[51]　Subsistence Management Regulations for Public Lands in Alaska, Subparts A, B, and C, 57 Fed. Reg. 22,940, 22,942 (May 29, 1992), codified at 36 C.F.R. Part 242 and 50 C.F.R. Part 100.

[52]　Alaska v. Babbitt, 72 F.3d 698 (9th Cir. 1995), cert. denied, 517 U.S. 1187 (1996).

[53]　Id. at 703.

[54]　Subsistence Management Regulations for Public Lands in Alaska, Subparts A, B, C, and D, Redefinition to Include Waters Subject to Subsistence Priority, 64 Fed. Reg. 1,276, 1,276 (Jan. 8, 1999), codified at 36 C.F.R. Part 242 and 50 C.F.R. Part 100.

[55]　John v. United States, 720 F.3d 1214, 1245 (9th Cir. 2013), cert. denied sub nom., Alaska v. Jewell, 134 S.Ct. 1759 (2014).

[56]　Act of June 18, 1934, c. 576, 48 Stat. 984, codified as amended at 25 U.S.C. §§ 5101 et seq.

[57]　Pub. L. 92–203, Dec. 18, 1971, 85 Stat. 688, codified at 43 U.S.C. §§ 1601 et seq.

[58]　Kristen A. Carpenter, Interpreting Indian Country in State of Alaska v. Native Village of Venetie, 35 Tulsa L.J. 73, 159 (1999).

Whether Alaska Native tribal governments or village were sovereign entities remained an open question until 1993 when the Interior Department listed Alaska Native villages as federally recognized Indian tribes.[59] In 1994, Congress ratified that understanding in the Federally Recognized Tribe List Act.[60]

However, Alaska is a mandatory Public Law 280 state,[61] meaning that the United States has required the state to assume civil and criminal jurisdiction over Indian country.[62] **See §§ 7.4, 13.5**.

John v. Baker

In *John v. Baker*,[63] the Alaska Supreme Court held that Alaska Native tribal government retain the inherent right to adjudicate child custody matters of tribal members in tribal courts.[64]

The question arose in a child custody dispute between a father, a member of the Northway Village, and a mother, a member of the Mentasta Village. The father brought a child custody action in the Northway Tribal Court, and the mother consented to that court's jurisdiction. The court issued a shared custody order, and the father brought a suit in state court seeking to undo the tribal court order. The state court refused to recognize the tribal court's order, and granted full custody to the father. The mother appealed.

The Alaska Supreme Court first addressed the question of Public Law 280. The father argued that the state court had jurisdiction over the child custody matter under Public Law 280. The Ninth Circuit had held that while Public Law 280 authorized the state court to assert jurisdiction, that statute did not strip the tribal courts of jurisdiction, rendering state jurisdiction merely concurrent and not exclusive.[65] The Alaska Supreme Court noted that the Supreme Court's decision in *Alaska v. Native Village of Venetie*, **see § 13.2**, all but eliminated Indian country in Alaska.[66] Public Law 280, according to the court, applied only to Indian country lands, and therefore *did not* apply to Alaska Native lands excluded from the Indian country definition in *Venetie*.[67]

---

[59] Indian Entities Recognized and Eligible to Receive Services from the United States Bureau of Indian Affairs, 58 Fed. Reg. 54,364, 54,368–69 (1993).

[60] 25 U.S.C. § 5130(2).

[61] Pub. L. 83–280, Aug. 15, 1953, 67 Stat. 588, codified in relevant part as amended at 18 U.S.C. § 1162 and 28 U.S.C. § 1360.

[62] Pub. L. 85–615, Aug. 8, 1958, 72 Stat. 545.

[63] 982 P.2d 738 (Alaska 1999), cert. denied, 528 U.S. 1182 (2000).

[64] Id. at 743.

[65] Id. at 746.

[66] Id. at 747.

[67] Id. at 748.

The court then addressed the legal implications of the federal government's recognition of the sovereignty of Alaska Native tribal governments. Reversing itself, the court applied the principle that Indian nations retain all aspects of tribal sovereignty unless Congress divests the tribe of authority to conclude that ANCSA and other relevant statutes have not divested Alaska Native tribal sovereignty.[68]

John v. Baker was a child custody case and did not implicate the Indian Child Welfare Act. The courts would later turn to that statute and Alaska Native tribal sovereignty.

Kaltag Tribal Council v. Jackson and *State v. Native Village of Tanana*

In *Kaltag Tribal Council v. Jackson*,[69] the Ninth Circuit held that Alaska Native tribal courts are entitled to full faith and credit under the Indian Child Welfare Act (ICWA).[70] **See § 8.8.** The Alaska Supreme Court reached a similar conclusion in *State v. Native Village of Tanana*.[71] Notably, the Alaska court held that an Alaska Native tribal government retains concurrent jurisdiction over Indian child welfare cases unless the government petitions to reassume exclusive jurisdiction under Public Law 280.[72]

The continuing and evolving understanding of the sovereign authority of Alaska Native tribal governments after the federal government's acknowledgement in 1993 has infiltrated other areas of tribal sovereignty. For example, in *Akiachak Native Community v. Salazar*,[73] the court invalidated an Interior Department regulation that treated Alaska Native tribal governments differently from other tribes under Section 5 of the Indian Reorganization Act, 25 U.S.C. § 5108, which allows the Secretary of Interior to acquire land in trust for the benefit of Indians and tribes.

---

[68] Id. at 751–59.

[69] No. 3:06–CV–211 TMB, 2008 WL 9434481 (D. Alaska, Feb. 22, 2008), aff'd, 344 Fed.Appx. 324 (9th Cir., Aug., 28, 2009), cert. denied sub nom., Hogan v. Kaltag Tribal Council, 562 U.S. 827 (2010).

[70] Pub. L. 95–608, Nov. 8, 1978, 92 Stat. 3069, codified at 25 U.S.C. §§ 1901 et seq.

[71] 249 P.3d 734 (Alaska 2011).

[72] Id. at 751.

[73] 935 F. Supp. 2d 195 (D.D.C.), appeal dismissed, 827 F.3d 100 (D.C. Cir. 2016).

§ 13.5   Public Law 280 and Alaska Indian Criminal Jurisdiction

Alaska is a so-called mandatory Public Law 280 state.[74] **See** **§ 7.5**. But the state's ability to effectively enforce criminal laws in the state's 229 Alaska Native villages is hampered by a lack of governmental capacity—people and resources—and the extraordinary distances law enforcement must travel.[75] Moreover, Alaska Native traditional justice may be at odds with state law, or is otherwise ineffective in handling on-the-ground community enforcement.[76]

In 2013, the Indian Law and Order Commission condemned the State of Alaska for its failures in protecting Alaska Natives from crime, especially Alaska Native women from sexual assault and domestic violence.[77]

Congress accepted one recommendation in repealing the Alaska exemption from the Violence Against Women Reauthorization Act.[78]

---

[74]   Pub. L. 83–280, Aug. 15, 1953, 67 Stat. 588, codified in relevant part as amended at 18 U.S.C. § 1162 and 28 U.S.C. § 1360.

[75]   Kristen A. Carpenter, Interpreting Indian Country in State of Alaska v. Native Village of Venetie, 35 Tulsa L.J. 73, 158 (1999).

[76]   Id. at 158–59.

[77]   Indian Law and Order Commission, A Roadmap For Making Native America Safer: Report To The President And Congress Of The United States, chap. 2 (Nov. 2013).

[78]   Pub. L. 113–275, December 18, 2014, 127 Stat. 2988.

Chapter 14

NATIVE HAWAIIANS

Analysis

§ 14.1 A Brief History

The volcanic island chain of Hawai'i is home to indigenous people usually known by Americans as Native Hawaiians. Native Hawaiians do not enjoy—and many Native Hawaiians would reject—the type of relationship with the federal government that 567 Indian nations know as federal recognition. For decades, Alaska Natives and Native Hawaiians were the indigenous peoples in the United States that did not have a relationship with the federal government similar to other Indian nations. Now that the federal government has formally recognized Alaska Native tribal governments, **see Chapter 13**, Native Hawaiians are the most prominent indigenous community in the United States to which the government has not yet established a similar formal relationship.

Prior to 1778, the Hawaiian Islands were isolated from non-Hawaiian contact.[1] After contact from the first European to reach the islands, Captain James Cook, the many independent high chiefs unified under King Kamehameha I. The unification of the Native Hawaiians offered some protection from foreigners that sought to dispossess the best lands from native ownership but also allowed foreigners to focus their efforts on one office. At first, the interests of the king, the high chiefs (ali'i), and Hawaiian commoners were aligned, but that quickly changed. In 1840, King Kamehameha III signed the first Hawaiian constitution, which declared that the

---

[1]   The historical survey that follows derives largely from David H. Getches, Charles F. Wilkinson, Robert A. Williams, Jr., Matthew L.M. Fletcher, and Kristen A. Carpenter, Cases and Materials on Federal Indian Law 994–1002 (7th ed. 2017), which is significantly informed by the work and assistance of Melody Kapilialoha MacKenzie, and Breann Swann Nu'uhiwa, Government of the People, By the People, For the People: Cultural Sovereignty, Civil Rights, and Good Native Hawaiian Governance, 14 Asian-Pac. L. & Pol'y J. 57 (2013). See also Native Hawaiian Land Law: A Treatise (Melody Kapilialoha MacKenzie ed. 2015).

king, the high chiefs, and the people owned Hawaiian land collectively. In 1848, however, during the "Great Mahele," the king and the chiefs secured all the land in a series of transactions, leaving little for the common people. The new land regime also lifted restrictions on alienation of Hawaiians lands to foreigners, effectively allowing foreigners to acquire much of the best land in Hawai'i.

By 1890, foreigners controlled 1 million of acres of land in Hawai'i. The United States had already considered Hawai'i a part of American strategic outreach for many years, starting by appointing a foreign minister to Hawai'i in 1848. American control was almost a foregone conclusion by the time the United States orchestrated an overthrow of the Hawaiian monarchy in 1893. Though President Cleveland passionately opposed Hawaiian annexation, his successor, President McKinley, pushed formal annexation through in 1898.

Monarchy controlled lands passed into federal government control at that time. The Organic Act of 1900 established Hawai'i as a territory, and established a territorial legislature.[2] Native Hawaiians suffered terribly through this period, as their mid-19th century efforts to wrest control of lands away from the Hawaiian monarchy and high chiefs failed, with little or no hope for relief from the new regime in the 20th century. In 1910, Congress enacted an amendment to the 1900 act allowing Native Hawaiians to make claims to the former monarch controlled lands, lands then controlled by the federal government. Sugar growers threatened by the 1910 act pushed through the Hawaiian Homes Commission Act of 1921.[3]

In the 1921 Act, Congress recognized that the federal government owed a duty to the Native Hawaiians akin to that duty owed by the government to American Indians.[4] Even then, the House of Representatives report defended the bill from critics who charged that the law was "unconstitutional class legislation."[5] The Act set aside 200,000 acres for Native Hawaiian land claims, but this land was usually unsuited to farming. The Act was "remarkably similar in purpose and effect to the General Allotment Act."[6] See § 3.6.

---

[2]   Pub. L. 56–331, April 30, 1900, 31 Stat. 141.

[3]   Act of July 9, 1921, 42 Stat. 108.

[4]   H.R. Rep. 66–839, at 4 (1920).

[5]   David H. Getches, Charles F. Wilkinson, Robert A. Williams, Jr., Matthew L.M. Fletcher, and Kristen A. Carpenter, Cases and Materials on Federal Indian Law 999 (7th ed. 2017).

[6]   Id.

In 1959, the United States admitted Hawai'i as a state.[7] Section 5(f) of the Act established a federal trust obligation, imposed on the new state, relating to lands transferred from the United States to the State. Even so, Native Hawaiians remain disadvantaged.

The citizens of Hawai'i have established the Office of Hawaiian Affairs (OHA) to manage trust funds arising from trust lands held and managed by a board of trustees.[8] The OHA-managed trust funds derive from 20 percent of the revenues derived from the so-called Section 5(b) lands.[9]

In 1993, Congress enacted a joint resolution acknowledging the 1893 overthrow of the Hawaiian monarchy that offered an apology to Native Hawaiians.[10]

§ 14.2   *Rice v. Cayetano*

In *Rice v. Cayetano*,[11] the Supreme Court struck down a state voting rule restricting the right to vote for the board of trustees of the Office of Hawaiian Affairs to descendants of the indigenous Hawaiians as a violation of the Fifteenth Amendment.

The dispute involved the Office of Hawaiian Affairs (OHA), established by the people of the State of Hawai'i in 1978.[12] The OHA was supervised by a nine-person board of trustees elected by "Hawaiians," defined by statute to mean "any descendant of the aboriginal peoples inhabiting the Hawaiian Islands which exercised sovereignty and subsisted in the Hawaiian Islands in 1778, and which peoples thereafter have continued to reside in Hawaii."[13] The statute also defined "Native Hawaiian" to mean "any descendant of not less than one-half part of the races inhabiting the Hawaiian Islands previous to 1778, as defined by the Hawaiian Homes Commission Act, 1920, as amended; provided that the term identically refers to the descendants of such blood quantum of such aboriginal peoples which exercised sovereignty and subsisted in the Hawaiian Islands in 1778 and which peoples thereafter continued to reside in Hawaii."[14]

---

[7]   Hawaii Admission Act, Pub. L. 86–3, March 18, 1959, 73 Stat. 4.

[8]   Haw. Const., Art. XII, § 5.

[9]   Haw. Rev. Stat. § 10–13.5.

[10]   Pub. L. 103–150, November 23, 1993, 107 Stat. 1510.

[11]   528 U.S. 495 (2000).

[12]   Haw. Const., Art. XII, § 5.

[13]   Haw. Rev. Stat. § 10–2.

[14]   Id.

The petitioner was a Hawaiian citizen who sought to vote in the state election to elect the OHA board of trustees. He did not qualify as a "Hawaiian" as the statute provided. He claimed that the Fifteenth Amendment prohibited the voting requirement. The State of Hawaii, represented by later-Chief Justice Roberts, argued that the United States and the State acknowledged an obligation to Native Hawaiians similar to that of the trust relationship with other Indian nations that precluded the application of the Fifteenth Amendment. The Supreme Court agreed with the petitioner.

Justice Kennedy's majority opinion held that the plain text of the Fifteenth Amendment prohibited any voting restriction created and applied on the basis of race, rejecting the federal and state arguments that the OHA statute was a classification established on the basis of the relationship between the United States and Native Hawaiians. The Court reaffirmed that Congress could create a political classification based on the treaty relationship between the United States and Indian nations, and that classification may apply to internal tribal elections or to federal employment preferences, as in *Morton v. Mancari*.[15] **See § 3.13**. But the Court held that the United States may not authorize a state to create voting restrictions in state elections.

The Court concluded by noting that the history of Native Hawaiians is troublesome but that governmental remedies may not run afoul of the Fifteenth Amendment, which "has become the heritage of all the citizens of Hawaii."[16]

§ 14.3 *Hawai'i v. Office of Hawaiian Affairs*

In *Hawai'i v. Office of Hawaiian Affairs*,[17] the Supreme Court held that the 1993 federal apology resolution did not impose additional trust duties on the State of Hawai'i preventing the state from alienating so-called Section 5(b) lands.

In the 1993 apology resolution, Congress:

(1) on the occasion of the 100th anniversary of the illegal overthrow of the Kingdom of Hawaii on January 17, 1893, acknowledges the historical significance of this event which resulted in the suppression of the inherent sovereignty of the Native Hawaiian people;

(2) recognizes and commends efforts of reconciliation initiated by the State of Hawaii and the United Church of Christ with Native Hawaiians;

---

[15]   417 U.S. 535 (1974).

[16]   Rice v. Cayetano, 528 U.S. 495, 524 (2000).

[17]   556 U.S. 163 (2009).

(3) apologizes to Native Hawaiians on behalf of the people of the United States for the overthrow of the Kingdom of Hawaii on January 17, 1893 with the participation of agents and citizens of the United States, and the deprivation of the rights of Native Hawaiians to self-determination;

(4) expresses its commitment to acknowledge the ramifications of the overthrow of the Kingdom of Hawaii, in order to provide a proper foundation for reconciliation between the United States and the Native Hawaiian people; and

(5) urges the President of the United States to also acknowledge the ramifications of the overthrow of the Kingdom of Hawaii and to support reconciliation efforts between the United States and the Native Hawaiian people.[18]

Section 3 of the resolution provided, "Nothing in this Joint Resolution is intended to serve as a settlement of any claims against the United States."[19] Several of the 37 "whereas" clauses preceding the apology's substance referenced the sorry history of American-Hawaiian relations, impliedly suggesting that Native Hawaiian land and sovereignty rights may still be extant. Most notably, one clause provided, "Whereas the indigenous Hawaiian people never directly relinquished their claims to their inherent sovereignty as a people or over their national lands to the United States, either through their monarchy or through a plebiscite or referendum."[20]

The dispute involved the state public housing agency's decision to acquire from the Office of Hawaiian Affairs Section 5(b) lands for purposes of redeveloping. OHA insisted the land purchase—and other transactions like it—be blocked unless and until potential Native Hawaiian land claims referenced in the apology resolution were resolved. OHA argued successfully before the Hawai'i Supreme Court that land transfers conducted before the land claims were resolved was a breach of trust.[21] The Hawaiian court relied in part on the "whereas" clauses as well.[22]

---

[18] Joint Resolution to Acknowledge the 100th Anniversary of the January 17, 1893 Overthrow of the Kingdom of Hawaii, Pub. L. 103–150, Nov. 23, 1993, 107 Stat. 1513.

[19] Id.

[20] Id.

[21] Office of Hawaiian Affairs v. Housing and Community Development Corp. of Hawaii, 177 P.3d 884, 898 (Haw. 2008), rev'd, 556 U.S. 163 (2009).

[22] Id. at 922.

The Supreme Court rejected the Hawaiian court's conclusions, holding that Congress could not impose a restriction of alienation or cloud on the title of state lands through a mechanism such as an apology resolution.[23]

Section 5(f) of the Hawaii Admission Act established the trust burden on the State, but several Hawaiian court cases had foreclosed the enforcement of the trust absent a waiver of state sovereign immunity.[24] Without the apology resolution, and absent a waiver of state immunity to allow the resolution of trust breach claims and other Native Hawaiian claims, there can be no resolution of those claims. The Hawaiian legislature did enact a rule that requires a two-thirds supermajority vote to alienate Section 5(b) lands.[25]

§ 14.4 The Future of Native Hawaiian Governance

For the most part, outside observers of Native Hawaiian affairs have focused on the efforts of Hawaii's congressional delegation to enact a bill, usually referred to as the Akaka bill after Sen. Daniel Akaka, to extend formal federal recognition to a Native Hawaiian government akin to the recognition extended to Indian nations.[26] So far the legislation has not been successful. And the Akaka bill is controversial even within Native Hawaiian communities.[27] In 2016, the Department of the Interior adopted procedures for the federal acknowledgement of a Native Hawaiian government, should one be established.[28]

Chief Justice William Richardson, the first Native Hawaiian chief justice, frequently invoked the concept of *kuleana* in important land use and environmental decisions issued by the Hawaii Supreme Court.[29] More than a decade after the Chief Justice

---

[23] Hawai'i v. Office of Hawaiian Affairs, 556 U.S. 163, 176 (2009).

[24] E.g., Pele Defense Fund v. Paty, 837 P.2d 1247 (Haw. 1992).

[25] David H. Getches, Charles F. Wilkinson, Robert A. Williams, Jr., Matthew L.M. Fletcher, and Kristen A. Carpenter, Cases and Materials on Federal Indian Law 1047 (7th ed. 2017).

[26] See generally Le'a Malia Kanehe, The Akaka Bill: The Native Hawaiians' Race for Federal Recognition, 23 U. Haw. L. Rev. 857 (2001); R. H K Lei Lindsey, Comment, Akaka Bill: Native Hawaiians, Legal Realities, and Politics As Usual, 24 U. Haw. L. Rev. 693 (2002).

[27] See generally Ryan William Nohea Garcia, Comment, Who is Hawaiian, What Begets Federal Recognition, and How Much Blood Matters, 11 Asian-Pac. L. & Pol'y J. 85 (2010).

[28] Procedures for Reestablishing a Government-to-Government Relationship with the Native. Hawaiian Community, 43 C.F.R. Part 50.

[29] See generally Symposium: Chief Justice William S. Richardson (1919–2010), 33 U. Haw. L. Rev. 1–138 (2010–2011); Breann Swann Nu'uhiwa, Government of the People, By the People, For the People: Cultural Sovereignty, Civil Rights, and Good Native Hawaiian Governance, 14 Asian-Pac. L. & Pol'y J. 57, 75–79 (2013).

stepped down, the Hawaii Supreme Court continued to apply *kuleana* to modern disputes. In *Public Access Shoreline Hawaii (PASH) v. Hawai'i County Planning Commission*,[30] for example, the court held that resort development projects in Hawaii that would shut off access to shorelines remain subject to traditional Hawaiian gathering practices. The court had long held before that decision that Western property rights notions do not always control over traditional Native Hawaiian rights. After, the Hawaiian people in the 1978 state constitution agreed to protect customary and traditional subsistence, cultural, and religious rights.[31]

---

[30]   903 P.2d 1246 (Haw. 1995), cert. denied, 517 U.S. 1163 (1997).

[31]   Haw. Const. Art. XII, § 7.

Table of Cases

Index

References are to Pages